Swami Chinmayananda

JOURNEY OF A MASTER

The Man, the Path, the Teaching

Nancy Freeman Patchen

Central Chinmaya Mission Trust

First Printed in the United states of America
Reprint in India in 1994 to 1996 - 6,000 copies
Revised Edition in India March 2005 to January 2021 - 14,500 copies
Reprint - October 2024 - 1,500 copies

Published by:
Chinmaya Prakashan
The Publications Division of
Central Chinmaya Mission Trust
Sandeepany Sādhanālaya
Saki Vihar Road, Mumbai 400072, India
Tel.: +91-22-2803 4900
Email: ccmtpublications@chinmayamission.com
Website: www.chinmayamission.com

Distribution Centre in the USA:
Chinmaya Publications West
560 Bridgetown Pike
Feasterville, PA 19053-7240, USA
Tel.: (215) 396-0390, Fax: (215) 396-9710
Email: publications@chinmayamission.org
Website: www.chinmayapublications.com

Designed by: Chinmaya Kalpanam, Mumbai

Printed by: SAP Print Solutions Pvt. Ltd., Mumbai

ISBN 978-81-7597-305-3

Publisher's Note

We have great pleasure in presenting this revised edition of *'Journey of a Master'* on the life of the spiritual giant of the Age, Pūjya Gurudev, Swami Chinmayananda.

This is the first biography of the great Master narrating his successful journey towards the highest goal.

The perennial demand for this book prompted us to bring its revised edition with lot of improvements in its look and other aspects like bigger font size and so on, for the comfort of the reader.

We trust that the study of life story of Pūjya Gurudev would certainly inspire the reader in his spiritual pursuits.

Chinmaya Prakashan
Books Division of CCMT

30th November, 2017
Tapovan Jayantī & Gītā Jayantī,
Mumbai-72

Transliteration and Pronunciation Guide

In this book, Devanagari characters are transliterated according to the scheme adopted by the International Congress of Orientalists at Athens in 1912. In it one fixed pronunciation value is given to each letter; f, q, w, x and z are not called to use.

Devanagari	Translit-eration	Sounds Like	Devanagari	Translit-eration	Sounds Like
अ	a	son	ढ्	ḍh	adhesive*
आ	ā	father	ण्	ṇ	under*
इ	i	different	त्	t	tabla
ई	ī	feel	थ्	th	thumb
उ	u	full	द्	d	this
ऊ	ū	boot	ध्	dh	Gandhi
ऋ	ṛ	rhythm*	न्	n	nose
ॠ	ṝ	**	प्	p	pen
ऌ	ḷ	**	फ्	ph	phantom*
ए	e	evade	ब्	b	boil
ऐ	ai	delight	भ्	bh	abhor
ओ	o	core	म्	m	mind
औ	au	now	य्	y	yes
क्	k	calm	र्	r	right
ख्	kh	khan	ल्	l	love
ग्	g	gate	व्	v	very
घ्	gh	ghost	श्	ś	shut
ङ्	ṅ	ankle*	ष्	ṣ	sugar
च्	c	chuckle	स्	s	simple
छ्	ch	witch*	ह्	h	happy
ज्	j	justice	ं	ṁ	improvise
झ्	jh	Jhansi	ः	ḥ	**
ञ्	ñ	banyan	क्ष्	kṣ	action
ट्	ṭ	tank	त्र्	tr	three*
ठ्	ṭh	**	ज्ञ्	jñ	gnosis
ड्	ḍ	dog	ऽ	’	a silent ‘a’

* These letters don’t have an exact English equivalent. An approximation is given here.
** These sounds cannot be approximated in English words.

Contents

Preface to Revised Edition 2000

With this edition I was asked to complete Swami Chinmayananda's life through his mahāsamādhi (death). In the first edition, several readers found several inconsistencies with regard to dates, which I have happily corrected. Others felt I had excluded certain names or anecdotes. These comments impelled me to consider why I had written the biography. No doubt I spent considerable time in research to be able to compile all the facts accurately. The many people I personally interviewed are acknowledged at the end of the book. Nonetheless, this compilation of facts was only the backdrop of the true reason for writing the book.

Swami Chinmayananda was a human being who had the courage, independence and innate intelligence to realize his divinity. He dedicated that same courage, independence and intelligence to point out to us that we too are divine. Had he not been a human being like us, his life's journey to the Truth would have had little meaning for us. Because he was a man, his life and his teachings offer us a model of what is 'humanly' possible. Certainly, we can worship Swamiji as God, but we must not fail to worship ourselves as God too. This incredible Truth was the essence of his teaching. Although each journey to this Truth is unique, I thought that his story would give us some hope, insight and courage to take our journey to the Self.

Life has its mystery, its majesty, its illusions, its deceptions. There are very few things one can be sure of, but I am absolutely certain of one thing. I am the person I am today only because I met a Master, Swami Chinmayananda. I remain forever grateful.

Author

Mumbai
January, 2000

To the Reader...

This book was not intended for scholars, but was written so that the average person interested in India would be able to gain a greater understanding of a Reality unknown to us in the West. Because of the many new ideas, one must read the book through with an open mind in order to get a complete picture before any assessments or judgements are made. Although I have attempted to communicate as clearly as possible, many new concepts and words of the Indian culture have made it difficult. Therefore, I suggest that if you do not comprehend the nuance of an idea or word you put it in the back of your mind, for the term will surely come up again in the text. In this manner, you will continue broadening your understanding of the various concepts.

Sanskrit is intimidating because there are no accurate English translations for many of the essential words. When the sense of a word has been narrowed by the English translation I have put the Sanskrit word in parentheses after it. In direct quotations, I did not take that liberty; there, I placed the English translations in brackets after the Sanskrit word. When the word was a common one, after using it several times, I began to incorporate the Sanskrit term into the text. A glossary is provided for a more elaborate definition of the Sanskrit words. For understanding of the spiritual concepts that are introduced in the text, the final section, 'The Teaching', brings together and elaborates on all the philosophical ideas.

New York City
December, 1988

Nancy Freeman Patchen

The Inspiration

Can I do it?

Can I face the educated class of India and bring to their faithless hearts at least a ray of understanding of what our wondrous culture stands for? Sitting on the banks of the roaring Ganga, I shivered as I pondered the thought. None could argue against the eternal truth that man is in essence God. But could I explain it to others? Sitting, watching the Mother Ganga in her incessant hurry, I seemed to hear the words interlaced in her roar, 'Son, don't you see me; born here in the Himalayas, I rush down to the planes taking with me both life and nourishment to all in my path. Fulfilment of any possession is in sharing it with others.' I felt encouraged, I felt reinforced. The urge became irresistible!

Thus was born the idea that was to take Swami Chinmayananda throughout India and to parts of the world never touched by the sacred waters of the Ganga to share the secrets of life that he had learned in the valleys of the Himalayan peaks. The Vedānta philosophy that he would teach was studied exclusively by scholars of religion in Indian universities and by Swamis in their huts and āśramas. But did this ancient knowledge have any significance for the average man struggling with his mundane problems in his daily life? This is the question that Swami Chinmayananda was to address in his life's mission.

In the forty-two years since that day of inspiration, Swami Chinmayananda has met and overcome many obstacles in his journey, as surely as the Ganga leaps high as she meets boulders in her course and lays out a new path when she encounters obstructions in her one-pointed concentration to bring her fresh waters to the Bay of Bengal.The Swami never seems to need rest as he meets his 365 day-a-year, sixteen hour daily schedule, including two or three public classes and lectures. His constant outpouring of love and humour, criticism and encouragement, insight and enthusiasm – with equal attention to both the spiritual and material needs of the students – has resulted in the transformed lives of thousands of people.

His life represented a model of one, who pursued a goal with concentrated dedication; thereby demonstrating in his own life the secrets of success that he shared with others. By the end of his life, with the assistance of many inspired workers, he built a foundation and structure for a spiritual renaissance in India.

The impact of his hundreds of lectures (discourses) on *Gītā*, Upaniṣads and contemporary subjects generated several activities – like Chinmaya Vidyalayas/Colleges (Chinmaya International Residential School (CIRS)), Chinmaya International Foundation (CIF – Research Centre on Indology) culminating in Chinmaya Vishwavidyapeeth, Chinmaya Naada Bindu (Gurukul for Indian Performing Arts), Bala Vihars for children, CHYKS for youth all over the world, Vanaprastha Sanstha for senior citizens, Super Speciality hospital and a worldwide rural service unit (CORD), besides transforming thousands of individual lives.

These projects, inspired, established and run by individuals from the community – furnish a field of service for those dedicated to the ideals of the eternal Truth expounded by Swami Chinmayananda, the Ageless Guru.

PART – I

The Preparation

1

Political Fugitive

We were accused of much more than we actually did, although we didn't mind – let those British think the worst of us! – that was our attitude.

– Swami Chinmayananda, 1958.

In 1951 when Swami Chinmayananda left the heights of the Himalayan valleys for the plane of his homeland, India was only four years into her independence from the British. His mission was a response to a restless society. Two hundred years of alien rule had left its scar in every arena of life – cultural, political, economic, religious – and, equally devastating, the loss of the natives' confidence in their self-worth. A religious and cultural identification had provided a unity for two thousand independent kingdoms of many languages and distinct customs for centuries. People of this region traced their origin to Bhārata (one who revels in light), the legendary king immortalized by the poet Kālidāsa in the great epic *Śākuntala*.

That which lies to the north of the oceans;
That which lies to the south of the snow-capped mountains;
That is named Bhārata; for, it is the home of the Bhāratīyas.

This unique cultural and religious foundation of unification on the Indian subcontinent had been seriously undermined by foreign rulers just at the time that consolidation into a nation was to occur. Consequently, a civilization of four thousand years was embarking on the monumental task of building a vital nation not as an organic, natural development, but in a great leap, without the roots of its foundation.

True, Bhārata had been conquered by Sultans from Turkey and Afghanistan, and later by Mughals of Mongolia, centuries before the British arrived. Some of these Muslims had come to destroy and pillage, but the majority came to settle and build wealthy empires. Although they brought many changes into the public life of the conquered, they encouraged economic growth since Bhārata also was their home and source of livelihood. In most areas, the rulers hardly interfered with the social and religious customs of the conquered. Therefore, the populace, divided into many small kingdoms, never attempted any united effort to expel the foreign overlords.

The wealth that had tempted many a foreign adventurer to Bhārata was so great that it could continue withstanding the 'hit and run' attacks of the Sultans, but the organized pillage policy of the British conquerors entirely upset the sub-continent's economic structure with its intricately woven social and religious culture. The British officials, along with their military forces who ran the government and regulated trade, had never really left home. They kept all their prejudices, class snobbery and religious conservatism of their native land.

The most serious undermining of the national self-image came through the Anglicization of the educational system. In British-styled schools, students were presented with all the ideas and ideals of Western thought. But this also turned out to be the undoing of the British because the future Indian rebels discovered the intriguing foreign ideas of 'equality', 'democracy', and 'autonomy'. They learned that as early as 1760, the statesman Edmund Burke had been advocating that government in India should be for the sake of the Indians. And the English education furnished them with another necessary tool for their self-government – a common language, English.

Since the British had allowed education only to enough natives to provide their government with clerks, only ten percent had a Western education and consequently, Western ideas. These educated Indians were the political and commercial leaders who were destined to guide the course of India's history. These leaders, who knew little of their religious and cultural heritage, were the ones Swami Chinmayananda came from the mountains to teach.

He had been one of the educated elite. He knew their weaknesses; he knew their strengths. In fact his activities as a socialist, inspired by the leader of the Indian Socialist Party, Jayaprakash Narayan, had taken him into the battlefield for the freedom of India from the British imperialists.

World War II had brought to a focus all the conflicts between the ruling and the ruled. In 1939, without her people or leaders being consulted, the British Viceroy announced that India, along with all the other nations of the British Empire, had declared war against Germany. Particularly agitated because Indians had thought India's independence imminent, the Indian leaders and general public rebelled against conscription. However, in 1941 when Roosevelt and Churchill declared in the Atlantic Charter that the war was being fought for 'the right of all people to choose the form of government under which they will live', the rebels took heart.

Their hope was short-lived. Winston Churchill, a vehement imperialist[1], announced within a month of its writing that the Charter did not apply to India or other parts of the British Empire. This meant that India was at war to ensure that other nations had the right to choose their own forms of government while being denied that option herself. The situation was stressed further when Singapore was attacked and fell to the Japanese. Insisting that the British presence in his country heightened the likelihood that she too would be attacked, Mahatma Gandhi demanded that India be left to deal with Japan with her own non-violent techniques,

1 Churchill had spent two years of military duty in India (1896-1898) playing polo, raising roses and collecting butterflies, while complaining that he was not in the Egyptian campaign where war medals, crucial to his political ambitions, were being won.

an urgent condition since Britain had not allowed any building of a national defence. Armies in India had been created for the protection of British trade interests. With emotion packed words of a man who had spent many years in British prisons, Gandhi implored: "Leave India to God; if that is too much, then leave her to anarchy... From there a true India will arise in place of the false one we now see." That was his last appeal to the British to 'Quit India'. It was a message to the people that at last Gandhi would not object to the use of mass civil disobedience if his mandate were not heeded. Jawaharlal Nehru pointed out to the British that the 'Quit India' resolution contained an assurance that a free India would be an ally of the United Nations; then, he officially added – 'The Committee resolves to sanction... the starting of a mass struggle on non-violent lines on the widest possible scale.'

The issue of India's independence had been debated without enthusiasm on the part of the British since 1857, the year of widespread rebellion in Northern India. As a result of atrocities committed by the British soldiers upon the Indian people in quelling that uprising; the power of government was transferred from the British East India Trading Company to the Crown in 1876. The British had won the battle, but they had lost the respect of the people. The Indians would never again be manipulated into thinking their rulers were a superior race.

Since India's freedom was contingent on the politicians in London, little progress was made in the ensuing forty years. At the beginning of World War I, the Indians had been promised dominion status after the termination of the war, and thereby were blackmailed into giving all-out support in the vicious struggle between the imperialist nations for colonies and raw materials in which India was a mere pawn. Even Gandhi and his more radical predecessor Bal Gangadhar Tilak had given their support to the British cause on the assumption of future independence. Over a million Indians fought in the Middle East, Africa, Iran and Afghanistan; the funds to provide for these forces were financed by doubled taxes in their homeland. The famine-stricken peasants saw wheat, rice, jute, tea and raw ore produced by their hard labour being shipped to England at the cheapest possible rates. The British Lord Chancellor Birkenhead later admitted, "Without India the war would have been immensely prolonged, if indeed without her help it could have been brought to a victorious conclusion."

Post-war India was a disaster. The high taxes and forced loans, the unchecked profiteering and price increases had thrust destitution on the populace. In addition, the spread of the worldwide influenza contagion to India, plus a pneumonia epidemic there, had killed at least thirteen million – a total comparable to the battle losses in all Europe. Indian leaders, particularly in Punjab, simmered with grievances due to methods of raising men and money during the war. After numerous protests that were met with British retaliation, including the bombing of Punjab, the Indian nationalists had made no progress toward their goal of self-rule. Frustrated and defiant, the Indians signed their declaration of Independence on the 26th of January 1930.

But the 1930s also saw England in an economic depression. Since decisions pertaining to India were, had been and would continue to be governed by economic concerns, even in 1935 Churchill was touting his imperial policy with the words: "Gandhi, and all he stands for, must be crushed." His real concern was that, aside from other losses, Indian self-rule would worsen the British unemployment problem.

It was not just the London politicians who were delaying the retirement of the British from India. The British ruling class in India was not anxious to give up their luxurious lifestyles. The Viceroy's lifestyle was comparable to the Queen of England – thrones, carriages and something even the Queen did not have – an elephant for state occasions. His entourage, complete with a red carpet, accompanied both him and his wife everywhere. Further, he enjoyed a salary five thousand times that of the average income of the native labourer. It was an opportunity for Britain's middle-class, from whom the officials of the Empire came, to live like noblemen. The ordinary cavalryman, with a retinue of up to ten servants, did not even dress or shave himself. In addition, the British were enchanted by the tropical paradise – abundant and diverse wildlife of rhino, elephant, panther, leopard, tigers (a soldier could bag one before breakfast); fragrant trees laden with purple, yellow, red or orange flowers; all kinds of sweet, juicy fruit to be plucked from trees in their gardens; long vacations in the cool Himalayan valleys; safaris, train journeys, river houseboats, picnics in the jungle. The children of the officials, sent back to dreary England for their proper education at six years of age, longed for the life, colour, variety of India, and often returned. True, the attitude of many had soured in the heat of the tropical sun, but they knew they could not duplicate their affluence back in England. Comforted by their whiskey and opium, they held firm to their status with the rationalization that the undeserving natives did not 'appreciate all that the British had done for them.'

At the beginning of Word War II, the Indian Congress did offer cooperation in the war effort on the condition of the immediate recognition of Indian independence and the establishment of a provisional National Government, which would organize the defence of India and the role of India in the war. The British Government turned down the offer.

When Gandhi, issued his 'Quit India' ultimatum in 1942, the betrayal was evident. The Indians were no closer to their goal of independence than in 1930, and the problems in India, due to the Empire's economic policies, were rapidly multiplying. With one all-out campaign the Indians hoped to finish the matter once and for all. Congress planned to catch Britain when it was weak – involved in a war in Europe and Asia – to make their final move. Nationwide strikes were called. The people paraded past the government buildings shouting: "No help for wars! Not a man! Not a rupee!" But the Indians had miscalculated their enemy's strength.

The government retaliated with a vengeance. The Indian Congress was declared illegal. Its leaders, including Gandhi and Nehru, were again imprisoned in the usual manner, no trial, no sentencing.

These arrests set off an electrifying response. The masses, passive no longer, demonstrated in every major city. Everyone from labourer to housewife took to the street singing nationalist songs and demanding the release of Gandhi, Nehru and the other political prisoners. Students poured out of the universities and instigated a campaign of sabotage throughout the militant northern provinces – telegraph and telephone lines were cut; trains were derailed; the benches tagged 'For Europeans Only' in the train stations and city parks were burned; peasants withheld taxes from the landholders; protest marches were held in every city.

Balakrishnan Menon, the future Swami Chinmayananda, was one of these students. He left Lucknow University to join others who were writing and distributing leaflets and giving speeches to stir up the populace to a national pride and an awareness of the inability of the British to comprehend, much less solve, the problems of India.

The British police and troops countered every demonstration with whips, guns and arrests. Within weeks one thousand Indians were dead, three thousand seriously wounded and over sixty thousand imprisoned. During these massive lock-ups a warrant was issued for the arrest of Balakrishnan Menon, a Madrasi. Menon was actually from Cochin, but the British did not recognize the distinct kingdoms and cultures of South India. To them it was all Madras, the central city of their southern trade headquarters. When word reached Menon that British officials were looking for him, he went undercover.

Balakrishnan Menon spent the following year moving around in the state of Kashmir, out of the range of political activity. During that time, though, he was able to take several trips to visit his former college roommate and close friend, Shroff, at his family home on the outskirts of Delhi. There Menon was able to keep up with the latest political news, incidents often withheld from the British owned and operated newspapers and radio waves. Except for these brief respites to get some fresh clothes and some decent food, there was neither time nor place to rest; constant movement was necessary to avoid any suspicion. In Kashmir many days no food was available. He starved rather than approach a stranger to ask for assistance for fear that the person might be sympathetic to the British. Then word could get around in this predominantly Muslim state that a 'Madrasi' – easily noticeable by his accent, dark skin and thin stature – was in the area.

After a year of hiding out, Menon left Kashmir and was travelling toward Delhi to catch up on the latest political news. Upon arriving in Abbottabad, he boarded a bus headed for the centre of the city, but at the next stop he saw an officer step into the bus and question the passengers, "Did anyone see a Madrasi here?" Not waiting to hear the reply, Menon scooted out the back door and around a corner. He knew nothing about the town and had no idea in which direction to head for safety. In his momentary disorientation, he looked up and noticed a sign reading 'Earn While You Learn'. He quickly ducked inside the opened door below this invitation.

He found himself in the military quarters of a British intelligence communications centre that was relaying coded messages for the allied war effort. Menon assumed the attitude of a young man simply looking for a job and was hired immediately as a machine operator. Since he intended to stay only for a few days until his trail cooled down, the menial nature of the task did not bother him.

Within a week the British officer who had hired him noticed that this young man was too intelligent for the job, so he asked Menon why he had to settle for such boring work. Appraising the officer to be of a sensitive character, Menon took a risk and confided the entire situation; he considered the job a temporary one and he would be taking off just as soon as he felt it was safe. Menon had assessed the officer correctly, for, he was a sympathizer with the Indian freedom cause. He advised Mr. Menon that he had better stay put, or he risked having the military police, as well as the regular police, looking for him.

The officer then made Mr. Menon his personal assistant, which meant that he would have good pay and comfortable living quarters inside the military compound – a safe hideaway. Life was quite luxurious on the base. Set up by the British to maintain their way of life, it had tennis court, a game room, bar with imported liquors and cigarettes, and dining hall with good food. Mr. Menon had stumbled out of poverty to one of the most comfortable jobs in India available to an Indian.

On the job he had few duties. He sat at a desk all day, ready to assist the officer with receiving calls, messages and an occasional visitor. So he took advantage of the time and the large library, to study for his last round of examinations at Lucknow University. To earn his degree in English literature, he had to take a gruelling exam that covered not only the final year's work, but also any previous years' material. He had been away from his studies for over a year, but wanted to take the exams as soon as he was free to do so.

Always an amiable person, and educated in their own language, Mr. Menon got along easily with the British officers. He only challenged them on the tennis court or over a game of chess. 'Extremely popular, an avid conversationalist – he seemed to put an extra touch on everything he did and to get an extra enjoyment out of any activity,' report Robert D'Souza, a co-worker of those days. 'Menon was meticulous in both his manners and dress,' he added.

Certainly, Menon took these officers for what they were; British citizens doing their duty in the war effort and not personally responsible for the policies of the government that was keeping India in the British Empire. India sympathized with the allied cause; however, considering her political position and the bitter memories of the breaking of promises after her contribution to the British in World War I, she remained less than enthusiastic about giving more than moral support to the Allies. Even at that time, there were Indian soldiers who had been caught in the political impasse and were fighting in Europe with the Allies.

During this period an old desire of Mr. Menon's surfaced, a fascination for flying. It was aroused when the Air Force announced examinations for pilot training in Cochin, the place of his birth. Since he was stuck in the armed forces and it was proving to be a safe haven, he took a short leave to take the examination for flight training. However, his hopes of flying were short-lived, for, his imperfect eyesight caused him to be eliminated on the first round of testing. Unexpectedly, he was unable to contact or meet his family on this trip because German submarines had been spotted off the coast of Cochin, so the coastal cities had been evacuated.

He returned to Abbottabad and settled in for the duration, which he assumed would be a long one. But luck seemed to be with him. Knowing that Mr. Menon had no real interest in continuing at the job, his overseeing officer was able to arrange the paperwork so that Menon could be released. After only eight months of service, he was able to depart with a training and a considerable cache of rupees from his accumulated salary.

Upon leaving Abbottabad, Menon ran into several freedom groups in Punjab, one of the most politically active states. Thinking that his case, now almost two years old, was long forgotten, he began advising some students on distributing leaflets and organizing public strikes, based on his previous experience. But government officials soon learned that a Madrasi was moving around in Punjab; he was picked up and imprisoned.

Winters in Delhi are cold and damp; this one was no exception. The prison was a makeshift – no heating or lights. In the cold, dark cells, the Indian revolutionaries waited for the passing of each day. They left their cells only for the daily interrogations accompanied by beatings with iron rods on the ankles where no telltale scars would be left. The British officials were convinced that there was a master plot to overthrow their regime in India.

But there was no such overall plan; the Indians were not that organized. Their subversive activities were carried out by individuals and by small independent groups who were bound only by their conviction in the cause of freedom from oppression for their countrymen. Nevertheless, the British continued their search for a plot and regularly called the prisoners to the interrogation room, hoping that one would finally break and disclose some conspiracy. The fact that none did – they stuck to the simple truth – only incensed the officials to increase the beatings.

Somehow it seemed appropriate that this drama was unfolding in Delhi. Vulnerable Delhi stands in the centre of a large plane at the crossroads of the trade routes from the West and North. Delhi stands, although invaded, looted and utterly destroyed by foreign invaders – the Turks in 1186, the Mongolians in 1398, the Persians in 1739 and finally the British in 1857. While many of the great cities of the past lie a desert wasteland, victims of similar wars and invasions, Delhi stands a testimony to the recuperative spirit of the people of Bhārata. Her soil now supported the prisons that contained the future leaders of India, the leaders who would make her the capital of their Republic.

Because of the prison's crowded, unhygienic conditions – the cracks in the walls provided the only ventilation – plus the small rations of poor quality food, disease was rampant. Many were dying, making known the severity of the conditions to those in the city who had to make arrangements for cremation of the bodies. The deaths of these political prisoners would not help the already precarious relations with the Indian nationalists in 1944. Fearful of an investigation the officials determined to avoid any more in-prison deaths. The dreadful typhus fever[1] had already taken its toll of inmate lives when Menon became ill. Weakened by months in jail, he quickly fell into a stupor from the disease. At that stage of typhus, there would have been little hope for his recovery even with proper treatment. Consequently, he was carried out into the night and tossed beside a road on the outskirts of the city.

The next morning an Indian lady was passing along that route and happened to notice a young man lying along the side of the road. At that moment he appeared to make a feeble movement. 'Was that a signal for help?' she wondered. She saw that he was dressed in rags (the remains of the one suit he had worn during the several months spent in prison), but she sensed he was not an ordinary beggar. On impulse, she had her driver stop the car to investigate.

She immediately realized that she had encountered a very sick person; he was delirious and burning with fever. She was sympathetic to his helpless plight; her own son was with the Indian troops in Europe. I must help this boy; even at this very moment someone may be aiding my son, she determined. Menon later quipped that it was his big nose that saved him – "It looked exactly like her son's!"

So the lady took Menon to her home and called a doctor who insisted that the young man be taken to a hospital immediately. The dear lady would not consider it because she knew she could give him better care than he would receive in a crowded Indian hospital. She also realized that her home was safer, for, a problem could arise in a hospital if questions were asked as to how the patient came to be in such an emaciated condition. Then too, the suspicious wounds from the floggings were visible.

She devotedly cared for Balakrishnan Menon as her own son, sparing no expense in seeing that he got proper diet and

[1] Typhus was often known as jail fever in the old world because overcrowding, bad ventilation and poor food favour its occurrence.

medicine. After several difficult weeks, Menon slowly regained strength enough to be able to be up and move around. Soon afterwards, he made the short journey to Baroda where he could fully recuperate at the home of his cousin, Achuthan Menon. Dressed in an old suit of her son's, Menon boarded the train north and bid the good Samaritans goodbye with loving thanks. This Christian lady never knew that she had saved the life of a future Hindu sage, for, she died a few years later. Her only son was killed in action and buried in Europe.

2

The Journalist

To produce, transport, distribute and consume is not all of life – these are accessories, no doubt unavoidable and necessary, but they are only subsidiary to the evolution of the individual.
– Swami Chinmayananda, 1958.

The cousin Achuthan Menon was a tall, muscular, handsome man, whose fame in his university days came from his skill at soccer. Upon receiving a degree in Forest Management, he joined the Indian National Forest Service. Balan (Balakrishnan) and Achu (Achuthan), the elder by thirteen years, had been raised in the same family household in Cochin. Due to their age difference, there had been little friendship; Achu had left for the university by the time Balan was of school age.

Achu was now stationed at Baroda, but spent most of his time away from home on various field assignments. Fortunately, on the day Balan arrived he was not out in an encampment, but was only away for the day, because Achu's servant refused to admit Balan on his word that he was Achu's cousin. The servant could not believe that such a sickly character in an old suit was a relative of his employer; he wanted confirmation of the claimed kinship. So Balan had no choice but to spend the afternoon waiting outside. Upon his return, Achu was surprised to see a beggar at the gate. Just as he was thinking, why hasn't the servant given this vagabond some food and sent him on his way, Balan spotted Achu approaching and roared a jovial greeting in his characteristic manner. Achu immediately recognized the voice and enthusiastically invited his long-lost cousin into his home.

After hearing of Balan's adventures and physical distress, Achu invited him to stay in his home. But Achu's duties as a Forest Officer took him away for weeks at a time; he simply would not be available to help out with the demands of caring for a convalescing person. The problem was solved when the servant who had tried to turn Balan away, Narayan (a name of Lord Vishnu), kindly volunteered to take over the extra responsibility of caring and cooking for him.

Narayan made sure that Balan had fresh fruits and vegetables along with plenty of fresh milk and yogurt each day. He cooked in the style of Balan's home state; the diet of rice and dal (split bean), instead of the roti (flat wheat bread) and spiced potato of the north, was recuperative in itself. Balan affectionately called the servant Baroda-Narayan, that is, the Lord of Baroda.

It was during this period that Balan took out Achu's typewriter and began a career in journalism. He chose the pseudonym of Mochi, 'street shoe cobbler', as the symbol through which to express the poor man's point of view. Along the pathways that skirt the streets of cities, the mochi sits under a tree. With bits of string and a simple metal punch, he repairs shoes in exchange for a few pennies. Consigned to a life of poverty, he can only hope to earn enough to buy food for his family each day. Through these articles by Mochi, Balan was able to put forth his own ideas of the imperative of socialism in a society in which the vast majority was poor. Although these short, critical satires were Balan's first journalistic efforts, they were soon published regularly in Indian nationalist newspapers. Each time Achu returned to Baroda, he would be surprised to find that more articles had been published and even paid for. He would carry the cheques to the bank to get them cashed. They still felt it wise for Balan to remain invisible.

An important phase of Balan's life was precipitated during his stay in Baroda. Here he was to discover, or rather rediscover, a subject he had left behind some fifteen years back – the Hindu religion. In prison, he had had plenty of time to reflect on the precarious nature of life. There had been too many first hand examples – he had seen lifeless bodies carried out daily – to ignore the reality of death. Also his own death had seemed inevitable. In such moments, one turns within to question – Can there be any meaning to such an impermanent life? If so, can man ever know it?

The impetus of this rediscovery came from an unlikely source – a women's magazine. Achu's wife remained in Cochin with her family to avoid the lonely periods that Achu was away from home. However, she came to Baroda regularly for long stays, particularly in the winter season when the weather would force Achu to be at his home station. When Balan arrived in Baroda, she had recently departed, leaving behind a stack of reading material that she always brought along to entertain herself. For this trip, the material included a large, bound volume of issues of '*My Magazine*', a general magazine with themes on every phase of living, from cooking, to gardening, to religion.

These particular issues happened to feature a series of articles on the lives of the saints in the Himalayas. Although the older generation had little contact or understanding of their ways of life, they still held an awe and respect for these holy men. In contrast, the younger generation had only a meagre interest, if not disdain, for, these apparent loafers who lived in caves and huts, completely detached from the problems of their fellow countrymen. However, since much of the ancient Hindu lore and history was centred around the Himalayas, even an agnostic would have some curiosity about the stories of these unusual men who had through the centuries safeguarded spiritual teachings unknown to the general public. In the long hours of free time, Balan leafed through these magazines and came upon the articles focusing on the values of the Hindu culture and religion. In one of the issues an article appeared by the president and founder of the Divine Life Society in Rishikesh, a dynamic, intelligent, educated Swami dedicated to the spiritual upliftment of his countrymen. This was Balan's first encounter with Swami Sivananda Saraswati who was later to perform the initiation ceremony in which Menon would begin his life as a Swami.

A self-proclaimed agnostic, Balan's only concerns were the political, economic and social reforms in India; he had no interest in religion. As a child, he had repeated his prayers in order to get his supper. On several occasions, he had been bounced on the knees of various holy men who had visited his childhood home, but he hardly remembered them.

These articles brought back haunting old memories of those long forgotten days – the ability to sleep well if he had repeated his mantra, the peace of an old grandmother who had dedicated her last years to chanting the name of Lord Kṛṣṇa, the knowing look of a holy man whom he had met in his college days. Could there possibly be anything to the idea of a divinity within, now obscured by clouds of worldly desires without?

The philosophical wanderings of Balan's mind were quickly checked by the practical realities of life. Eager to get on with a career and gain success in the world, he left Baroda as soon as he felt strong enough. Convinced that newsprint was the best and easiest means to reach the public, he returned to the university at Lucknow where he took several courses in journalism and completed his M.A. in English literature with Honours. With this background, he was able to get some editing work at a local newspaper. As an editor, however, he felt separated from the complete process. He was convinced that to be an editor 'worth his salt', he should know everything about the news business from gathering of stories to the actual printing.

The opportunity to extend his expertise came unexpectedly. Several acquaintances were involved in the making of a film in Bombay and invited Balan to join them. They thought with his experience in drama at the university, extroverted nature and speaking ability, he would be perfect for one of the parts. Balan decided to take the opportunity to go, not only for the amusement of working with the film, but to continue with his chosen profession by working on a small independent newspaper, *The Free Press*. Although the film project soon fell through, Balan continued working at *The Free Press*, experiencing first hand all the phases of the process of publishing a newspaper.

> "I was learning the real inside of the news business. How the news was twisted with an appropriate flavour according to the country it was sent out to. In some it was the advantage to say the Muslims had attacked the Hindus; in others, to have it slanted to imply the Hindus had attacked the Muslims. Of course, it all took attention from the real issue: the fact that the British had not left India, as they had been promising."

The Free Press was useful for training, but the pay was low and his views were often too liberal for the small paper. Menon caught on fast to the details of the business and was soon practically running the paper, or at least attempting to do so. Although the owner considered Menon a competent, enthusiastic and dedicated worker, he thought Menon's ideas too radical and his manner too aggressive. So as soon as Menon decided that he had gotten the background he had wanted in journalism and newspaper operations, he and the newspaper owner parted company. Menon returned to Delhi.

In 1945 Delhi remained the centre of political activity. The headquarters of the *National Herald*, the national newspaper of the Indians, was located there. Menon was able to secure a position as a sub-editor with the paper. It was not exactly the position Menon thought he deserved, but Delhi would have several surprises for his ego.

He had left the university, proud and confident with a master's degree in English literature to substantiate his vanity.

He expected that any desire would come to him easily, just at the wanting of it. This would have been true had he lived in Cochin with his family who were related to the consort of the raja (king) and an uncle who was the Chief Justice of the state. His father, a court magistrate, would have dotingly supplied all of his son's needs. But in Delhi the game was different – it was every man for himself.

Menon was taken aback to find that he was not welcomed into the society of the educated wealthy of Delhi. To them Cochin was far away and little known; any social contacts there were useless. Nevertheless, he was determined that he would manipulate his way into the elite circle to enjoy the fruits of the good life. He knew he would get what he wanted; he always did.

In those days, Menon was lean and tall with his hair oiled and combed perfectly in place. He was a zealous follower of fashion; the homespun cotton of his student activist days had given way to the British made sharkskin suits. A vivacious conversationalist, he was always welcomed at the evening discussions at the local club, which was an imitation of the British clubs where no Indian would be allowed. His jovial manner and boisterous laughter invariably attracted a group to his table. He had an unfailing ability to come up with a joke on any occasion and bring out the comical side of any situation.

Nor did he pass up an opportunity for a lively debate on the more serious subjects of social and political issues. The changes that India's freedom would bring remained his principal interest. It was an assumed fact that the British would be leaving India; it was only a question of time. He foresaw that freedom for India meant more than the departure of the British; freedom could not be accomplished until there was social and economic justice for the people.

Menon turned to the *National Herald* as a medium to voice his critiques and to suggest solutions for India's problems. In addition, the journal carried other essays by him on every aspect of life, from history and culture to public lectures. He quickly gained a reputation as a controversial character as he was willing to speak out against anyone, even the news media that supported him. However, his major emphasis was the plight of the poor and underprivileged including the soldiers, postmen and the shoe cobbler.

In the *National Herald*, December 1945, in an article headlined 'Honour to Released INA Men', Menon reported that little had been done to aid the released Indian National Army men as they returned to civilian life, particularly in the area of employment, upon their release from the military. Menon recommended that INA Central Committee open a Labour Bureau. "Let us show the world outside that besides mere declarations of our firm belief in the sincerity of INA men, we are ready as a nation to honour them with our respect and love."

In March 1946 edition of the *Herald*, Menon comments in an article headed 'In praise of postmen' that only in the moment of the impending strike of postmen had their value been realized, for, they did deserve fair compensation for their work. 'With their soulful devotion to their duty, these messengers of our Age deserve better pay and more respect. These niṣkāma karma yogīs (those who work unselfishly) serve only for the sake of serving.'

Again in the *Herald* in December 1946, under the headline of 'The Mochi – Symbol of Craftsmanship', Menon laments that the occupations of the shoe cobbler only pays pennies a day. Then he makes a philosophical comment on the cobbler's manner of working – 'With concentrated devotion to torn shoes, he sits working by the wayside with a disinterest for the modern world, which is rotting with its own false sense of values, its meaningless strife and its ridiculous prejudices. In mending soles, he mends the souls of those who care to watch him, for, from his serene face, the world can learn a sacred lesson.'

Early in 1947, a new series, 'The view from the footpath' by Mr. Tramp, was started for a publication named *The Commonweal.* These articles were actually an elaboration of social criticisms in the style of the earlier Baroda articles by the Mochi. However, his name was now too well-known to miss out on the prestige gained by revealing that Mr. Tramp was actually P. Balakrishnan Menon. Using first person singular, he would take the point of view of an underprivileged person facing the daily drudge of living in the shanties that line the city streets. Drawing on his personal experiences from living a year in the streets of Kashmir, he empathetically described the feelings of the poor as the wealthy rushed by them as if they were inanimate objects. One particularly touching article was the story of a beggar's son as he watched his mother die because there was no money to pay for medical care.

THIS WE CALL A DAY BY MR. TRAMP
Views from the Footpath/2nd in a series
The Commonweal, Thursday, February 13, 1947

It was the coldest of nights. After sleepless hours of waiting, the dawn at last grudgingly peeped out. From my corner under a wooden staircase which leads to the tinkling sanctums of a prosperous bank, I came out. Numb with cold, slightly giddy with exhaustion and hunger, I stood on the open footpath watching the empty streets. All slept; the entire bazaar was ominously silent. Leaning against a cold concrete pillar, I remained gazing into the dimly lit void of the sky.

What is the use of this existence? The only blood relation who I ever knew was my mother; she died a month back. It was good that she had died; she was suffering from her ancient stomach ache and no hospital had ever accepted her. Yet she always believed that one day some doctor would take pity and admit her, so everyday she visited the Government Hospital and patiently waited in a corner of its veranda.

I well remember that day, for, I had accompanied her. She sat in her usual corner. Then suddenly – that was the first time I had ever heard her complain – a painful cry burst out from her lips and she lay herself on the bare floor. Bending down on all fours, I tried to comfort her. She turned and rolled and twisted and bent in two. With set teeth she tried to suffer silently her agonising pain. Her grip on my arms tightened; I was surprised to feel her strength. Then once more she cried, or rather she howled.

The shrill dying cry brought out a furious compounder babu (assistant) and a wild doctorsahib (respected doctor). Threateningly, they closed down upon us; I could make no excuse. But as soon as the doctorsahib saw her, he softened. I allowed him to examine her. He pressed her belly – a crumbled, skinny, furrowed old belly. "Merā beṭā, merā beṭā," (my son, my son) called my Ma. I again bent over her; her bony hands groped for me. Her futile eyes stared vacantly. "Ma, Ma", I softly called. No answer! Her hands fell heavily on the floor by her side. I felt alone, lost and stunned.

Why didn't she get any treatment? Why didn't they save her? As though in answer to a host of similar questions that rose up in me, I heard the doctorsahib telling the compounder babu, "Pity, we had no space. What else could we have done? What about the victims of the riots? Certainly they should be given preference, shouldn't they?"

"That is right, Sir", conceded the babu. Then to console himself and his sahib, he added, "What if a poor beggar woman dies? She has to die anyway. Even if we had admitted her, how could she have purchased the medicines she needed? What could we have done for her?"

"Yes, what if a beggar woman dies?" When they both left, I looked into my mother's face – "Do you want anything, Ma? How are you feeling now? Better?" Her glassy eyes stared and remained open. I closed them reverently. What am I to do with her body? I asked myself. Funerals and ceremonies are for the rich. We, the rabble and the stray animals, often die, but are left to be removed and disposed of by others. We don't take care of the carcasses. Although we, no doubt, respect the dead, we can't afford to honour dead bodies.

I was heartened as I watched an innocent happiness beaming on my mother's face. After all, she must be happier now than ever she was in this life, this wretched life, where you feel the poignancy of cold and the bitterness of hunger. Those twin burning tortures that dog at our heels wherever we may go, however hard we may strive! Leaving her still body there on the dusty, cold hospital veranda, I walked off. I don't know what they did with her body. All I know is what the babus and the sahibs did for her while she was living – which was precious nothing! Now that she is dead, why should I care? None of us do. We, the poor ignorant brutes. We, the citizens of the slums!

Thus had my thoughts raced back as I stood on the footpath gazing at the void skies. I suppose the early morning hours have a bewitchery about them, they can obliterate the present, arrest the flow of hopes for the future, and push you headlong into your blasted past. Nothing like the dawn or the dusk to take up dull reminiscences within the dead souls of a cursed lot who strive endlessly in penury, want and starvation; this especially so when all these happen for no obvious fault of the hapless sufferers!

For how long I stood there thus lost in my own thoughts, I don't know. It was a loving hand on my shoulders that woke me up to the realities around me, to the cold morning, to the crowded traffic, to the hurrying pedestrians. "Why, you are hungry. Come on, I have something for you." The lame Mohammed Aslam has a way of reading one's thoughts and coming to everyone's help at dire moments. He is a benefactor in this Republic of the Rabble.

"Thank you very much." I was really hungry. "Honestly, I never thought that I was so hungry", I confessed as I rubbed my hands together after the third substantial roti.

"Allah be merciful! Last night I didn't sleep a bit. I was feeling that I was wrong in stealing a few handfuls of flour to make these rotis from that ration-shop of the lālā (shopkeeper), as I found no one to share it with me, no one who was as much in need of it as I was yesterday. Now I am happy because I can share with you today," explained Mohammed Aslam. (Though immoral ones, we too have our strict morals.)

"But certainly nothing is wrong in stealing something to eat when one is hungry," I consoled him. Aslam, leaning on his crutches raised his hand in a warning gesture. "Let us not discuss what is right and what is wrong. Leave it all for Allah to decide. Now both of us are no more hungry; let us go out." We strolled into the bazaar roads. Leaving Aslam at his usual seat on the Mithaiwala street, I started for the city.

At three o'clock in the afternoon I was still with my fellow sufferers, all of us hopefully expecting some odd job or other to come our way. None came to hire us... Or perhaps to say that is not to tell the entire truth. What happened was this – At about seven in the morning we were herded out by the agent of a rich contractor, hired at fourteen annas (nickels) per head, to move some bricks to the site of a new building that was under construction. We were at it for some three hours, until at about ten o' clock, the great contractor himself came. He saw us working, threw a fit, then called the manager and ordered him to dismiss us on the spot. We were accordingly turned out with one anna pay each. The contractor sahib insisted that, because of the distance the bricks were to be transferred, it was cheaper to engage a truck! But "Oh mighty contractor sahib," what about us!

Maybe the contractor was right in engaging the truck; how could we know? We are ever the ignorant. We know no calculations! However, we knew well one thing – that instead of getting a belly-full of grub, we ultimately got that day almost nothing. We were dismissed at 11 o'clock, and we knew that no one would hire us for the rest of the day.

Dusk descended without a warning, as it does in the north during the winter. Shivering in body and soul, we silently lumbered along, a jogging caravan of desperadoes, disillusioned and sorely frustrated. On the way we collected the blind, the ailing, the deformed and the diseased from their respective posts of duty. Some of them had earned a good number of copper coins.

Those who earned, fed the others; those who collected eatables, shared; those who came upon some discarded cloth pieces gave them away to those who needed them most. There is always a family feeling of oneness among us all. We are not mere citizens of a kingdom, but we are a well-knit, misery-bound community of strong men, patient and silent.

Now we wait for the gaudy shop-windows to close, for the lālās to retire, for the streets to empty. By ten at night the commercial hum dies out. We, in small groups, enter our respective sheltered corners. There, the unsatisfied children cry and whimper; the disillusioned youth grumble and curse; the resigned elders pray and silently suffer. Only a negligible few seriously talk of revolt and riot, of looting and murder, of violence and vengeance. All of us are drunk by bedtime – some with country liquor, others with regrets and all of us equally with despair.

Shivering in the cold we lie nestled together, a stinking mass of humanity, disinherited by society, condemned by the rich, neglected by the government, exiled from every respect that is due to man.

As we lie thus under our rags, this we call a DAY!!

3

Spiritual Practice Begins

Each one of us is in the right atmosphere and environment for our evolution. Don't try to be more intelligent than universal intelligence – Stay where you are and start opening!

—Swami Chinmayananda, 1972.

Menon's innate compassion for his fellowmen was quite evident in his journalism. But his sympathy was not only with the poor; his alert eye was carefully observing and measuring the benefits of the wealthy, fortunate few. As he watched their daily lives, he wondered if the economic improvement of the people was what was needed. With time he began to conclude that the wealthy, who had everything money could buy, exhibited neither happiness nor satisfaction with their lives.

With the combination of his journalist credentials, an extroverted personality and skill on the tennis court, he was soon able to accomplish his goal of entrance into the social world of the privileged wealthy. The occasion was a grand ball in one of the Delhi palaces with all the dignitaries of government and magnates of business on the guest list. That evening, his previous peripheral suspicions were confirmed. He observed first hand the 'good life'. That experience was one that would direct his future course. He later described the impact of that event.

A roaring welter of unnatural values! Impossible behaviours! Sick and suffering was this generation of hollow, lifeless creatures in the hustle and bustle within those stuffy palace walls. In their studied smiles

> were dormant tears; in their insincere, made to order laughter were sighs of voiceless, deep regrets. Their heartless love concealed stormy hatreds, grudging sympathies and poisonous rivalries. Each suffered and contributed lavishly to the suffering of others.
>
> This was sufficient for Mr. Balakrishnan Menon. At that ball, he saw what a godless animal life could be, even at the level that most considered to be the best. He decided on the very first day of gate crashing into this 'Palace of Life' to quit it for good. Beyond the palace walls lay uncharted deserts of the unknown. To walk out of life is easy; no questions are asked upon departing at the gate. No lies need be told, for, no one bothers to notice. But Menon had to answer his own questions – To whither, ye miserable stranger? He decided to seek for himself the lonely path of the Divine Life that promises to lead all pilgrims to the brilliant domain of perfection. This path might perhaps make life worth living. If this other be life, there was certainly nothing to lose!

....

On that day this lone traveller, equipped with courage, determination and intelligence, started forth on a course that would set an example for those whom he would some day teach – spiritual practices are to be done in the exact setting in which the seeker finds himself or herself. He later described the changes in his activities during this period.

....

> The mantra (sacred word or phrase) that he had repeated as a child came back to Menon. He took it up again, not in a spirit of defeatism, but with the refreshing realization that he was mere pilgrim on an unknown path. He must discover for himself the turns on the route and the charms of the destination. He did not know at that time just what the goal

was, or where the paths of spiritual practices would lead. But it was consolation enough, and sufficient encouragement for Menon to recognize the simple fact that the path of the 'Divine Life' was not running parallel to the tarred roads leading to the deceptive 'Palace of Life'.

For three years Menon secretly pursued a life of strict spiritual practices, while remaining in the very mainstream of life, always noisy with its gruesome agitation. He was never idle – he reacted to every solution, suggested plan, discussed scheme and manifesto; each social, national, international and one-world programme. Those in power devised ideologies to excuse their barbarous selfishness, discovered engines of cruelty to crush their fellow beings, perfected their arguments to torture the poor, enunciated laws to tyrannise over the weak and honest. They manoeuvred a revolution to bring about – not happiness to many – but power to the few.

....

Soon after his resolution to pursue philosophical studies, he had the opportunity to move in with an uncle, V. K. Govind Menon, and his son, B. Gopinath, who had come to Delhi for an extended stay to transact some business. He enjoyed their company and found that with fewer expenses he was able to spend less time writing to earn a living and more time reading. His uncle recalled that Balan would often be found curled up with a book.

His first endeavour was an intense study of philosophy, mainly European thought. Hoping for some insight to disperse his doubts about life, he poured over the books for months. Yet, dry philosophy gave little compensation to one burning for first hand experience. The words spoke not to the desire roaring in his heart, demanding expression in his own experience.

However, his personal studies did not keep him away from the world with which he continued to interact in his daily social encounters. Each evening, he, Gopinath and Shivadas (a cousin of Gopinath) would head for the local club to discuss the current events. "He was completely out of the ordinary. No obligations to anyone, he was a real gentleman at large. He was meticulous and careful in his actions. He was also very conscious of his appearance and would always remember to arrange his coat and trousers as he sat down so as not to wrinkle them," his cousin described the Menon of those days. "He paid careful attention to whatever he did and succeeded in every endeavour." These daily meetings continued to be a major source of information to follow up for his newspaper articles, so that he could spend the majority of his hours in pursuit of his spiritual and philosophical interests.

The uniqueness of the eternal Truth (Sanātana-dharma) of the Vedas is that in Bhārata there are great messengers born each century to interpret the ancient scriptures according to the needs of that particular era. The truths and values remain eternally the same, but the manner in which they are lived changed in the context of the current social pressures, economic necessities and individual lifestyles. These sages lead an exemplary life and take on a one-pointed mission to guide others in their spiritual evolution. They have discovered the truth of the spiritual goals described in the scriptures and give out their message to their generation in light of these two sources, their own personal illumination and the authority of the scriptures. Only a person with both of these qualifications is considered to be a true Teacher. This tradition assures the continuation of the authority of the original scriptures as well as a living example of the possibility of human achievement of the divine goals indicated in the scriptures.

The first half of the twentieth century had been kind to Bhārata in this respect. It was as if the needs of those years of crisis brought forth an extra allotment of these teachers. They gave spiritual guidance to the people of Bhārata as it endured the labour pangs into the birth of a nation with a name bestowed by foreign invaders, India. Swami Vivekananda, Swami Dayanand Saraswati, Swami Sivananda, Swami Rama Tirtha, Śrī Aurobindo and Ramana Maharshi had achieved such recognition that they were known in Europe and the United States. Three of them had also been active in India's demand for freedom from the British. These holy men were well-known since they spoke English and came in contact with large number of people. However, there were many others who lived quietly in their little huts in the forests giving guidance to those who searched them out.

It was at the crucial moment when it seemed that his questions about life were not answerable, though thundering louder then ever, that Menon turned to the words of these great saints. Truth cannot be disguised to a sincere seeker. When discovered, it is as if an inner light flashes; it is immediately known to be the Truth that one is seeking. Now Menon had some guidance and direction for his effort. He devoured the books written by and about these great sages. In the end he found the answers to his questions from his own countrymen.

There were no notable changes in his external life as he continued to keep his inner life to himself. However, he did question his uncle Govind and was able to learn something about the Hindu religion from this devout man, who was a scholar of the scriptures. Many Indians of the older generation, particularly from the south, where the political turmoil had been of less consequence than in the north, had upheld the traditional religious practices. The uncle also knew Ramana Maharshi and explained to his inquiring nephew the fame and greatness of this simple, devout sage who had left Menon with a memory that he could never quite forget.

This sage resides at Arunachala, a mountain peak of less than 3000 feet, but visible for miles as it rises up from the flat planes of southeast India. This was an area of India, like the majority of the rural region, that had been untouched by the influence of the British. Old India remained as it always had been – peaceful villages adorned with a small temple dome, dusty dirt roads across green fields, mud huts of poor peasants, washermen pounding clothes in the ponds, crows circling overhead, scorching summer sun, monsoon floods.

Swami Chinmayanada describes his first visit to Arunachala

It was the summer season, about 1936, when I was a student at St. Thomas College in Trichur. That year the southern railroad offered a student pass. For some nominal fee one could travel on any train in Southern India during the vacation period. I just took off. I had no destination, no schedule – I would just pick a town that interested me, get off the train, explore, and talk to people, then when I was inclined I would get on the next train passing through. It didn't matter what direction it was headed. I was just enjoying seeing a big chunk of my homeland and talking to people. I was young, about twenty years old, and very curious to see how others thought and lived.

As I had always lived in Cochin with its lush forests and fields, it was a shocking contrast to see the poor people eking out a livelihood in the desert areas. Once when we were passing through one of these desolate regions, a barren, red mountain loomed in the distance. Suddenly all the people in the coach jumped up and ran to one side of the train, looking in that direction. When I asked what was going on, I was told that this was the famous Arunachala Hill, mentioned in the Purāṇas (Hindu epics) as the centre of the universe. I was further informed that a great sage now lived at its base. Observing all this enthusiasm, I of course, was quite curious and thought it should be an interesting phenomena to investigate. So, I got off the train at the next stop and began inquiring the directions to the hermitage of this supposedly great man.

It was really quite far from the train station, especially by foot power, but I plodded along in that burning, bright sun of Tamil Nadu. I asked directions along the way until I finally arrived at a large thatched hut that served as a meeting hall. It was just about noon and the sun of June (India's hottest month) was nearly unbearable, so upon entering that dim room I was momentarily blinded. As my eyes began to adjust, I made out shapes of people sitting, all facing in the same direction. So I made my way up to the front where I noticed that there was a kind of low platform. Seeing some space over to the side of it, I sat down to await whatever it was that everyone else was waiting for.

As I was sitting, feeling the relief of being out of that blistering heat, I looked up and noted to my surprise that there was a human form on the platform. When my eyes adjusted to the dim light, I discerned the form of a human body stretched out with his feet in my direction. My eyes began to slowly scan the body starting at the feet, part by part – his legs, his hips (he wore only a simple loin cloth), his chest, his arms. He had one forearm up and was resting his head in that hand. As my eyes travelled up, they finally reached his face, then the area of his eyes. They were closed; he seemed to be sleeping. But just at the moment my eyes focused on his eyes, his eyes suddenly popped open and he looked straight into mine. I knew, in that one moment, with that one look that he knew everything about me – even things that I did not know myself. I sat there transfixed as if seeing my whole life go up in a wave. Then he quietly closed his eyes again. I continued to sit there for a short time; I really don't know for how long. When I was again aware of my body and surroundings, I forced myself to get up, wondering what had happened. I shook my head to clear my thinking – 'Nothing has happened to me', I rationalised. 'This man is a hypnotist.'

Later, while talking with his uncle in Delhi, Menon realized that he had been a fool not to value this experience of being in the presence of a Man of Wisdom. Something had 'happened', but his mind had not been pure enough to grasp its significance. Rationalizations and doubts had come in to cover over the impact of this encounter with a true Master.

Through his reading and study, questions kept tugging at Menon's mind. Was there any truth to what the Hindu sages were saying? If they were really concerned about mankind, why weren't they down there with him trying to improve the society in which man was destined to live? How could they justify their retired life along the holy rivers and in the sacred mountains when Bhārata was suffering under the distress of centuries of foreign domination? If the scriptures that the sages carefully preserved were not of any use to man in his struggle to meet his everyday life and improve its conditions, should not the scriptures be thrown out and a new system be devised? Haunted by such doubts and confusion, at last Menon determined that he would set out for the Himalayas to find the answers to these questions for himself.

It was at this time that another change came into his life. His uncle and cousin had completed their business in Delhi and were moving back to Cochin, leaving Menon without a home. This was an opportune moment for him to make a move; he was ready for seclusion. He rented a small room in a boarding house where he could have complete privacy for his study, contemplation and meditation. As the men said their goodbyes, Menon confided in his uncle, "I am going to the Himalayas to see what those holy men really do. I'm going to get the inside story!"

4

The Sage, Swami Sivananda[1]

Swami Sivananda is a name to be remembered not only for his own spiritual achievements, but also for the approach he has been advocating to stimulate the modern man's eagerness to learn and practice the great Vedāntic teachings.
—Swami Chinmayananda, 1947.

Swami Sivananda was born in September 1887, as Kuppuswami Iyer, in rural Tamil Nadu. A typical southern village, it was surrounded by green rice fields and mango groves. His family had a long tradition of scholarliness and saintliness. The young Kuppu enjoyed the advantages of both a religious home and material comforts, for, even though his father, Śrī P.S. Vengu Iyer, was a Brāhmaṇa priest, he worked for a salary as a revenue official. Mr. Iyer was respected as a saintly person, who dealt kindly and fairly with his friends, family and neighbours, as well as the gods, as he performed the rituals prescribed for Brāhmaṇas in his home daily. These religious values were to guide the son Kuppu throughout his life.

During his school years in an English medium school, funded by the local raja, he excelled in both sports and academics. Self-assured, extroverted and friendly, he was a favourite among the students and teachers alike. His passion for gymnastics was so great that he would get up as early as 3 a.m. After carefully arranging the bed covers so that he would not be missed, he would hurry to the empty gym so that he could use all the equipment.

[1] Compiled from information in the *Autobiography of Swami Sivananda* and other sources published by the Divine Life Society, Yoga-Vedanta Forest Press, P.O. Sivanandanagar, Dt. Tehri-Garhwal, U.P., Himalayas, India.

His scholastic achievements merited him entrance into a strict Jesuit college. There he imbibed a thorough knowledge of the Bible, and a fascination for Christ and the Christian mystics.

His outgoing personality was always turned toward others, whether helping them with schoolwork, solving personal problems or arbitrating a quarrel. Therefore, it was no surprise when he chose the service oriented career of medicine. His medical studies began at the Tanjore Medical Institute in 1905, but were interrupted by an urgent letter. His father had died suddenly and his mother had fallen ill.

Kuppu hurried home to console and care for his mother, and to face a new problem – economic. The family finances had been dependent on the regular income of his father. Without these funds, Kuppu had to come up with a source of income to support his mother and himself. Determined to remain with his ailing mother, he came up with the solution – he would start a medical journal right there in his home. Ambrosia included results of the latest medical research as well as articles of general interest to the public. He was editor, manager, distributor and chief contributor, although he masked this fact by assigning various pseudonyms to many of the articles that he wrote, thereby making it appear as if the journal had a regular contributing staff.

He took advantage of this break from his formal scholastic studies to pursue his personal interests of philosophy and religion, both Hindu and Christian. With the required subjects at the university, he had found too little time to study these subjects in depth. Putting into practice what he read in the books, he began a daily routine of yoga postures, breathing exercises and meditation, using both Hindu and Christian (Catholic) meditation techniques.

Reputed for its reliable information, Ambrosia was well accepted by the medical community; however, the distribution remained small. Finally Kuppu Iyer was forced to seek additional income and took a position at a pharmacy in Madras (now

Chennai). Soon after, he learned of a job opportunity in British Malaya (a part of modern Malaysia) as the manager of a hospital maintained by a large rubber plantation that employed many indentured Indian workers. There he could obtain his training as an intern and complete his medical education. Overruling the protests from his family, he chose his own path, for, he realized that selfless service to mankind was, in his own words, 'the most potent weapon to thin out the ego'. He accepted the job in Malaya and boarded the ship for the journey.

After completing his internship and examinations in that country, he moved from a managerial position at the hospital to the medical staff as a full-time doctor. Dr. Iyer's attitude of helping others without thought of personal gain endeared him to all his superiors and colleagues. He was a favourite among the patients who joined this young, devout doctor as he led them in a prayer meeting each Friday. His generosity was well-known to all; he personally financed the medical care of some of the poor patients and was known to distribute coins among the patients so that they could afford a book or candy. A nutritious meal was assured for anyone at his home – whether friend, beggar or stray dog.

After several years, Dr. Iyer moved to a larger hospital outside of Singapore, which gradually increased his fame and financial security. There he published his first medical book and continued his numerous contributions to medical journals. He was a man of tremendous energy and easily found time from his busy routine to continue his spiritual disciplines. Each day he rose by 4 a.m. for yoga and meditation, even when hospital duties had kept him up until midnight. Through these years, his mind was becoming calmer and purer, thus the joy of his relation to the Lord increased as he served, prayed, meditated and sang the devotional hymns that he loved so well.

His daily observations of poverty and sickness taught him an acute lesson about life. He described his feelings at that time.

> 'People are sick physically and mentally. To some, life is but a lingering death; to some, death is more welcome than life. Some lead a miserable life, unable to face death; some invite death by suicide, unable to face life. An aspiration began to grow within me that, if God had not made this world merely as a hell for hexed people to be thrown in to suffer, and, if there is (as I intuitively felt there should be) something other than this misery and this helpless existence, I must know and experience it.'

His longing to learn more of the true purpose of life brought a poor, very ill, Swami to his door one day. The holy man was impressed by the capacity for caring and devotion of Dr. Iyer. The young man took advantage of the opportunity to discuss spiritual themes as soon as the patient's health returned. Observing the seeker's ardent desire for true knowledge, the Swami gave him his one possession, a text of Vedānta, a philosophical treatise on the nature of life. Reading the truths in this book, Dr. Iyer began to feel an overwhelming desire to devote himself totally to spiritual pursuits. "The positive aspects of this earthly life and the real purpose of this life were made apparent" – "this drew me from Malaya to Himalaya," Dr. Iyer disclosed.

Thus in 1923 after ten years of service in the two hospitals, the decision was made. He left no task unfinished; his life in the world was complete. He packed up the barest necessities and returned to his homeland. Back in India, his pilgrimage began in Varanasi, long revered as holy ground both as a residence and meeting place of many holy men through the centuries. Although today Varanasi remains a centre for scholarly scriptural study, the bustle of commerce has sent the present-day saints to higher altitudes. However, in 1923 it was still possible to meet holy men and learned Swamis passing along the banks of the Ganga. From Varanasi, Dr. Iyer travelled to other noted places of spiritual pilgrimage. He lived a life of complete renunciation, which meant having only one set of clothes, taking a daily bath in the Ganga and eating only begged food, a difficult practice for one accustomed to doing all the giving. Slowly, he made his way to Rishikesh, where he received the formal renunciation vows from Swami Vishnudevananda, the head of the esteemed Kailash Ashram. The new Swami was given the name Swami Sivananda Saraswati and a set of saffron clothes. His daily life changed little, for, he continued to live a simple life, so that he could spend all of his waking hours in constant contemplation on the truths of the scriptures. The essence in them was gradually transformed from the precepts of intellectual knowledge into his own personal experience of direct knowledge during these years of his wanderings.

By 1930 the depth of his realization was apparent by his blissful countenance, serene composure and divine utterances. His love and compassion for mankind compelled him to begin teaching others. Soon a group of disciples gathered around him to reap the benefits of hearing the eternal Truth (Sanātana-dharma) from one who knew it first hand. "I have begun to roar like a lion of Vedānta", he confided to a friend, for the depth of his words surprised even him. Around 1934, he and a few followers established a small āśrama, Ananda Kutir (Cottage of Bliss), on the banks of the Ganga at Rishikesh. They also started a small charity hospital to serve the poor and to provide medical service to the many itinerant Swamis. In his wanderings, Swami Sivananda had been caring for any sick, ailing Swami whom he happened to meet. Their sufferings from malnutrition, fever and dysentery had been unbearable for him, yet he could do little to aid them with his limited resources. At Ananda Kutir the Swamis would have a free hospital so they could receive proper care.

As years passed the āśrama and its operations expanded, a non-profit trust organization was founded and named, Divine Life Society. An herbal medicine pharmacy, a printing press, cottages for new disciples and visitors – year by year new structures were added to accommodate the expansion of the charitable work. The *Divine Life* magazine was published; funds came for a free kitchen for the Swamis in the area; the hospital was expanded.

People from the planes of India were generously supporting the activities at the 'Cottage of Bliss'.

Swami Sivananda felt that practices such as devotional singing and meditation sped up spiritual evolution. Not only did he lead the daily services at Ananda Kutir, but during the 1930s, he travelled throughout the northern regions from Kashmir to Calcutta (now Kolkata) giving lectures and singing bhajanas (devotional songs). Wherever he travelled he organized centres to perpetuate spiritual practice in the area.

In his autobiography, he declared, "I want my disciples to be like myself in applying themselves in an all-round manner to the propagation of the Lord's message, the development of divine qualities in themselves and their inculcation in others." In preparing for the task, he advised one of them –

> "Wherever you go, give, distribute, and disseminate your ideas, mottoes and ideals. Broadcast your spiritual feelings. Share with others. Always give, give, give. Give all. Ask nothing. The present work you do is a greater yoga than the impotent, so-called meditation – sleeping and building of (dream) castles combined – done by Vedāntins of the present-day. This work is a great yajña or sacrifice. Work like a lion. Roar like a lion."

In 1950 the dynamic Teacher completed a tour of India and Ceylon to disperse the spiritual values of Hinduism. He visited all the important cities where he gave talks on spiritual practices and led singing of bhajanas. After listening to his melodious, devotion filled voice, many in the audience were filled with such joy that they joined with him in dancing in ecstasy.

It was to this hive of spiritual and charitable activities that the journalist Mr. P. Balakrishnan Menon of the *National Herald* headed, armed with a pen, pad of paper, and an inquiring mind.

5

Meeting the Sage

Serve, Love, Purify, Meditate, Realize and Be Free – Practice of these became my life.

—Swami Chinmayananada, 1947.

It was the summer season of 1947 when Mr. Menon at last set out for Rishikesh. "I am going to find out how those holy men are keeping up the bluff! I am prepared to expose the whole racket", he declared to his friends. Menon planned to conduct his interviews with the critical mind of a journalist, yet he knew he was seeking more than he admitted to others. At that point the true question in his mind was whether it was possible to find peace and tranquillity by going to an āśrama and leading a spiritual life. And he wasn't even sure what a 'spiritual life' meant, but he was determined to find out.

Rishikesh was the most likely place to find a person of wisdom. Situated at the base of the Himalayas where the Ganga broadens into a smooth river after its tumultuous journey from the high altitudes of snow-capped peaks, Rishikesh was named for an ancient seer ṛṣi), who became Master of himself – achieved Enlightenment – at this spot. Through the centuries, many saints, Swamis and ascetics who travelled through the Himalayan ranges, have frequented it. It had once been a primeval forest of pines, cedars and bamboos, interlaced and decorated with many varieties of flowering and fruit bearing vines. Elephants, bears and tigers were found there in abundant numbers, but the tooting of cars and the whistling of trains had replaced the cries of wild animals as they gradually retreated to more remote safety. Only the mischievous monkeys and a few strutting peacock remained as reminders of its primeval past.

After the twenty-four hour train ride from Delhi Menon set out immediately on the one-mile trek along the north bank of the Ganga to the āśrama of Swami Sivananda. Upon reaching the grounds, he encountered several of the Swami's disciples. He introduced himself and explained that he had come up from Delhi to meet an authentic sage in person and to see what life in an āśrama was like. Menon was kindly received, given the customary cup of tea, and then the disciples made arrangements for his lodging in the guest hostel. An āśrama was considered to be the home of the Swami and any visitor to it was treated as his personal guest.

After disposing of his luggage in the small, sparsely furnished room, Menon was conversing with a group of residents in the shade of a spreading mango tree when Swami Sivananda approached them from the rear. It was about noon and he was walking from his office to his personal cottage where he would eat and rest. As was customary, everyone rose and greeted him, as did Menon. He recognized the Swami immediately as he had seen his photograph in various publications. One in the group introduced Mr. Menon and mentioned to the Swami that he had just arrived as a guest. Swami Sivananda greeted him and asked him a few personal questions. Menon explained that he was a journalist from Delhi and had come up to see the land of the holy sages, as he had never had the opportunity to see this area that figured so prominently in the spiritual history of India. Continuing, he added that he intended to write a story on the area and had read some of the Swami's works; for this reason, he had come specifically to Ananda Kutir.

Swami Sivananda asked Menon how long he would be staying. Mr. Menon replied that he could probably collect the information he needed in a day or two. "What's your hurry? You should take your time and satisfy yourself that you see everything. Stay at least a few days; anyway you are welcome to stay as long as you like."

Menon soon observed that this Swami was no hermit sitting in the retirement of meditation; he was busy seven days a week without holidays or vacations. His daily routine included correspondence with spiritual seekers around the world, writing articles and books on religious subjects, receiving guests at the āśrama and managing the hospital. In addition, he would sit in the main hall each evening with his disciples and guests to answer their spiritual questions and doubts, then conduct an evening service of singing devotional hymns, followed by a discourse on a spiritual text. In spite of his busy schedule, he would often take tea to a visiting Swami, or carry fruits and sweets to the hospital for the patients. He was the humblest of men; there was no job too small for him and no day too short to complete his work, yet he always exuded a dynamic peace through all his activities.

Finding Swami Sivananda such a kind and generous, as well as a godly person, Menon was quite inspired and gradually extended his stay to several days, then a few more. The days grew into weeks; the weeks into a month. During this period, Swami Sivananda would now and again prod him, saying, "God has blessed you with such intelligence; why don't you use it to analyse and see that the worldly life is only misery. Observe. Think about the life you are living down in the plane. Then draw your own conclusion!"

There was little doubt in the eyes of the disciples that this Balakrishnan Menon was receiving special attention from the Swami, and they could not see why. There did not appear to be a spiritual bone in his body – he was an extrovert, always on the move, forever talking, constantly drilling everyone like the reporter that he was. They never saw him in meditative mood; instead, his main interest seemed to be his ever present cigarette and a cup of tea. Of course, there were no complaints when he treated them to a cup at the local tea shop. Yet they did admit that he had those big, bulging yogic eyes and extra long arms, which are both considered outward signs of a great yogī of supernatural powers in a previous birth. "There must be some spiritual tendencies from previous lives. If our Swami is interested in Menon, it is definitely the result of karma-phala (fruits of past actions)", they concluded as they watched Menon trudge to the train station for his return to Delhi.

September 8, 1947 was the Diamond Jubilee Birthday of Swami Sivananda. This particular birthday, the sixtieth, is always honoured by special celebrations. Sixty is the number of years it took a certain comet known in ancient times to complete its cycle; therefore, this number is considered to have a special significance in an individual's life cycle. For Swami Sivananda's sixtieth year, there was to be a big celebration for Ananda Kutir. Devotees were to arrive from all over India to join in the tribute.

To commemorate the occasion, a souvenir book was to be released. This book would include some articles on the Swami's life and projects as well as various spiritual subjects. The disciples and devotees would write the material, but there was no one at Ananda Kutir who was qualified to take on the arduous task of editing it. Then Swami Sivananda's secretary, Mr. Dar Rao[1], came up with the solution. He recommended that they send a request to the journalist in Delhi who had recently visited the āśrama. He would surely be willing to help and be able do a professional job.

Throughout his life Balakrishnan Menon had been lean and wiry. However, when he arrived at the āśrama to start editing the commemorative book, everyone was shocked – he was nothing but skin and bones. Rumours spread that he had fasted for forty days. Menon ignored the indirect allusions to the fasting, and no one felt it proper to ask him directly for information that he didn't volunteer. In spite of his appearance, everyone observed that he was as alert and active as ever; so they concluded his emaciated look was from fasting, not from illness. "Certainly his

[1] Mr. Rao was later initiated as Swami Chidananda.

chain smoking and heavy tea drinking habits were not daunted", they critically observed.

During the day Mr. Menon worked on the editing of the articles for the commemorative book. Mornings and evenings he joined the resident disciples in the daily routine of the āśrama, as did all of the guests. Days followed a general schedule – a 4 a.m. bath in the cold waters of the Ganga, meditation, then breakfast, assigned tasks or study, lunch, rest, study and the evening service.

The editing of the souvenir book was soon completed, but with some objections. Mr. Menon had ruthlessly cut the articles, even some which were written by important persons. Swami Sivananda feared they might be offended. Menon stood his ground. He assured the Swami that the essence of the articles had remained, and that the message was even clearer when the extraneous material was removed. In the end, all the articles stood as edited.

When the celebration day arrived, everyone was in an especially festive mood. They were not only commemorating the Swami's birth, but also the birth of a free India. The transfer from the British had occurred the previous month on August 15. Everyone was very optimistic; they were free after a long, hard struggle – twenty-seven gruelling years since they had officially declared their independence in 1930. There had been tens of thousands of martyrs to the cause, but the days of poverty, prison and submission were believed to be over.

Menon stayed on to participate in the celebration and to continue with his own programme of studies. At one evening service, always a rather informal, spontaneous event, Mr. Rao gave a talk on a spiritual topic. Then out of the blue Swami Sivananda called on Mr. Menon to get up and speak.

"Me? What will I talk about? I don't know this spiritual subject like you. Isn't that why I am here?" queried Menon, hesitant to put the ideas he had been reading into words.

"So talk on anything, something you do know about – your trip up to Rishikesh!" persisted the Swami.

"Well, I came up from Delhi", Menon began. His mind flashed back to the village, the wide planes of wheat racing by the train window, but there was nothing distinctive about that. He simply could not continue. This was one of the rare occasions that Mr. Menon was at a loss for words.

At last Swami Sivananda interrupted the silence, "It's okay – you'll get another chance."

The service continued on with the uplifting chanting of the Lord's name – Om Namaḥ Śivāya. Menon smiled inwardly as he listened to the words of his childhood mantra.

"What is this, an M.A., a successful journalist, not able to give a short, impromptu discourse", Swami Sivananda commented as he stopped Menon on the way out of the hall. "You had better prepare yourself for tomorrow evening's meetings as I'm sure to call on you again." Then he started for his cottage, but turned back, "Say, why don't you take the theme of śreyas and preyas as your first topic."

The following day Menon researched the suggested theme. After some time of contemplation on the subject, he carefully wrote out his thoughts. Then an elder Swami volunteered to check over the ideas to make sure he had caught the import of the concepts. That evening Mr. Menon gave his first spiritual discourse. The subject was one that has puzzled many keen observers of life, why is it that man knowing good from bad, and, although desiring to do good, still does what he considers bad and even harmful to himself or others. The discourse on the path of the sensually pleasant (preyas) versus the path of the morally good (śreyas) would not qualify as his most brilliant, but with it Swami Sivananda launched Mr. P. Balakrishnan Menon on a lifework of giving spiritual discourses.

The Swami continued to call on Menon to give a short talk from time to time. So he spent a portion of each day studying and reviewing a particular spiritual topic, then carefully assimilating the ideas into a clear, succinct presentation. Swami Maunananda would then go over his notes to clarify or elaborate on some of the points. To that Swami's surprise Menon often did not use his suggestions, but would leave the talks in their original form. Menon felt that it was better to use the ideas of his own reflection and contemplation, even if they were not yet totally correct, than to blindly imitate someone else's words. When the Swami questioned him about forgetting to use his comments, Menon would simply say, "Oh, these people at the meeting won't know the difference anyway." There are no secrets in an āśrama, so the gossip circulated, "Menon thinks he knows more than the Swamis!"

Menon later commented on those visits to Ananda Kutir.

> At first I was mechanically imitating the routine to look like a serious seeker, for, these were the things they believed any serious seeker must do – although I was not convinced. I took the Ganga bath with them at dawn, attended the evening service, chanted the hymns, worked at the āśrama chores, helped in the office and served the elder Swamis – in short, served as an obliging errand boy for all. Throughout the day, I consumed the books from the extensive library. At night there was no light since the āśrama was not electrified yet. In the darkness – through the long nights – I had time to rethink what I had read during the day.

Swami Sivananda was a model Swami in his discipline and his service, but there were other Swamis to observe. On the day of Swami Sivananda's birthday, a huge crowd gathered to celebrate and partake of a special feast. As a resident, even though a temporary one, Menon helped to serve the food. The dessert was laḍḍū[1] so plentiful that they were served in buckets. The servers went around several times passing out two or three to each Swami. Then one Swami signalled for more, then more, then again for another one. Menon estimated that the count for the glutton was at least a dozen laḍḍūs. If the Swami had no self-control, Menon would provide it; he pretended that he did not see the Swami's signal for more.

On another occasion when he was walking along the Ganga that ran beside the āśrama, a Swami who maintained silence as a spiritual discipline signalled to him. After five minutes of signalling and deciphering, Menon finally figured out that all the man wanted was a cup of tea. Menon then purchased it for him, but not without a mental comment – What a stupid waste of time. In ten seconds, he could have simply told me what he wanted. How can one consider this nonsense spiritual? Menon lamented these practices as he continued down the path that runs along the river.

He silently made these observations and persisted with his own study. He was clearly seeing the value of moving the thoughts and contemplation from the misty regions of the head into concrete words to explain to others during the evening services. In the process his understanding of spiritual concepts and ideas was getting clearer and clearer.

Yet he remained silent when Swami Sivananda again suggested, "God blessed you with such intelligence, why don't you use it for Him? You can join us – become a Swami like us! Keep this idea in mind, even as you continue with your life out in the world."

After three months of āśrama life, Menon returned to Delhi. He picked up his daily life and career as he had left them. From all external appearances life went on as usual. As he explained –

[1] A sweet combination of sugar, spices and yellow dal that is rolled into a two-inch ball.

> "These trips to Rishikesh did not have too much of an effect on my actions. It was my thoughts and ideas, my concepts and visions, my values and principles, that were changing in the relentless logic of the great books of Hinduism. So whether I was in Delhi or in Rishikesh the place did not change my daily thought life as I took up whatever actions there were to be done. I remained active with my work and with running from Delhi to Rishikesh, but these physical movements were perhaps my mind's attempts to run away from its own growing conviction that I had wasted my life up until then."

When he left Ananda Kutir, he carried a bundle of books from the Divine Life printing press, all written by Swami Sivananda. Many were verse by verse commentaries on the various scriptures of Vedānta; others were transcripts of his public lectures, discussions and talks, which had been given on Indian radio. The Swami's personal spiritual insight lent inspiration as well as practical application to these ancient teachings of the spiritual giants of India. Educated in British styled schools and in a Christian college, Swami Sivananda both lectured and wrote in English, so none of his knowledge was lost or misinterpreted through translation into English from an Indian language. To date, all of his commentaries and original works remain among the most respected by Hindu religious authorities.

At this time a new subject entered into Menon's newspaper articles – reviews of books dealing with spiritual matters. Although religious terms and concepts had been appearing in his articles for several years, he now made public this personal interest. Reviews of books from the Forest Press at Ananda Kutir were included in the *National Herald* and *Champion Magazine*. Of Swami Sivananda's *Light Fountain* he comments, "Although the title may be a bit far-fetched, the volume is an interesting study of a St. Francis-like saint of the Himalayas, who is doing yeoman service for the revival of spirituality in India and abroad." Reviewing *The Philosophy and Teachings* of Swami Sivananda Saraswati, he praises the Swami's "happy combination of theory and practical tips". Further, "his use of many apt illustrations drawn from ordinary life hits so close to home that even a casual perusal brings out the entire significance, alive and palpitating." He continues in the article –

> "The striking feature in this Swami's works seems to be his almost contagious self-confidence and convincing methods. He proves to be one who has not only studied and commented on the Prasthāna Trayī[1], which form the rock bottom foundation of all of the many Hindu philosophical schools, but has actually lived them to a degree of perfection not yet known to have been achieved by any except the ancient seers and sages who have now become mere mythological characters to us. It reads as though it were a volume that has come out of the pen of one who has just stepped out from among those perfect Masters of our classical Sanskrit poets."

Menon's book reviews also included several selections from the Aurobindo Ashram. In 1910 after imprisonment by the British Government with the charge of 'advocating terrorism and violence,' Śrī Aurobindo Ghose experienced enlightenment while incarcerated. He then retreated to the small French territory of Pondicherry (now Puducherry). Menon wrote a review of *The World Crisis – Śrī Aurobindo's Vision of the Future,* in which the sage developed the premise that the present world crisis was but a birth pang of mankind, one of nature's catalysts for advancing human evolution to a new era of hope and salvation in the world community. Another review summarised the biography of one of

[1] The three principal scriptures of Vedānta – *Brahmasūtras,* the Upaniṣads and the *Bhagavad-gītā.*

Śrī Aurobindo's disciples, Yogī Shuddhananda Bharati, known for his research into all of the major religions and philosophies. From these studies, he synthesized a śuddha sanmārga, 'pure spiritual path', for all of humanity to follow in order to attain harmonious peace in the world.

The idea of world community must have particularly appealed to the socialist Menon as he also reviewed another work on the subject, *The Streamers of Light from the New World*, published in Los Angeles, California. Menon's review included these comments –

> "Altogether *Streamers of Light*, is an exceptionally decent volume, providing a vivid picture of the author's vision of a new, ideal world with a new race characterised by width of tolerance, height of vision and depth of insight, and imbued with an enduring peace passed from generation to generation. To work out the dream we will have to train a generation to be perfect, a generation who are masters of themselves. In this feat, I find no impossibility. Perhaps, some millenniums will be necessary to achieve this degree of perfection – but the goal is worth the attempt and the ultimate achievement worth the waiting."

Menon's words read like a prophecy of the work that he would be attempting in the world within a few years. Such ideals were the result of his having encountered a Master of Swami Sivananda's advanced state of spiritual realization, a model to serve as a living example that such self-perfection was indeed possible.

Menon continued to divide his time between his mundane life in Delhi and the spiritual life in Rishikesh. Special spiritual camps of ten days commemorating the many Hindu holy festivals were regularly held at Ananda Kutir. These particular days are considered to be auspicious times for meditation because the earth is in a balanced relation to the sun and moon. These configurations have a calming, quieting effect on the restless mind, which aids in the transcendence of the mind during meditation. On these holidays there would be special chanting of the Lord's name, often continuously for several days and nights, ending with Swami Sivananda leading a peaceful meditation.

Swami Sivananda continued to ask Mr. Menon to participate in the evening services and Menon did not object. On the contrary, he welcomed such opportunities to clarify his ideas, often choosing topics upon which he had doubts, so that with his research he could illuminate his own mind on the subject. This was his constant concern – enhancing the quality of his own understanding.

Swami Sivananda loved thinking of new ways to present the truths of spiritual life to his disciples and guests at the āśrama. On one occasion he organized a short drama from the life of Gautama Buddha, based on the story in which a distraught mother came to the Buddha holding her dead child in her arms. Weeping over her loss, she implored the great one to give life back to her only child. The Buddha, in his wisdom, instructed her to go out into the village, inquire at each house and bring back a mustard seed from any household that had escaped the tragedy of death. If she brought back even one mustard seed, he would surely give life to the child. The woman went out for her investigation but did not return, for, it was impossible to find even one household that Lord Death (Dharmarāja) had not visited.

The Swami selected Menon to participate in the drama as the distraught mother. With a scarf draped around his head and a cloth-bundle baby cuddled in his arms, he made such a caricature of the dejected little lady, elaborated with a display of weeping and wailing, that the whole audience exploded into laughter. Swami Sivananda was delighted with the performance. "The best I've seen", he declared as he wiped the tears of glee from his eyes. Later when a special guest arrived at the āśrama, he would command a repeat performance from Menon. However, the Swami himself, with his great capacity for joy, enjoyed the repeat performances more than anyone else did.

Finally, Menon asked Swami Sivananda about the possibility of being initiated to become a Swami. But to his surprise, the Swami advised him to be cautious, "There's no hurry. You're still so young. You go on with your newspaper work in Delhi. That's the Lord's work too. You must be sure you've tasted all of the worldly life. Let's give you plenty of time to be sure that this is a true desire for the spiritual life, not just a temporary moment of disenchantment with the world."

One preoccupation that brought Menon back to Delhi regularly was concern for his long-time friend, Shroff, who was suffering from a terminal illness. Menon felt helpless in the confrontation with his friend's physical and mental anguish.

> Each time I ran down to the bedside of my dear friend who was suffering endlessly from a mortal disease, the more I grew confirmed in my present, growing conviction that wealth, position, loving parents, wife, child – all of these might be there, as Shroff himself had achieved – but nothing of the world can really console, comfort and stand by one when one is suffering. Life is empty and shallow without the inner expansion, the inner depth. This inner wealth alone can reinforce against the sledgehammer strokes of destiny, the conspiracy woven by the circumstances of life.

After several years of intense suffering Shroff breathed his last breath. The body was cremated according to Hindu custom, accompanied by the traditional rituals performed by a priest to invoke a safe passage of the soul into the afterlife. The elder Mr. Shroff was quite old and the loss of his only son, born late in his life after much prayer and with much thanksgiving, was a heavy blow. He did not feel well enough to make the trip to Rishikesh, yet he wanted the ashes of his son dispersed in the holy Ganga. Upon his request, Menon, who was like a second son to him, agreed to take on the responsibility. It required no extra effort since he was spending nearly all his time at Rishikesh anyway. He had intended to return there after his friend's cremation ritual.

The following day, the solemn Menon entered the first-class compartment where he would be spending the next twenty-four hours alone with the sole remains of one who had been a vibrant, lively, intelligent companion. Mr. Shroff's servant carefully secured the basket, which held the sealed pot of ashes, on the overhead rack. The family bid him a safe journey from the platform as they bravely held back their tears. With a puff of black smoke, the train lurched forward beginning its journey across the Indian planes, then up to the foothills of the Himalayas.

Menon tried to read to pass the time, but his attention kept being diverted to the pot overhead. It seemed to rattle with the motion of the train. He and Shroff had passed many hours in a train compartment like this one – those were happy, carefree hours, coming down to Delhi from Lucknow University to spend the holidays with Shroff's family. The recurring thought kept circulating through his mind –

> *"The man who is usually with me is now in that small basket – a few bones and ashes are all that remain. Flesh and life are gone. Flesh and life are gone."*

6

Pilgrimage in the Himalayas

Pilgrimage is a very powerful means of self-purification; for, if the pilgrim has eyes and ears to watch and experience the beauty and majesty of nature, then his capacity to contemplate explodes within himself and he reaches hitherto unknown depths.

—Swami Chinmayananda, 1982.

By the spring of 1948, for all practical purposes, Menon had taken up permanent residence at Ananda Kutir; from there he was able to continue his career by mailing his articles down to Delhi. During this time, he received a letter from a cousin, Bhaskar Menon. Bhaskar did not think of himself as a religious man; actually, he claimed to be a total agnostic. Nevertheless, he had followed a strict ethical and moral code that he considered common sense, not religion. Yet he found that he had to regularly compromise his ideals in his chosen profession as a lawyer. He disclosed in his letter that this disenchantment had led him to reflect on the value of the impermanent life and its short-lived joys. Thereafter he had spent his vacation time in making regular pilgrimages to holy places and temples in Kerala. Now, after careful consideration, he had decided to leave everything and go to the Himalayas to renounce the world by taking the sannyāsa vows to become a Swami. Bhaskar had heard that his cousin was a regular visitor at the Sivananda Ashram and thought Menon might be able to assist him in fulfilling this desire.

Menon showed the letter to Swami Sivananda, describing Bhaskar's past and his naturally sincere, austere, honest character.

Although he was unpractised in religion, he had read books of philosophy and was a deep thinker on the nature of life. Bhaskar had been a man of strict self-discipline his entire life. Such a person can easily take to the hardships necessary to renounce the pleasures and luxuries of the world. Swami Sivananda requested that Menon write to his cousin to come to Rishikesh immediately.

When Bhaskar Menon arrived at Rishikesh, Swami Sivananda, perceiving his quality of character and his determination to lead a spiritual life, soon gave him the sannyāsa initiation to become a Swami. Bhaskar reverently donned the saffron robe and received a new name, Swami Jnanananda. The Swami's dearest desire was to visit the great pilgrimage centres of the Himalayas. He planned to set out immediately and invited his younger cousin to accompany him on the journey.

Menon was a self-confessed scorner of exercise. In an article only a year earlier in the *National Herald*, he had admitted, "Personally I am one of those who hates to cause consciously the slightest unnecessary strain to any of my tender muscles." The article was the report of an interview with Mr. Ramu from South India who had developed a series of exercises that he claimed were so beneficial to muscle development and general health that even Menon was convinced to experiment himself, until he thought better of it.

> I almost felt like taking some of the severe exercises myself; thus shortening my sojourn among the sub-editors of this world, like one of the zoologist's dogs or hares. But just in time I remembered the famous prescription of the sensible Robert Hutchins of the University of Chicago. He confessed for the benefit of the misled generality of mankind that 'whenever I feel like taking exercise, I just lie down until the feeling goes away'. I switched off the light and went to bed.

When invited on this pilgrimage by Bhaskar, however, Menon had no second thoughts. He enthusiastically agreed to join him. It would be quite an adventure and he could collect information for articles on Bhārata's holiest places. Any further aspiration for his own spiritual growth was kept to himself once again. The two men began their pilgrimage, joined by Śrī Ramesh Gautam, a householder devotee of Swami Sivananda, and a local young man to carry the necessary cooking utensils, hygienic supplies, clothing and an extra bundle of paper, pens and books. The journalist planned to keep a diary of his experiences and post dispatches to the Sivananda Ashram and several newspapers along the way.

The grand chain of white capped mountains that makes up the Himalayas stretches out 1,500 miles in length, with widths varying from 125 to 250 miles. They encompass thirty of the world's highest peaks; all exceed 24,000 feet, including the 29,028 foot Mt. Everest. Their natural beauty and pure air have made these mountainous regions a favoured spot for spiritual retreat.

The excursion would take the pilgrims to the four great Himalayan spiritual centres – Yamnotri, Gangotri, Kedarnath and Badarinath. Throughout the centuries these places have been considered the holiest locations in the Indian Himalayas and have been frequented by many great sages whose meditation and prayers for the well-being of mankind have sanctified the atmosphere. It is believed that any pilgrim who manages to visit these four shrines in one arduous journey receives such merit that he only has to contemplate continually on any desire, whether material or spiritual, and his wish will be granted. Balakrishnan Menon vowed to repeat the Lord Śiva's name throughout the pilgrimage; for, his true motivation was to attain Enlightenment. However, an avenue that could help him accomplish his goal repeatedly surfaced in his mind, to study with the Vedāntic scholar, Swami Tapovanam.

On April 24, 1948 just one day before Menon's 32nd birthday, the pilgrims set out for Yamnotri, which lies 120 miles northwest of

Rishikesh. Travelling on the footpaths that skirt the swift Yamuna river, they reached their destination after nine days of relentless climbing, relieved only by level passes and sharp descents, often more difficult to negotiate than the ascents. Upon arrival at the eleven thousand foot peak, they gave their bodies a rejuvenating soak in one of the celebrated hot springs in that area. The water of one of the springs was hot enough to cook rice, placed in a cloth bag, in a matter of minutes. After meditating on the banks of the river, they departed the following morning, retracing their footsteps down to the path that would take them eastward.

The route to Gangotri and Kedarnath passes through Uttarkashi, the dwelling place of Swami Tapovanam, a Master of the scriptures as well as austerities. He was reputed to be among the wisest of sages in the Himalayas. So when the band of pilgrims arrived in Uttarkashi, they immediately sought out the renowned Master and spent the evening in discussion with him. Swami Tapovanam, customarily called by the Hindi version of his name Swami Tapovan, had travelled many years in the hallowed altitudes and had recorded his spiritual ecstasies and personal experiences in a journal, *Wanderings in the Himalayas*. When Menon returned the following morning to bid the Swami farewell, Swami Tapovanam advised him, "During the entire journey, keep a continuous unbroken Brahman vicāra (reflection on the Truth); just as, even while one is walking, he remembers a loved one who is far away." Then to the surprise of the young pilgrim, the sage asked him if he needed anything, like warm clothes, for the pilgrimage and offered to arrange for his needs. Such an offer seemed out of character, for, Swami Tapovanam had no conglomeration of buildings like those mushrooming at Ananda Kutir. Tapovanam Kutir was a simple one-room hut with mud walls and native slate stones for the roof. He encouraged no students, nor supplied them with anything. He had always refused to be involved in the world even to the extent of performing the renunciation ceremony for others; by his own choice, he had no disciples.

But unknown to this passing pilgrim, Swami Tapovanam knew of Menon through his articles published in the *National Herald*. His reviews of spiritual books had been brought to the Swami's attention. Tradition holds that a Guru (spiritual Teacher) waits for the mature student, who will understand the true meaning of the teachings in order to pass the knowledge on to others. From his reading of Menon's work, Swami Tapovanam knew that this young man had a good education and an alert mind, so he would be a promising student of the logic of Vedānta. Menon would not have suspected that the Swami read the *National Herald*, for, he did not know the Swami knew English. Several years later an Australian passed by Tapovanam Kutir and stopped to chat. To Menon's surprise, Swami Tapovanam conversed with him in perfect English.

At this first meeting, Menon assured the Swami that they had all necessary supplies. Bidding him farewell, the pilgrims set out for the higher altitudes by following the banks of the Ganga up to its source, except where steep cliffs forced them to take long detours.

In Menon's daily reports, he took great delight at the awesome beauty of nature in the Himalayas – the rushing, leaping rivers, the snow-capped mountains, and the flower decked meadows. At the end of the first week, he wrote in his journal.

> As we turned the corner, we suddenly heard the familiar music – the inimitable, celestial music of the Ganga as she rolls over the rugged rocks, just a loop of green water gurgling in silvery form, but sufficient to refresh the tired pilgrim and to bring into him a feeling of exultation and utter peace. Automatically, the pilgrim stops, leans on the mossy mountainsides, gazes across tall pine groves and drinking in this strange nectarine happiness, is refreshed beyond words. The music soothes away his exhaustion. Wave upon wave of the mountain breeze gently takes away his weariness.

The trek was tiring, and often treacherous. The pilgrims climbed steep trails strewn with loose rock, crossed makeshift bridges over deep gorges, hiked through mountain passes covered with snow and walked over sharp rocks – barefoot. Unfortunately, Menon's simple sandals had given out. The absence of anything resembling a shoe store in those remote areas forced him to continue the journey with the pain of sore, blistered feet.

On a typical day, the group rose at 4 a.m. However, on the days that they planned to cover extra miles; they were up and on the trail by 3 a.m. They averaged about fifteen miles a day, depending on the terrain and the effectiveness of the prodding of Swami Jnanananda, who at times seemed to be on a foot race. Since he was a Swami and an elder, Menon was obligated to show him a certain deference. Nevertheless, the senior could be trying when he insisted that they push on to the next temple or shelter even before they had unpacked, eaten and rested at the present one.

It was understandable that the elder wanted to reach Gangotri as soon as possible, for, it was known to be the haven of many authentic holy men. Situated at 8,000 ft., Gangotri is nestled in the centre of the Himalayan range and surrounded by a crown of perpetually white peaks. In a giant ice cave fourteen miles to the north, the Ganga originates its life in a tiny pool of glacial waters, decorated with the yellow flowers of the Brahma lotus. The site is called Gomukh (13,500 ft.), the symbolic source of creation, 'where shadows struggle into form against the vast white canvas of eternity.' Quickly amassing her strength as trickles of melted snow and mountain springs join it, the trickle becomes a river that rushes through the valleys and leaps down mountain slopes to purify, refresh and nourish the dry planes below.

A special blessing for Bhārata has been that a number of Masters have continued to live in these mountainous regions, preserving the inspiration of the eternal Truth (Sanātana-dharma), not the letter of the scripture, but the spirit of it, living a life of meditation. They exist as reminders of the possibility that man can know his own divine essence. Gangotri has long been a favoured spot of these ascetics because, until recent years, it could only be reached by foot, while snow protected it for six months of the year from even foot travellers. Most of these ascetic yogīs have not taken the formal vows of renunciation, as they consider even that ceremony too worldly for their consideration. These are the natural renunciates, whose attachments to the world and its attractions are so minimal they have virtually nothing to renounce.

The three pilgrims were able to meet with several of the recluses. Śrī Phalahari Baba, dressed only in a loincloth, spent his days in continual meditation. Not interested in wasting time or energy in speaking, he observed continuous silence (mauna). When it was necessary to communicate, he used hand signals or wrote in the sandy floor of his handmade hut. When they met the Bābā, he was in the middle of a one month fast and he appeared somewhat weak. When they asked about his health, he simply wrote in the sand, "It is the nature of all flesh to be now healthy, now sick, now fat, now lean. We are not to be concerned with these transformations of the body, for, we are the indestructible supreme Spirit!" As the three sat in the presence of this Bābā, his eyes radiating a divine glow, they forgot all the problems of their little worlds, for, they were lost in a deep peace within themselves.

Nearby was the slightly larger hut – one was able to stand up straight in it – of Śrī Raghunath Das. After asking the three seekers where they came from, he sat facing them in total silence for some ten minutes. At once it seemed as though time stood still and the world ceased to be. "If we do not receive the meaning of this silence, it could only mean a weakness in our own understanding. The true life is in meditation and in renunciation," Menon concluded to himself as they took their leave from the Mahātmā (great soul).

It was in the quiet, peaceful moments of twilight when the sun had already disappeared behind the mountains, leaving the valley in a cool, peaceful shadow, that Menon sat beside the

Ganga for two hours of meditation. He described those precious moments in a journal.

> Wonderful! No words to describe the inner peace I enjoyed, the concentration I achieved, the entire world forgotten. Forgotten are all worldly contacts, for, here I have come to live in myself. For the first time I tasted bliss in meditation which I know is but an iota of what one can have from deep, long, steady and powerful meditation. My only prayer to my divine Guru and to the divine Lord is that, by their grace, I may never fall and that I may drink deeper at the fountain of the eternal divine nectar!

The following morning, Menon met with Śrī Krishnashram, a naked ascetic who also remained in continuous silence. When Menon asked him for a message for his fellow aspirants at the Sivananda Ashram, he wrote:

> Drink the true, pure Ganga water, not this river water. Visit the inner source. The guide to lead you is in you. You must only develop faith and love. There is no God beyond or besides you. God's grace is really your own efforts.
>
> Karma-yoga is not for renunciates. Writing books, opening schools, hospitals – these are the duty of a charitable householder. One need not take to the spiritual path for this purpose. Nowadays, everybody writes. But what for? They are only culling ideas from old books and expressing them in their own language. This is a sheer waste.
>
> Write when new experiences and truths gurgle forth from the inner Consciousness. Ādi Śaṅkara wrote and he was justified. In such instances, the author is only

a divine instrument. It means the time has come for those particular ideas to be given to this generation. Accept renunciation and end all outer activities. Delve within and reach the inner source. Drink the true Ganga water.

....

On a cold morning in mid-May, the pilgrims began the beautiful, although arduous, 115-mile trip to Kedarnath. Advancing through thick forests of fragrant cedars, green meadows scattered with wild flowers and passes with vistas of peaks with perennial glaciers, the pilgrims continuously experienced an inner joy as they silently viewed the magnificence of the mountain terrain. After a steep ascent of seven miles, they reached the Kedar temple, situated on a marshy meadow between two ranges of snow-capped mountains. Tradition holds that the Pāṇḍavas of the epic *Mahābhārata* built this temple. A large, irregularly shaped stone that seems to have grown up naturally from the earth serves as the object of worship. Many find it difficult to understand the revering of a stone as a symbol of God, but Hindus consider the entire universe as the body of God – everyone and everything merits worship. "God shines everywhere – in stone, in plants, in water, in the sky – but those who have not overcome their ego fail to find God anywhere," Swami Tapovanam used to say.

After spending only a day in the cold of Kedarnath's twelve thousand foot altitudes, the pilgrims started downhill for the 105-mile hike to the fourth and last holy shrine, Badarinath. Situated in a valley between mountain ranges its long history includes several great sages – Śrī Vyāsa, Śrī Śuka and his disciple, Śrī Gauḍapāda. The small, smooth rock where Gauḍapāda sat to compose his commentary on the *Māṇḍūkya-upaniṣad* is still visible on the left bank of the Alaknanda river. In the vicinity is the cave where Vyāsa, the compiler of the Vedas, lived for several years. Once the temple was taken over by Buddhists, but in the eighth century Ādi Śaṅkara re-consecrated the temple, installed a new idol and brought priests from his homeland of Malabar to assure the rituals were done properly and regularly.

Menon had obtained permission in advance to stay at Badarinath for a month. The priests were glad to arrange accommodations for a visitor from their ancestral home.[1] As the others set off for their return to Rishikesh, Menon organized his belongings in the provided shelter. The only thing disturbing the peaceful environment was Menon's own excitement at having such an opportunity to be alone at this beautiful sacred place without having to rush to the next shrine. Since he was acclimatized to travel, it would take several days before the tendency to be active dissolved away.

It was around this time that he took a hike over to the cave of an aged *sādhu* (renunciate), who was in poor health with an ulcerous sore on his leg. Menon was horrified to note there were actually maggots on the wound. Just at the moment that he had intended to suggest that he take the sādhu to a doctor, one of the maggots fell from the leg. The sādhu picked it up, placed it back on the leg, and told it, "There, my son." Then he looked straight into the eyes of Menon and told him, "Don't you know that it is all only matter. Matter feeding matter," Menon would never forget this first hand lesson of enduring what must have been incredible pain without complaint. Mind is matter and is affected by its companion, the body. However, a Master's inner peace is not disturbed by the agonies of his body nor the ravings of his mind. The sādhu was found dead on his straw mat the next morning.

Menon spent the long summer days of July enjoying the natural splendour of the region and assimilating the experiences of his encounters with holy men during the past weeks. In the dynamic peace of the Himalayas, he spent long hours contemplating and meditating. The events of this pilgrimage were to have a marked influence on the path that he would choose to take at this juncture.

---

[1] Based on their common history, culture and language – Malayalam – the kingdoms along the Malabar coast, including Cochin, Calicut and Travancore, were combined to make the state of Kerala in 1951.

7

The Renunciation Rites

I was born on that Śivarātri day. The past of this body and mind has nothing to do with me.

—Swami Chinmayananda, 1962.

When Menon returned to Ananda Kutir in late August, he knew the moment had arrived to take the renunciation ceremony, thereby becoming a Swami. Swami Sivananda seemed to know it too, for he told Menon to write to his father to obtain permission. Before giving renunciation vows to a person younger than retirement age, some Swamis require that permission be obtained from the parents. This practice reflects respect for the Hindu parents and their wishes. It also assures that the person, particularly a son, is free from responsibility to his family and would not be called upon should the family be in need of assistance.

Menon did witness such a case at the Sivananda Ashram. Daily all the students (brahmacārīs) and young Swamis performed some service (karma-yoga) in the āśrama – cleaning, carrying wood, cooking and serving food, caring for the elder Swamis or whatever tasks were needed. One young brahmacārī helped the cooks prepare the simple daily fare – rice, unleavened flat wheat bread (roti) and some variety of split bean (dal), cooked with a vegetable and spices (when available). One afternoon Menon and several others were in the kitchen cleaning the large cooking pots when Swami Sivananda walked in. "Go!" he ordered, looking directly at the cook's assistant. Everyone was quite surprised to see the indicated man drop everything and walk out without saying a word. "What in the world has he done?" wondered all the onlookers. They later found out that a problem had come up in the young man's family. Swami Sivananda perceived that this matter needed to be tended to or his mind would be constantly troubled with thoughts of home. A couple of years later, after having helped his family, he returned to Ananda Kutir to take up his āśrama duties and spiritual disciplines.

A Hindu son is responsible for the welfare of his parents after their retirement; he is their social security and medical insurance. This responsibility is not taken lightly and can be foregone only if there is another son in the house capable of taking on the duty, or if the parents are quite wealthy. As both were true in the case of Menon, the request for approval from the father was a matter of formality.

The letter to his father was especially meaningful for this young Swami to be. Menon had not communicated directly with his father for seven years. During his years as a fugitive, he could not write for fear of being traced. Then he had not wanted to worry his father with the facts of his imprisonment and convalescence. Although his father learned news of him through Achuthan Menon in Baroda and Govind Menon in Delhi, father and son had had no direct contact. This lack of communication reflected not only the disorder of those years, but also past tension with his father over his spendthrift habits when he was at the university. His father had then complained that Balan was living like a prince, while he, the father, lacked the king's treasury to support him in such style. Hoping to quell the impression left by his university days of only writing when he needed money, Balakrishnan Menon had waited until he had a firm economic base to write to his father. But by the time he was making a decent income from journalism, he had changed his interest to the spiritual quest. The son had a lot of explaining to do.

Menon wrote an eight page letter, detailing all the pertinent events – his political activities, his imprisonment, his work as a journalist – then he described his inner feelings and thoughts about life lived only to 'eat, sleep and breed'. Continuing, he explained how his personal doubts had led him to investigate into the spiritual life and his eventual meeting of the sage, Swami Sivananda.

Upon receipt of the letter, the elder Menon was shocked that his son, who had openly criticized religion and who had been such a decadent student that his only concern seemed to be the acquisition of the finest things money could buy, could even consider to become a renunciate. And he was not overjoyed at the prospect of his son giving up the life of the world. Like every father, he relished the prospect of seeing his son with a successful career, good wife and many dear children. Even the most religious Hindu father wants his son to complete the three stages (āśrama) of life – brahmacarya, student (birth to 25 years of age); gṛhastha, householder (25 to 50 years); and vānaprastha, semi-retired (50 to 75 years) – before entering the fourth āśrama, sannyāsa, the life of renunciation. The Vedas that prescribed this tradition also allowed for the exception by stating that one could take sannyāsa the instant one became imbued with true renunciation. Also, historically Buddhist practices influenced Hindus to begin monastic life at a younger age.

In spite of his personal reservations, the elder Menon sent off his letter of permission to Swami Sivananda. The father explained to the family, who were surprised at his quick capitulation, "This boy always does exactly what he wants, it's useless for me to try to stand in his way!" In his reply, his father expressed his surprise at learning of the decision and commented further that Balan must have met a very great saint indeed to be influenced so greatly. "Go ahead, I give my permission," he completed the letter.

Balakrishnan Menon received the initiation into the sannyāsa āśrama from Swami Sivananda on the 25th of February, 1949, on the auspicious Śivarātri day, along with five other initiates. Sannyāsa is taken to reach a goal – the spiritual goal of Self-realization. The crucial step in this process is the setting aside, the forsaking of, all other goals; therefore, a Hindu monk is called a renunciate, a sannyāsī. The external ceremony of renunciation is an aid to enlightenment, a symbol of the inner renunciation. After enlightenment there is nothing to renounce, so many a Hindu saint has never become a sannyāsī. The Vaidika ṛṣis were not renunciates, for, they comprehended the freedom beyond the laws, rituals and orders without any ceremony.

The entrance to each āśrama is commemorated with a religious rite. For the initiation into sannyāsa, a ritual fire is built according to exact prescriptions from the Vedas. First, a priest chants incantations to sanctify the undertaking. Each element of the ceremony is a physical representation of a mental process. The fire represents the burning of any dross that may remain from previous associations with the world. Just as all matter is consumed by fire, the fire of Knowledge consumes all previous misconceptions about the Truth.

The initiates arrived at the ritual site after a purifying bath in the Ganga river and the shaving of the head, leaving only a tuft on the crown to represent the remaining desirable attachments – the Guru and the scriptures. The Vaidika sages had used the metaphor that the desires of man's mind are as numerous as the hair on his head; therefore, the shaving of the head has developed as a symbol for cleaning the mind. In any case, it is a deed that creates humility in the shaved one.

At the ritual fire, the initiate purifies his mind as he mentally surrenders any desire, emotion or thought of his past into the sacrificial fire while he is repeating the vows –

> From this moment onwards, I will not be enemy of the flying birds, running rivers, flowering trees and plants, animals and small creatures, and they will not be an enemy to me. I renounce all desire for wealth, spouse, name and fame.

This ceremony is the initiate's last ritual. From this moment forward, the fire of purification is ablaze in the mind of the renunciate. Having completed these vows with a devout and sincere mind, Menon and the five others plunged three times, representing the three worlds of experience, into the Ganga's chilly waters. With each immersion a vow of renunciation was enunciated –

....

> Bhū sannyastha mayā. (the physical world, which includes the body and all objects of the world, is renounced.)
>
> Bhuva sannyastha mayā. (the astral world, which includes the emotions and all ancestors, is renounced.)
>
> Sva sannyastha mayā. (the celestial world, which includes higher thoughts and all gods, is renounced.)

....

These vows are a promise to the five elements that constitute each of the worlds – material, subtle and causal – that the sannyāsī will no longer be a contender for their possession. Since he does not desire any object of the world, the world no longer has the power to hurt him. Therefore, he will now be fearless as he travels through life. The sannyāsī is immune to enjoyment of the sense objects; his only pursuit is the dissolution of his ego.

To complete the ceremony, the Guru cuts the last tuft of hair, which means the attachment to the Guru and the scriptures have also been renounced. He then gives the Swami a new name to represent the birth into spiritual life. The past is dead and a new life has begun. The sannyāsī has no rights in the society – no property, no family, no vote, no I. D. card. If he is not given food, shelter or clothes, he does without.

The name given to the renunciate often indicates the goal he is now seeking, but it can represent some attribute that is predominant in his character, or even a quality that needs to be developed. The choice of the name comes from the insight of the initiating Swami. 'Chinmayananda Saraswati' was the name that Swami Sivananda Saraswati gave the man formerly known as P. Balakrishnan Menon. Literally, Cit means 'Consciousness', maya means 'composed of', or 'of the nature of,' Ānanda means 'Bliss'. His new name loosely translated is 'one who revels in the bliss that is composed of pure Consciousness.' The ending of the name, in this case Ānanda – plus 'Saraswati' which indicates a scholarly order – is taken from the name of the initiating Swami and represents the lineage of that particular Swami.

The suffixes, such as ānanda, vanam, puri, tirtha, giri, ashram, designate in which of the four spiritual centres (maṭha), which were founded by Ādi Śaṅkaracārya, a particular line of Swamis originated. In this case, the ending 'Ananda Saraswati' indicates that the name originated with a holy preceptor at the Sringeri Matha in the southern district. For the sake of brevity and humility, Swami Chinmayananda has declined to use the 'Saraswati' with his name, as did his Guru. The title of respect, 'Swami', which literally means 'one who is with oneself', is added to the name of the sannyāsī.

Along with the new name, Swami Sivananda handed an orange robe to Swami Chinmayananda. The saffron cloth is worn by Swamis as a physical reminder of the vows that they have taken. The colour represents the mental flame in which all desires are to be extinguished. "Even if the members of the society do not offer him respect, at least they don't approach the Swami with suggestions of making money on the black market, or marrying the sister. So the physical symbol offers the wearer some protection as he pursues his spiritual life," concluded Swami Chinmayananda with his broad smile and twinkling eyes after he had worn the saffron robe for many years.

Swami Chinmayananda, a product of his British styled education, could not accept anything on pure faith. He wanted to know the true import of the scriptures, Sanskrit words which were often uttered mechanically without understanding and even sometimes with misunderstanding. "You want to master the scriptures. Go to Swami Tapovanam, the great Teacher from Kerala, your own home state." With these words, Swami Sivananda sent his disciple to Swami Tapovanam with a package, as it was his custom to send food to the sages when their wanderings brought them to Rishikesh for the cold season.

Swami Chinmayananda crossed the Ganga to the opposite shore and proceeded to the Brahmananda Ashram where Swami Tapovanam stayed a few months each spring. After he greeted the Mahātmā and presented him with the package from Swami Sivananda, he asked the Swami if it would be possible to study Vedānta with him. He then explained his great desire to study the subtleties of the highest philosophy from a Master who really understood what the seeming contradictions of the scriptures were indicating. Swami Tapovanam replied that he would be willing to give classes; however, it would be up to the student to take the treasures of the scriptures and apply them in private contemplation to discover their value for himself. "I can teach, but it is you who must understand," the Swami told his prospective student.

Each holy man is a unique manifestation of the divine song; it is as if the Creator deifies man's attempts to stereotype his chosen servants. The two major influences in Swami Chinmayananda's spiritual life, Swami Tapovanam and Swami Sivananda, to all appearances, were as diverse as nature itself. Yet the experience of God-realization of these two Masters was identical despite all external appearances indicated by the activity of the body and mind. According to their own innate nature, they were used as instruments of universal intelligence. Swami Sivananda was full of dynamic energy; whereas, Swami Tapovanam manifested a subtler vibration. Ananda Kutir had grown into a small community. Swami Sivananda's enthusiastic energy enabled him to keep in touch with every resident and every detail of the āśrama. In contrast, Tapovanam Kutir was a simple, one room hut where Swami Tapovanam lived only a few months of the year with no concern for the coming and going of students. He offered no food or accommodation to any of his students.

Finally, after a lengthy discussion, Swami Tapovanam told Swami Chinmayananda that he would be returning to Uttarkashi before the monsoon rains began in May. The younger Swami could follow him there and begin classes then.

> When I went to Swami Tapovanam to study I had no idea of serving mankind. All I wanted was fuller confirmation of what I had gathered from books in the library, that is, a direct glimpse of the ideas and arguments of the ṛṣis as they were expressed in their original texts – the Upaniṣads and the *Gītā*. These texts are written in Sanskrit – I had only an elementary knowledge of this language. Swamiji[1] was an authority in Sanskrit. He had even developed a style of his own in his poetic works written in that language. I went to him with the desire to know directly what the scriptures say in their profound declarations.

Swami Chinmayananda had learned only the basics of Sanskrit from his early secular education; this was only a small aid in the complicated classical Sanskrit of the scriptures. Sanskrit literally means 'complete' or 'perfected" because its thirteen vowel sounds and thirty-three consonants are said to include every possible sound of the human voice. Individual words are joined together according to several combining rules; therefore, any one 'word' may actually be a phrase that contains a half dozen words. A real expertise is necessary to untangle them to

[1] The suffix 'ji' is added to a name to show respect. Swamiji is the term of direct address to a Swami.

derive the content intended by the original author. The process is complicated further by changes in letters as words join, so that one line of script may be separated into different words to have distinct meanings. Many words have several meanings according to context. In addition, verbs are conjugated in ten tenses in singular, dual and plural. Nouns have eight case endings according to their usage and are also conjugated in singular, dual and plural in the three genders – masculine, feminine and neuter. These complexities add their share of difficulty, as well as accuracy, to the ancient language.

In the late 1940s, there were four great Enlightened Masters of Vedānta living in the Himalayas – Swami Vishnudevananda, Swami Tapovanam, Brahmaprakasa Udasina and Devagiri Swami. However, all but Swami Tapovanam preferred to give their classes entirely in Sanskrit. He used both Sanskrit and Hindi. Although Swami Chinmayananda only had the basics in Sanskrit, it was sufficient to follow Swami Tapovanam with some extra homework. In the process, he would also improve his knowledge of the ancient language directly from the scriptures instead of wasting time memorising long lists of vocabulary from Sanskrit grammar books according to the traditional method.

8

My Teacher Swami Tapovanam[1]

by Swami Chinmayananda

All I am, all I have done, is only because of my Teacher, Swami Tapovan Mahārāja.

—Swami Chinmayananda, 1978.

Just as the biography of a man starts with his birth, and does not go behind it to trace the biological growth and development of the seed in the womb, so too, to write the life of a Realized saint of the stature of Swami Tapovanam, is to trace the adventures of his soul in its onward flights to God-realization. A Mahātmā starts his life, in a new world, with a new personality, and maintains absolutely a new set of relationships. Upon becoming a sannyāsī, he becomes dead to his entire past. Yet we often have curiosity to trace the life of the Mahātmā (Enlightened Master) before he reached the gate of the inner temple to ring the bell in adoration of the Infinite.

Śrī Swamiji was no tame individual of whom, even after years of intimate service, and total surrender, could I discover the necessary courage to ask about his personal life before he took sannyāsa. Some fragments are available in his own writings[2] and I am tracing them here as best I can.

In a house called Puthan Veedu (New House), in 1889, a baby boy was born to Smt. Balamba and Sri Achuthan Nair in

[1] Written in 1965 as an introduction to Swami Tapovanam's *Hymn to Badarīnātha*.

[2] He has written in his life in a Sanskrit work of both poetry and prose, entitled *Īśvara Darśana*, in which he has condescended to reveal a bit of the landmarks of his life.

Palghat district in Mudappallur, a medium-sized village in Kerala. The child was named Subramanyam, but his parents called him by the pet name, Chippu Kutty, which was taken up by his friends and admirers all his life, until he took the vows of renunciation.

His early education started with the village teacher where he soon completed the elementary level. However, the educational system then available and the subjects taught were not to his taste; so at the young age of fourteen, the boy returned home one day to declare to his father his decision to quit school.

These words were a great disappointment to his father, a fairly wealthy landlord (Kṣatriya), who had his own ambitions to see his son educated and employed as a government official in a high position. Śrī Swamiji himself remembered the painful exchange with his father. Expressing his utter disappointment, the loving father exclaimed, "What a pity, when hundreds and thousands of children bemoan that they have not the means to educate themselves, you, who have sufficient means, decide not to continue your education."

Chippu Kutty did not run away from the school because of idleness – he had the greatest reverence for knowledge and a true thirst for learning. He had independently thought of the situation and had come to his own conclusions regarding the type of education that would satisfy him. The boy replied, "Father, I have not discarded education. I have only stopped attending school." Thereafter, with the help of some well-educated persons in the vicinity, the extremely bright boy started his own schedule of study.

The loving father arranged for two tutors to attend to the child's education, one to instruct him in English and the other to educate him in Sanskrit. Within a short period, the boy gained mastery in both languages. Then realising the hollowness of the content of English literature, he switched to a deeper and more exhaustive study of Sanskrit and vernacular Malayalam (the native language of Kerala). Under competent teachers, he mastered poems, dramas, grammar and logic in both languages. Simultaneously, he read and made a study of all available religious literature in both Malayalam and Sanskrit, including the philosophy of Vedānta.

The boy grew physically and developed mentally. At seventeen years, Chippu Kutty Nair had become a noted personality among Malayalam writers and speakers and had developed a style of his own that enriched the Malayalam language. At the age of eighteen, he composed the poem, *'Vibhākara'*. It attracted the attention of all the literary scholars of the time. When they came to know of the young heart behind the work, he received endless applauses. Even at that age Chippu Kutty began feeling an urge for an intense study of philosophy and the scriptures. The usual weaknesses of young men of his age, who are materially well off and quite independent, had not touched him. Solitude and books were his companions. He liked to spend much of his time in the jungles near his beloved father's house. He spent his time regularly in japa (repetition of the mantra) and meditation upon the form of Śrī Śiva.[1] Om Namaḥ Śivāya was his mantra.

The untimely death of his father when he was only twenty-one shook him considerably. To bring his mind back to equilibrium he turned the impulses of despair at his loss into a poetic inspiration and wrote a prayerful poem *'Viṣṇu Yamakam'* (in memoriam). This shock of experiencing the impermanence of life first hand awakened the spirit of renunciation, which had been dormant in his bosom.

At this time, his only brother was still in college; therefore, Chippu Kutty was head of the family and he could not shirk this

[1] Śiva is one of the three gods of the Hindu Trinity. See glossary for more information.

responsibility. However, he still managed to spend most of his time in religious pursuits and study of the spiritual texts. During these days, Chippu Kutty was able to leave Kerala for a short visit to Bhavnagar in Saurashtra. There, at the feet of Swami Shantyananda Saraswati, he studied two great Vedāntic texts – *Saṁkṣepa Śarīrikam* and *Vedānta Paribhāṣā*.

Upon returning to Palghat, in the spirit of service to the community, he took up the publishing and editing of a monthly journal that he named *Gopal Krishna*. The journal contained discussions on such relevant topics as ethics, education, character development, literature and other such non-political themes of social importance. During this period the young man often addressed the public on religious or social themes, especially in the southern districts of Kerala. He also regularly contributed articles to newspapers published in the state.

His mother, Balamba, was a traditional woman who had plans for seeing her son married and settled in life. She often pointed out the girl she had chosen for him and said, "This is the perfect girl for you to marry. When are you going to marry?" Chippu Kutty's usual answer was rather evasive – "Yes, I shall marry; and when I marry, you will see who it is. You will have no reason for regret."

All through this period of external activities, his personal spiritual practices were never given up; his inward development ultimately conquered all his attention. The publishing and editing, the writing and the lecture tours – all had completely dried away by the time Chippu Kutty entered the twenty-eighth year of his life.

Spiritual pilgrimage was the only recreation for this young man. During this period he visited many South Indian pilgrimage centres including Madurai, Srirangam, Chidambaram, Arunagiri and Rameswaram. At Chidambaram, he met the great spiritual preceptor Śrī Daṇḍapāṇi Dikshitar and had discussions with him.

In this way he cleared many of the questions which had arisen during his independent study of the scriptures. In Madras (now Chennai), he met and discussed various spiritual themes with Swami Sarvananda, President of the Ramakrishna Math there. On his return journey he visited Cape Comorin (now Kanyakumari), the Śrī Ananta Padmanabha Temple in Trivandrum, and the sacred temple of Ādi Śaṅkarācārya in Kaladi.

In addition, he had been corresponding with Swami Shantyanada, the Śaṅkarācārya of the Dwarka Maṭha, who was then visiting Calcutta (now Kolkata). At his invitation, Chippu Kutty left to spend a few months in Bengal. He took this opportunity to meet and discuss spiritual themes with other outstanding priests and scholars there. He spent much of his spare time in lonely parks meditating upon the effulgent, divine Self. Pleased by the young man's spiritual unfoldment, the Śaṅkarācārya gave him the title of 'Chidvilasa' (one who shines from Knowledge).

From Calcutta (now Kolkata), he travelled to the spiritual centres along the holy Ganga – Varanasi, Haridwar and Rishikesh – where he met many priests, sages and saints. He visited all the sacred temples and bathed in the sacred rivers. After staying at each for a few days and tasting the joys of solitary meditation in these holy places, the young man started his journey home to return to his duties there. As he said his farewell, he humbly prayed to the Lord of the Himalayas to call him back speedily, so that he might serve the true Himalayan mission by achieving spiritual perfection in these immortal and glorious peaks.

This visit to the north completed the transformation of Chippu Kutty. He returned to Kerala a true spiritual renunciate. There he erected a humble thatched hut a furlong away from his family home in the coconut grove on the edge of the extensive fields of cultivation. Within he sat reading, contemplating, worshipping, praying and meditating all day long. Once a day, at noon, he walked to his ancestral home, of which he was still head, to partake of his one daily meal of rice and sambar (spiced bean soup). For two hours only he rested in the night; his bed was the bare floor. Early morning, after his bath, he put on the same wet towel, a single piece of white cloth, as his sole apparel. Thus, in such tapas (austerities) lived the young man, Chippu Kutty, for three years as a Cidvilāsa indeed.

His contemporaries remember how they would occasionally meet the young man living in his hut in the open field, sleeping on the ground and clothed with one single cloth as his sole personal possession. They confess that, though he appeared to be extremely intelligent, they took him to be 'slightly mad'.

When his younger brother returned home after having completed his education, Chippu Kutty ordered a small feast in his family home. All the members of the family were invited. They were surprised because he offered no explanation for this special dinner that for him would be the last meal with his family. After the dinner he officially entrusted the responsibility of the estate and family to his brother. A couple of days later, Chippu Kutty approached the brother, saying, "You are now the head of the family; therefore, I ask your permission to go on a pilgrimage to visit the Hari Hara Temple on the banks of the Tungabhadra (river)."

On the auspicious Kṛṣṇāṣṭamī day (Kṛṣṇā's birthday), accompanied by his brother, Chippu Kutty reached the railway station. As the train was steaming out, the brother called out, "Do not stay too long! Come back soon!" The ominous silence was broken only by the shriek of the whistle as the train pulled out of the station.

From whom and what sources Swami Tapovanam gathered his inspirations are not very well-known. By the time I had the good fortune to surrender myself at his feet, he had soared so high in his realization that looking back upon the past was to him a meaningless and purposeless pursuit.

However, he did speak of a great sannyāsī, who he mentioned twice as his Guru, and at whose feet he must have studied. But he did not give Swami Tapovanam the sannyāsa initiation, for, when he had asked to receive the initiation, his Guru had told him, "Sannyāsa need not be given to you. You take it yourself. You are already a true sannyāsī." Therefore, on the banks of the Tungabhadra river, obeying the great call within him, this born Yogī accepted sannyāsa for himself. Thereafter, for seven years, he lived in rigorous tapas in many places in India.

After these wanderings, he reached Rishikesh. There on a tiny island (Purana Jhadi) in the Ganga in a grass hut, he lived peacefully practising meditation. At that time he was given the traditional sannyāsa initiation by Swami Janardanagiri of Kailash Ashram. Thus Chippu Kutty became Swami Tapovanam, meaning, 'forest of austerities'.

Even today his life as a young sannyāsī is glorified and pointed out as the ideal for new initiates to aspire to and emulate. Many eager to study Vedānta from such a pure soul came to sit at his feet as he spoke on the scriptures for one hour each morning. Swami Tapovanam was one who through long years of discussion with Mahātmās, studies of the scriptures, and arduous disciplines had confirmed by his own personal experience the truths that he had once only intellectually appreciated. He was so saturated in the Bliss Divine that he could not but share the bountifulness of God-realization as experienced by him and verified by the scriptures and Masters throughout India's history. As the crowds increased, each student vying to serve the Teacher-Saint, Swami Tapovanam retreated to higher altitudes where he could live in the solitude of communion with nature, which he loved so dearly.

An intuitive poet, he had a mad passion for witnessing nature's beauty unrolling itself on the canvas of the unfrequented peaks and valleys of the Himalayas. Moving from place to place and roaming from peak to peak, he visited almost all the areas from Kashmir to Almora, including the great Mt. Kailash, the holy shrine of Hindus and Buddhists alike. He is known today even in the remotest villages of the Himalayan ranges.

As he roamed about, his pen was constantly scribbling down the beauties he discovered and the thoughts passing through his sacred bosom. This Master of Vedānta developed an essentially new style of literature with his poetry on nature and philosophical travelogues. He reported his travels in two splendid volumes, both written in Malayalam – *Himagiri Vihāram* (*Wanderings in the Himalayas*) and *Kailāsa Yātrā* (Pilgrimage to Kailash).

In addition to these two important books, Swami Tapovanam wrote a few volumes in a beautiful, yet efficient Sanskrit. His masterpiece is the thick volume called *Īśvara Darśana* (Vision of the Lord) that is a garland of the spiritual thoughts of a Man of Realization as he waded through the welter of life. An autobiographical sketch forms the framework on which the philosophy rests. This book, written in prose and interspersed with poetry, has been much commented upon, not only for its style of easy flow and sureness of stroke, but also for its depth of insight.

Apart from this main work, he wrote smaller pieces, all in Sanskrit metre, such as *'Śrī Saumya Kāśīśa Stotram'*. Each hymn is a glorification of some splendid abode of divine association where he had lived and spent his glorious life of perfection, places of pilgrimages such as Uttarkashi, Gangotri, Gomukh and Badarinath. In essence, each contains an exquisite summary of the difficult Vedāntic philosophy.

Throughout his life, Swami Tapovanam had been teaching the students who voluntarily requested that he instruct them in a text of Vedānta. He never encouraged disciples to come for teaching, nor did he believe in opening āśramas. He firmly believed that a true seeker would be guided to a true Teacher by the Lord. In fact, many of the Swamis who are today working outside of India, belonging to the various missions of India, came in contact at some time or the other with Swami Tapovan Mahārāja[1]. Each of them was initiated by him into at least one of the Upaniṣads or an introductory textbook of Vedānta.

It must be said that since he was a very strict disciplinarian only rarely could his students remain long enough to complete their studies with him. I myself belong to the last group that Swamiji taught, and even during my years of study and practice I can count only a handful of students. All came with divine enthusiasm, but alas none could keep it up for more than a year or so. The severity of the climate, the unavailability of any living convenience, lack of nutritive, not to mention tasty food, the chilly bath twice a day in the Ganga, the hard study and the unrelenting discipline – all contributed their share of discomforts. Together they became a suffocating tyranny for those who could not get any glimpse of the yonder.

However, had they spent at least a part of their time in reflection and meditation, instead of merely reading, they could have discovered the endless source of joy that would have made it worthwhile to endure the discomforts of Uttarkashi. This failure was certainly their own doing.

During the Uttarakhand (the northern region) pilgrimage season all varieties and types of seekers came to the Swami and he gave his advice as best suited to their temperaments and natures. In the beginning his way of teaching was rather confusing for me. An educated priest from Varanasi would come to discuss with him some portions of the *Ṛg-veda*. The discussions would be entirely in Sanskrit. The conversation was held in aphoristic style, implying subtle logic and significant lines of philosophical argument. At this moment would enter a heaving old lady – an uneducated, ordinary woman – from the village of Rajasthan on her way to Gangotri. To the utter discomfort of the priest, Swamiji would suddenly leave the philosophical heights of his talk to

[1] great king of the spiritual world in this context.

inquire of the woman's children at home or of her relations. Then he would encourage her that surely all she had to do was visit the sacred Gangotri and she would return home with all her sins completely cleansed.

This capacity to sing in all tunes and with all notes is unavoidable in a great Teacher occupying a place of reverence and glory. It took years for others around him to understand the necessity for such an agile mind in a Teacher. For, there is no doubt in my mind that the faith – in the words of a sage and in the benefit of pilgrimages – of this simple-minded woman was such that when she returned to her village she was not the same person who left it.

Never did Swami Tapovanam try to keep in contact with his devotees or disciples. He invariably discouraged anyone from even writing a letter to him and, as a general rule, he replied to only a few. Living thus sequestered, seeking only solitude and contemplation, he never encouraged anyone to have a close relationship with him. Nevertheless, he was always ready to give a discourse on a scripture or have a spiritual discussion. He lived a life of his own, chaste and pure, ever content in his Self nature.

9

The Teaching

The perfect seer experiences his own Self in everything and roams around the world experiencing the divine presence everywhere at all times. To one who is thus living inwardly this constant God experience, to him every incident – every thing and being – is but a fugitive note from the infinite song. Swami Tapovan Mahārāja was a reveller of this type as he lived in the valleys of the Himalayas.

—Swami Chinmayananda, 1960.

The month following his initiation by Swami Sivananda, Swami Chinmayananda packed and set out for the long trek by foot up to Uttarkashi. He was accompanied by a Nepalese brahmacārī who was also anxious to study a text from the Master of Vedanta. As one winds his way up into the mountains, following the route of the Ganga, one naturally forgets worldly preoccupations in the presence of the grandeur of a panorama of nature untouched by any modern change or strife. Some one hundred miles distance through the foothills – dotted with grand old forests and an occasional simple village – stands the great mountain Vāraṇāvata, celebrated in the Hindu epics (Purāṇas). In its eastern valley lies a small plane on the banks of the Ganga. On this meadow is perched the tiny, unadorned village of Uttarkashi, the marketplace for the people of the local mountain villages.

Uttarkashi is revered as a holy place not only for its history, but also because at this place the sacred Ganga makes a long sweeping curve and turns back to flow in the direction of its source for a short distance. Similar places along the Ganga have been held as a symbolic representation of what the mind of man must achieve

– turn back the flow of thought toward its very source – and they are considered holy for that reason. The mountains that surround the village are dotted with caves where great sages passed their lives in meditation and penance. Those who have mystical vision see a spiritual light radiating in all directions in this region. To the east lies the Vālakhilya mountain with a large cave that is said to have been the meeting place of the ancient sages (ṛṣis).

Swami Tapovanam was not one to provide any room or board for his students; he believed that any Mahātmā who opened an āśrama was quickly reduced to the life of a manager of an inn for pilgrims (dharmaśālā). Anyone who came to him for teaching was surely sent by the Lord, and that same Lord would surely provide shelter and food for the seeker. Accommodation was found for the new students just down the path from Tapovanam Kutir at the Devgiri Ashram with the kind aid of Swami Govindagiri, a student of Swami Tapovanam and long-time resident of the Himalayan ranges.

Jagdish, a local villager, served Swami Tapovanam with loving devotion whenever the sage stayed in Uttarkashi by cleaning, cooking and delivering daily milk from his home. This assistant later reported the arrival of Swami Chinmayananda –

> "The greatest, most glorious event of the thirty or so years of my service to Swami Tapovan Mahārāja happened some ten years ago. It was the arrival of a sweet boy full of ardour, every part of him throbbing to learn Vedānta under the Master, who had found his way to Tapovanam Kutir. One wondered in those days, looking at the tall, frail Swami Chinmayananda, whether he could stand all the weight of knowledge that his Master was going to unload on him.

Chinmaya, as Swami Chinmayananda was called by his Guru and other disciples, was anxious to begin a Vedāntic text, but there was no hurrying Swami Tapovanam. "We'll start next month after we go up to Gangotri," he responded to the enthusiastic inquiry by Chinmaya as to when classes would begin. "You contemplate on what you have already studied. Get those ideas clear before you add on more!"

In addition to the intellectual learning, the Guru knew that there must be daily chores to release some of the natural energy of this young student and to maintain his physical vigour.

"Chinmaya, make a garden for us here in front of my hut," requested Swami Tapovanam one sunny day. "Some fresh vegetables would be appreciated by all of us."

"But Swamiji, there's no water supply up here on the hill," replied his disciple.

"What! The mighty Ganga is roaring down at the bottom of the hill – and here's a bucket. You can bring up plenty of water for a garden."

"Yes, of course. Yes, Sir," Chinmaya muttered unenthusiastically as he eyed the sixty-foot steep climb up a winding path to Tapovanam Kutir from the banks of the Ganga.

When the hot summer season started, as was his custom, Swami Tapovanam packed his begging bowl and one extra cotton robe to journey to the higher altitudes of the Himalayas. In addition to the advantage of the cooler temperatures, he would be removed from the havoc caused by the influx of pilgrims who flooded the lower ranges during the warm weather.

So after a month of settling into the mental peace that is conducive for the study of the scriptures, Swami Tapovanam, Swami Govindagiri, Swami Chinmayananda and the Nepalese brahmacārī began the trip of fifty-six miles that would take five days by footpath. Along the way there were shelters for pilgrims, placed every eight miles, where the local villagers provided food for the travelling Swamis – flour to make unleavened flat bread (roti) and an occasional vegetable, the potato being the most abundant. The Swamis would cook the food, eat and take a short rest, then start up again, travelling from dawn until dusk.

Gangotri was certainly removed from the comforts of civilization – nutritious food, warm clothing, adequate shelter. One attached to worldly pleasures could not have remained there for long. It is well suited for reflection on the truths of the scriptures and for meditation. However, the glory of the place is so evident that it has an immediate influence on the mind, rendering it naturally peaceful. Therefore, Swami Chinmayananda braved the difficulties without complaint because he had an intense desire to study and understand the philosophy of Vedānta.

Each morning the students began the day with a bath in the icy waters of the Ganga, a feat that causes excruciating pain to the human body, but wakes it up for the morning class at 6 a.m. like no other exercise could. The students then assembled in front of the cedar hut of Swami Tapovanam. The class began with a prayer chanted in unison by the Teacher and students to attune themselves to the omniscient God Principle (Brahman) and to invoke the best effort from both the Teacher and the taught.

> Om. May He protect us both. May He bless us with the bliss of Knowledge. May we both concentrate equally. May our studies be thorough and faithful. May we never misunderstand each other.
>
> Om. May my limbs, speech, vital system, eyes, ears, strength of all my senses grow vigorous. All is the Brahman of the Upaniṣads. May I never deny the Brahman. May the Brahman never spurn me. May there be no denial of the Brahman. Let all the virtues recited by the Upaniṣads repose in me as I delight in the supreme Self.
>
> Om. Peace. Peace. Peace.[1]

[1] The prayer verse from the group of Upaniṣads in the *Sāma-veda.*
ॐ सह नाववतु। .... ॐ शान्तिः! शान्तिः!! शान्तिः!!! – कठोपनिषद्-शान्तिपाठः
ॐ वाङ् मे मनसि प्रतिष्ठिता .... ॐ शान्तिः! शान्तिः!! शान्तिः!!!
– ऐतरेयोपनिषद्-शान्तिपाठः

Their first text, *Pañcadaśī*, was written in Sanskrit by Swami Vidyāraṇya, the eleventh Śaṅkarācārya of the Sringeri Matha, who was both an Enlightened sage and a Master of the scriptures. It is considered a beginning text of Vedānta as it explains all the concepts and terminology used in the Upaniṣads. The thick book is so comprehensive that no philosophical idea of the Vedāntic scriptures is left unelaborated, yet it adds practical guidance to spiritual seekers. It is called *Pañcadaśī* because it contains fifteen chapters, the chapters are grouped into three sections treating the subjects of discrimination of the Real from the non-real; an explanation of the nature of the Self as pure Consciousness; and an exposition of the nature of Brahman as Bliss.

This lengthy text gave Swami Chinmayananda the fundamentals of understanding the essence of the scriptures as well as the Sanskrit terms used in scriptures. Swami Tapovanam would read out one verse of the text, then give the equivalent meaning in Hindi. Word by word, he explained the Sanskrit, giving the rules of grammar and the meaning as well as possible misinterpretations of the meaning. He would follow with a commentary and often an example to illustrate the meaning. As the Guru spoke in Hindi, Chinmaya was meticulously translating everything into English because he wanted all of his notes in the language most familiar to him. Swami Govindagiri, himself a Master of the scriptures, remembers those first classes with the eager, new student of Vedānta.

> The subject matter of *Pañcadaśī* is so subtle that it takes a brilliant, penetrating mind to comprehend the contents and grasp the abstruse meanings that lie hidden beneath the words themselves. At that time I had studied several texts with Swami Tapovanam and had not once dared to question him during class, but not this Chinmaya – he would put so many questions to Swami Tapovanam. He was not willing to move on to the next topic until every doubt on the present subject was removed by the Teacher.

Often Swami Tapovanam would repeat at the end of his class that what he had discussed was only the conditioned. "Remove the conditioning and realize the Self," he would conclude the class.

After contemplating these words for several days, Chinmaya felt compelled to ask the Guru during the next class, "Swamiji, why not remove the conditioning and explain the pure Brahman? Why do you say that it is the eye of the eye without the eye-conditioning?" The Guru paused for a moment, then continued the class without giving any direct reply. As the lesson proceeded, Chinmaya's mind became so involved in the logic of the concepts that he had forgotten his earlier question.

All of a sudden Swami Tapovanam said to him, "Chinmaya, get me some water to drink." The disciple was somewhat surprised because it was unusual to be thirsty in the cold climate of Gangotri at such an early hour. Nevertheless, he quickly brought a pail of fresh water and placed it in front of the Guru.

"What is this?" asked the Guru in an assumed air of anger.

"Swamiji, this is the water you wanted," murmured the awed disciple.

"But did I ask for a pail?" roared the Master, "Or for water? Take that pail away and bring me the water."

"But Swamiji, how. . . without a pail? How. . . can I carry. . . water?" stammered the confused and confounded Chinmaya.

"Never mind", said the Master, in a soft, encouraging tone. "Nobody can convey water without a vessel; it is the same in conveying the knowledge of Truth. The Absolute cannot be explained in words, just as you cannot bring water without a vessel. We cannot express Truth except through the medium of one or the other of its conditionings, in this case, words. Hence, it is that the scriptures as well as the Gurus explain only the conditioned Truth, instead of the absolute Truth."

After class the students would take care of any necessary chores and prepare breakfast. The only readily available food was dry roti – that is, wheat flour and water mixed together and patted into a flat disc, then baked on a skillet (frying pan) on an open fire, without any oil or butter to flavour it. Chinmaya did not have to lose any of his study time in acquiring the flour and occasional vegetable or dal as the Nepalese brahmacārī took the responsibility of going out and collecting bhikṣā (begged food) for the Swamis each morning. The food was uncooked, so Chinmaya would often cook the food for his Guru, as he was somewhat more familiar with Indian food preparation than the Nepalese. But not much – his expertise had been in eating and enjoying food – not cooking it.

South Indians are rice-eaters; rotis are eaten in the north, so Chinmaya was at a loss when it came to the art of producing the thin, soft, round rotis. Sometimes Swami Tapovanam would give a quizzical look at the questionable nature of the misshapen, thick and dry rotis brought to him by his student. But he must have known the good intentions of the cook, for, he ate them without comment. Once, out of earshot of Chinmaya, with a chuckle he told a student "See, one never gets to give up tapas (austerities) in these Himalayas," demonstrating one of Chinmaya's rotis.

Since Swami Tapovanam was well-known to the surrounding villagers as a great sage, often one of them would bring him bhikṣā of a spicy vegetable dish to go with the rotis. On such occasions Swami Tapovanam might call out, "Chinmaya! Come!" He would give his student just a bite of the savoury dish. Just enough to whet his appetite! Some opined that it was a generous gesture on the part of the Swami, knowing what a luxurious life filled with good food Chinmaya had forsaken. Others were sure that it was a test of whether the flavours of his previous lifestyle would cause a disturbance in his mind.

The tall shadows of the mountain peaks fell early across the valley bringing a rapid nightfall. There was no electricity for reading and no talking was allowed among the students, not with this disciplinarian for a Guru. Swami Tapovanam thought that talking was a waste of time and that no one had any time to waste in the great pilgrimage to the divine goal. With the exception of class time, if the students even approached him while he was sitting on the veranda of his hut, he would chide them – "What are you doing hanging around here? Don't waste a minute! You go, do your own reflection. It's all in you!"

With the setting sun, Chinmaya retired to his humble shelter – an old cow shed, walled in only on the north side to hold back the drifting snows in the winter. The straw-thatched roof, so low that Chinmaya had to stoop over when inside, had housed many a generation of birds. He spent long, cool nights contemplating the words of his Guru, then meditating on the Truth revealed. In this manner, the student passed his days, delving deeper and deeper into the Truth that lies hidden in oneself.

As the cold winter winds began to blow, around October in those altitudes, the group undertook the journey back down to Uttarkashi. Only Swami Chinmayananda accompanied Swami Tapovanam on the return trip as the other students were going to another pilgrimage site en route. As the Guru and student stopped in the shelters along the route, the student cooked the food and served his Teacher. Following the course of the Ganga as she slips through the mountain valleys, they went along conversing in their native language, Malayalam.

Swami Tapovanam was such a pure soul that he saw God in everything. Along the way he would stop and point out the majestic scenery. "Look at those clouds, Chinmaya. So beautiful is all of nature. How can anyone not believe the grace and beauty of the Lord when they see his form manifested in this wonderful world of nature." Try as he might, Chinmaya just could not quite see what it was that Swami Tapovanam was seeing in those clouds.

Chinmaya later wrote of those blissful days with his Teacher –

> "When we used to move back and forth from Uttarkashi to Gangotri, Swamiji would often stop abruptly in the trail, alert and thrilled, tense and silent. I watched him – now lost in wonder at the snow peaks, now aghast at the thundering laughter of the Ganga in her panting speed; even a long-tailed, tiny bird fluttering across the path was sufficient to tickle Swamiji into a visible rapture. At these times he would stand still, bathed in a vivid glow of joy, whispering silently his homage to the Creator.

In the early years of my study, he had once stopped en route to point out to me a spot in the distant sky where the golden colour had suddenly changed in a mighty stroke of an inscrutable artistic inspiration into a blue splash! On another occasion he cried out to me, 'Why can't man see the divinity behind the ecstatic artist who has painted this inspired beauty?'

I could fill up a big volume with the instances when he took such effort to point out to me scenes from the divine play of the Creator – a crab returning to its hideout or a spider weaving its web under our feet, leaves dancing in the passing breeze while embracing an opening flower bud, the mighty pines secretly whispering and nodding to each other in an eloquent rhythm, the majestic peaks of snow-capped mountains, divinely glistening above the lower hills, here an insignificant bull, there an uninviting herd of tired sheep, elsewhere an ugly rustic singing a disgusting tune with a joyous abandon – at a thousand such instances he rejoiced and laboured to direct my attention to SEE. But, alas, immature, unpoetic and intellectually sophisticated as I considered myself to be then, in all these instances I must have sadly disappointed him in my blindness.

But I sensed what he felt, for, I felt the warmth of his ardour, the thrill of his ecstasy, the serenity of his mad joy. I often watched his breathless expectancy, his trembling lips and his eyes welling with tears, as he stood dissolved in a visible divine harmony with nature. At such inspired moments, an unearthly tranquillity used to descend around him in which I have vividly basked many a time."

Upon their return to Uttarkashi, the discussions continued in such an intense manner that others were intimidated to approach the two as they sat on the veranda of Tapovanam Kutir. After a week Swami Govindagiri and the brahmacārī returned, and the classes resumed with their logical analysis for the intellectual understanding of the scriptures. However, there were activities for other aspects of the personality, such as service to the Guru and the elder Swamis to develop the qualities of kindness and compassion.

One such project taken on by Chinmaya was to be at the Guru's door with a cup of tea when he arose at 4 a.m. Accustomed to the āśrama life at Ananda Kutir, Swami Chinmayananda woke up automatically by that hour, but now he would have to rise, bathe and have water boiled by that hour – and there was no alarm clock. He was determined that he would not oversleep, so each night he used a large stone for a pillow, which kept him from going into a deep sleep. With this system he was at the door of Swami Tapovanam at 4 a.m. sharp with a cup of steaming tea in hand.

Although Swami Tapovanam allowed no comforts for himself and had lived years without them, he was able to use objects of the world for the sake of the training of his students. And the lesson of the Guru was often one that the student did not expect, for example, when the Swami left the full cup of tea sitting untouched after all the student's effort.

Another time the Swami handed some plain cotton cloth, which had been given to him as a gift, to Chinmaya and another student. He requested that they make one of his simple robes. They carefully cut the fabric, stitched it by hand, dyed it orange with saffron, and then laid it out Indian-style, over some bushes, to dry. Afterwards, they folded it carefully, put it in a plain paper wrapping, and presented it to Swami Tapovanam. Somehow, after he took off the wrapping, he found a tear in robe, or at least he claimed he did.

"Look! You tore it. You were careless when you took it off the shrubs!" He looked straight at Chinmaya.

"No, I was very careful, Swamiji," the student bravely defended himself. "Let me see it. I can't understand how it got torn."

"I was watching you take it off those shrubs and you were careless. Your attention was not on what you were doing. You are surely lying now!"

That was a heavy blow for Chinmaya – to be called a liar – especially when he was sure he was telling the truth. After that, when Chinmaya approached his hut, Swami Tapovanam would taunt him – "Liar". Chinmaya's anger and frustration stirred to the boiling point. He did not think that he had torn the garment, but he did not see how he was going to convince the Teacher.

After a couple of days of this harassment, Chinmaya could bear it no longer. How could this Teacher be such a Master anyway, if he was so concerned over a torn piece of cloth? He kept his rationalizations to himself, but in the end, he made up his mind to leave and study on his own 'without all the guru nonsense.' Fortunately, an older Swami, who understood the Guru's ways, saw the young Swami making preparations to leave and called him aside. "Look, son. He is only testing you," he persuaded the young man.

The next time Swami Tapovanam called out "Liar!" to Chinmaya, he was ready. "Perhaps", he retorted with a knowing smile.

"Oh, so now you see! This whole creation is a lie. Why make a big deal over one little lie!" the Swami retorted with a chuckle.

He never missed an opportunity to teach the ideals of spiritual discipline in practical situations. His goal was to turn the student's mind beyond material concerns even in their daily routines. Not only did he not allow comforts for himself, he sanctioned none for his students. If anyone even suggested an idea for a non-essential item, he would huff, "What do you think we have here, a dharmaśālā?"

Occasionally people would send Swami Tapovanam candy or hard biscuits – the equivalent to ambrosia in the austere setting. He would direct the postman to set the package on the corner of the veranda, then without opening the packet he would have a student carry it down the winding path to the Ganga to dump it in the river.

"Swamiji, we know that you do not want to eat these things, but couldn't you at least give them to us. . . or someone?" cautiously ventured a student at the delivery of a promising looking parcel. "Why waste it?"

"Look, it's their karma (duty) to send sweets, but here we have no karma (destiny) to eat them. Here we're interested in more worthwhile pursuits," he roared, leaving no doubt as to the fate of the package of biscuits.

One afternoon a basket of laḍḍūs arrived just as the class began, so everyone got a chance to eye it well. The laḍḍū had earned the distinction of being the favoured sweet of holy men and everyone felt sure that the Teacher would allow each student just one. Most of those present had studied with Swami Tapovanam only a short time and had not witnessed his previous record of requiring all goodies to be tossed into the river.

"Put it inside!" he tersely ordered one of the students.

Since there was no evening meal at Tapovanam Kutir, the students thought, tomorrow he will distribute them with the noon meal. But noon meals came and went and no laḍḍūs appeared. After a few days the students' minds became disturbed, thinking – this is some Master, hogging all the laḍḍūs for himself! Several actually became so disenchanted that they left, for, they did not want to study the scriptures from such a greedy character. Chinmaya tried to convince them of the Guru's austere way of life, explaining that he often used such incidents as practical examples of teaching. But he was not so sure what was going on himself; Swami Tapovanam had never allowed even a grain of rice inside his hut before. The next day, the Teacher noted that the attendance in the class had abruptly dropped; two of the students had left without even bidding him goodbye.

"What's happened? Where are the other two?" he questioned, for, no one dared arrive late to his classes.

"They left", came a timid reply from someone in the group.

"Chinmaya, come here. Now, go and take that basket from my room."

Chinmaya went inside and found the basket of laḍḍū exactly as it had arrived, not one was missing.

"Bring it here!" he ordered.

Chinmaya followed the order, thinking (as was everyone), "Good, now he is going to give them out." Mouths that had not savoured a sweet for many months were watering at the thought.

"To the Ganga! Throw them out!" he ordered. "When you take sannyāsa, you are supposed to have control over your senses. Just look at the quality of your minds, agitated over a paltry basket of sweets. I saw your distractions and knew what was going on, so I didn't want to continue to encourage it. We're here to study the Upaniṣads, not to eat laḍḍū!"

Living the life of a sannyāsī meant no money in the pocket for any purchases; however, Swami Chinmayananda was regularly seen with a cigarette. Even in that remote corner of the world someone could be found to reinforce one's worldly habits. His fondness for smoking was known to the villagers and they would give a few bidis, hand-rolled cigarettes, to the young Swami as a 'service'. One day some zealous soul reported to Swami Tapovanam, "Swamiji, do you know that your disciple Chinmaya is seen smoking regularly."

"Humph, I'm only concerned with the inner smoke; this outer smoke is of no importance – it will take care of itself in time," he replied simply.

While Swami Tapovanam and his students were at Uttarkashi, many pilgrims who were passing through on their way to Gangotri travelled the path up to Tapovanam Kutir. Everyone knew of the great Mahātmā who lived there, and none would miss an opportunity of receiving the blessing of seeing such a Master. These visitors often caused a disturbance if they arrived during class time, but they also provided an opportunity for some unique lessons.

On one such occasion a devotee who visited Swami Tapovanam regularly came trudging up the hillside carrying two bundles of groceries for the Master, one in each hand. The Swami spotted him coming up the path and called out to him, "Drop it!" The poor fellow, not knowing exactly what the Swami meant, but wanting to follow his instructions, obligingly dropped one bundle. "Drop it!" called out the Swami again; so the man dropped the other bundle. By this time he had approached nearer the hut, when the Swami looked him straight in the eyes and repeated with an emphatic firmness, "Drop it, I say!" Since the devotee had dropped all of the external packages, there was nothing left to drop but the internal bundle – the mind. When the light dawned of what Swami Tapovanam meant, the devotee sat down on the spot and entered samādhi, a state of bliss. The students observing the encounter were dumbfounded.

Before snowfall, Swami Tapovanam went down to Rishikesh with his disciple Chinmaya, who returned to Ananda Kutir to stay while the Teacher took a boat across the river to stay at his usual quarters at Brahmananda Ashram. Reunited with his former companions at the āśrama, Swami Chinmayananda shared with them the new insights from his study of the scriptures while lavishly praising Swami Tapovanam's expertise as well as his exemplary life of discipline. Interested in the progress of this disciple, Swami Sivananda listened to the lively and loving reports – it seemed that Chinmaya had found his true Guru and was going to be able to bear the life of austerity necessary to study with him.

At that time Swami Sivananda received a letter from Swami Chinmayananda's father. Mr. Menon, a diabetic for many years, was ill and had written requesting that his son be allowed to visit him. Swami Sivananda granted the permission, so Chinmaya left for the long journey, five days by train, down to Kerala. When he arrived there, he went first to the home of his maternal uncle Govind, who lived in Ottappalam. As a formality, he asked his elder to please accompany him to Trichur to the home of his father since Swamis do not stay in their family home in order to help insulate them from any latent attachments to their past. Happy to see his nephew, Uncle Govind gladly agreed and the two set out for Trichur.

Mr. Menon, retired from his career, was sitting out on veranda to catch the rays of the winter sunshine before the noon meal. Suddenly a streak of orange came racing through the gate and up the walk. Before he knew what had happened there was a Swami prostrating at his very feet. For a moment he was completely taken aback at seeing a holy man bow to him. Momentarily, he realized that it was his own son who for so many years had bowed and touched his feet each morning in a gesture of respect. As he hugged his son, they both shed tears of joy. A small group of family members quickly gathered around the two, adding their own happy tears to the homecoming.

Ten years had passed since they had seen him. He had not only changed from a twenty-year old youth named Menon to a thirty-year old man, he had become a Swami named Chinmayananda. At first, the family was slightly apprehensive of this new person, a religious monk. However, they were soon relieved, for, he acted like his old cheerful self. He even joked with his father, "See, I had my head shaved, so you wouldn't have to do it!" In years past, his father had threatened to shave his son's head because he wore it in the fashion of his peers – too long and too oily. Everyone had a good laugh. Then the Swami gave everyone his energetic hug. He could recognize his sisters, Kanakam and Padmini, but his half-brother and sisters, just small children when he left for Lucknow University, had to tell him who they were.

The Swami had asked his uncle to accompany him to his father's home, but no such formality was necessary at his mother's ancestral home, Poothampalli, meaning, 'place of the Lord'. Whenever the family assembled to dine, the place at the head of the table was always set and left vacant, held ready to serve any holy man who happened to be passing that way. Therefore, the family got a big surprise when the door burst open and the holy man that rushed in and sat at their table was none other than their own beloved nephew. The whole household rippled with enthusiasm as his aunts brought out the special pickles, favourite deep fried pepper chillies and delicious sweets reserved for holidays for this special bhikṣā.

Swami Chinmayananda remained for a couple of weeks in Kerala. He spent his time visiting temples, spiritual centres and talking to the spiritual Teachers in the area. Because of his connection with the Divine Life Society, he was asked to give several lectures at its centres. His own father recovered his health sufficiently to accompany him to one of the talks. He described it when he wrote to notify Swami Sivananda of his son's return to Rishikesh –

....

> Salutations and adorations!
>
> Many thanks for allowing Swami Chinmayananda to visit me in my sickness. He had been sent back from here on February 8th and is expected to reach there for Śivarātri, as ordered by you.
>
> Swami Chinmayananda visited the Divine Life Society at Ottappalam and at Calicut. He went twice to Calicut at their special request and I accompanied him on the second visit. I listened to his lecture on the Divine Life on Feb. 2, 1950 and to his answers to various questions put by the audience. I was really surprised at the knowledge you have been kind enough to impart to him in such a short period of time. The lecture was so instructive. I am convinced that the whole audience was

impressed by him. His solving the various doubts was so clear and convincing that the audience had no further questions to ask him after his explanations. There was a photo of yours placed behind the dais he was sitting on, and I felt that you were quite pleased with the way he handled the subject and was therefore smiling.

I feel myself much honoured and blessed by having such a son for whom God has been pleased to give such a saintly Guru. I have no regret at all that I had given my free consent to him to be a pupil under you and to serve you for all time.

With prema and praṇāmas,
Your humble sevaka and admirer,
V. K. Kuttan Menon

....

Soon after Swami Chinmayananda reached Ananda Kutir, several of his old associates, reporters from Delhi, were curious enough to make the trip up to Rishikesh to meet their former colleague. They wanted to see how things were going with his life as a Swami. When they were allowed an interview with him, they were quite open in their questioning. Following is the first part of the interview as it appeared in the *Champion* magazine –

INTERVIEW WITH *CHAMPION* MAGAZINE, 1950

At Rishikesh on the banks of the Ganga's silvery March sits Ananda Kutir, Śrī Swami Sivananda's āśrama. Amazed at the institution and its varied activities of guiding, instructing and encouraging the saint's numerous disciples from all over the world, we silently watched. The more we watched the more we learned. It was most fortunate that we could get Swami Chinmayananda to ourselves for an hour one afternoon and we shot dozens of questions at him. The cool confidence and sympathetic understanding with which he answered all our sceptical questions on God and spiritual life gave us the courage to expose the worst of our own curiosity.

"Swamiji, excuse us, but could we ask a personal question?" we ventured.

"Certainly. Why not?" smiled back the Swami.

Knowing very well that it is unpardonable to ask any monk about his life prior to becoming a renunciate, we asked, "Swamiji, why did you take sannyāsa?"

There was a visible tension in his calm face. He was alert. His eyes wandered for a moment among the correspondence, typewriter and the many volumes that lay scattered about him. "What would you have me do," he shot at us, "marry, breed, fight and talk shop until, wrecked with age and sorrow, this body drops down dead?"

The criticism on life was quite clear. It set us thinking. We remained silent. Our usual professional satisfaction was replaced by a welling gush of futility. From where it came, we knew not.

"Chinmaya was tired of living in the tomb, so he walked out into the open to breathe, to bask, to work and to live." The Swami was all ablaze. None of us had even suspected that such a frail body could contain such a consuming fire of earnestness and sincerity.

All of us were silent. The song of the waters of the Ganga rose up to reach the modest room of Chinmaya. The Swami sat looking out into the glittering flow of the immortal river. It was a roar of silence that smothered our values and lay heavy on our sinned bosom.

"Yes", the Swami spoke at last, almost to himself. "It was at this realization of the uselessness of the worldly values and goals of life that P. B. K. Menon, curious to know what an āśrama life would be like, and eagerly thirsting to meet his saviour and unknown Master, one day reached Rishikesh. This sādhu (Swami) must confess," confided Swamiji, "that Balakrishnan Menon reached the feet of his Guru more as a deserter of life, than as a discoverer of some new shores."

10

Tuning the Instrument

I was miserably disillusioned and disappointed at the working plans of all the āśramas and temples, at the stuff that was doled out as the best of Hinduism.

—Swami Chinmayananda, 1951.

Swami Tapovanam had developed a regular schedule in his later years. At the beginning of April, he left Rishikesh for the higher altitudes of Uttarkashi where he spent the spring season. In July he went up to Gangotri for the summer. By November he returned to Uttarkashi to stay until February, when he departed for Rishikesh to spend the coldest winter months there. His classes on the scriptures continued at Uttarkashi and Gangotri. Normally, he gave daily lessons in the morning for one and a half hours, except in the winter sessions at Uttarkashi. Because of the cold at those altitudes he conducted the classes there in the afternoon from 2 to 3:30 p.m., taking advantage of the few hours when the sun reached the outdoor classroom in front of his veranda.

When summer's arrival brought its warm sun to melt the snows of the higher altitudes, Swami Tapovanam and Swami Chinmayananda set out for Gangotri. There the study of the Upaniṣads continued each morning. The daily schedule was always the same; Swami Tapovanam did not allow any interruption from the outside world to change it for him. He knew what really mattered in the world, by taking care of That all else would take care of itself.

Thus Chinmaya's time was spent with the Guru, serving him with loving devotion, listening to the words of the holy scriptures, and contemplating to realize the meaning of the words. It was evident among the other students who had joined the classes that Swami Chinmayananda displayed all the qualifications of one ready for the final plunge – the dive into Self-realization.

Through the generations, the teachers of the scriptures in general, and Vedānta in particular, have discussed and made an attempt to understand why it was that some of their students were able to catch the truth behind the words of the scriptures and transcend the realm of logic, while others only intellectually understood the words, and still other students never even seemed to hear the words correctly. The sages concluded that the successful students had certain mental qualities that they enumerated as the four prerequisites of the 'successful' spiritual student –

First, viveka, the capacity to discriminate the Real from the unreal, that is, the permanent from the impermanent, the changeless from the changing.

Second, vairāgya, detachment from that unreal through logic and intellectual discrimination.

Third, ṣaṭka-sampattiḥ, the six moral and mental qualities (1) śama, control of mind and ability to remain focused on one's objective; (2) dama, control of the organs of perception and organs of action; (3) uparati, the ability to cease all activity; (4) titikṣā, fortitude or endurance; (5) śraddhā, faith based on an intellectual appreciation of the truths of the scriptures, and (6) samādhāna, a tranquil, steady mind that is born of the contemplation on the Truth.

Fourth, mumukṣutva, the compelling desire to leave the limitations of the world to reach the final divine goal of freedom from all bondage, both mental and physical.

The student who possessed these four necessary qualities was ready to discover the divine essence within. Therefore, if the student did not merge into Self-realization at hearing the esoteric truths from the Guru, the fault was with the student's mental preparation, not the scriptures or the Guru.

The illuminated sages and Masters rarely mention their own personal struggles along the path to the final Realization, their experience of oneness with the Divine. First, they know none of their struggles really happened, so there is no purpose in talking about them, thereby giving emphasis to the details of one's own personal illusions. The Buddha declared that, upon experiencing Nirvāṇa, what he realized was that he was always Enlightened. Secondly, each person's path to the Truth is so distinct, so unique, that to verbalise the particulars misleads others into inflexible beliefs and false imitation, which are always detrimental on the spiritual path. Therefore, all great teachers speak in universal terms, maintaining a distance from their own personal experience.

Likewise, Swami Chinmayananda has said little of his inner evolution. His fellow classmates observed the outer discipline, but the real transformation was known only to himself and his Master.

During the four-month stay at Gangotri, Swami Tapovanam took up the teaching of the celebrated *Māṇḍūkya-upaniṣad*, accompanied by its lengthy gloss, the *Kārikā*. Swami Chinmayananda had already completed the study of several Upaniṣads and was delighted to take up the study of the great text of which it is said – Having understood this scripture, there is nothing else to know. In twelve short mantras (verses), the *Māṇḍūkya* unfolds a complete philosophy of life; that is, it gives an exposition of all fields of experience and all states of Consciousness.

The mantras of the Upaniṣad point out the Truth without decoration or a single extra word, while Śrī Gauḍapāda, the author of the *Kārikā* (commentary), elucidated the terms and concepts that warranted clarification, so not a single gem of the wisdom in the mantras was missed. Aside from expounding and illuminating the ideas of the mantras, Śrī Gauḍapāda applied an exhaustive logic to prove the illusory nature of the pluralistic world, followed by a careful exposition to prove that the advaita (non-dual) Reality revealed in the *Māṇḍūkya* is not illusory. Further, he systematised the logic of Vedāntic philosophy by adding another section to bring together all the valid tenets to establish that the supreme Truth is non-dual, uncreated and eternal. As was characteristic of all the ancient ṛṣis (sages), Śrī Gauḍapāda was equally at home with poetry and hard logic, so he composed the 215 verses of the *Kārikā* gloss in metric form. This style added to its elegance and made it easier for the students to memorise, since the scriptures were handed down orally from Teacher to student.

The Upaniṣads, the fourth section of the Vedas, are discussions between disciple and the Master in which the Master reveals the highest Truth. The unwritten words were remembered by the disciple and passed on to his disciples. The Sanskrit word, 'Upaniṣad', is composed of three syllables – upa – near; ni – below; sad – to sit; meaning, a treatise given by a Guru to a student who was sitting near and below, that is, the student sat nearby in a physical and mental posture of reverence.

The avatāra, Śrī Rāma, had given his disciple Hanumāna a necklace of 108 pearls on which were inscribed the most important mantra from each Upaniṣad. Through the centuries many of those 108 Upaniṣads have been lost, but tradition holds that it is not necessary to study all 108 treatises. A serious student should first study *Māṇḍūkya*. If that text is understood to the fullest, further study is not necessary. If God-realization is not experienced, one should take up the study of the ten major Upaniṣads, that is, *Aitareya, Bṛhadāraṇyaka, Chāndogya, Īśa, Kaivalya, Kaṭha, Kena, Muṇḍaka, Praśna* and *Taittirīya*. After the thorough study of these ten, if the goal is still not attained, the student should continue his study of the remaining Upaniṣads.

Swami Chinmayananda was enthralled with the sureness and completeness of the transcendental knowledge as expounded in the *Māṇḍūkya* and its *Kārikā*. As was his custom he took careful notes, spending hours after each lesson going over each word to be sure no term was forgotten, no thought left incomplete, no insight left undigested, for, he was planning to share this divine wisdom with the disciples at Rishikesh. "This is the most thrilling text that you could ever imagine!" he wrote to Swami Chaitanyananda, a fellow disciple there. "When I return there, we will study it together."

Silently, the Teacher observed his student. Although Swami Tapovanam was not one to compliment his students directly, he used to tell others. "Chinmaya is very intelligent." However, he was always alert to the necessity of eradicating the student's ego. So to the student, his words were most often reproving. "Chinmaya, you are so carried away by the non-dual philosophy! In the morning you are studying the non-dual Reality in *Māṇḍūkya Kārikā*, yet at 4 p.m. you are in duality writing letters!"

But Chinmaya was never intimidated in sharing what he had learned. He was most liberal in offering advice to assist others with their spiritual understanding. He corresponded regularly concerning religious matters with several family members and seekers who were indeed living in the duality of the world.

He consoles a friend in a letter dated 5th February 1950 –

"As to our lot in life, remember always, no circumstance is a special packet of sorrow sent to us as special punishment. No family is without its own sorrow; nobody is without his own silent accompaniments of pain while living upon this reeling globe of ours! But the solace is in the fact that none of this is infinite – even our sorrows must end, as must all our joys.

If Vijayam is not healthy now, it cannot be forever. She has to live through the results of her own past actions; as you too must live out the impressions gathered in your past. At each hour of pain and anxiety, a true devotee of the Lord learns to feel great consolation – "Oh, my sweet Lord, in Thy grace I am going doubly fast through the results of past actions and thoughts, with each sigh and tear I am getting so much nearer to Thee!"

He advises in another letter written the same day –

"Each day after meditation and worship, sit for a while both morning and evening, for some fifteen minutes to start with. Don't worry about your breath or the correct posture, just sit in peace and watch the flow of thoughts. Now, do not identify with these thoughts – Be a witness of them. Remember there must be a 'lighter' of these thoughts, or else you would not be able to perceive them. The lighter is the witness – you, yourself, at this moment. Forget or reject entirely the body and all of its relations – the house, the dinner, family and friends. Nothing else IS but this Awareness – THAT I AM!"

In another letter he inspires a friend suffering from mental anguish to continue with her spiritual practices.

"In pain I come to thee" is the Lord's own promise. Therefore, to every devotee painful circumstances are the approaching music of the Lord's own procession! Develop more depth to your devotion. Up until now your practice has been submissive, surrendering and humble. Now make the practice positive. That is, up until now you have been removing the dirt of the mind; you have done enough of that. Now don't stay where you are – take a step higher. Be positive by asserting,

> "The Lord is near NOW; I am in His safekeeping. Even these pains are to cut asunder my false sense of attachments to my husband and daughter. I am not the guardian of my children's future or of my husband's joys. Until now in my delusion I thought so; now Goddess Mother is correcting me. I surrender all to Thee; I only ask for Wisdom."

....

That winter Swami Chinmayananda flew on wings of love down to his old quarters at Ananda Kutir. Bubbling with enthusiasm to share the wisdom he had absorbed, he entered the familiar gates. "The world is unreal! It never came into existence!" He would rave on for hours – "like a man possessed" a cohort described him. He didn't even think of food or his beloved tea. The Swamis who were already harbouring a bit of jealousy over his ability to stick it out with the great disciplinarian Swami Tapovanam were somewhat intimidated. They did not know what to think of this transformation. But they were soon delighted to catch him lighting up a cigarette.

"See what kind of man you are – talking scriptures one minute and then smoking the next!"

"Don't you see? In a dream what does it matter if the dreamer has a dream cigarette. This creation is all non-existent, like a dreamworld," he responded with blissful chuckle.

They, without the depth in themselves to perceive the source of happiness within, retorted, "When it suits you, you talk Vedānta."

Many think that āśramas are havens of peace and tranquillity. That is the ideal, but often not the reality. As āśrama is not a group of buildings, but the people who inhabit them. The seekers are under a tremendous strain; they have given up the pleasures of the worldly life, but have not reached the contentment of the spiritual life. They have come to the āśrama to develop themselves. In the process of purifying the mind, the impurities surface to discolour and distort everything and everyone, these projections are inevitable. Understanding the nature of the mind, Chinmaya was not fazed by the comments or criticisms. He was dwelling in his Self – not in an āśrama.

Upon his return to Uttarkashi in the spring, Swami Tapovanam had planned to give classes on the *Bhagavad-gītā*, but developed a severe cough. Hardly able to speak without a spasm of coughing, he told his disciple, "Okay, I've taught you the Upaniṣads, now you study the *Gītā* on your own. If you have a question, we'll discuss it." With these words Swami Tapovanam ended Chinmaya's studies from a textbook. But learning from the Teacher did not stop; he would spend another six years communicating with the Master.

In the *Bhagavad-gītā*, Lord Kṛṣṇa strung together the ideas of the Upaniṣads in a divine song in such a manner that the common laity could comprehend the Truth, the play of the Divine and man's relation to it. The actual writing of the *Gītā* is attributed to the great-seer, Vyāsa, who produced such a quantity of literary works in his lifetime that modern scholars have assigned him to the realms of mythology.

First Vyāsa took up the task of actually writing down the Vedas, which had been preserved through the centuries by an oral tradition. Perceiving that the minds of his contemporaries were becoming more agitated by the stress of daily living and would not be sufficiently calm to retain the long treatises by rote, he codified the Vedas into a more manageable form of four books – *Ṛg, Yajur, Sāma, Atharva*. Having completed this compilation, with an aspiration to relate the divine truths in a simpler manner, he wrote the outstanding epic *Mahābhārata* (the great revelling in light), a history of several lineages of ancient Hindu kings. In the middle of the narrative, he discretely included a treatise that illuminates the advanced tenets of Vedāntic philosophy of the Upaniṣads. In 700 verses of conversation, later named the *Bhagavad-gītā* ('Song of the Lord'), Lord Kṛṣṇa taught his student Arjuna the highest truths of life. Upon completing the *Mahābhārata*, the genius Vyāsa composed a collection of shorter epics called the Purāṇas (stories of old), which illustrate in story form the deeper philosophy of the scriptures. These stories of gods, great deeds and heroes of the past are still told to Hindu children to teach them the values of living in harmony with the higher Reality.

Set on a battlefield on the eve of combat, the *Gītā* relates to men of action facing the troubled situations of life, not just to sages in contemplation in the mountains. For this reason, it would later become the primary text in Swami Chinmayananda's mission to teach other.

In fact, Chinmaya had already undertaken its study when he was a journalist in Delhi, and again with the assistance of Swami Govindagiri the previous year. Adept in both Sanskrit and the scriptures, Swami Govindagiri had studied the *Gītā* with several sages during his twenty-five years in the Himalayas. He was not inclined to do any teaching, but he had been willing to discuss the verses and point out some of the hidden treasures with this sincere seeker. "Chinmaya practised an intense sādhanā (spiritual discipline) all during his period of study with Swami Tapovanam. I often saw him sitting all night in meditation in a quiet corner of the forest or sometimes on a boulder beside the Ganga," recalled Swami Govindagiri.

At one point Chinmaya decided that even the proximity of Swami Tapovanam and his fellow students was a hindrance to the solitary existence that was necessary for meditation. As the wail of a temple conch pierced the darkness of early morning, Chinmaya started down a trail toward the deep forest. But his solitary form alerted his Master who sent another student to bring back the wandering monk. "Never forget the peace you are seeking is within," his Guru cautioned him. "The few noises and irritations you have around here are only the Lord's way of turning you to the silence within."

At Gangotri as the Ganga emerges from a gorge of high rock surrounded by tall trees, it makes a wide turn and cuts out a small peninsula. Embraced on three sides by the holy Ganga, it was favoured spot for the holy men in the area to sit out in the sun to discuss Vedānta. These sophists would debate for hours, competing to show their vast intellectual knowledge. The logic of Vedānta is exhaustive as a means to dismiss the changing, temporary world and to affirm the permanent, spiritual Reality. Nonetheless, it has also been acknowledged by Hindu sages that all the scriptures are intended for the purpose of answering the mind's questions and thereby quietening it, for, it is only in a silenced mind that the Truth beyond the mind is reflected. The competition among these ascetics revealed no interest in the dissolution of the mind. As Swami Chinmayananda described, it was quite the contrary.

> We called it 'Fakirastāna' (place of the wise). There the elderly Mahātmās discussed Ādi Śaṅkarācārya's commentaries among themselves and asserted vehemently some conclusion or other, often without much logical argument. It was out of court to interrupt the divine prattlers, even if it were to inquire for the logic of a deduction. I was often snubbed by them as 'one who will never understand Vedānta.'
>
> These daily discussions gave me a peep into what these Mahātmās were saying in the cities, and how much their words must be affecting, adversely no doubt, the educated, thinking class. I was terribly disappointed. Slowly, I left them for my own personal reflections and meditation.

It was after one of these encounters, while he was sitting on a large boulder on the banks of the Ganga in its infant state, that the inspiration to take the truth of the Hindu scriptures – as taught by the Master Tapovanam and realized by the student – to his fellow countrymen, dawned in the heart of Swami Chinmayananda.

But there were obstacles to actualising his plan. A seemingly insurmountable one was his own Guru. Swami Tapovanam had not once left the climes of the Himalayas since his renunciation. He was a staunch believer that a Swami should lead a life of retirement. Although retirement did not mean inactivity, he wrote in his travelogue that a Swami should remain active in studying the scriptures, taking pilgrimages, and teaching those who came to him. But he thought that the highest philosophy of Vedānta should not be taught to the general public, as it might do more harm than good. Since the ordinary man was so consumed by desires, he lacked the subtle mind to be able to understand the paradoxes of the scriptures correctly. Swami Tapovanam considered that man should be left to come naturally to the phase in life when he was ready to investigate the true nature of things. At the right moment, he would be led by the Lord to a worthy Teacher. "You can't treat this knowledge like your newspaper business," he admonished his student. Respecting his Guru's convictions, Swami Chinmayananda put the idea aside, again and again.

> The vague mental suggestion when suppressed became almost a mighty call – an urge that could no more be controlled. One day, therefore, taking courage literally in both my hands, I declared my intentions to my Guru. I remember even today how his heavy brows came down, clouded by anxiety, almost stunned with surprise at my determination. "You don't know what you are asking for! You will get permanently caught up in the wheel of work. That is the nature of all activities. We start the action, and later the activities themselves take charge of us!"

It was not that Swami Tapovanam did not have sympathy for those who were living without the blessing and guidance of their ancient culture. He deplored the plight of men so busy with worldly concerns that they had no time to consider and discover the inner Spirit. He had written in *Wanderings in the Himalayas* –

"I must confess, I can hardly pass through the solitary valleys in the lonely Himalayan region without casting a longing, lingering look at the past and without being saddened by the changes that have come over our motherland. I believe that no man who loves his native land and who has some power of thought still left in him can traverse these regions without feeling a touch of melancholy for the loss of our great culture.

Nearly a month had passed since Chinmaya's declaration of his intentions when Swami Tapovanam called his student and suggested that he take a trip down to planes wandering around as a renunciate, living as a beggar among those he had once emulated. "This will rub out your ego! To have the experience of the Divine is not enough. You must be able to keep that vision through all your activities. Go down to the planes and keep your mananam (continual reflection) going there where it is the most difficult. When you face the adversities of life there, you will not fall into the dangers of complacency and self-contentment in your spiritual discipline."

Chinmaya wrote of that journey –

Thus it was that I, in May 1951, walked down from the heights of Gangotri to Rishikesh and from there moved on to Delhi with a plan to set out on an all-India pilgrimage, visiting all the important spiritual centres to see how others were serving the Hindu brethren. I travelled on foot some six months; living on bhikṣā (begged food), sleeping in āśramas, temples, under wayside trees. Swamiji was correct – it was quite an experience in rubbing off the ego. Education, social status, family connections, prejudices, sham values – these were no longer mine. When people do not know who you are, they consider you an inconvenient beggar, a worthless monk, an unproductive member of the community. And they insult you with looks of abhorrence as if you were something the cat dragged in. If you ask me, this kind of discipline is the best cure for the ego-disease.

....

It was a long journey, down to Delhi, over to Madras (now Chennai) through the state of Andhra Pradesh, then across South India. Swami Chinmayananda followed the general route of the railway lines. All along the way he talked to people and listened to them, always observing and assessing. The people in the cities were an aimless crowd, out of contact with the values in their own traditional culture. Those who did observe some of the religious rituals and disciplines did so mechanically, without discernment of the meaning of their actions; therefore, they were deriving no spiritual benefit. A well of empathy began building up in Chinmaya, which would be the source of his overflowing love for his countrymen. That love would sustain him for some forty years of constant teaching. "I am more attached to the world than you! I love everyone and everything in it, whereas you love only a few paltry items!" he later exclaimed to a group of students.

Swami Tapovanam had visited the Ramana Ashram during his early travels and Ramana Maharshi recalled him as he had had occasional news of the Swami from wandering sādhus (monks). He did not recall the brief visit Swami Chinmayananda had made to Arunachala twelve years earlier as Balakrishnan Menon.

Swami Chinmayananda then continued south to visit Cape Comorin (now Kanyakumari) at the southernmost tip of India, where in 1888, Swami Vivekananda was inspired to begin his campaign for the spiritual upliftment and political freedom of his countrymen. Circling up the western coast, Chinmaya finally reached his hometown in Kerala.

The family was interested in his spiritual life, as well as his ideas to bring the true light of the Hindu scriptures to the people. "To convert Hindus to Hinduism," as he succinctly stated his mission. His stepmother and a former schoolmate, Shankaran Marar, organized his first public talks. Spending five rupees (forty cents) for the printing of a small flier, they advertised the event and gathered a small group of a dozen people to hear a talk on the scriptures. Several attended just out of curiosity – Could this Swami possibly be that worthless Balakrishnan Menon of Trichur?

Parukutty Menon, Mother of
Balakrishnan Menon

Balakrishnan in intermediate school

The Menon Family:
(L to R) Padmini (sister),
Balakrishnan, V. K. Kuttan (father),
Kanakam (sister)

Swami Sivananda with the newly initiated Swamis on February 25, 1945
(Swami Chinmayananda third from Right)

The student in front of a thatched hut at Uttarkashi

ॐ

THE DIVINE LIFE SOCIETY

AIM:
Dissemination of
Spiritual Knowledge.

ANANDA KUTIR POST

Rishikesh, 14th Oct 1951.

Sri Swami Chinmayananda,
UTTARKASHI

Glorious Immortal Self,

Sàlutations and adorations. Om Namo Narayanaya.

Thy kind letter.

It is a grand idea. Spread of the Message of the Upanishads is the need of the hour. You will be doing the greatest service to the Lord's children by taking to their very doors the sublimest of wisdom.

The Rishis will shower their blessings upon you. The Lord's Grace will enable you to attain success in this divine undertaking. May God bless you with health, long life, peace, prosperity and Kaivalya Moksha!

Thy own Self,

Sivananda

The student with Guru, Swami Tapovanam in front of Tapovanam Kutir, Uttarkashi

Swami Chinmayananda, the Teacher

The brahmacārīs leading Swamiji to the temple for his birthday celebration at Sandeepany Sadhanalaya, 1975

PART – II

The Foundation

11

A Loving Start

The Hindu joint family is important to the continuation of our culture; it affords the members all of their needs in whatever crisis.

—Swami Chinmayananda, 1964.

Kerala, a narrow strip of land that runs along the western coast of South India, has had the advantage of a fertile soil and a tropical climate that have facilitated a comfortable prosperity for its inhabitants. The Arabian Sea to the west brought traders from afar who stabilized its economy, while the mountain range, the Western Ghats, on its eastern border, protected it from the outside invaders who have continually upset the more accessible regions of India.

The seaports of Kerala welcomed those who came to trade, bringing with them products and ideas from many foreign regions. In ancient times, Keralites exchanged goods with Egypt, Babylonia and Greece. The Chinese arrived from the Far East leaving their fishing nets, a particular style still used by the fishermen of the region. Recent excavations have verified trade with the Romans during their early Empire. In the first century St. Thomas came to this region in his missionary efforts. He died and was buried in South India. A community of Jewish merchants arrived in the third century, fleeing persecution. Their synagogue in Cochin remains the oldest continuously active one in the world. Arabian traders reached these shores about 800 AD to set up maritime communities on this bountiful, tropical coast. When the Europeans landed on the Kerala (then called Malabar) coast in 1498, they found Christians, Jews, Muslims and Hindus living and working side by side in a harmony unequalled on this planet.

In spite of the many contacts with the outside world, the native people of Kerala maintained their own simple, distinct lifestyle. In fact, the various foreign settlers often adopted their customs. Taking advantage of the fertile soil, the inhabitants had spread throughout the countryside. In the early 1900s, Kerala was one large continuous village except for the several towns along the coast where the Portuguese and Dutch, then British, had built their large warehouses to serve as trade centers.

Situated approximately at the midpoint of the coastline, Ernakulam was a thriving town located next to the busy port of Cochin. Its people, a mix of many cultures and ethnic groups, had welcomed the Europeans as traders, assuming that they would settle in the area and contribute to the flourishing economy as the traders of the past had done. They had no idea that the Europeans had come only to exploit, not to initiate commerce for mutual benefit.

The region came under British authority in the 1790s when both the Kings of Cochin and Travancore, weakened militarily from fighting between themselves, asked the British for protection from the destructive invasions of Muslims from the nearby state of Mysore. Unfortunately, after the victory, the 'protectors' proceeded to usurp both kingdoms. Two attempts, a decade later, to oust the British resulted in the martyrdom of these two objecting kings.

Except for the large brick warehouses, built by the Dutch in the 1600s, but in British hands by the 1700s, as well as an occasional mission church, school or bank, the British were hardly visible. They had built their spacious headquarters on an island in the bay from where they could administer their trading affairs without having to mingle with the 'niggers', as the officials called the natives among themselves. While criticizing the Hindus for their caste system, the British took advantage of it by placing themselves at the top. They defined their dealings in terms of only two groups – us and the untouchables – all those who were not white-skinned Europeans. Even a rumour of 'the touch of the tarbrush' in the genealogy would cause complete ostracism from the 'us' group. However, this maintenance of a cultural barrier allowed the life of the Keralites to continue as it had for centuries in their tropical paradise.

Water was plentiful. The numerous lakes, rivers, lagoons and ponds furnished a home for a multitude of sea birds and fish. The waterways were decorated with red and white water lilies, pink and white lotuses and blue water hyacinths. In addition they served as a watering hole for indigenous elephant, panther, bison and an occasional thirsty tiger. The undulating mountains of the ghats contained isolated green valleys planted in tea and coffee, whereas the jungles offered a refuge for some of India's most backward tribes. The fields were a patchwork of bright green, dark green, or light green, depending on the ripeness of the rice paddy, and were edged with stately coconut palms and small groves of betel nut trees. Situated among the shady groves were the two-room palm-thatched huts of the labourers, one room for living quarters for the family and the second for their animals – goats for daily milk, as cows were too expensive, and a few chickens for eggs. In contrast to the green of the fields and gray of the huts, the roadsides exploded with colour from a profusion of flowering trees and vines in vibrating shades of red, orange, hot-pink and bright yellow.

The economy of Kerala remained agricultural. When towns began to develop, Keralites kept the simple, functional style of the homes of their country estates. The sprawling one or two storied houses were surrounded by a parcel of land, enclosed by a high, thick mud wall with a peaked entrance gate, topped with a tile roof over which spilled branches of fuchsia and orange bougainvillea. This compound contained the necessities for daily living – several coconut palms, a couple of varieties of banana trees, a spreading mango tree, as well as vegetables and spices such as coriander, chilli peppers, black pepper and curry leaf, which furnished the special ingredients of the cuisine. A stone encased well furnished fresh water and a small tank doubled as a bathtub and laundry vat, as well as a swimming hole for the children. A large flower garden produced the colourful marigolds, huge crimson hibiscus, and fragrant jasmine blossoms that were offered in the daily worship service. Reminiscent of the true spirit of the ancient Indus Civilization, a crude stone altar was perched among the gnarled roots of the oldest tree, placed there in times forgotten.

In one corner of the compound, there was a shed to shelter the cow that supplied the daily milk. When extra milk was needed, it was guaranteed fresh – the dairyman arrived at the gate with his buffalo. Upon hearing the bell, the cook would run out with a pail to witness the milking. When the garden was short of vegetables, they were purchased from the vendor who carried his basket woven of palm leaves down the lanes, hawking the produce he had picked fresh that morning. Traditionally, a relay of runners between the towns delivered the mail, using a tinkling bell to caution the drivers of ox carts, rickshaws and bicycles to give the right of way.

A large rambling house of sun-dried mud bricks – coated with white wash and topped with a red tile roof with a carved 'Malabar' gable – was home for a large extended family. A stiff ocean wind was caught by the coastal palms and converted into a pleasant breeze that drifted through the wide verandas and open courtyards to provide a natural air-conditioning system. The open windows, unglassed and unscreened, were barred to deter the monkeys and shuttered against the fierce monsoon rains.

The home and properties were jointly owned and managed by the women in the family. The matriarchal system, like a mother's love, was based on unconditional acceptance. This custom probably evolved to protect the woman's rights should her husband not return from war, since the nobleman warrior

(Kṣatriya) was the region's predominant caste. This practice was unlike the rest of India, where a widow was often left penniless because all of her property belonged to her husband's family. In Kerala, after the marriage ceremony, the groom came to live in the family home of his wife. The system has been strained by the need to move into the cities to find jobs, but regardless of where she lived, the woman continued to possess her proportionate ownership of the family property. The tradition provided material security as well as protection from the distress of a bad marriage. If the husband was courageous enough to mistreat his wife under the noses of her mother, father, brothers and sisters, the wife could obtain a separation simply by mutual consent, or in some areas by placing the husband's shoes on the doorstep. So, when he came home from the fields and saw his shoes, he got the message. The influence of the women in Kerala was also notable in that sati was not practised and widows were allowed to remarry. Although the elder women owned the house, it was home for all the family members. The joint family lived, worked and prayed together in a mutual cooperation system that allotted extra mothers and fathers and many sister cousins and brother cousins for each child.

Into such a home in Ernakulam, Balakrishnan Menon was born on the 26th Mesham, 1091 of the Kollam era[1] (May 8, 1916) at 7:30 P.M. with Punarvasu on the ascendant in the position of rāja-yoga (Master of yoga). The Malayalam calendar, like that of other parts of India, is based on a lunar month in which each day is named for the constellation through which the moon is travelling. The father, Vadakke Kurupath Kuttan Menon, was from an aristocratic family of the landed gentry of the Kurupath House. His mother's cousin, Sittassi, had married the Mahārājā of Cochin. His father had been a landowner Nambūdiri priest. In Kerala, in the priest caste only the eldest son married a woman from the Nambūdiri caste to carry on the priestly tradition.

[1] Kollam era began in 825 AD on the Malabar coast of South India.

Marriages for the remaining sons were arranged with women from the other castes. Since Kuttan Menon was not the eldest, he married into the Kṣatriya caste. Until recently, the oldest son was free to take four wives – one from each of the four castes – in order to assist him with all aspects of his priestly duties. This custom was prevalent in the Vaidika times when the sage scholars had several wives to help with their schools in which the students always lived with the teacher. Because of these marriage practices, the caste system in Kerala remained flexible and open. For this reason, even today at the regional meetings for debate on the scriptures up to half of the participants are Śūdras of the lowest caste.

Kuttan Menon's family had resided on ancestral properties in Trichur. But after receiving a degree in law, he took a position in Ernakulam as a munsif (judge) in the local court, a justice system instigated by and imitative of the British. In feudal India, law and punishment were taken care of within the family group. In serious cases affecting the community, the king or his appointed ministers administered the law.

Kuttan Menon's marriage had been arranged with Parukutti (Manku) Menon[1], sister of P. Neelakanta Menon, Chief Justice of Cochin. After deliberations as to the pertinent points of compatibility of age, personality, wealth, health, profession and genealogy, then finally a consultation with the priest-astrologer, the parents of both Manku and Kuttan agreed to the match. Traditionally, the priest would preside over a ceremony in which the woman would select her future husband, but the custom had been eradicated by contact with other Indian cultures. The wedding had been a happy and elaborate affair with relatives coming from afar to celebrate the union. Accompanied by days of feasting, the lavish banquets represented the fertility that was

1 Menon was a title conferred by the kings on Nair nobleman to show favour or as a reward for services. It became a special caste group, so Menons only married Menons until recent years.

to manifest in the couple. Each day the guests were feted with heaping plates of rice, vegetables cooked in coconut milk spiced with black mustard seed and green chillies, breadfruit coated with spices and coconut, mangoes in a buttermilk curry, lime and mango pickles. The desserts included the customary sweet milk pudding, subtly flavoured with saffron and cardamon, along with huge silver trays piled with bananas, melons, mangoes, guavas, custard fruits and large red orange papayas.

As was the convention among the Menon nobility, the wedding was officiated by Manku's eldest maternal uncle and aunt. At the appointed time, the groom arrived with his gifts for the bride, usually two expensive saris and a gold necklace or a pair of gold bangles. Bedecked in their clothes of finest woven cotton cloth, both the bride and groom sat on a platform before a large barrel of rice. In its centre sat the flower of a coconut palm tree and an oil lamp – the lamp of wisdom with its five flames – which took the place of the ritual fire used in most of India. Facing each other in an east and west direction, the bride and groom exchanged voluminous, fragrant garlands and gold rings. Then joining hands, they circled the lamp three times.

After the ceremony, the parents of both the bride and groom escorted them to Poothampalli House, Manku's family home. Upon entering the home, Manku scattered grains of rice over the threshold; then she was received with honour with the lamp from the prayer room by Kouchi Narayani, the eldest woman of the household. The young couple was then fed fruit and milk by a number of their relatives. In this loving and supporting environment, Kuttan and Manku spent the early years of their marriage.

The birth of their first child was an occasion for rejoicing in the household. Kuttan was overjoyed that the child was a boy who could follow in his footsteps, pursuing a law career. Although Yogīrāja Bhairavananda, the kula-guru (spiritual preceptor of the household) and regular guest at the

Poothampalli House, had predicted the child would be a boy, the proud father was happy to see the actual confirmation. The Brāhmaṇa astrologer-priest was called immediately to the home to cast the baby's horoscope. He candidly informed them that the position in rāja-yoga meant that the child would become a great man; there was even potential for worldwide repute. The family was quite pleased to hear this forecast. They felt sure it meant that the progeny would not only have a successful law career, but would surely become an important British official. However, even at that moment India's fate was turning in a new direction, for Bal Gangadhar Tilak had formed the Indian Home Rule League only days before Balan's birth. The astrologer-priest did not mention any connection with a spiritual life or work. At that time, no one imagined that the success would be in the spiritual sphere.

At the time of his birth there lived in Poothampalli House (abode of effulgent Consciousness), Kouchi Narayani, a widow with four children, and her oldest brother Govind and his family, along with several unmarried sisters. Since their mother had died, Kouchi Narayani, the eldest daughter, had taken over the duties as the manager of the household. She was a sweet woman, small of stature, but with a commanding power and a firm will that got things done – and always done well.

This orthodox Hindu family followed all the religious rites and injunctions for the householder (gṛhasthāśrama) stage of life. Manku's father, Choppully Kunjkittu Menon, was particularly devout and known for his kindness and generosity. Holy men or Swamis often stopped for a rest during their travels because the environment at the Poothampalli House was a sanctified and peaceful one. To the Hindus any guest is considered to be a visit from the Lord, so to receive these holy men into their home was held as a special blessing. Śrī Menon had built a separate guest house in the compound to accommodate these ascetics, so that they would be comfortably away from the worldly goings-on of the household and could talk privately to those who came seeking spiritual guidance.

During the week of the infant's delivery, a Swami was visiting the Poothampalli Menons. Chattambi Swamigal was actually more than a Swami; he was a Yogī who had mastered all branches of yoga and was said to have the power to be in three places at the same time. The parents, desiring the blessings of this great man for their son, asked him to name their baby. With an appropriate ceremony the name Balakrishnan, meaning, 'the child Kṛṣṇa', was bestowed on the four day old boy. In Kerala, the family house name precedes the given name, so the full name was Poothampalli Balakrishnan Menon. He was called Balan for short.

Balan was welcomed into a loving and religious family with all the ancestral rites and rituals. To give him a healthy start in life, at twenty-eight days, Balan was bathed and given a mixture of locally grown herbs to which was added a dash of powdered gold. Daily for six months he was given the Vayambu herbal paste with powered gold. The consumed gold was intended to give the child a clear complexion throughout life.

During the first year of Balan's life, he received the other rituals prescribed by the scriptures for the Hindu child. These ceremonies were meant to attract favourable influences, as well as ward off negative ones. In addition to the name giving ceremony, there was a short ritual before the baby's first outing – always to the temple – to ask favour from the gods for his physical well-being and to impress on his young mind the magnitude and grandeur of the creation. To ensure a long life, his head was officially shaved. Also there was a ceremony at the taking of his first solid food at six months of age. Around the end of that year, his ears were pierced and gold earrings were inserted. This practice served both for decoration and prevention of disease, particularly hernia.

His first years were passed with all the attention and affection possible with a mother and four aunties in the household to take care of his every need. His six cousins, ranging in age from four to ten, looked for any chance to hold and play with the baby.

When Balan was around two years of age, Chattambi Swamigal returned to the Menon home. He always displayed a special affection for children and seemed to hold them entranced as he whirled them and danced with them. And they seemingly entranced him too, for, often the reason he gave for being late to a meal or spiritual discussion (satsaṅga) was that he had been enjoying himself playing with the children. But the satsaṅgas with the Swamigal were always worth waiting for. His vast knowledge included the major scriptures both in Sanskrit and Tamil. This intellectual knowledge, along with his own personal experiences and contacts with other holy men, made him a fountain of inspiration. The Menons and their neighbours who came to the satsaṅgas loved to hear him recount these stories from his life. The satsaṅga often ended with a performance on the stringed Vīṇā. The music could last for hours. No one ever complained – meals were postponed and appointments were forgotten in the peaceful presence of this saint.

On this visit, the Swami paid particular attention to Balan. After eating the noonday meal, he would retire for his customary rest, lying on a cot on the wide, shady veranda. He then would call Manku to bring Balan to him. Taking the boy, he would sit him on his chest and begin to tease and jostle him in a playful manner. On several occasions, he spoke to the boy in a strange language, unknown to anyone in the household. Balan's mother did not know whether it was just a childish gibberish or a language that was foreign to her. Her curiosity prompted her to timidly question the Swami, "What are you telling this boy? What language are you speaking?"

"Don't worry, this is only between him and me," he replied with a bright smile. "Look at his face! See! He understands what I am saying. It's just between the two of us." During a later visit, he remarked, "Don't worry, I've taught him everything."

The Swamigal was again present to preside over Balan's initiation to begin his more traditional education – a short ritual in which the first letter of the alphabet is spelled out with rice on the child's tongue. The ceremony took place in the prayer room in the presence of the deity of the house. As soon as their young cousin was initiated into the world of reading, writing and arithmetic, the older children immediately took up the task of teaching him to write the letters 'BALAN' in a tray of rice, which could be easily shaken when a fresh start was necessary.

Celebrations and ceremony were an integral part of home life in Kerala. For each person's birthday there was a ceremony in which Manku Amma lit the lamp, the symbol of wisdom, and served the rice, the symbol of prosperity. Then a feast was served and the sweets brought out. Since Balan's birthday fell on the same day as Vilasini, a sister cousin, the day was celebrated with lavish festivities. After dinner, the children took the tray of specially prepared candies around, serving the elders first. Throughout India a person gives to others to commemorate a birthday.

Holidays and festivals were also important occasions for merrymaking in Kerala. Many of them honoured the birthdays of saints, while others marked the changing of seasons. But New Year's Day, Viśu Day, was the children's favourite; they looked forward to it in the same way as Western youngsters anticipated Christmas Day. On the morning of Viśu Day, the children were carried to the prayer room with closed eyes and placed in front of the Lord's picture. When they opened their eyes, they beheld the deity's picture, which was placed behind a large decorated bowl that was filled with gold coins, fruits and a glowing butter lamp. The head of the household distributed the coins and fruits to the children and other family members, as a manifestation of the abundance of the Lord's gifts to them and a symbol of prosperity in the coming year. New Year's Day fell in April and coincided with the spring festival, which is the custom in several Indian provinces. It marked the beginning of the planting the major crops of rice and sugar cane.

At harvest time each year, there was another major festival, Oṇam, which originated in Kerala's pre-Āryan past. Legend told of a great, wise, wealthy king, Mahābali, who ruled in the utopian days of Kerala when the entire populace was happy, healthy and wealthy. To commemorate this well respected and long remembered king, ten days were set aside each year after the harvest when the storerooms were filled with grain and fruits, as they had been maintained during the reign of Mahābali. On the morning of full moon day in Ciṅgom (August-September) the houses were scrubbed inside and out, and the walls were whitewashed. At the front door the women artfully arranged a large circular maṇḍala made from the colourful petals of flowers picked from the garden by the children. Outfitted in new clothes of simple white cotton – the women in a two-piece sari edged with a small stripe of black, red or green, and the men in wraparound cloth (lungi) with a top cloth (muṇḍu) folded over the shoulder – everyone feasted and danced until the wee hours of the morning. This was the night that the legendary king made his annual visit to his blessed land of Kerala. Oṇam celebrations continued even after the Āryan Hindu conquerors tried to dissuade the people from honouring a king who, they claimed, was in fact a demon, which probably meant that he was non-European.

Balan actively participated in all festivals. He grew up steeped in a dual heritage of the Āryan invaders and the native South Indian Dravidians. An unusually attractive child, the boy evoked comments that he had the look of a great man. Quite intelligent also, he soon mastered the art of getting his way. Balan was particularly fond of his eldest aunt, Kouchi Amma, who the children called Kouchi Narayani (feminine form of 'Lord'), for, she treated all the children lovingly, as if they were her own. He quite naturally called the dear soul 'Mother'. In fact Balan used to tell Manku that Kouchi Amma was his real mother. He later commented that she was a mother to everyone – "My mother had her own welfare department. Anyone in need knew where the door to Poothampalli House was. She never had to leave her own home and family to do volunteer work as do the women of today. She practised charity right in her home."

Balan was always alert and inquisitive. One early fascination was airplanes. He loved to draw them. On the rare occasion when one flew overhead, he became ecstatic. "I am going to fly in a plane when I grow up," he assured his mother. "I'll lean out and yell to you 'Hello, Mother' from the sky." By the age of four, he was a challenge to his mother and aunts who were hard put to keep him entertained while his older cousins were in school. His youngest aunt solved the problem. As she was a teacher in the St. Teresa's Convent College, she took the four year old along to her classes each mornings. Another aunt picked him up at lunchtime, before he became restless. He looked forward to these visits because he loved the attention of the older children.

Too soon tragedy struck in the idyllic life of this precocious lad. As a consequence of his prosperity, his father had purchased a separate home for his family of four; Balan now had a younger sister, Padmini. When Manku was blessed with the conception of a third child, she and the children returned to Poothampalli House to live temporarily. According to Hindu custom, she was to remain there until three months after the baby was born. In her family home, she would be relieved of any household duties and receive extra care from her own sisters, who would administer the proper herbal medicinal baths according to Ayurvedic prescriptions.

The actual birth of Kanakam went without any difficulty or problem. In fact, the doctor had left the room to wash up and announce the birth of a new daughter. In the few moments of his absence, Manku's vital signs ceased suddenly. The doctor reasoned that it was a heart attack that took the young mother who had previously seemed in good health.

The five year old Balan immediately sensed that something was wrong. He began to ask for, then demand, his mother.

His Velya Amma (Govind's wife) told him, "She has gone to Ernamkulathappan (the local temple)." But he was not to be put off so easily. "I want to go too! Take me there! I want my mother!" he wailed. Never before had his mother failed to appear at his demand. Velya Amma and her children kept the boy distracted until a message was sent to the father and he could get away from court to pick up Balan. The father and son spent the evening together, as had been their practice during Manku's confinement with the pregnancy.

After the funeral rites were completed, it was decided that the children would remain at Poothampalli House where they had several mothers to give them the love, care and affection, the foundation of a matriarchal upbringing. Balan soon adjusted to the new situation; for, he had a great affection for Kouchi Amma; therefore, he would do anything she asked. Gradually, she took over the entire responsibility of mothering of the three children. Each evening after completing his duties at court, their father joined them for dinner. The children were always happy to see him, although he seemed to be quieter and more serious now. To show his affection, he always brought a box of candy, which assured him a very warm welcome from all the children of the household.

Another regular visitor to the house was the Swamigal. During the next few years, he returned several times for short visits. On warm, spring afternoons with the scent of jasmine floating through the air and the sun dancing on the white walls between the shadows of the nodding flowers, he would sit out on the shady veranda. Chattambi Swamigal emitted an aura of peace to which Balan was drawn. He sat at the Swami's side pulling and twisting his long gray beard as Padmini attempted to do some fancy braids on the other half. Although there seemed to be no special interaction with Balan during these stays, all the children thought the Swami favoured Balan.

When he took his leave after a visit, the Swamigal would always repeat the suggestion that they take good care of the child, as if the loving women of the household needed such advice. So the loss of his own mother had not brought any changes in Balan's care. The women were determined to give him a happy and healthy start in life, for, he surely had many life experiences to reap before he would become the 'great person', as predicted by the astrologer. The Swamigal, they recalled, had also mentioned that Balakrishnan would be famous. "But first he will have to suffer greatly," he had added.

12

A South Indian Yogī[1]

I only have a very dim memory of him. And yet, the flashes that rise in my bosom are unfailingly clear. They have been a silent inspiration. They have helped me more often than I dare to confess.

—Swami Chinmayananda, 1967.

Chattambi Swamigal (1853-1924) was one of those rare persons through whom the true essence of the Hindu scriptures has been preserved as a live, lived experience. He was one who dared to give up the joys (and sorrows) of a life in the world to pursue the knowledge experienced and taught by the ancient sages. For these courageous few, the traditional renunciation at the last stage of life is superceded by a seemingly inborn knowledge that the joys of the world are but a superficial reflection of the Divine. They seem to have an innate desire to experience that Divine that is in and through the eternal play of life. Therefore, they live their own unique lives.

Born in Kerala into the home of a poor, low sect Brāhmaṇa couple, Kunjan Pillai daily heard his father chant the ancient mantras and hymns from the Vaidika rituals. His father also told him the stories of the great sages of old; they no doubt impressed his bright young mind. When Kunjan was only five, his father initiated him into the study of the scriptures. Surely this incarnation was the type that Lord Kṛṣṇa noted in the *Bhagavad-gītā*. In the sixth chapter, he assured Arjuna that

[1] Compiled from information in the booklet, *Chattambi Swamigal – The Great Scholar Saint of India*, written by K.P.K. Menon (1967), published by P.G. Narayana Pillai.

anyone who spends time in spiritual practices, but dies before reaching the goal of enlightenment, will be reborn into a devout household where he will be able to continue his journey toward the transcendental knowledge without interruption.

Kunjan also learned of the physical realities of the world early in life. To help in supporting his family, each morning he would pick flowers from the neighbouring forests, string the blossoms into garlands, and sell them to devotees at the temple gate. During the autumn harvest season, he also collected wild root vegetables in the marshes, to exchange for rice and salt in the temple kitchen.

When Kunjan was about eight years, a relative noted that the young boy was particularly bright and sent him to a school in Trivandrum, paying all the expenses. There Kunjan learned Tamil and Sanskrit and was able to read the scriptural classics in these languages for himself. His scholarship and discipline were such that he acquired the name Chattambi, 'monitor', because he was asked to be in charge when the teacher had to be away from the classroom.

Chattambi's facility in languages made it easy for him to obtain jobs as a scribe copying manuscripts, so he was able to continue helping with the support of his parents. Only after the death of both parents did he consider his responsibilities in the world completed. He was then free to cast off all worldly concerns and live the life of a wandering mendicant, trusting that the Divine would take care of any physical needs, so that he could devote full time to the pursuit of his spiritual goal.

He then left Kerala for Tamil Nadu (ca.1873) where he joined a group of scholarly men and was able to study the scriptures, discuss religion and take classes in music. Meeting daily with this group, Chattambi learned some English and heard discourses on Vedānta. Through them, he also met the great scholar Subba Jatavallabhar, a Master of Sanskrit, Tamil, Vedānta and Yoga. Anxious to study with this Guru, Chattambi obtained his permission and went to live with him as a student for four years. There he completed his mastery of the major scriptures in both Sanskrit and Tamil and continued with his music classes.

Considering mere book learning useless unless it was employed as a basis for first hand observation and contemplation, Chattambi was not satisfied until he personally delved into a subject to discover its truths for himself. He applied this spirit of inquiry not only to the scriptures, but also to all fields of his studies – yoga, geology, botany, geography and medicine. He was not content until he mastered whatever he attempted.

A great lover of music, Chattambi played twelve different instruments. His love of music was not out of character for a holy man. In India, music is considered a means to counterpoint, and thereby point out, the silence on which the diversities of the creation play. Once the performer states the basic melody pattern (rāga), the music is evolved spontaneously with embellishment of variations of the pattern with grace notes. The music evokes memories from within the deep recesses of the soul – haunting intimations of the inner harmony, beauty and peace.

He was also an expert in all the specialised postures of Kathakali, the native folk dance drama of Kerala. After learning the traditional dramas, he produced several new ones. Kathakali consists of pantomimes of hundreds of specific gestures and postures that require years to master. The various contortions of the face, exaggerations of eyes, caricatures of expression, sudden leaps, spins and freeze stances are combined to narrate the various religious epics. As with all forms of Indian dance, Kathakali is of a sacred nature and originated in the temples, not merely to entertain, but to evoke a spiritual experience in the spectators.

Throughout his entire life, Chattambi's true love was the study and understanding of Vedānta. He would regularly spend days in solitary meditation in the jungle or in a cave. His heart longed to know that experience of experiences described by the saints of Bhārata. As is usually the case, the occasion came unexpectedly. One day while he was walking through a village, he noted a beggar with a pair of stray dogs digging in the leftovers from a feast at the temple. A group of small boys started throwing stones at the trio, but they didn't seem to notice. As Chattambi was taking note of this peculiar event, the beggar perceived that he was being watched and shot Chattambi a quick glance, then scuttled off into the woods. Chattambi sensed something unusual about this vagrant – clothed in rags, hair matted, bone thin – for, there was a certain penetrating depth in that glance. Immediately, Chattambi ran after him, but soon lost his trail. Determined not to give up, he continued running at a frenzied pace until he fell into a swoon.

When the old sage found the young man unconscious under a tree, he intuitively knew that Chattambi was ready to receive a direct experience of his essential Self. He waited until Chattambi regained normal consciousness, then guided him into experiencing the divine Realization.

Spiritual renunciates, such as this beggar, who leave the world totally, without compromise, rarely share the mystical knowledge they have achieved with others. Bhārata's social environment has always allowed for individual expression; mystical experiences are considered significant and are encouraged. Because of this prevalent attitude, such experiences are not considered extraordinary, or labelled insane. In cases like this beggar, the person can become so lost in divine ecstasy that he forgets his body and the necessity of caring for it. To the imperceptive ones, these Yogīs can appear to be ordinary paupers.

After the initiation from the old sage, Chattambi spent long periods in isolation. In 1882, he met Śrī Narayana Guru Swami. They spent months together living in the forests and mountains, living on wild roots and berries, drinking fresh water from mountain streams, and practising meditation and yoga. During these wanderings, Chattambi became well-established in the knowledge of the divine Self.

He then began to have some contact with people, advising all who came to him seeking spiritual or personal advice. They now added 'Swamigal', an honorific form of Swami, to his name. He travelled throughout Kerala equally happy in the hut of a poor man or the house of a wealthy landowner. He shocked many orthodox Brāhmaṇas because he defied customs by refusing to pay any attention to a person's caste or creed. Further, one of his spiritual Teachers had been a Muslim mystic. However, he did refuse to eat food prepared in a kitchen where non-vegetarian food was cooked. He was also known to refuse invitations to wealthy homes where they had taken up 'the foreign evil of drinking liquor'.

For physical strength and agility, Chattambi Swamigal had practised wrestling and yoga postures (āsanas) for many years. He had cultivated mental control with the use of several mantras and the practice of deep meditation (samādhi) every evening from the time of his school years. On several occasions, the Swamigal demonstrated his mental power by taming wild animals. Once a ferocious guard dog broke loose, bit several people, and was terrorising the neighbourhood. Just when Swamigal arrived in the village, a local policeman had climbed a tree and was about to shoot the dog. "Doesn't man have more mental strength than a dog?" Swamigal chided the frightened crowd. Just then, to the onlookers' horror, the dog lunged for the Swami. But one moment later, he was humming a tune and leading the dog by the ear to its owner.

Once Chattambi Swamigal had the opportunity to use this ability to teach a lesson to a tax collector who had a well-known reputation for dishonesty. Probably hoping to cancel out some of his sins by doing a good deed, this official invited the Swamigal to his home for dinner. The Swamigal graciously accepted the invitation with the provision that he could bring some of his disciples. The greedy official was quite happy to accommodate the request, for, he thought the more holy men, the more merit he would gain by feeding them. On the specified date, at the specified time, the Swamigal arrived alone at the door. Expressing his disappointment, the official inquired as to the whereabouts of the disciples. The Swamigal assured him that they were waiting outside and would come in as soon as the meal was served. As is customary in South India, long woven straw mats were rolled out to seat the guests on the floor; fresh green leaves of a banana tree were laid out to serve as plates; then the hot rice and sambar with vegetables were served.

When everything was ready, Swamigal stepped outside to call in his disciples. To the host's surprise and dismay, a pack of stray dogs obediently entered the door, took a seat in front of each banana leaf and began quietly and politely dining. The inspector was speechless, not only at having dogs for guests, but also at seeing this normally rowdy, quarrelsome lot of mongrels behaving so meekly. The Swamigal, upon seeing the collector's shocked look, responded nonchalantly – "These dogs were tax officials in their last life. Corruption, greed, plunder and other crimes of which they were guilty have led to their being reborn as dogs. The wages of sin are sure to be paid, if not in this life, then in the next." The Swamigal continued eating calmly, confident that the corrupt official had gotten the point.

This ability to communicate with animals came not only from his yogic powers, but also from his genuine love and concern for all earthly creatures. As he travelled from place to place, staying at homes like Poothampalli House in Ernakulam, numerous examples of his friendship with animals were often observed. Ants used to line up patiently to wait until he was served his meal, for, they knew they would get a generous offering. Often he would have both a snake and a frog, natural predator and prey, in his room at the same time; on another occasion it was full of little frogs that had taken safe shelter there. In one household, he called out the mice and admonished them for chewing up some beautiful linens belonging to his hostess, then he gave them a meal to eat.

On all of his travels he continued his first hand botanical study. His diligence in learning the secrets of herbal medicine was so consuming that the occupants of one village where he had spent some time in his younger days began to call him 'Goat Kunjan Pillai'. He went from plant to plant with his notebook, collecting leaves, munching on them and noting his observations. He felt that nature in her abundance had provided plants for healing and they should be used whenever possible.

When an emergency arose, however, he would use his yogic powers. In one such case, he received an urgent message to go to the home of a relative whose wife suffered from epilepsy and a chronic stomach ailment. With a simple ritual, Chattambi Swamigal blessed her with a new life of health. There were many first hand reports of such healings, carried out only when traditional herbal remedies had failed, and always in a quiet, unobtrusive manner. He would never speak about these instances when later questioned.

He wore no saffron robes, nor any marks of saintliness, but his fame spread far and wide. Scholars and spiritual seekers from all over India came to learn from him. His knowledge and powers were such that he intuitively knew just what lesson to teach the seekers and the best way for them to learn. Once a greedy man associated himself with Swamigal for the purpose of learning the art of transmuting copper into gold. Later this disciple and the Swamigal were crossing a river in a small canoe. They hit a whirlpool and the canoe capsized, throwing them both into the deep water. The Swamigal was a strong swimmer, but his student was thrashing about, trying desperately to keep himself afloat. Swamigal asked him if he were now ready to learn the knowledge of turning metal into gold. The drowning man renounced his interest in gold and proclaimed that he only wanted to save his life. Then the Swamigal helped him reach the shore safely.

On another occasion, the Swamigal was travelling in Kerala with two companions and an oarsman in a boat. Suddenly high winds and waves came up and ferociously rocked the small boat. The oarsman's efforts were useless against the force and he sank back in the helm, overcome with grief of the impending disaster.

As the wind and current propelled the boat to the open sea, the two companions resigned themselves to death and called out in fear to the Swamigal. Sitting peacefully in his seat, he assured them that there was no danger. The two could not quite believe his prediction, but ten minutes later the boat had crossed the currents and ebb tide and landed safely some two miles away – right in front of a temple.

Chattambi Swamigal continued to travel, write and study until the end of his life. His depth of thought and broad experience assured a distinctive place for all his writings, both for their spiritual knowledge and literary excellence. Enriching the lives of all around him, he only lived to serve mankind in whatever way he was able.

About a week before he died, he was invited to Quilon, a town in south Kerala. He replied to the invitation, "Wait until after the 23rd, then I will go south." Everyone assumed he meant that he would be going to Quilon; no one realized that he was using a play on words. 'To go south' is an expression that can also signify, 'to die'. On the 23rd after having lunch and giving a performance on his vīṇā, he went to his room, sat cross-legged on his bed, and entered into a deep meditative state (samādhi). After some hours, his hosts realized that he had departed from his physical body.

Śrī Narayana Guru Swami composed the following verse to commemorate the spiritual Teacher.

> The all-knowing seer, the Teacher of Truth has flown along the track of eternal Bliss.
>
> Like the full moon, he shines in the highest firmament in the plenitude of his aesthetic luster.
>
> The great Teacher, after spending his days in divine play and discarding his mortal frame, has attained his inherent divine Self.

13

Religious Training

It was during those days waiting for the conclusion of the worship service that Swami Chinmayananda was born.

—Swami Chinmayananda, 1950.

As the sun sends its first thin rays to light up the golden temple domes in South India, holy sounds fill the morning air. In each temple the priests chant the words from the *Ṛg-veda*, dedicated to the solar deity Sāvitrī –

Let us meditate on the most excellent

Light of Sāvitrī;

May she guide our intellect.[1]

This verse, along with other sacred mantras and prayers from the Vedas, has been chanted throughout Bhārata for thousands of years, thereby giving meaning and unity to a civilization that has withstood so many disruptions from other cultures and religions.

India was not born by an edict of the British. It had long been united by a common belief system based on the scriptures which Āryan invaders had brought to the region in 1500 BC and continued compiling as they met with the indigenous cultures. Although the Āryans had begun their conquest with swords in the Indus Valley, they completed it with the word. The holy Vedas have been recited for centuries in their original Sanskrit from Kashmir to Kerala, just as they continue to be. From ancient times, learned men all across the subcontinent communicated

[1] Gāyatrī Mantra from *Ṛg-veda*-3.62.10

in this language. Ādi Śaṅkarācārya, the great saint, scholar and mystic from Kerala, made three pilgrimages around the entire sub-continent in the early decades of the eighth century, conversing with all the holy men and philosophers in Sanskrit. He established four centres (maṭhas) to serve as the pillars of Sanātana-dharma, a belief system that by 700 AD – four hundred years before William, the conqueror reached what is now called Britain – had provided Hindu Bhārata with an integral unity. The many divisions in the land remained political, economic and linguistic, but the underlying foundation of the spiritual ideals of the Vedas was deeply rooted in the daily life of the Indian people.

In the India of Balan's boyhood these ideals continued to guide daily activities. The most auspicious way to start the day was to go to the temple or the prayer room in the home to see the form of the Lord. Just to behold the deity's image, either as a picture or a sculpture, was considered worship. Even a glance reminded one of the Lord's qualities of goodness, kindness and charity, and a mind filled with such thoughts was automatically deemed a worshipful mind. Since the European influence was still only minimal in South India, the sacred routine was followed in homes as it had been for centuries. By 5 a.m., every household was astir with activity. Upon arising, adults bathed in the outdoor tanks and dressed in clean clothes for their daily pilgrimage to the temple. The women at Poothampalli House, carrying the younger children with them, were back home by 6:30 a.m. The older children would then be rising for their baths and would soon be ready for morning coffee – hot milk with enough coffee for flavour.

In many households in Kerala, the children were required to go to the temple each morning. They would not be served breakfast until they displayed the sandalwood paste on their foreheads as proof of the visit. This was not the practice in Balan's home, however, and, although some children did choose to go along with the adults, Balan was not among them.

However, the flexibility of choice did not extend to the daily evening service. As the sun descended behind the fringed palms and stretched its last orange rays across the lagoons and rice paddies, the family gathered in the prayer room. An oil lamp, the first light of the night, was lit. Balan, his sisters and cousins, fresh from a bath in the tank, lined up along the back wall with the greatest intention to stay awake and participate – no prayers, no supper. And there was another incentive to wait, the consecrated offering of sweets and fruit that was passed among the worshippers as blessed food (prasādam) after the service; that is, if Balan didn't get to it first.

With the lighting of the lamp, the service started with a simple devotional song (bhajana)[1] – in praise and adoration of the Lord Kṛṣṇa. The children joined in and often had a contest among themselves to see who could sing the loudest.

After some fifteen minutes of singing bhajanas, the adult women began the service proper, chanting the one thousand names of each of the three favourite deities of the house – Viṣṇu, the deity of preservation of the creation, Lalitā, the Goddess of power of the creation, and Lakṣmī. As the Goddess of wealth, Lakṣmī was invoked in every household.

The ancient sages of Bhārata saw that every form of this physical world is but a manifestation of the one supreme unmanifest. Therefore, to adore these manifestations of the Lord is one way of identifying with the Lord himself. In chanting the one thousand names of a single deity, the worshipper is reminded that the Lord is omnipotent and omnipresent – in every action, every form, every thought, every emotion.

anantarūpaḥ (one of infinite forms)

anantaśrīḥ (one of infinite glories)

jitamanyuḥ (one who has conquered anger)

---

[1] *'anjana śrīdhara cāru mūrti kṛṣṇa'*

bhayāpahaḥ (one who destroys all fears)

caturasraḥ (one who deals fairly with all)

gambhīrātmaḥ (one whose true nature is unfathomable)

The long recitations droned on and on as an aunt offered a flower petal with each exultation to Lord Viṣṇu...

janajanmādiḥ (the sole cause for all living creatures)

bhīmaḥ (one whose form is frightening to sinners)

bhīmaparākramaḥ (one whose prowess causes fear in his enemies)

ādhāranilayaḥ (one who is the supreme controller)

puṣpahāsaḥ (one who shines like on open flower)

prajāgaraḥ (one who knows no sleep)

ūrdhvagaḥ (one who is the highest of the high)

satpathācāraḥ (one who walks the path of Truth)

prāṇadaḥ (one who gives life to all)

praṇavaḥ (one who is the sacred Om mantra)

paṇaḥ (one who is supreme manager of the universe)[1]

One thousand names and one thousand flower petals were offered. Endless repetitions, which Balan began to resent. The two long hours were sheer misery for this active young body. "I used to wonder how even a goddess could endure so much chanting," later confessed Swami Chinmayananda. "It seemed an unending torture, not only for my restless little body, but I felt that the goddess herself must be suffering under the weight of the mounting heap of flowers that was presented to her at the recitation of each of the one thousand names."

In the first fifteen minutes of singing bhajanas (devotional songs), Balan did join in with some enthusiasm. But as time

1 *Viṣṇu Sahasranāma,* verses 932-937, 947-957

dragged his mind soon turned inward to daydreaming – anything to pass the long hours. And he dared not fall asleep, for, this would surely invite a reprimand from his aunts. They made the children feel that in the illustrious line of Poothampalli Menons such a demon who could fall asleep in the worship service would bring the displeasure and vengeance of the gods upon everyone. Such a responsibility was quite a burden for the children. So, the fear of divine retribution exacted obedience from them, almost as surely as the dread of sharp pinches from a zealous aunt when she caught any of them dozing.

Balan's daydreaming took many forms. One was to study the various gods presented in the coloured paintings on the altar and to make up stories about each one or to mentally enact and embellish the many stories his aunts had read to him about the great deeds of these deities. The deity who best suited his adventurous temperament was the portrait of Candrakalādhara, a form of Lord Śiva. The Lord was depicted with the waters of the holy Ganga flowing out of his long hair, which was beautifully gathered into a mountainous heap on the top of his head. 'The crescent moon poised on his broad forehead, the smiling eyes of compassion, the serpent coiled around his blue neck, the beaming mouth that seemed to be ready to speak of tenderness and affection from behind his moustache. This splendid Śiva was the ideal of young Balan's own heart,' as Balan later described his attraction to the picture. At the time he did not question the meaning of the symbol of mental self-control. The cobra faced outward so that it would never bite Śiva, but would be alert to destroy any evil that approached his Master.

Seeking refuge in the grandeur of this great Lord and his smile, the child managed to sit through the long hours each evening. 'It was during those days of waiting for the conclusion of the worship service that Swami Chinmayananda was born, in Balan, only a frail child,' Swami Chinmayananda later explained. 'Somehow Balan had stumbled onto this new game. He would look at the picture of the Lord, then would shut his eyes to see Lord Śiva in the darkness within, exactly as he was in the picture on the altar. This gave Balan a game so sweet and pleasant that it became a habit to call up this picture onto his mental screen behind his closed eyelids at all hours of the day. The picture came readily as soon as it was ordered; his wonder grew at this success.'

Inadvertently, Balan had discovered a technique of meditation called upāsanā; that is, mental visualization of a deity. Upāsanā has two benefits – First, it uplifts and purifies the mind by placing a positive thought form into it. Second, it concentrates the mind and makes it one pointed by maintaining one thought, thereby halting the usual mental chatter.

Lord Śiva is but one of the 330,000 gods and goddesses said to exist in the Hindu pantheon. However, the understanding of the three principal gods can clarify the basic roles of all of them. The three gods each represent a distinct aspect of the eternal cycle of the creation – Brahmā, the Creator; Viṣṇu, the Sustainer; and Śiva, the Destroyer. Since the material world is a duality of positive/ negative and masculine/feminine, each God has his respective consort. In order to create, the Creator must have a workable plan; therefore, Brahmā is wedded to knowledge, Sarasvatī. The sustainer of the creation needs material to maintain the universe, so Viṣṇu is married to wealth, Lakṣmī. To be able to destroy the present creation to allow the space, material and energy for new life, Śiva needs power, which is supplied by his consort, Pārvatī. These six deities comprise the entire cycle of creation, so there is nothing outside of their dominion.

The other numerous gods are these six disguised according to a particular role in the creation or an aspect of the mind. For instance, the elephant God Gaṇeśa, the child of Śiva and Pārvatī, is known to be a powerful deity. From his parents, he inherited both physical strength and wisdom. Therefore, he is invoked to remove all obstacles in daily life as well as in spiritual life. With the removal of ignorance, wisdom is born. The majority of the thousands of gods were popular local deities that were later incorporated into the Hindu pantheon, for, the Vaidika gods of the conquering Āryans were the forces of the mysterious and unfathomable nature.

The Āryan invaders idealised power. With the invention of a sword, which could be wielded from a horse and a light two-wheeled chariot, the age-old tendency of barbarians to prey on the wealth of settled civilizations became a simple, although brutal affair. When the Āryans entered Bhārata by crossing the Indus river in several excursions beginning around 1500 BC, they encountered the Indus Valley Civilization. The settled, agricultural people were helpless in the hands of these sword wielding, nomadic hunters. The Āryan Vedas include hymns of triumph over what was described as a great and powerful enemy –

'With all outstripping chariot wheel, O Indra,

Thou art famed, you have overthrown the twice ten kings of men with sixty thousand and nine and ninety followers.

Thou go'st on from fight to fight causing great fear,

Destroying fort after fort here with strength.'

The Indus Valley Civilization, dating from 4000 BC, or earlier, was unique among the ancient civilizations in that it was composed of over one hundred settlements scattered along one thousand miles of the Indus riverbanks. The two principal cities were probably the largest cities on the planet at that time and were unusual because they were built with the same master plan. All the buildings, made of kiln fired plain red bricks, were laid out on parallel streets, the main avenues being some thirty feet wide. In the large residential section, homes of two floors contained small rooms with windows opening to a central court. Doors opened onto narrow lanes that connected to the main streets. Each home had a bathroom set up for the style of bathing still common in India today – pouring water over one's body with a small pitcher. All buildings were linked by an elaborate drainage system that was comparable only to the sanitary system of Crete. Both cities had an identical citadel, a thickly walled artificial mound fifty feet high. On the plateau stood a large granary, a building containing a large rectangular tank surrounded by many small rooms, plus a variety of other small structures, including platforms and watch towers. There was another unprecedented aspect of these two cities – neither palace nor temple was found in the ruins.

It has been conjectured that the precise planning and the longevity of the civilization indicate a cooperative religious order rather than a power oriented secular one. The large tank atop the citadel could have had a religious function; it is not likely that it was used for bathing, since each home had its own facilities. The dead were buried in an extended position with the head oriented to the north, adorned with a variety of finely executed and polished jewellery and surrounded by an assortment of utensils and pots, indicating that the people must have believed in an afterlife. In the excavations, the top half of a small statue with a remarkable resemblance to a present-day South Indian priest was found. The absence of temples might indicate that the invading Āryans encountered a religion similar to their own, for, they worshipped the powers of nature under the canopy of the heavens. They needed no man-made temples.

The secret of the longevity of this unique Indus Valley culture may remain forever silent. The inhabitants did not leave a proliferation of writing as did the Babylonians and Egyptians. Archeologists found all of the buildings and homes surprisingly empty of any possessions; either the inhabitants fled with their belongings or the invaders meticulously ransacked every structure. Since all of the buildings and most of the pottery found in the layers of artifacts remained unadorned, the only potential clue to their intellectual life is some two thousand small square and rectangular shaped clay seals found scattered throughout the ancient dust of both cities. For the most part the seals were decorated with designs of real or mythological animals. However, several indicate a naturalistic orientation to the sacred. Some half-dozen depict a yogī seated cross-legged (lotus pose) surrounded by a variety of beasts, while others bear the image of a goddess with a trident crown surrounded by serpents.

These seals, probably used for trade, were also found in Sargon (Mesopotamian city of 2300-2400 BC). Trade records of Sumeria as early as 2450 BC refer to the two cities of Dilmun and Meluhha[1] in the 'place where the sun rises'. These registers indicate an exchange with a flourishing, even wealthy, economy. The Sumerian imports included timber, gold, ivory and perhaps cotton. The Indus Valley people cultivated cotton, the earliest found anywhere in the world, as well as wheat, barley, peas, melons, sesame and dates. As indicated by their seals, they had domesticated the humped cow, camel, horse and their beast of burden, the bullock.

Modern scholars will long wonder what manner of people lived in this valley complex in peaceful harmony and cooperation for thousands of years. Although the art of tempering and casting iron developed in India long before it is known to have appeared in Europe, archaeologists have been puzzled by the lack of ancient hunting tools in the major centres of population through the subcontinent of India.

There is evidence that the Indus agricultural community was vegetarian. In fact, vegetarianism may have been prevalent in this subtropical land where nature yielded up bountiful gains – in some regions rice and wheat fields bear three crops a year – and many nutritious vegetables, roots, nuts and berries. They enjoyed such an abundant supply of luscious tropical fruits that in the south the papaya was considered the poor man's fruit. Nature was an all-giving, all-loving, benevolent mother that gave to mankind, not a brute force to be harnessed and controlled for survival.

---

[1] In the *Ṛg-veda*, the Āryans called the conquered people by a similar name, mleñccha.

As the Āryan invaders slowly spread out over the countryside, they encountered many indigenous tribes. Excavations give evidence of settlements along the entire length of the Ganga river planes. The native Dravidians, called Dasyus by their conquerors, were described as 'strange, noseless, dark skinned devils'. Thus began the first sprouts of a two caste system that would evolve into a thousand branches. A large number of the native populations fled south, a theory confirmed by the close relationship of the Tamil spoken in South India and the Brahui language of East Baluchistan and Sind (in the region of the Indus river) in present-day Pakistan. In their flight from the sword, the Indus Valley dwellers no doubt encountered other native cultures in what is now South India. For example, in the Mysore region there is a continuity of ruins from 4,000 BC.

These native people were in contact with, if not relatives of, the Indus Valley dwellers. Dwelling in tropical villages along the many rivers, they led a life of respectable dignity and cultural organization. They had their own deities, designating Mother Earth, as the principal goddess. She is still worshipped by tribal people in Bengal, Bihar and Orissa. Even though the Āryans indiscriminately killed hundreds as they passed into the interior native settlements, the sword wielding conquerors (and the rifle wielding Europeans who later followed them) held it despicable that the natives of some areas practised human sacrifice in their annual spring festival. In an elaborate ceremony of prayers and offerings to the Goddess Kālī, a young female virgin was sacrificed in a ritual symbolizing the death from which life springs in nature's ever creating, ever dying cycle.

As time passed, the Āryans, probably tired of fighting and no doubt influenced by the peaceful prosperity they had encountered, began to settle and intermarry with the native women. They did not insist that the vanquished Dravidians change their gods, but simply incorporated the various native gods into the Āryan pantheon according to the role each God played in creation. Therefore, in the southern regions, which the Āryans reached in approximately 300 BC, Lord Śiva is often called by the local name of Candraśekhara (one with the moon on his forehead), Candrakalādhara (one as pleasant as moonlight) and Naṭarāja (the cosmic dancer). In this manner, through the centuries, the Āryan gods were accepted and interwoven in and through all of the local religions while some of the original Sanskrit names were changed or forgotten.

It was not until the excavations of the Indus Valley Civilization in 1921 by the Englishman John Marshall that scholars had to finally acknowledge the indigenous Dravidian cultural influence on the Āryan Hindus. Based on a change of attitude in the Vedas, which were composed over a four thousand year period, European Sanskrit scholars had already conjectured a foreign influence on the development of the Vedas. The early Vedas portray a boastful, demanding petitioner who called on the nature gods for his own benefit.

I call upon Agni (fire) first, for welfare;

I call upon Mitra Varuṇa (the supreme lawgiver) for aid;

I call upon Rātri (night), who brings the world to rest;

I call upon Sāvitrī (sun) for support.

The mid period Vedas reflect a change from the impersonal, faraway power to a more personal God. The worshippers rejoiced in the possibility of spiritual experience, sometimes gained from a drink derived from the soma plant, which they boasted enabled them to go to the abode of the gods and to become immortal.

In the last section of the Vedas, the Upaniṣads, new concepts are presented that are not found in the earlier books of knowledge. Reincarnation, the possibility of the release from the cycle of rebirth, the disciplines of yoga, reverence for animals, vegetarianism and purification by water are all later developments in the Vedas. Therefore, evidence is presented in the Upaniṣads themselves that the Āryan Brāhmaṇas met this new philosophy during their conquests.

The one central theme expressed throughout the Upaniṣads is God-realization. The philosophy is beyond ritual knowledge and was not necessarily taught by Brāhmaṇas, but by Realized sages. In two early Upaniṣads, a king was named as the 'Knower of the Truth.' A Brāhmaṇa priest went to the Enlightened king to seek this knowledge. One of the early Upaniṣads, the *Chāndogya-upaniṣad,* clearly states that until that encounter of king and priest, a Brāhmaṇa priest had never been taught this Knowledge of knowledges. The King Ajātaśatru, who taught a Brāhmaṇa student in the *Bṛhadāraṇyaka-upaniṣad,* has a suspiciously non-Āryan name.

This was the flexible era of Hinduism when ideas and concepts were tried, experienced, then added to the scriptures after being tested and deemed valid by other sages. The Brāhmaṇas had the role of preserving the knowledge. This flexibility turned into a rigidity in an effort to protect, then defend, their religion as one foreign invader after another plundered India with not only greed, but with a religious prejudice.

But before the ideas of the philosophy of the Upaniṣads fully crystallized in the land of their origin, they would spread throughout the intellectual community of Greece and Europe. In 600 BC, when the Greeks sought rational and consistent answers to the life of the world and humans, they sought out the oriental philosophies. For example, Pythagoras spent 30 years collecting ideas in travels through India, Arabia, Syria and Egypt before he began to develop his own philosophy.

During the early centuries before the Christian era, philosophical thought in Bhārata was also influenced by the two great saints, Gautama Buddha (563-483 BC) and Mahāvīra (549-477 BC). Both advocated a reverence for all life, vegetarianism, identified the release from rebirth as the goal of life, and rejected the Vedas and their priests because they dealt with the mundane matters of attaining wealth and heaven. This was an important step in the evolution of Vedānta 'the end of the Vedas', since it holds these same beliefs.

Following the entry of Alexander the Great's army into India, Pyrrho studied with the philosophers there in 312 BC. Several ideas of Vedānta entered into the philosophy he later compiled –

> Neither the senses nor reason can give us sure knowledge, the senses distort the object in perceiving it, and reason is merely the sophist servant of desire.

Revolutionary words, considering the Greek's adoration of the intellect, but they demonstrate Pyrrho's understanding of the Vedāntic philosophy of the Upaniṣads. Although intellectual discrimination has been important in the evolution of mankind, he understood that it was not the crown jewel of attainment.

The Greek influence in India was terminated within ten years when Chandragupta's armies overran what remained of Alexander's garrisons in the north. The young king (r. 322-298 BC) then went on to conquer the large Magadha kingdom on the Gangetic plane, which began a historical Golden Age that lasted for several hundred years. Students from East and West flocked to the university at Takṣaśilā in North India where all the arts and sciences, including medicine, could be studied under eminent professors. Trade flourished to such an extent that the Indian merchants became wealthier, thus more powerful, than many of the land-owning nobility, and certainly richer than the poor priests who could accept no money, but only cows and goods, for their services. The arts and crafts of India were highly developed and the craftsmen began to form guilds to protect their skills and wealth. The intricacies and contradictions of the caste system were gradually multiplying.

When Magasthenes, the ambassador for the King of Syria, visited India in 300 BC, he was amazed to find a Civilization that he described to the incredulous Greeks – still in their zenith – as entirely equal to their own. In the royal palaces, he was amazed to find interiors luxuriously furnished and adorned with many pillars plated with gold, artfully ornamented with designs of bird life and plant foliage. The king himself was a model of disciplined life, he meditated and prayed for ninety minutes at dawn and dusk; then, divided the remainder of the day into fourteen ninety minute segments to fulfil all of his earthly duties, reserving the last three for sleep.

His grandson, Aśoka (273-232 BC), led the Mauryan Empire, which reached as far south as Madurai, in the height of its glory. After a particularly bloody battle early in his reign, Aśoka renounced violence and war, then became a Buddhist. He sent Buddhist ambassadors to the West where they conferred with Greek philosophers and Egyptian priests. Concerned with the welfare of the people, he built roads, irrigation projects and dams; he also set up pillars – carved with enlightened and tolerant edicts – throughout the land, some of them still stand today. The first mention of the region of Kerala was inscribed on one of these pillars.

When Europe was still enshrouded in superstition and barbarism, the Hindu had developed logic and systematised human knowledge. Buddha expounded an analysis of the psychology of man even before the birth of Socrates. There is little reason to doubt that the development of philosophical thought in the West has been greatly influenced by the philosophy of ancient Bhārata.

14

School Days

> *Yes, there always was a horoscope cast at birth, but my parents never told me anything about it. I was always so sure of myself, they wouldn't have wanted to encourage me more!*
>
> —Swami Chinmayananda, 1978.

Morning was a leisurely time for the early risers at Poothampalli House. The men relaxed with the newspaper and discussed business matters in the sitting room, while the women gathered in the kitchen to gossip over coffee and plan the household duties of the day. Having been up for some four hours, at 9 a.m. everyone was ready for the hearty breakfast of rice and sambar – a combination of a split yellow bean, tomatoes, hot chillies, and spices. Minutes before 10 a.m. the children headed for school and the men for the office.

Balan officially started his education in the Śrī Rama Varma boys' school in the fall of 1921 at five years of age. The school was taught in English with the native language, Malayalam, as an elective. The entire system was patterned after the British. Even the textbooks showed English children in English homes with English pets, even the farms, the countryside, the trees and plants were from England. The stories and pictures completely ignored India's abundance of flora, fauna, heroes and history.

In 1834, Lord Macaulay, a British administrator in India, set down in exacting terms the standard for educating the natives. The education of the Indians was solely to create 'a class who may be interpreters between us and the millions we govern. . . Indians in blood and colour, but English in taste, in opinions, in morals and in intellect.'

In other words, the education of the natives was to be solely for the benefit of the British and should be accomplished only to the extent that these intermediary interpreters were necessary. The medium of education would be English, for, the multicultured Indians were to be ruled as a domain of the Empire and should have a common language with the other domains of the Empire. Even if they wanted to, it was not feasible for the British officials to learn the Indian languages; there were too many. On the subcontinent there were about twelve completely distinct languages, with their own unique alphabetic script, along with hundreds of different dialects of each. To produce the officials that the British needed to handle the lower levels of the administration of the government, English-speaking Indians were imperative.

Traditionally, the Indian boys had been educated in the homes of the priests. The unique Vaidika civilization was a forest culture of scattered hermitages and small villages, not an urban civilization with monumental palaces and temples. Depending upon their caste, at the age of six to eight, the male child was given the upanayanam (bringing near) initiation, in which the boy was 'brought near' to his spiritual essence through the recitation of the sacred Gāyatrī Mantra, the daily salutation to the sun. The Vaidika scriptures glorify this initiation and declare that with this ceremony the boy begins his transformation into a spiritual life.

> The father and mother have given birth to him from mutual desire, so that he is born in the womb, let this be known as the physical birth.
>
> But that birth which is given, according to the ordinance, through the Sāvitrī by the priest who has mastered the Vedas, that is the true birth, the ageless and immortal.[1]

[1] Code of Manu 2.147-148

The upanayanam initiation was officiated by a local priest and the student's father. After the chanting of rituals, the priest placed the sacred thread over the boy's shoulder, across his chest and tied it at the waist to remain as a symbol of his second birth. His head was then shaved except for one tuft on top, which represented the attachment to the teacher and the scriptures. The twice-born then left his parental home to live and study for twelve years in the forest hermitage of a Teacher, a Brāhmaṇa priest.

The relationship between the teacher and the young child was of mutual respect. The student gave the teacher the same reverence – including the morning salutation of touching the mentor's feet and deference in all matters – that he had given his own parents. For his part, the teacher took on the task of educating the boy as a sacred duty. Some of the ancient Vaidika scholarly priests had several wives, ideally one from each caste, to ensure that their charges were given the best of care.

The scriptures were the actual textbooks in the classroom. The study and memorization of these lengthy treatises was the principal occupation of the students. However, the Vedas emphasize not only a spiritual and ethical life, but also include, particularly in the most recent *Atharva-veda,* rites for such practical matters as acquiring a wife, producing a son, curing oneself from disease and protecting oneself from serpents. Herbal medicine (Āyurveda), music, astrology and martial arts such as archery were also taught.

Traditionally, there was never any fee asked, or expected, of the student. One role of the Brāhmaṇa priest was to teach; he accepted this privilege as an honour. This has been one factor of the enigma that those of the highest priestly caste have often been the poorest of the four castes. These hermitage schools were run by donations, usually grains and cows, from the kings and graduates who became successful landowners. By using the scriptures and Sanskrit as the education medium, a common culture was assured throughout Bhārata.

In ancient days, the young girls also had the upanayanam ceremony performed, chanted the Gāyatrī Mantra, studied and even were taught the Vedas. Enlightened woman sages are mentioned in both the Upaniṣads and Purāṇas. The later interpretive scriptures state that the spiritual practice of women was so powerful that their benefits were shared by the husband, children, and the entire society, whereas the effects of the practice of the men was theirs alone.

However, through the centuries, many changes occurred in the religious customs to reflect the conditions in the society. In some areas, including Kerala, the upanayanam had become reserved exclusively for the priest caste. In addition to the practices in the society at large, each region had its own wealth of saints who set to words their spiritual insights. These works in the vernacular languages had been gradually incorporated into the curriculum.

Although the Muslim population had tended to gather in a few large cities, the Hindu population had remained in scattered villages – when the British arrived Calcutta (now Kolkata) was only a line of thatched huts; Bombay was a swamp. But education had not been neglected; at that time there were 100,000 schools throughout India. The priests then taught in the village itself, in the temple or a school built by the local raja (king). If the child lived too far from a school, he would live with the teacher's family, or the family of a classmate or relative.

It was one of these raja supported schools, but with a modern curriculum, that Balan attended. His early years at school, first through seventh standard, presented Balan with no problems, even though it was a regimented life with a caning by the headmaster when anyone failed to conform to the rules. Quite intelligent, Balan completed his lessons easily and always did his recitations with confidence. More likely a result of his own disposition than the threat of a caning, Balan was considered an ideal student. He could be depended upon to do his work without prompting. His love for reading also contributed to his success in school. There was never any report of a problem with discipline from any teacher. His aunts remember him as being a self-fulfilled and happy youngster.

During grades one to four Balan selected Malayalam as his second language. Malayalam had evolved from the Dravidian language, Tamil, with modifications according to local customs and also with additions of vocabulary from Sanskrit. In the fifth grade he switched to Sanskrit, which he studied for the following five years. His teacher, a Brāhmaṇa, who had received his education from his own father, was a brilliant Sanskrit scholar who had a knack for making the difficult language more palatable by showing his students the similarities between it and their native Malayalam. "Yet he is one who would be considered among the illiterate because he had received no English styled education," Swami Chinmayananda would later lament, when criticizing his country's modern standards of education.

The school was close by so the children from Poothampalli House went home for a hot lunch. If the students did live far away, the cook from each household brought their meal, steaming hot in metal canisters, for a picnic under the trees in the schoolyard. When classes ended at 4 p.m., Balan biked home for a quick snack, served with tea, then ran outdoors to play, preferably soccer and badminton, a local variation that used a ball instead of a shuttlecock. The badminton net was a permanent fixture in the compound and only the rains of the monsoon kept Balan away from it. He didn't care for other forms of exercise though. He had joined the Boy Scouts to be with some friends, but quit after only a couple of month with the allegation that all they did was go on long hikes.

The routine of Balan's life was regularly broken up by trips to visit relatives during school vacations or for special occasions. When he was eleven years old, the family went to Trichur for the marriage of his father's younger sister. Weddings, while considered the most important sacrament in a Hindu's life, was also an opportunity for the family to gather for a holiday.

One of Balan's favourite vacation spots was the palace of Cochin. His mother's cousin, the wife of the raja, had several sons who welcomed visits from their cousins, Gopinath and Balan. Often they would play the drums, feigning imitation of the skilled temple drummers of Kerala who performed at the festivals. Sometimes at dusk, they would create their own ceremony, auspiciously announcing the ending of the day with resounding drumbeats while marching around the billiard table. Most likely, Balan beat the loudest, happy to be relieved of the tiresome religious ceremony at Poothampalli House.

When Balan was twelve, he spent the summer with his cousin, Kuttappan, who lived on a large country estate. There Balan was able to perefct his skill at swimming in the large pond. He and Kuttappan, already an expert swimmer, had many strenuous races. By the end of the summer, Balan could beat his cousin. Balan's enjoyment of swimming has remained. After he became a Swami, devotees have been startled to see him diving into a holy river or the sea and swimming out until he was but a speck in the distance – even after he was sixty years of age.

During his entire life, Balan treated his two sisters, Padmini and Kanakam, with special consideration. "He was a very good kind brother, but a real tease. There was always lots of hollering and fussing going on when he was around," Padmini remembered. There was one younger aunt in the household who was very strict and took it upon herself to discipline all the children. Whenever they make any loud noise in their play, she would appear with a threatening cane. To the delight of his sisters and cousins, Balan called her the 'home police' behind her back.

Their older brother, 'Balachettan' (little Balan) as they affectionately called him, was also a solace to his younger sisters. They report he never complained when they pestered him to play with them or to help them with their homework. Sometimes he would hurry them up with the promise of a ghost story after they were finished, but he always emphasized that their studies were very important. Except one evening when, in frustration, he told Kanakam, "You better forget studies; you just don't have a head for it."

His siblings always looked to their wiser older brother and he liked to be helpful. However, there were times when Balachettan took advantage of their confidence. Once, when Kanakam was going through a phase when she was fearful of the night, Balachettan, with great ceremony, tied a string talisman around her wrist. In his usual verbose manner, he told how both the priest and Lord Śiva had blessed the string and that no evil – human or spirit – would dare come near her as long as she wore it. Kanakam suspected that he had just grabbed any string out of the desk drawer (which he had), but she was afraid to get rid of it "just in case what he said was true." Finally, one day when she was playing out in the yard, she threw the dirty string away. That evening at dinner when Balachettan spotted that it was missing from her arm, he tantalized her, "A ghost will come and get you now for sure." Of course, she really didn't believe him – he was such a tease – but. . . So that night she took a lantern and searched the compound yard to retrieve the talisman and return it to her wrist before retiring.

Throughout his boyhood, Balan was sure of himself, so that he always managed to get what he wanted. When preparations were being made for the sixtieth birthday celebration of one of his uncles, Balan decided that he wanted to sample some of the food put aside for the feast before the day arrived. So he went to the locked storeroom where a stalk of special, small bananas was hanging and managed to squeeze his thin body between the bars that were intended to keep the monkeys out. After having himself a banana feast, he called his sisters and cousins over and handed out a good ration of the tasty bananas to them. When their mother discovered the indulgence, she demanded, "What have you done?" Balan shrugged nonchalantly and replied, "I just ate some bananas. I wanted some; there they were, so I ate them. Father can get some more for the birthday dinner."

Balan's aunts catered to his every need to assure that he would not suffer any emotional deprivation from the loss of his mother. If Kouchi Amma did have to discipline him for coming in late from play, he would win her over with his sweet and sunny disposition, massaging her back until he was sure that he was forgiven. However, he usually stayed on her good side and would not intentionally disobey her. Of course, his father remained willing to indulge his only son in his slightest desire. Not only did Balan bask in attention at home, but at school also. As the son of a District Judge and the nephew of the Police Commissioner, he enjoyed a special status. The inevitable happened, Balakrishnan became spoiled.

So by the time he reached thirteen and began classes at the Maharaja's College, Balan had become a less respectable student. At first, he joined the older boys in pulling pranks on the teachers, but before long he instigated the mayhem. He resorted to any method for a little merriment to break up the boredom of the class, a loud noise when the teacher looked away, a book or paper taken from the teacher's desk and hidden, a ball tossed to a friend across the room. The boys gave a particularly hard time to the drawing teacher since he made the mistake of reacting to their pranks.

Shankar, one of Balan's cohorts in those days, was living with poor relatives who could not afford the extra expense. So Balan made him a simple offer, he would furnish his schoolbooks if Shankar supplied Balan's homework. Sometimes Balan also paid Shankar's school fees on their due date telling Shankar to pay him back later, whenever he had it. But if the money did not materialise, Balan would pay the next term's fees without ever making a comment to Shankar.

During these days of adolescence, Balan was hardly ever at home after school. Instead he played ball with his classmates in the schoolyard or just hung around on the street corners. He loved to talk and tease, and sometimes when enough boys gathered to make an audience he would give extemporaneous discourses. "He would launch out on any subject at random, not knowing where to begin or how to end," remembered Shankar. He was great at imitations and would send the rowdy boys into peals of laughter when he mocked their teachers or the town merchants. He was always full of ideas and advice, given out in an embellished form with gestures and jokes. Balan's family frowned upon these street corner packs. His uncle even warned a couple of the boys not to associate with his nephew or they would become spoiled like him. But his peers thought he was the greatest; there was always some boisterous fun going on when he was around.

Nobody could deny that he had a serious side, for, he was always a loyal, dependable friend. "Even in those days he seemed to have a double head; that is, he always had such a devil-may-care attitude. But there were also moments when he seemed to have a deep depression, especially when he questioned about life itself and could not find any meaning or purpose to it. I thought it indicated a spiritual bent of mind that he even thought about such deep questions. I used to tell him so," reminisced Shankar concerning his childhood friend.

Perhaps this spiritual inclination prompted his uncharacteristic behaviour after he turned twelve. At this age, he was no longer required to attend the evening worship service, but he made it a point to make sure his sisters were there, bathed, on time and alert. Sometimes he would hide behind the prayer room door to check on them. After all, he reminded them, it was the woman's duty to carry on the religious ceremonies. If they made a mistake in chanting or whispered or giggled during the service, he would give them a stern reprimand and make them promise to behave properly in the future. They never knew whether he was serious or if he was just making sure they suffered through what he had endured for his first twelve years.

Personally, he had little use for any ritual. He never went to the temple and ridiculed those who did. "If you want to pray, you can pray anywhere!" he taunted. To further shock his cousins and sisters, he made up several terrible tales that even ridiculed their religion. "How could he dare," they said, worrying over his sins, even as they enjoyed his defiance. His sisters remembered one particularly 'bad' story from those days:

> As you know everyone has to go to heaven or hell – so I will be going to hell for sure. Now, when I go I will take a pineapple and a palm leaf with me. The record keeper will call 'Balakrishnan Menon' and will begin reading out all my sins. I will make a great noise by shaking the palm leaf, and the record keeper will be so glad to see that I have brought a leaf for him to use to write his records. As you know there are no palm trees where he is, and there are so many going to hell these days, so he is always running short of palm leaves. He will tell me all my sins are erased for being so helpful. Then he'll see the pineapple and he'll be very pleased because there are no pineapples in hell either. Accepting this gift, he will grant me a special boon – anything I would like. I will ask for the Milky Ocean that the Lord Viṣṇu sleeps on and a gigantic bag of sugar. With the milk and sugar, I'll make buckets of milk pudding for everyone to enjoy. Then I'll urinate in what's left of the Milky Ocean and it will turn into yogurt for everyone to have their fill – just think, a limitless supply of yogurt for all of us!

When the Yogīrāja Bhairavananda and other Swamis occasionally came to the house, Balan would ridicule his sisters and cousins who humbly prostrated in the traditional Hindu greeting of a holy man, "Go fall at his feet! What do you think it will get you!" The Yogīrāja, who lived to see the day that this cynical youth would take the sannyāsa vows, never seemed to notice his failure to greet him properly. He treated Balan with the same kindness and interest that he did the other children.

Regardless of what others thought, Balakrishnan played on. He was pursuing a science major; botany, biology and chemistry were included in his studies. But the active youth found classes boring and missed them at the least excuse. "I could always find something more interesting to do, even if it were reading book. Never one assigned by the teachers, of course, but one of my own choosing. Usually, I would round up a gang of friends to just hang around with." When he did attend classes, his teachers wished he hadn't, for, he passed the time cracking jokes aloud and making a general disturbance.

Final exams for completion of the intermediate course of study arrived too soon for the unenthusiastic student. Until this point, Balakrishnan was still passing easily even though he hardly studied. At exam time, he would gather Shankar and a couple of other friends together and listen to their discussions on the main points of the subjects. That was enough – he was prepared! But these yearly exams were different. They included several unexpected questions, to which his answers brought not unexpected results. In the English literature section, the essay question asked for a character sketch of one of the leading roles in a Shakespearean play. Balan quickly sketched a picture of a sixteenth century Englishman and flipped over to the chemistry section. After a glance, he quickly surmised that he didn't have a prayer. So he simply copied the question paper on to the answer paper and turned in the exam. That experience marked the end of his science career. Soon afterward, he moved to Trichur, enrolled in St. Thomas College, and changed his major to liberal arts.

15

The College Years

I had everything I wanted in my childhood. I never thought of the future.

—Swami Chinmayananda, 1978.

Just when Balan completed intermediate school, his father was transferred to Trichur to a higher position in the regional courts. Wishing to take his children with him and provide a home for them, Kuttan agreed to a marriage arranged by his family with Devaki Menon, a progressive, intelligent woman who had earned a B.A. in Sanskrit, specialising in the Hindu Purāṇas. They moved into Patinjaresrambi House, a large, rambling two storey adobe structure, which would hold Kuttan Menon's family along with several cousins who came from country estates to stay in Trichur in order to get a proper English education. With time the union of Kuttan and Devaki brought four children into the household: three daughters and one son.

An arrogant teenager, Balakrishnan considered himself quite an intellectual. When he thought of God it was only with a negative doubt. Who is God? Where is God? But he did not let go of his relationship with Lord Candrakalādhara. Every night before going to sleep, he would sit in his bed, mentally visualise this form of Lord Śiva. Then he would silently repeat the universal mantra, Om Namaḥ Śivāya, before lying down to sleep. This habit was so ingrained he thought it essential for good sleep, and perhaps even helpful for staving off any bad dreams or nightmares. Kanakam and Padmini watched him sitting up straight and still in his bed each night before sleeping and knew he was doing japa (repetition of a mantra). They wanted to tease the self-proclaimed atheist for it, but they knew that he would pull a trick on them to get even, so they kept quiet.

Not only had Balan rejected God, he had also rejected all the superstitious rituals. All those baths, that was another stupidity about the Hindu religion, he claimed. In his opinion, one bath in the morning was enough unless one got dirty during the day. Everyone else had a bath before the evening service, but since Balan no longer joined it, the rule was that he had to bathe before eating supper. If he felt like taking one, he took one, if not he omitted it. Sometimes he would throw a damp towel around his shoulders to make it look like he had just come from the tank. His sisters knew what he was doing, but they knew better than to tell. "If you don't mind me, I'll have my friends tease you after school," he would threaten them.

One evening he came in and his stepmother asked: "Have you had your bath?" "Sure", he replied. "Good, because the priest is just arriving to do the funeral rituals for your auntie." Even to this non superstitious intellectual having to bathe in order to eat was somehow different from having to bathe to attend a funeral ritual. Unnoticed he slipped out back to the tank, took a dip and melted back into the group in time for the ceremony.

During the funeral ritual the officiating priest chanted a hymn from the *Ṛg-veda* addressed to Agni, God of fire –

'Carry him, Agni, in your arms gently;

Give him a perfect body, a bright body.

Carry him where the ancestors live,

Where there is no more death.'

The ceremony was oriented toward invoking the spirit to leave its attachment to the physical body and to pass into the subtle realms of the afterlife where experiences gained and lessons learned are of a different nature. The Hindu understood that lamenting over the dead could cause the spirit to cling to the physical world where it no longer has the physical vehicle necessary to gain experience, thereby impeding its evolution in other realms. A mourning period for each caste was designated in the ṣcriptural injunctions – a few days for the Brāhmaṇas, who ideally have the subtle mind to understand the nature of death, to three weeks for the lowest caste. This group were more attached to worldly relations and possessions; therefore, they would need more time to assimilate the loss.

Although Balan always seemed to manage to get his way, it was not without some scolding from his father who was a strict, serious man. Balan's extravagant tastes were becoming a noticeable expense. He had taken to wearing silk shirts rather than the traditional cotton ones. He wore gold chains around his neck, waist and arm. But his oily hair was what irritated his father the most. "So much hair dressing is bound to make you bald," his father scolded him. "Then you'll see how much oil you will need." But these criticisms had no effect on Balan, he continued to dress in the style he considered the most elegant. He had no use for the older generation's opinion on fashion.

Although Kuttan Menon had a serious side, he was a generous and affectionate father who loved to have good time. One could often hear the roar of loud laughter and disputes over a card game coming from the veranda of Patinjaresrambi House in the evenings. Balan's stepmother also joined in the game playing.

Mr. Menon had a habit of working on Saturday mornings for three or four hours to clear off his desk and prepare for the following week's docket. He issued an ultimatum that Balan must study during the time he was at the court. Thinking he was going to give the boy a break, one Saturday he returned home early after only two hours to find Balan and Kuttappan having a great time playing badminton. The father was quite shocked at such an overt display of disobedience. He gave Balan an unmerciful scolding and went into the house shaking his head. But he never held a grudge. Ten minutes later he was out on the veranda with the chessboard. He loved the game and Balan and Kuttappan were his only available opponents. Kuttan loved his son's charm, intelligence and wit, but he also feared for his future. What would become of this arrogant lad who had no interest whatsoever in his studies, nor had any ambition at all?

As a last resort, a tutor was hired for Balan. After some six hours in the classroom, he would have to come straight home, do his school homework with the tutor, and then do extra homework that the tutor would assign. He continually complained and lamented his ill fate of having no freedom for playing sports with his friends after school. The tutor was known to be a tyrant. There were even rumours of beatings with the cane whip. Not one to take such treatment without some revenge, Balan would get even by playing tricks on the teacher. Once he removed the bar from the canvas lounge chair that the teacher always sat in. When he arrived and sat in the chair, he crashed to the floor. Another time Balan poured black ink on a wooden chair moments before the teacher sat in it, thereby ruining his immaculate suit of white clothing.

Although Balan was a jovial character on the streets with his friends, he always exhibited a genuine love and caring for his family, particularly the elders. He used to sit on the bench with his father's mother, a widow who lived in their house. Always dressed in her three-piece white luṅgīs, the customary dress of old Kerala, her only activity was participating in the daily evening worship service. The semi renunciate passed each day in sitting on a plane wooden bench in her attic room doing japa, silently repeating the name of Lord Kṛṣṇa. The elderly look forward to their retirement when they can devote full time to spiritual pursuits. It is a time of preparation for the coming change of consciousness into the heavenly realms and a future birth, which is determined by the spiritual merit accumulated in the present life.

Although it was not unusual for a person to spend his retirement in such a manner, Balan thought it a terribly dull existence for his grandmother and took it upon himself to entertain her by telling her jokes or urging her to join in the celebrations at a temple festival. "No", she insisted, "I have no interest in those things, for, I have enjoyed them all in my day. The little joy from that music and dancing is nothing in comparison to the joy I now know. Don't worry, you will understand some day." The remembrance of Lord Kṛṣṇa filled her mind and being with peace. This dear lady had never read a book on philosophy; she just lived with a simple first hand knowledge that 'God is love'. "Now when I recall our conversations, I realize how much she did understand about life and God, although she had never studied the scriptures," Swami Chinmayananda said of her, long after her death.

The temple festivals regularly broke up the monotony of the daily routine. Most of them date from pre-Āryan times and were unique to this region. In the month of Medam (April-May) when the moon was in the constellation of Pūram, the spring festival was celebrated in a grand style throughout Kerala. The most magnificent celebration was the Pūram at Trichur when the many relatives from miles around gathered at Patinjaresrambi House to participate in the festivities. Each day everyone would go to the temple grounds to wander about the colourful carnival tents filled with food, games and handicrafts. A fifty piece orchestra furnished the background music for the celebrating. The temple drummers showed their skill by competitions in which each attempted an intricate rhythm so difficult that the others could not follow. Every evening there was a fireworks display, followed by a long drama from one of the classical epics. At about three in the morning, the sleepy playgoers wandered home down lanes lit with oil lamps and festooned with palm leaves, coloured banners and flower garlands.

The most spectacular event of the Pūram was the parade of elephants that arrived from the Śiva and Devī temples all over Kerala. As they passed through villages on their journey to Trichur, they were greeted and fed at each temple along the way.

The venerated animals entered the temple grounds decked out in gold plated chain with bright flowers painted on the exposed parts of their heads and hips. On their backs rode a small idol and a priest carrying a colourful silk parasol, a long handled whisk and peacock feather fans, which were twirled in unison during the parade. The procession started off by circling the temple to the rhythm of a Chenda Melam, a drum beat distinctive to Kerala. The religious devotees lined the avenue to throw rice and flowers as they passed. Following the afternoon break, the procession was repeated after dark with the priests whirling flaming torches on the backs of the plodding elephants. On the last day of the festival, two local temples competed for the best performance and quality of some fifteen elephants, judged by their overall size and beauty of eyes, ears, trunk and toenails. The festival ended with a dazzling display of fireworks.

These temple festivals were local holidays provided for by the local kings. In the early eighteenth century, a prosperous Mahārājā of Cochin initiated the special Trichur Pūram to give the villagers and country folk something to look forward to as they toiled in their daily chores. The peasants also used it as an opportunity to make some extra money. Throughout the year, they would weave rope or mats from coconut husks or make decorative crafts to sell in decorated stalls in their spare time.

Always ready for a good time, Balan had been the first one to arrive at any festival in his younger days. But he now thought it all a bore, particularly because of the religious connotations of the fanfare. So he took it upon himself to liven up the crowd. He would grab the hands of his friends and pull them through the thick crowds. Like lightning he would take off, banging and jostling the crowd, with his friends fearful for their own safety as well as that of the mob. And Balan played on.

All of his friends considered Balan big-hearted. As the gang leader, he treated everyone equally and put pressure on the others to do the same. However, his extroverted friendliness took on a negative bent when it was directed toward the shy Hindu girls. He and his gang would stand near the temple entrance to catch the girls with a suggestive whistle or a compliment on their beauty. As the embarrassed girls blushed and hurried off, the boys would break into peals of taunting laughter. The young ladies of Trichur did not consider this complimentary and were known to detour past the street where he lived to avoid the teasing of the 'tiger', as they called him. But the tiger was hard to avoid, for, he was seen touring around town in a new automobile.

Balan's uncle Neelakantha Menon, Police Commissioner of Cochin, and later Chief Justice, was one of the few persons in town who owned a car. No one was allowed to even touch it – except his driver and Balan. Everyone wondered how Balan managed to talk his uncle into letting him use the vehicle. Perhaps, it was because of Balan's inclination to perfectionism in caring for things. He began tinkering with the car, for, he always knew when it had any problem. The slightest squeak or rumble and he would be under the hood until he was satisfied that all the parts were humming smoothly.

The ambitious uncle had graduated from Oxford Law School and hoped that his nephew would follow in his footsteps. He knew that Balan was a dedicated loafer, but he also saw his potential. Often he would send a messenger to call Balan to his home for dinner with the greatest intention of getting the young man straightened out. Determined to fire up some ambition in him, he would start off the sermon in a stern voice on the evils of laziness, the virtue of hard work and the absolute necessity of having a career to pay for the things that Balan enjoyed. But he would soon succumb to the charm of Balan's jokes and excuses, he would end up laughing with his nephew, for, uncle Neelakantha had confidence that such a brilliant one would somehow find his place in society.

His uncle was not the only family member who was distressed over Balakrishnan's behaviour. His father was also deeply concerned and openly disappointed about his son's performance. On one occasion an acquaintance, who was an inspector of schools in Cochin, came for a visit. He was a bachelor, strictly self-disciplined in his daily life, and financially successful. Kuttan Menon called in his son to meet the man. "I want you to meet this man because at forty-two years of age he does not have a single bad habit." He then proceeded to deliver a thorough lecture right in front of his guest. "At not even twenty years of age you have all the vices possible. Can't you see for yourself that this man leads the type of life that gives one the most happiness? Why do you have to destroy yourself and your chances for a future with such foolish habits?"

Although they felt helpless to do anything, his sisters and cousins were also anxious and thought it would be a disaster if he did not get the education needed for a public service career with the British Government. One cousin who lived in Patinjaresrambi House during the school session even stayed up late one night reading Balan's history lessons to him when he had a fever, so that he would be prepared for an exam the following day.

In a last attempt to make his son qualified for a job in the Civil Service, Mr. Menon dismissed the tutor and moved his studious classmate, Shankar, right into their home. Now Balan's behaviour affected Shankar's grades as well as his own. Ordered by his father to be in the room with Shankar at study time, Balan would bother his companion by tapping out a rhythm on the desk or hurrying him so they would have time to go for a coffee before bedtime. But these nightly trips to the coffee house were cause for tension to Shankar. The only coffee house open at late hours was a Muslim restaurant. Hindus did not eat in Muslim restaurants because Muslims ate meat and Hindus do not even eat out of a pot in which meat has been cooked. "What's the worry? They don't cook meat in the coffee pot!" the impetuous Balan assured Shankar and his other doubtful friends who went along with Balan, since he always paid the bill. But they were secretly hoping that they would not be seen by anyone.

Although Kerala remained apart from most of the political unrest of the 1920s, there were several notable exceptions. In late 1921, because of the British interference with the Caliph in Turkey, the Muslim peasantry in Cochin rebelled against the British rule. On November 21, 1921, seventy of these peasants were arrested and locked into an airtight railroad car. When the authorities opened the doors the next day, all had suffocated. It took nine months and three thousand dead Muslim peasants before the British crushed the rebellion. It was a forewarning of the cruelty the British would be capable of in the approaching thirty years.

Gandhi visited Kerala several times in the late 1920s on his tours of India. Balan's uncle, Puthezhath Menon, served as the translator for Gandhi's talks in Trichur. Balan joined the crowd who gathered to hear him, but the young man was not impressed; for, at that age he had no interest in politics. Gandhi also came to Kerala to witness a protest of the prohibition of untouchables from entering the Vykom temple. The temple priests finally capitulated to Gandhi's argument that if India were going to get rid of the British, the Indians had to take responsibility for the social improvement of the citizenry and allow everyone to enter the temple.

Balan was not particularly interested in religion either. He had even used Hindu concepts to carefully rationalise his position as an agnostic. Swami Chinmayananda later described his thoughts on religion during that period.

> Years passed by. The tall, slender Balakrishnan Menon reached college. By then he had become extremely bloated in head and intoxicated at heart. His early habit of asking questions about everything, including God, grew with his bones. He came to ask such dangerous questions as "Why should there be God?"
>
> You see this was what happened to Balakrishnan. He had heard the various spiritual teachers who visited his home describing God. They said if God is

the sun, every living being is but a ray of him. If God is the conflagration, the individuals were mere sparks. If God is the whole, each of us is only a part of the whole. This set the boy thinking and, in his immaturity of thought, he came to the conclusion that, since even in the best of us there was only a tiny part, scarcely twenty percent, of goodness then what must be the whole but a huge cauldron of stinking evil. Again, if the various individuals are all different rays of God, then only because of all these people like Balan could there even be a God. In short, Balan was really the source of God, not God the source of Balan. Why then should Balan pray to God? So argued the stupid youth.

Alas, with these fallacious arguments, Balan divorced himself from God and wandered aimlessly through an empty life of inner gloom. Yet he did question anyone he felt safe to open up with about his spiritual doubts, for, he was never sure that it was really possible to overthrow God with such easy arguments. But he kept up the questioning, for, something kept on warning him in his heart that there was a serious flaw somewhere in his line of logic. But his intellectual honesty would not countenance any blind faith.

Even in those days, pocketing all self dignity, he used to do his japa secretly in bed. The compromise was painful – yet, strangely enough, he went on submitting to his own inner voice for a long time. The spiritual Balan persisted as only a shadow in the background of the unconvinced sophist Balan until the day when he left home to enter Lucknow University.

16

The University Days

Balakrishnan Menon of Lucknow University is, even today, a topic to moralise and an instance to quote when the staff and students sit around to discuss the depths of degradation into which the modern students have sunk.

—Swami Chinmayananda, 1950.

The history of the Lucknow area stretches back to the glorious days of the ancient kingdom of Ayodhya, one of the seven sacred cities of India and the birthplace of Rāma. It is also tradition that the Buddha resided there for a time; therefore, by the fifth century the area was the site of a hundred Buddhist monasteries. Lucknow itself was a stately city, built by the Muslim Nawab (prince) of Oudh on the shores of the Gomati river in the fourteenth century.

The city was adorned with colleges, mosques, a large palace and houses for courtiers. It had a cosmopolitan atmosphere; the finer things of life were taken for granted. It was to the palaces of Lucknow that the respectable landed gentry sent their daughters, well chaperoned, of course, to be schooled in the fine arts of culture, languages, deportment and conversation by the palace courtesans, who were considered to be the most erudite and cultured women in all of India. In literary circles, the kingdom of Oudh was well-known for its all night soirees of poetry reading.

Such was life before the British occupied the land. In a scenario similar to dramas re-enacted across the sub-continent, the British East India Company took advantage of court intrigues, struggles for the right of succession, Hindu kings chaffing against cruel Muslim overlords, and, when those attempts failed, down and out treachery to take over the wealthy Indian kingdoms. Ironically, these English conquerors, like all of the foreign invaders before them, excused their immoral behaviour with rationalizations of racial and religious superiority.

Actually, it was in Lucknow that Warren Hastings, the first governor general of Bengal, met his Waterloo, for immoral excesses not even the British public would abide. The seeds of his fall were planted when the Hindu raja asked the governor general to help free Varanasi from the authority of the Muslim Nawab of Oudh – with a generous payment for his services. The crafty Hastings agreed, on the condition that the rights to Varanasi be ceded over to the Company Protectorate and a large annual tribute be paid in exchange for the British protection. Then Hastings began to ask the Raja Cheyte Singh for more and larger payments – up to an additional fifty thousand pounds on several occasions. It was 1780 and extra funds were needed. The East India Company was at war with France over the Indian trade routes. In addition, the rebellious Marathas in Bombay and Gujarat were still vigorously resisting British rule.

When at last the raja refused to be blackmailed, he fell into the trap that Hastings had set. It was the excuse Hastings was waiting for to overrun the palace and claim the royal treasury. But the people of Varanasi resisted with unexpected fury, and the invasion turned into a massacre. The raja barely escaped with his life, never to return to his kingdom, but certainly a lot wiser about the definition of 'cruel overlords'. The British East India Company was then owner of Varanasi along with its royal treasury. The cache of two hundred fifty thousand pounds sterling found in the treasury was a disappointment to the Company army and officials; they had expected to divide up at least one million pounds.

On the wings of his victory in Varanasi, Hastings proceeded to Lucknow, the wealthy capital of Oudh. In order to ascertain the whereabouts of their fortune, he had the two dowager princesses almost starved to death and the two old eunuchs in their employ arrested and cruelly tortured. But before these methods gained him the booty, Hastings was recalled to England by the House of Commons for high crimes and misdemeanors. However, his only punishment was a grueling seven years of court proceedings, after which he was acquitted.

So it was left to General Outram, after the Indian uprising of 1857, to deprive the Oudh royal family of its right to rule. Lucknow played a leading role in this general rebellion of the Hindus and Muslims against the British. With the treasures of the nobles and merchants carried off, the British interest in Lucknow quickly dissipated. They left the grand old palatial buildings to fall to ruin. The old traditions were disturbed but by no means obliterated; Lucknow remained a centre of culture despite its somewhat dilapidated appearance.

Even in 1940, when Menon went to the university, Lucknow had an intellectual and literary community of no small repute. This sophisticated character from the small kingdom of Cochin – tall and lean, hollow cheeks, bulging eyes, tobacco-stained fingers – at first glance appeared hard and cold. But his classmates were soon to discover that Balakrishnan Menon was a riotous companion; always ready for a good time and with plenty of money to pay his own way, as well as that of others, should they be short of cash.

Madras University would have been the usual choice for a South Indian, but Balakrishnan's grades prevented his acceptance there. Lucknow University offered him the opportunity to take a master's degree in his favourite subject, English literature, while at the same time take a secondary course in law. The year 1940 was a precarious time to start a law degree, as the inevitable departure of the British would bring major changes in the legal system. But Balakrishnan decided to go ahead with the law courses as the degree would give him a preparation for further studies in law. Not that he was enthusiastic about a career in law; he had agreed to go along with his family's wishes since he had no particular ambition. He persevered even though he seriously doubted there was a possibility for him in law. Once he had questioned an eminent barrister as to what was his secret of success. The reply – lots of hard work – was contrary to his specific talents.

But reading, on any subject that interested him, was not hard work for Balakrishnan. He excelled in his literature courses, covering all of the classics, including Shakespeare, Swift and Milton. He particularly admired George Bernard Shaw and was somewhat influenced by the Shavian manner of social and religious criticism later in his own journalism. He enjoyed all the poets of the romantic period, Shelley being his favourite. Balakrishnan loved to talk about his favourite books and would often corner the distinguished scholar and professor of literature, Sri Vilasan Nair (a fellow Keralite), for long discussions.

On the other hand, Balakrishnan ignored the subjects that didn't appeal to him, so he had plenty of time for extracurricular activities. He was on the university tennis team, literary committee and the debating team. He also participated in the theatrical activities, appearing in several dramas. But his favoured activity was the all night card games. Although he ignored the need for sleep, he watched his diet to keep himself in top physical shape for his tennis matches. He took his tennis seriously, and did well at it. He represented Lucknow University in singles against Ghaus Mohmed, the Indian competitor at the Wimbledon Tournament.

How did he ever manage to pass the courses he ignored? He just managed. Some things never change, notes were available for a price from previous examinations. They included enough questions and answers to succeed. But to satisfy attendance requirements took more complicated maneuvering. Through a little research, he found out that the professor of a course in which he did not have the required attendance was very religious and always went to a particular temple. Balakrishnan carefully laid out his scheme. He arrived a few minutes before the hour of the professor's daily visit and positioned himself with hands clasped in great devotion in front of the sanctum sanctorum. The professor, coming upon him, was surprised; he knew his student well enough to know of his worldly reputation.

"Do you come here often?" the professor inquired.

"Oh, yes, Sir," his student answered with marked enthusiasm that came from his joy that the professor had shown up and had spoken to him – the scene was going according to plan. "Yes, especially now, as I have a particular problem. If the great Lord Hanumāna cannot help me, I fear no one can."

"Just what is your problem," the professor asked, his curiosity aroused.

"I find that university records show that I don't have sufficient attendance to appear for the examinations," Menon explained. The professor, impressed, or rather deceived, promised to take care of the situation.

The temple was typical of the simple structures of North India in comparison to the ornate temples of the south, which are adorned with gold plated domes and intricately carved entrance towers. In the north, Hindus had finally lost their fervour for rebuilding the ornate temples that were annually looted and razed to the ground by Muslim invaders. Simple temples were easy to rebuild and it was hoped that their modest appearance would not invite the raiders' proclaimed duty to destroy the temples of the infidels.

The first Muslim raiders arrived in India, known throughout the Middle East and Europe as the richest country in the world, when an Afghan sultan realized that India was a relatively easy solution to the empty condition of his royal coffers. Beginning in 1008 AD, Mahmud of Gazni and his highly trained army annually crossed into the Punjab area, looting and killing until they had loaded up all the slaves, gold and precious jewels, including diamonds said to be the size of pomegranates, that they could carry home. These excursions went deeper and deeper into India until the Mahmud reached the famous Mathura temple on the banks of the Yamuna river. After relieving the temple of its golden idols covered with precious gems and its coffers of gold, silver and jewellery, he expressed his admiration for the architecture of this great shrine. Assessing that its duplication would cost one hundred million dinars[1] and the labour of two hundred years, he then ordered it razed to the ground. This prosperous Sultan of Gazni, represented as the greatest monarch of all time in Muslim history books, generated a gross national income for 30 years solely from his forays into India.

And he proved to be the model and inspiration to future aspiring young sultans with financial problems. However, some of the sultans remained in India to build great empires on the planes of Delhi. The natives of the area had allowed the strength of the era of Aśoka's Golden Age to dissipate in internal squabbles. Also, they had adopted the non-violent precepts of Buddhism and Jainism; even the Brāhmaṇa priests had incorporated the ideals of non-violence and vegetarianism into Hinduism. The Indian Āryans, like those they had conquered three thousand years before, no longer had the taste, skill or organization for war.

The stories of conquest throughout the chronicles of mankind have often been detailed. As the historian Will Durant described it in *Our Oriental Heritage*, the first volume of *The Story of Civilization* –

> 'The Mohammedan Conquest of India is probably the bloodiest story in history. It is a discouraging tale, for, its evident moral is that civilization is a precarious thing, whose delicate complex of order and liberty, culture and peace may at any time be overthrown by barbarians invading from without or multiplying within.'

[1] Dinar – lowest unit of money in Persia.

For 700 years, Hindus suffered unique tortures from the Afghan, and later Turk sultans, at times in such excess that even the Muslim population protested against their leaders. Simultaneously, this was a period of great prosperity for the Muslim Empire in India. For five centuries, the Muslims led the world in power and wealth, in scholarship, government, physical and social sciences, literature and art – and India, from Delhi to Hyderabad, was part of this premier economic and scientific age. Many Hindus in India, some to protect their lives, and some for economic reasons, accepted the faith of the rulers. Many Hindu merchants became extremely wealthy from the trade with the Muslims both in India and to the West. Others fled south to establish the Vijayanagar Empire in the early 1300s.

This noble empire, the last stronghold of the Hindus, was devastated in 1565 by an alliance of sultans of several small kingdoms. Having received word that Muslim armies were marching on Vijayanagar, the last great Hindu king, Rāma raja, set out with an army of half a million men. But they were no match for the skilled, experienced soldiers of the conquering troops, and the defeat was such that the streams ran red with their blood. The conquerors then sacked the wealthy capital, making it their solemn duty to destroy all sculpture and art – a task that would take five months. Afterwards, they set fire to anything that would burn including the abundant crops in the surrounding fields. Loaded with loot and slaves, they marched home proclaiming that there was not a breathing creature – neither man nor beast – left in a fifty-mile radius of the capital city of the empire.

Today from a nearby hilltop, the expansive ruins of a half-dozen temples are still visible. The man-made structures and aqueducts that connect them indicate the spiritual community and cooperation that once existed in the present wasteland. The greatest tragedy of Vijayanagar (place of victory) was not limited to the physical destruction of the populace, the temples and homes, the crops and animals. The true destruction was that of the inspiration that envisioned it, the intelligence that planned it, and the talent that executed it.

Late in sixteenth century, the Mughal Akbara took over the throne and widened his dominion from one-eighth of India to the entire subcontinent. In his more mature years, like Aśoka, he replaced the violent tendencies of his youth with a virtuous and benevolent administration of his kingdom. As a ruler, he exhibited the tolerant character of early Islam. His empire thrived as the cities of Renaissance Europe demanded more and more of India's treasures: ivory, ebony, sandalwood, indigo, pearls, onyx, amethyst, diamonds, silk textiles, iron products, cosmetics, pepper and spices to fulfil the growing Italian appetite for new luxuries.

With the royal treasury replete and the people happy, Akbara turned to his greatest pleasure – the study of philosophy. He invited the representatives of all religions to his palace to participate in discussions: Muslim mullahs, Christian priests, Hindu Brāhmaṇas, Buddhist monks. All attended and were equally welcomed. From the accumulation of these diverse ideas, along with his own insights, Akbara proposed a new religion, which encompassed the essentials of all the great religions, with the admirable hope that the inhabitants of India might become brothers.

But his dream was not to be. History has repeatedly demonstrated the liability of succession through heredity; the son of Akbara was no exception. He and those who followed him – decadent, extravagant rulers – led India again into military vulnerability, one that the Afghan Muslims would return to exploit. Nadir Shah sent armies into the Punjab and Delhi nine times to carry away the wealth of the temples, mosques and palaces of the weak Mughal rulers, who were addicted to war, liquor, opium and women.

A brief moment of hope for tolerance and justice was crushed when the mystic and philosopher Dārā Śikoh, the great-grandson of Akbara, was killed by his tyrannical younger brother Auraṅgazeba. He then proceeded to kill their remaining two brothers, imprison their father, and proclaim himself Emperor. Auraṅgazeba spent his entire thirty-year reign slaughtering the infidel Hindus and rebellious factions of the descendants of the Mughal rulers, Shia Muslims in Hyderabad and Bijapur. With his death, the Muslim Empire was left in chaos and confusion, vulnerable to the next siege of wealth seekers – the Europeans.

Under the British Raj, the people of India suffered bitter subjugation and economic adversity. Yet, they were able to recuperate the intellectual and leadership void left by the centuries of Muslim domination. With the formation of an Oriental Royal Society, Sir William Jones brought together a small group of English scholars, historians, archaeologists and philologists. It was the work of these scholars that gave Indians a connection to the roots of their varied history – the Indus Valley Civilization, the Āryan ancestry of the Hindus, and the Golden Age of Aśoka's Empire – long obliterated and forgotten in the battles of the past millennium. Many literary and spiritual Sanskrit works were translated into English and published for the European elite. However, these volumes were not added to any curriculum in Britain or India. In fact, they were most often used by the British to further their propaganda to demonstrate to the Indians they were a spiritual people and should not complain of their poverty while the British shipped their wealth out of their country. Nevertheless, the acceptance of the validity and depth of these inspired scriptures by foreign intellectuals would influence the Indians' opinion of their heritage and set the stage for the spiritual renaissance in the cities that Balakrishnan Menon, as Swami Chinmayananda, would initiate.

Each of Bhārata's spiritual revolutionaries has had a unique character and personality. Each brought to the task a unique life experience and particular secular knowledge to play a specific role in the revelation of the eternal Truth of Sanātana-dharma to mankind. Surely, no one but the Creator Himself could have known the mission designed for the unlikely servant, Balakrishnan Menon. But his courage, independence, energy and sense of humour stood him in good stead when he later applied these qualities to spiritual goals. He was determined to turn the children of Bhārata once again toward the treasures of their ancient heritage as elucidated in the Sanskrit scriptures.

PART – III

The Mission

17

The Yajña Plan

Hindu Religion is a science of self-perfection, comprising a complete technique of Self-realization.

—Swami Chinmayananda, 1952.

In November of 1951, Swami Chinmayananda completed his tour of India and returned to Tapovanam Kutir in Uttarkashi. He had witnessed the spiritual and economic degradation throughout his homeland, and was resolved to plan a series of Upaniṣad jñāna-yajñas in all of the great cities of India. He had taken the term, 'jñāna-yajña', from the *Bhagavad-gītā.*[1]

In the concluding verses, Lord Kṛṣṇa praises both the Teacher and student of the *Bhagavad-gītā* by stating that he who studies the sacred dialogue is performing a ritual of worship at the altar of wisdom. Through this worship (yajña) of invoking divine wisdom (jñāna), Swami Chinmayananda envisioned a revival of moral values and spiritual goals. The need for such a direction in India's recently won independence was great. Educated Hindus, who were now leading the country, had become disconnected from their cultural roots. The priest caste upheld only the letter, not the spirit, of their religion. The philosophy of Sanātana-dharma had been lost in the chaos and the economic reality of recent history. The need for basic necessities was extreme and the desire for luxuries was excessive, so Hindus turned to the old gods for help. In two thousand years, exotic India – land of untold riches, gold, jewels and spices – had been wrung dry.

[1] *adhyeṣyate ca ya imaṁ dharmyaṁ saṁvādam-āvayoḥ,*
jñānayajñena tenāham-iṣṭaḥ syām-iti me matiḥ. – Bhagavad-gītā-18.70

Foreign invaders had depleted her coffers and her hopes. The temple priests were happy to assist the populace, by invoking the deity of wealth – for a fee.

Swami Chinmayananda's hope was that large numbers of the educated, constituting the growing middle class in the overpopulated cities, could be inspired with the values, ethics and pride of their ancient culture. Several experienced businessmen advised the young Swami that the timing was not appropriate for spiritual development in light of the economic and the political crisis the new nation was facing. But that was the real crux of the plan – a large mass of people imbued with spiritual ideas and guidance could lead the country in a positive direction for the benefit of all. They would give it a strong foundation built on Vaidika ideals of mutual cooperation among men and the gods.

To accomplish this goal, Swami Chinmayananda planned to teach directly from the scriptures. This is the paramparā, tradition, a system in which the eternal Truth is imparted from an Enlightened Master to an earnest student through the medium of the scriptures. In Sanātana-dharma (eternal Truth), the name the Bhāratīyas called their religion, an individual's unique experience was never considered a valid path for others to follow. Instead the authority of teaching comes from the words of the ancient ṛṣis whose divine experience and insight has been verified again and again by a succession of Masters through the ages. Hinduism, or Sanātana-dharma, is the only major religion not founded upon the revelations of one man, but upon those of a great number of Masters through the centuries, working together, verifying, clarifying and the most essential – personally experiencing – the supreme goal set forth in the scriptures.

For his first lecture series Swami Chinmayananda considered Poona[1] ideal, for, it was a small, pleasant city developed during the British Raj. Although built as a military centre, Poona was known for its many educational institutions

[1] now Pune

that had produced a sizeable number of learned Hindus. Swami Chinmayananda visited the city on his pilgrimage around India and stayed at the home of Mr. Nanda whom he had met previously at Ananda Kutir. At that time, they had hiked together to visit an ascetic saint, Vasishta Gupta, who lived in a cave in the hills beyond Rishikesh. Upon their return to Ananda Kutir, Mr. Nanda had given the Swami his address with an invitation to visit his home should he ever be in Poona. When the Swami arrived during his all-India pilgrimage, Mr. Nanda welcomed him and listened to his plan for a series of lectures on the scriptures in somewhat the same format that Swami Sivananda had used in his tour in 1950. Mr. Nanda invited some friends over to discuss the possibility of having an Upaniṣad jñāna-yajña in Poona. Their willingness to help with the details of the organization had encouraged the young Swami in his plans.

"Poona! There are so many Brāhmaṇa Sanskrit scholars in Poona! How will you tackle them? They'll never countenance a Swami talking on the scriptures that they consider their private domain," roared Swami Tapovanam. "Anyway it's not for a sannyāsī to go and do this type of serious work. You will get caught up; it is the nature of action." This was the Guru's reply when Chinmaya mentioned to him that he had spoken to some persons in Poona who would be interested in talks on the Upaniṣads. But after the Guru made his statement, he kept quiet. "Perhaps, it is a test," hoped the disciple. Chinmaya knew that the Master was correct. There was a risk that someone would misunderstand the words and be thrown off course. But there was also a possibility that someone would hear the silent melody beneath the words and taste the divine ecstasy.

The text *Yogavāsiṣṭha* outlines the qualities of an Enlightened one – sāmya – calm and quiet as the moon with the mind constantly one-pointed in reflection on the Self; prasanna vadanam – a glow on the face of absolute satisfaction; rasavān – fullness or revelling in bliss. When one manifests these signs for a period of time it is an affirmation that his knowledge of the divine Self is established. At that moment, he is no longer considered a disciple, but a Master himself. Having seen these qualities on the face of his student and perceiving the nobility of his purpose, Swami Tapovanam allowed Chinmaya to choose his own path.

But the decision had already been contracted. Chinmaya's experiences during the five months of exploring India had strengthened his conviction. He felt impelled to give his plan a try. With a solemn farewell and prostration to his Guru, Swami Chinmayananda set out for Rishikesh on the first leg of his journey to execute the 'Gangotri Plan,' as he termed it, because the inspiration had dawned on him while at Gangotri. At Ananda Kutir, he met with several of the Swamis and informed them of his plan to give talks on Vedānta in Poona.

"What if the response is not good and the people don't appreciate what you are saying. What will you do then?" questioned one of them.

"Do? I'm a sannyāsī. I'll keep my bags packed. If they like what I say, I'll stay. If they don't, I'll leave. It's as simple as that!" replied Swami Chinmayananda.

In contrast to Swami Tapovanam, Swami Sivananda heartily approved and encouraged the Upaniṣad jñāna-yajña plan. The previous year he had completed a tour of India giving talks on the scriptures and he felt that the people sincerely wanted such knowledge. He even presented Chinmaya with a message to be read aloud in his first talk. In the service that evening Swami Sivananda announced the proposed discourses in case those present had relatives or acquaintances in Poona. "Go roar like Vivekananda!" extolled the seasoned sage to the inexperienced Swami.

With only the clothes on his back, a trunk filled with an accumulation of notes and books with the words DIVINE MISSION carefully lettered on its top, and just enough money to buy a ticket to Hyderabad, Swami Chinmayananda boarded the train for South India. He was leaving the peace and security of the mountains and the tradition of the spiritual Masters who spent their secluded lives in the cave of the Himalayan ranges. Instead, he dared to live among the people, to share the life they lived, and to address the problems they encountered.

With four nickels (annās) in his pocket, Swami Chinmayananda arrived at Poona on December 23, 1951. He was greeted at the railroad station by a small group with the traditional flower garland. He had only reached Poona because in Hyderabad he was able to contact Śrī Gopal Reddy, a devotee of Swami Sivananda. Śrī Reddy had requested Swami Chinmayananda to stay in his home for a few days so that he could invite friends to his home for satsaṅga (spiritual discussion) with the young Swami. Then Mr. Reddy bought him a ticket and sent him on his way to Poona.

The first yajña committee, composed of three men who had met with the Swami on his previous visit, had already planned an introductory talk for that very evening to introduce the content of the upcoming one hundred days Upaniṣad yajña. In his first talk, entitled 'Let Us Be Hindus', Swami Chinmayananda outlined a plan for the spiritual renaissance that has remained his goal throughout his lifelong mission. He was not leaving the contemplation of the Divine when he left the Himalayas. His dedication was to the service of the Divine – the Divine as revealed through humanity.

This dedication is clearly expressed in his first public address.

LET US BE HINDUS

December 23, 1951

A Hindu Swami to talk. A Hindu temple for the background. A crowded hall with a Hindu audience, and the subject for discussion, 'Let Us Be Hindus'. Strange! It sounds like a ridiculous paradox and a meaningless contradiction. I can very well see that you are surprised at the audacity of this sādhu (Swami)!

It has become a new fashion with the educated Hindu to turn up his nose and sneer in contempt at the very mention of his religion in any discussion. Personally, I too belong in my sympathies to these critics of our religion. But when this thoughtless team begins to declare that we will benefit ourselves socially and nationally by running away from our sacred religion, I have to pause to reconsider my own stand.

At the present state of moral, ethical and cultural degradation in our country, to totally dispose of religion would be making our dash to ruin even quicker. However decadent our religion may be, it is far better than having none at all. My proposal is that the wise thing would be for us to try and bring about a renaissance of Hinduism so that under its greatness – proved through many centuries – we may come to grow into the very heights of culture and civilization that was ours in the historical past.

No doubt, in India, Hinduism has come to mean nothing more than a bundle of sacred superstitions, or a certain way of dressing, cooking, eating, talking and so on. Our gods have fallen to the mortal level of administration officers at whose altars the faithful Hindu might pray in order to get special permits for the things he desires; that is, if he pays the required fee to the priest!

This degradation is not the product of any accidental and sudden historical upheaval. For the past two hundred years, Hinduism has remained an unwanted orphan without any patronage of the state and little encouragement of the rich. Once upon a time, the learned philosophers were rightly the advisers of the state. But then the quality of the adviser class (Brāhmaṇa) and the ruler class (Kṣatriya) deteriorated. By slowly putrefying themselves in the leprous warmth of luxury and power, they have taken us to the regrettable stage in which we find ourselves now. The general cry of the educated class is really against this un-religion. However, it is only the thoughtless, uninformed leaders who call this Hinduism.

Certainly, if Hinduism can breed for us only heartless lālās (shopkeepers), corrupt babus (clerks), cowardly men, loveless masters and faithless servants; if Hinduism can give us only a state of social living in which each man is put against his brother; if Hinduism can give us only starvation, nakedness and destitution; if Hinduism can encourage us only to plunder, to loot and to steal; if Hinduism can preach to us only intolerance, fanaticism, hard-heartedness and cruelty; then I too cry, 'Down, Down' with that Hinduism.

And yet the above is a realistic picture of the sad condition and plight into which the Hindu people as a nation have allowed themselves to fall. This is the tragic picture of the great Hindu disaster in present-day India.

But Hinduism is not this external show that we have learned to parade about in our daily life. Hinduism is a science of perfection. There is in it an answer to every individual, social, national or international problem. But unfortunately the religion that we have come to follow blindly is not the grand true Hinduism. It is only the treacherous scheme thrust upon us some time in the past by the selfish, arrogant, power-mad priest caste whose intention was to make us slaves of their plans and our own passions. The present-day Hindu ignoramuses prove the tragic success of these religious saboteurs. With their guidance we overlook the fundamental tenets in our sacred scriptures that are the very backbone of Hinduism. True Hinduism is the Sanātana-dharma of the Upaniṣads.

The Upaniṣads declare in unmistakable terms that in reality, man – at the peak of his achievement – is God himself. He is advised to live his day-to-day experiences in life in such a systematic and scientific way that, hour by hour, he is consciously cleansing himself of all the encrustation of imperfections that have gathered to conceal the beauty and divinity of the true eternal personality in him. The methods by which an individual can consciously purify and evolve by his self-effort to regain the status of his true nature are the content of Hinduism. Hinduism, in its vast amphitheatre, has been preserved and worshipped under the camouflage of the heavy descriptions contained in the Purāṇas (epics) and śāstras (scriptures), along with their commentaries of a thousand different interpretations. This overgrowth has so effectively come to conceal the real beauty and grandeur of the tiny temple of Truth that today the college educated illiterates, in their ignorance of the language and style of the ancient Sanskrit writers, miss the temple amidst its own festoons!

To inquire into the very textbooks of our religion with a view to understanding what Hinduism has to teach and how its message can be used to serve us as we face the problems of our daily life is the aim of our upcoming lectures. This one hundred day Upaniṣad jñāna-yajña is now proposed to commence on December 31, 1951, here in Poona.

Religion becomes dead and ineffectual if the seekers are not ready to live its ideals. For that matter is there any philosophy – political, social or cultural – that can take us to its promised land of success without our following its principles in our day-to-day living?

However great our culture might have been in the past, that dead glory, which has been reported in the pages of history books, is not going to help us in our present trials. If the barbarous cavemen of the unexplored jungles want to become as civilized as the man of modern nation, they cannot achieve this total revolution through mere discourses, or even through an exhaustive study of the literature describing the ways of modern civilized nations. They will have to know and then live the civilized values of life. A mere knowledge of the values will not help them. They can claim the blessing of their knowledge only if they are ready to live what they know. In order to live as civilized men, they will have to renounce completely their ways of uncivilized thinking and acting.

In fact without renunciation no progress is ever possible. We must renounce the thrills of our childhood games in order to grow to be young men of noble actions. Again, unless we renounce our youthful spirit, we cannot come to the reverence of old age.

Unless we are ready to renounce the low animal values of material life and replace them with the noble values of the true religious life, we cannot hope to gain the blessings of religion. A study of a cookbook, however thorough it might be, will not satisfy our hunger. No matter how long we meditate upon and repeat the name of a medicine, we cannot get the cure we need until we actually take the medicine. Similarly, the blessings of religion can be ours only when we are ready to live the recommended values. To condemn unpractised religion is as meaningless as those cavemen sitting around their open fire and querulously decrying advanced civilization.

During these one hundred days of the Upaniṣad jñāna-yajña, we shall be trying to discover the eternal happiness and bliss that is the essence of all true religions. In the light of the principles of Truth declared in the Upaniṣads, we shall be trying to get at the scientific significance of the various practices that are considered part of our religion. In a spirit of communal living for these one hundred days, we shall come to discover the science of perfection, the true essence of Hinduism.

Let us know what Hinduism is! Let us take an honest oath for ourselves, not only for our own sake, but for the sake of the entire world. That we shall, when once we are convinced of the validity of the eternal Truth, try honestly to live as consistently as possible the values advocated by this ancient and sacred religion.

Let us be Hindus, and thus build up a true Hindustāna (home of the Hindus) peopled with thousands of Śaṅkaras, hundreds of Buddhas, and dozens of Vivekanandas!

Om Om Om

18

The First Yajña

We only have to turn inward. Turn within – about face – and you are face to face with what you are seeking.
—Swami Chinmayananda, 1951.

The evening of the first Upaniṣad discourse arrived. The Swami quietly slipped in and took his seat on a simple mat on the temple floor. He was facing a group of eighteen people – some were sincere spiritual seekers, a few were curiosity seekers, and several were professional priests who came to criticize. The members of the committee who helped organize the yajña were rather disappointed at the small turnout; however, they were surprised to note that Swamiji[1] showed no sign of disappointment. In fact he was thrilled. Swami Tapovanam had warned him when he left Uttarkashi, "Consider yourself lucky if you find 10 or 15 listeners for Vedānta especially when you actually take up an Upaniṣad as a textbook. Scriptures have no charm at all for the ordinary folk." There were more than the predicted fifteen who were interested (for whatever reason), so he considered himself lucky indeed.

Swamiji began his lecture as if the entire hall were filled with interested students. He put aside all concerns for the failure or success of the project and spontaneously expounded upon the wonders of the scriptures. During the first seven days of the jñāna-yajña he introduced the terms and language of the Upaniṣads to prepare the audience for the first scriptural text, *Kenopaniṣad*. As the Swami's sonorous voice rang out with the eternal truths of

[1] For the remainder of the book, 'Swamiji' (the term of direct address to a Swami) will refer to Swami Chinmayananda.

life in a straightforward manner and modern language, a quiet hush settled over the listeners. His delivery was both wonderful and startling.

He invited the questioning mind to protest against tradition, to challenge ancient dogma and accept neither the words of the scriptures nor the interpretation of the sages on blind faith – the ideas were to be tested by individual contemplation, integration and experience. As he moved into the text of *Kenopaniṣad,* his vivacity and animated explanations erased the misgivings of even those who had come to scoff. He roused his listeners with thundering declarations, then coaxed them into blissful silence with subtle profundities. The Swami was answering questions about life that had long been in their hearts and minds; the questions that come to a thinking man observing his daily life – Is life only a pilgrimage between the office and home for the purpose of eating and sleeping? If so, is it worth it? Is there a true meaning of life?

The Swami also initiated a carefully designed programme of spiritual development to accompany the discourses. The one hundred days were to be used as an opportunity for intense sādhanā (discipline) even though the audience would be carrying on with their normal daily routines at home or in the office. The evening lecture for one and a half hours would be for the intellectual understanding of the divine goal. For the emotional personality, a continual chanting (akhaṇḍa kīrtana) for forty days of the Mahā Mantra[1] was begun after the first week of introductory classes. Participants signed up to commit to chant for at least one hour each day in front of a small altar – a small table with an oil lamp, incense and pictures of Lord Rāma and Lord Kṛṣṇa. In this way the chanting was unbroken except during the hours of the class. This daily repetition of the Lords' names developed concentration as well as increased devotion toward the spiritual goal in the hearts of the participants.

[1] Hare Kṛṣṇa, Hare Kṛṣṇa; Kṛṣṇa Kṛṣṇa, Hare Hare.
Hare Rāma, Hare Rāma; Rāma Rāma, Hare Hare.

In addition, the seekers were asked to carefully keep their attention on whatever action they were undertaking in their daily activities. Swamiji explained the value of this observing attitude to quiet and focus the mind. As added disciplines, the seekers were asked to abstain from sexual contact, movies and rich, spicy foods for the duration of the yajña, in order to aid in concentrating the mind toward the spiritual goal. This path of Vedānta was not a daily trip to hear a lecture, Swamiji emphasized, but a programme of conscious and dedicated living of daily life.

The Swami was striking a chord of truth in the heart of his students. The energy that has poured into the 'Divine Mission' from a host of selfless, dedicated workers even from the beginning of the mission has been both a barometer of, and a cause for its success. From the very first day, there were enthusiastic workers who had the foresight to record each talk in shorthand, so that the message could be shared with others. By the second week, a routine was maintained. Śrī S. Mani Iyer took down the lecture, transcribed it, and typed it out the following day. Then that same day Śrī S. Seshadri edited the manuscript and rushed it to the printer. Consequently, twenty-four hours after the lecture was completed, a copy of the talk was in print for distribution. Three or four daily discourses were then combined into booklets, named *Yajña Prasāda,* and were mailed out free of charge to anyone who requested them. In addition to the lectures, the publication included other items of interest concerning the yajña.

The first mailing list was made up of friends and relatives of the Poona audience, but requests for the publication started arriving in surprising numbers. An appeal for donations to cover the mailing costs had to be made. The budget was 1,000 rupees ($80 dollars) and the necessary amount began to arrive from all parts of India, Bombay, Delhi, Madras, and, naturally, the towns of Kerala.

When anyone came to see Swamiji during the day, they were immediately put to work, putting *Yajña Prasādas* into mailing wrappers, addressing them, and placing a stamp on them. Swamiji gave clear instructions, then observed closely to make sure they were carried out. Every wrapper had to be perfectly straight, every address clearly legible, every stamp upright, or he would instruct the person to redo it properly. "Every action must be done consciously and attentively. The attention of the mind is to be on the hand. Even with just this one practice you can become a great yogī," he would remind them.

The mail bags grew in number, but the first two copies of *Yajña Prasāda* from every batch were always addressed to 'Śrī Swami Tapovanam, Tapovanam Kutir, Uttarkashi' and to "Śrī Swami Sivananda, Ananda Kutir, Rishikesh' with the words, "With prostrations, Chinmaya", scrawled in Sanskrit across the title page. A reply addressed to Śrī Swami Chinmayanada, dated January 20, 1952, was quick in coming from Swami Sivananda.

> 'You have asked the aspirants to observe brahmācarya (celibacy), and a sāttvika diet (pure, natural food) and not to go to cinemas during the period of the grand yajña worship. It is very good; this is tapas (austerities).

> May Lord bless you and your work.'

Then a letter arrived from Swami Tapovanam dated January 22, 1952. His message was one of encouragement to the spiritual seekers of the yajña programme. There was no indication as to whether his feelings had changed toward the yajña plan itself, but he was generous in giving out his knowledge and blessings. After succinctly pointing out the transcendent goal to be reached, the causes for missing it, and the methods for reaching it, he closed the message with these loving words –

> 'Therefore, diligently and constantly practise with a long and intense pursuit the paths of devotion, selfless

action and yoga. One who has thus purified and disciplined his inner personality comes to experience intimately the Absolute Truth beyond all qualities, conditionings and limitations, and attains godhood.

May you all reach that eternal state of perfection and divinity in this very birth. May the blessings of the Upaniṣad ṛṣis be ever upon you all!

OM TAT SAT

.....

The frontispiece of the first *Yajña Prasāda* contained the only words with which Swamiji has ever spoken of his enlightenment –

.....

'Chinmaya's work is dedicated to the Śrutis (scriptures)

That told me what the Reality is;

To Swami Tapovanam Mahārāja of Uttarkashi

Who guided me to the end and pushed me into the Beyond;

And to Satgurudev Swami Sivananda Mahārāja of Rishikesh

Who showed me in his life how to live and act

In God as God!'

.....

These *Yajña Prasādas* from the Poona yajña were later combined to make up the textbook of the *Kenopaniṣad*. Therefore, its introduction and appendix is a record of the introductory talks given at the initial yajña in 1952 and the commentary section is the actual transcript of Swamiji's first talks on the scriptures.

The attendance at the yajña sessions grew along with the enthusiasm. By the end of the second week the walls of the Sri Hara Bhajana Samajam Temple could hardly hold the crowd. People also flocked to Swamiji's place of residence where he welcomed discussions each morning after breakfast and each afternoon at tea time. The enthusiastic crowd came to ask both spiritual and personal questions that had been bothering them. Sometimes it seemed as if the more questions they asked, the more they had, as new insights surfaced when each concept was made clear. These Hindus had indeed lost the meaning of their religion. The rituals of their grandparents were a mystery to them, as were the stories of the great sages of their epics. At last they were getting some answers. Swamiji always had light, comic parables for every situation to bring home the truth of the matter. He kept everyone laughing at themselves and their own foolish misconceptions.

There was a group of young students at his first yajña who soon began to shoulder many secretarial and organizational tasks in helping Swamiji in his work. In one of the daily satsaṅgas with Swamiji, one girl ventured a simple question, "Why is it that, even though we know a child is innocent, we are attached to the clean one and are repelled from a dirty one?" Someone in the group immediately criticized her for asking such an unimportant question to a Swami. "No! No question is unimportant", Swamiji corrected him. "These girls are just beginning to learn about the nature of the mind. They have to start with simple questions."

The Swami's residence had been arranged at the home of Mr. Jaya Bala, only four blocks away from the temple that was serving as the yajña hall. Ten minutes before the talk a large group would assemble to accompany Swamiji to the temple. He would walk there in a dignified manner, straight and tall, yet at such a speed that it was hard to keep up with him. Beginning with that first yajña, he had strict rules about starting exactly on the minute of the appointed hour. After the talk started if anyone caused a disturbance, he would stop the talk and ask the person to please consider the others who were trying to listen. "You may already understand what I am explaining, or perhaps you find the talk uninteresting and want to leave, but please have the human kindness to keep still for the sake of the others who are listening."

As the yajña continued, Swamiji incorporated several new elements into the programme. Swami Rampremi arrived from Ananda Kutir to lead bhajanas before the daily lectures to bring the mind to a peaceful state after the day's activities; a peaceful mind was better prepared for the subtle ideas presented in the lectures. At the end of the forty days of continuous chanting, which coincided with the midpoint of the 100-day yajña, a four-day traditional Vaidika havana ritual was initiated. For the first three days of the ceremony, Brāhmaṇa priests chanted the entire four Vedas and made certain prescribed offerings of clarified butter (ghī).

To conclude the ceremony, on the fourth day, the entire crowd of students of Vedānta sat in a circle around the ritual fire for the chanting of the scriptures. To the surprise of the Brāhmaṇa priests, everyone in the audience, including the women, businessmen and lower caste students, joined in the chanting. Sanskrit was no longer the personal language of the priests. Swamiji then carefully explained the symbolism of the distinct parts of the ritual.

At the end of the ritual, each person was to make an offering of nine different types of grain, symbolizing the many varieties of ignorance and wrong values. As the participants circled the fire pit, each one was to imagine that the grains held all of their negative mental qualities. When they threw the grains into the fire, these tendencies would be destroyed, leaving a clean, purified mind in which the divine essence could reflect. After the clear explanation, everyone solemnly rose and began to circle the altar while chanting in unison the Mahā Mṛtyuñjaya Mantra to invoke long life and good health. When the altar had been circled three times, each person tossed the grains into the flames, then returned to the mat to meditate.

Swamiji realized that the revitalization of the culture meant the proper use of these traditional practices of rituals, chanting and pilgrimage. He too had left these customs in his youth, but after understanding the whole of the religion, he realized that these practices had a valuable purpose. The rituals done with single pointed attention served to concentrate the mind to make it capable of meditation.

The ash that remains from a havana ritual was considered a sacred symbol of the dust to which all matter returns. Each participant took home a packet of ash to smear on the forehead each morning before meditation as a reminder of the attitude created in the ritual. Also the ash was believed to have absorbed a unique vibration because of the four days of chanting of the Vedas.

Everyone was watching the Swami – did he practise what he preached? His daily life was the epitome of discipline. He had only one meal a day, at lunch, and only one cup of coffee or tea with a piece of fruit at breakfast and dinner. In his every action, there was a certain attention to detail as if no task were too small for his undivided attention. But the question was bound to come up, "Swamiji, why do you smoke?" The courageous one who asked the question was quickly joined by others who admitted that the cigarettes had caused them some misgivings also.

In fact, Swami Sivananda had already mentioned this habit to Chinmaya. Someone had gone to Rishikesh and reported to him – "Your disciple, Chinmaya, is giving very good lectures. The audience is enthralled, but he is giving a bad impression with his smoking." Using a humorous play on words, Swami Sivananda wrote to his disciple. "The Upaniṣad yajña (knowledge ritual) will be greatly improved if you stop your own personal yajña (fire ritual)." Chinmaya promised his Guru, "With your blessings I will stop smoking after this yajña." He had smoked for so many years that he assumed that quitting would take his undivided attention. The middle of the yajña was not the moment to risk a struggle.

But nature intervened, for, Swamiji came down with typhoid. There was a five-day pause in the Upaniṣad discourses to enable him to rest and overcome the effects of the fever. During this time he did not smoke; the world with its cigarettes were far away from his consciousness. When he recovered, he did not take up the habit again. "I thought about how it would appear to me if I saw someone discussing spiritual philosophy while puffing away on a cigarette, so I stopped," he explained.

The freedom of a sannyāsī is such that he desires and expects nothing from the world. He has no vested interests, no loyalties, no obligations to anyone. He is free to treat all equally. And it was with equality that Swamiji treated the audience without regard for their profession or status, except for an occasional extra criticism of the Brāhmaṇa priests. And the criticism was not entirely undeserved. Although South India, with its educated people and its intellectual approach to religion, was the logical place for the first Upaniṣad yajña, it was also the stronghold of the Brāhmaṇa caste with their self-appointed rights to be the only ones who could read or study the scriptures. And to teach the sacred texts in English, the language of the foreign devils... unheard of! Regularly, Swamiji received letters and visits from these misguided priests. They had little reason to protest, for, had they been aware of their own history and scriptures, they would have known that many of the great sages of India had been of the Kṣatriya (king-warrior) caste, including Rāma, Kṛṣṇa and the Buddha. The scriptures also contain stories of priests seeking out Enlightened kings to learn the Knowledge of knowledge.

So Swamiji would criticize the Brāhmaṇas, comparing them to a donkey that carried gold on its back. Others might make use of the gold, but the donkey would not benefit. Many Brāhmaṇas came to listen only to be able to criticize. But among them were those who had developed a keen, alert mind from their spiritual disciplines and study of the scripture; therefore, they perceived the essence of the message of Vedānta and became diligent workers and loyal supporters of the 'Divine Mission'.

Many other Brāhmaṇas, however, quoted some verses from the scriptures in their determination not to give up any of their territory. One of their scriptural-based objections was that Vedānta should only be taught in the last stage of life, that is, to sannyāsīs. This meant that everyone should first spend their life as a householder (gṛhasthāśrama) performing all the daily and special rites prescribed in the ritual section of the Vedas. The Vaidika seers had appreciated the great mystery of life and envisioned the participation in these daily rituals as a method to imbue life with a sacred quality, thereby making man aware of life's rhythms. Then each person was to spend period in retirement, studying and practising the mental exercises and meditations of the Āraṇyaka section of the Vedas. The rituals and mental exercises gradually refined the mind; only then was the seeker fit for the highest Knowledge (*Brahmavidyā*). This preparation was necessary, so that one had the purified mind to be able to see first hand the sacredness of life and one's relation to the great mystery.

But this approach was not a definitive interpretation. The question had been discussed thoroughly by Ādi Śaṅkarācārya in his commentary on the *Brahmasūtras*. He clearly states that this knowledge of Brahman was to be studied by whosoever desired to know Brahman . No doubt it was a sign of the genius of the ancient Vaidika sages to prescribe certain rituals and mental exercises for the ordinary people, so that they could concentrate and purify their minds during their daily lives, instead of giving them a long list of don'ts, which seemed to be the central feature of most religions. But that was not to mean, argued Ādi Śaṅkarācārya, that one who already possessed the quality of mind aimed for in the exercises had to wait until the age of retirement to begin study. He had begun his study of the Vedāntic texts when he was a teenager. The second text to be taught by Swamiji in a yajña, *Kaṭhopaniṣad*, had been taught by Lord Death (Dharma Rāja) to a boy, who was thought to be in his teens.

To contribute to the necessary mental refinement, Swamiji gave personal initiations into the practice of meditation every

Thursday morning before sunrise. "Have a bath. Take your usual cup of tea. If you come with a completely empty stomach, you'll only be meditating on the rumblings of your stomach," Swamiji instructed the initiates. He would talk individually to each of the thirty to forty people who lined up at the front door. First he would ask them if they had already established a special connection with a deity or a mantra. If not, he gave them a general mantra, often the one associated with the region they were from or his own childhood mantra, Om Namaḥ Śivāya. To assist them in achieving a habit of meditation, he would have a ten to fifteen minute period of meditation at the end of each Upaniṣad class.

Swamiji exuded an aura of love and confidence in all his activities, a holiness not of a quiet contemplative, morose demeanor, but of a dynamic, joyful enthusiasm that presented a model of what a life lived by precise disciplines and spiritual insights can be. One moment he might be cheering on someone applying for a job, the next, tenderly sympathizing and uplifting a bereaved mother, or assuring a grandmother that the Lord always heard her prayers. But in every situation he always pointed his listeners to a fuller, freer attitude to guide their lives.

19

The Preceptor – Ādi Śaṅkarācārya

Whenever political tyranny comes to a community the importance of the individuals is eliminated as the tyrant elevates himself. Or, as in modern politics, the leaders glorify the state or the nation, and the individual faces are completely ignored. When man thus becomes faceless, he no longer has any enthusiasm to live a noble life. He doesn't bother to put forth the effort to fight against his base, lower impulses. He just relaxes and lives an animal existence because he feels that his actions do not contribute to the country.

It was in such a period of decadent Hinduism in the eighth century that the revivalist, the eminent, saintly philosopher, Ādi Śaṅkarācārya, appeared. His contribution to the Advaita philosophy is to be praised both for its noble content and its timeliness in history. It is this background that has given his accomplishments relevance in our disintegrated society of today. National revival, economic development and social justice are not possible because there is neither cohesion in the community nor balance in the individual personality.

Ādi Śaṅkarācārya was an extremely effective missionary of his era. He was able to revive the old heritage by expressing the ancient ideas in the language of his day, so that they were grasped and understood. This process has been repeated time after time in India. Whenever there is national disintegration, we have always returned to the sources of our heritage, and a revival movement began because each individual, to the extent that he was able to appreciate the subtle, great climes of thought that our forefathers had attained, started respecting himself and revering the divinity within. Thus, when the importance of the individual is recognized, each individual thereafter strives to live a nobler life.

—-Swami Chinmayananda, 1968.

The future Ādi Śaṅkarācārya was born to devout parents in the quiet village of Kalady on the banks of the Pūrṇā river (now Periyar) in the region now named Kerala. At the birth of this first child, his Brāhmaṇa parents were well advanced in age. They had remained childless even though they had attempted to enhance fertility, as well produce a healthy child, by practicing sexual abstention for long periods, as prescribed by the scriptures. As a last resort, they made a pilgrimage to a famous Śiva temple to pray for a son. Afterwards, his mother had a vision in which Lord Śiva appeared and told her that he would grant her wish for a son, but that she would have to make a choice, a son of long years, but of dull wit, or a son of few years, but of a brilliant intellect. The pious couple prayed to Lord Śiva for the second choice.

In response to the devotion and sincerity of this couple, Lord Śiva incarnated as their son, Śaṅkara (a South Indian name for Śiva). He was such a precocious child that he had completed his formal education by the age of eight. His father died in that year, leaving the son to the care of his mother.

Even at this early age, the child Śaṅkara had definite tendencies of an ascetic nature. Due to the understanding he had gained from study of the scriptures and his own innate capacity of discrimination, he wished to become a sannyāsī and dedicate himself totally to the quest for the Absolute Truth. But his devout mother was too attached to him to consider such a proposition and started to make arrangements for a future bride to entice the boy into a worldly life. However, Śaṅkara made his own plans.

One morning he was taking his daily bath in the river while his mother was washing clothes on the nearby stones. Suddenly, a crocodile appeared and caught the boy by the leg. "Mother, mother! My time has come. Please give your permission for my taking the renunciation vows," cried the boy. His mother could not refuse. The taking of these vows before an imminent death was a traditional practice. Quickly, she yielded her consent, and the boy solemnly repeated the vows. Then suddenly and mysteriously, the crocodile disappeared as quickly as it had appeared.

Therefore, as a renunciate, Śaṅkara left his home and mother at eight years of age to look for a spiritual Guru. Travelling north he found a renowned Teacher, Śrī Govinda Bhagavatpāda, living in a cave near the banks of the Narmada river with a group of learned disciples. He approached the Guru, prostrated, and requested that he be officially initiated into sannyāsa. Although he had not complied with the injunction for the completion of the first three stages of life, the Guru intuitively perceived the qualifications of the boy and performed the formalities.

After his initiation, Śaṅkara remained at the hermitage of the Guru, receiving instruction in all the foremost books of Vedānta. During this period, there was a terrible flooding of the Narmada river that threatened destruction of the small villages that lined its banks. The villagers were panic-stricken, but the compassionate Śaṅkara recited a mantra and placed a water pot on the earth to contain the abundant water and avert the disaster. This miracle was regarded as an enactment of a prophecy by the Sage Atri. The one who was able to stop the floods of the Narmada would be the proper person to write a commentary on the terse aphorisms of Sage Vyāsa's *Brahmasūtras.*

Perceiving the qualities of his disciple and having seen the revelatory sign, Śrī Govinda Bhagavatpāda authorised Śaṅkara to go to Varanasi, the intellectual centre of Hinduism, and expound the meaning of the *Brahmasūtras* to its scholars. The lad went there and expounded the ideas of all the Vedāntic texts with a clear and unfailing logic. Several brilliant scholars of the scriptures were so impressed with his knowledge that they became his disciples.

One morning after their bath in the sacred Ganga, he and his disciples were winding their way through the narrow streets when a Cāṇḍāla (untouchable) approached them. According to custom the Brāhmaṇa had the right of way, so, without thinking, Śrī Śaṅkara ordered the Cāṇḍāla to step aside. The untouchable asked him to be more specific – Did Śaṅkara want him to put aside the body, which was of equal composition in all people, or the Self, which was one and all-pervading, therefore impossible to move. Śrī Śaṅkara immediately realized that this was no ordinary man; it was the Lord Śiva himself who had come in the disguise of an untouchable to teach him the valuable lesson of practising the concept of non-duality (Advaita) in the mundane world. Recognising the untouchable as a form of Lord Śiva, Śaṅkara prostrated to him and spontaneously sang a hymn of praise in which he declared that one who has realized the oneness behind all forms is a Master, whether he be a Brāhmaṇa or a Cāṇḍāla.

Śrī Śaṅkara then set out for Badarinath in the Himalayas to meet Śrī Gauḍapāda[1], the most revered and accomplished Guru of his own Teacher, and to receive his blessings. Upon his return to Varanasi he started the work of formally writing the commentaries of the Prasthāna Traya. During their composition, Sage Vyāsa, the compiler of the Vedas, appeared and challenged Śaṅkara to defend his exposition of Vyāsa's *Brahmasūtras*. The debate between the two went on for hours touching the minutest details of the sūtras. The disciples who were listening wearied, but the two debaters never fatigued. Finally one of the disciples interrupted them by interjecting that there would be no peace if Lord Viṣṇu, in the form of Vyāsa, and the Lord Śiva, incarnated as Śaṅkara, kept up these endless arguments. Sage Vyāsa then granted his approval of Śaṅkara's commentaries, blessed the young man, and bestowed a boon – an extension of his life from

[1] The author of the *Māṇḍūkya Kārikā.*

sixteen to thirty-two years to enable him to travel around Bhārata and spread the concepts of Vedānta to the people, particularly the scholars.

Śrī Śaṅkara travelled throughout the land, teaching, founding and consecrating temples, then establishing four institutions for the preservation of the Hindu scriptures – Dwarka on the western border, Badarinath in the Himalayas to the north, Puri on the eastern coast of Orissa, and Sringeri in the south. He took on a unique mission, for, he was not a teacher of the masses, but of the philosophers and religious teachers. He set out to enlighten the preachers. In that era the religious climate was such that spiritual Teachers and monks welcomed debate. The vanquished was then obligated to give his allegiance to the philosophy of the winner.

On one such occasion, Ādi Śaṅkara was to debate a famous scholar, Maṇḍana Miśra, known as 'the jewel of scholars'. His wife, Bhāratī, was designated to act as referee. Quite an intellect in her own right, she placed a garland of flowers around each of the contestants and announced that the one whose flowers had not withered at the end of the debate would be proclaimed the winner. Both scholars exhibited a profound knowledge of the Vedas and the dialectical match lasted for eighteen days. On the last day, Ādi Śaṅkara's garland was quite fresh, while the other one had begun to wilt. In a last effort to save face for her husband, Bhāratī challenged the philosopher to a debate on the art of lovemaking. She had discovered an area in which the celibate monk was totally unschooled. He requested, and received, forty days to prepare himself for the contest.

By coincidence, an old king of a nearby kingdom was at the point of death. Just at the moment of his expiration, Ādi Śaṅkarācārya, also an accomplished Yogī, was able to enter the king's body so that he could use it as a vehicle for experience. The young maidens of the extensive harem were delighted at the sudden recovery of their master especially since he appeared more virile and vigorous than ever before. For over a month, Śaṅkara experienced first hand the intricacies of the sensual arts in such a manner that, as reported in some accounts, his disciples had to search him out to remind him of his actual identity. In any case, he did return to conquer Bhāratī in debate. Accordingly, she and her husband became Śaṅkara's disciples.

Ādi Śaṅkarācārya is credited with the final defeat of Buddhism in India because he vanquished in debate all leading Buddhist philosophers with his infallible logic. With this method, many great spiritual leaders became disciples and teachers of the Advaita non-dual philosophy of the Upaniṣads – Man is in essence, God.

20

Madras Yajña

This is a jñāna-yajña wherein we offer oblations of our own wrong notions and values of life into the well lit fires of our own discrimination and will.

—-Swami Chinmayananda, April 26, 1953.

The Poona yajña was a great success, indicating the divine providence behind Swamiji's approach to teaching the scriptures. Before it had ended, he had talked to people from several other cities about possibilities for the next yajña. First though, he needed to spend some time regaining the strength depleted by the attack of typhoid fever. Bombay (now Mumbai) was close by, so he went there to stay with Śrī P. M. Narayanaswami, a disciple of Ramana Maharshi. Śrī Narayanaswami and a group of Ramana's disciples were planning to publish a monthly booklet, *The Call Divine*, with articles by Ramana Maharshi and other sages. Swamiji helped them with the planning and editing of articles. He continued to assist them for several years until his own work grew to the point that he had no extra time. During his mission he would continue to support the work of other spiritual Teachers when the opportunity arose.

As soon as his health permitted, Swamiji set out northward toward the Himalayas, for, the monsoon would soon make travel difficult. Even while en route he did not miss an occasion to carry on with his mission. He stopped a few days in Delhi for satsaṅga at the home of the Shroff family. In between fielding questions from their friends and neighbours, he suggested a yajña in Delhi, the home of the new breed of Indian intellectuals – the perfect spot for a jñāna-yajña, 'a ritual of wisdom'. In his conscientious manner, he described step by step the different phases of the yajña in Poona – discourses on the Upaniṣads, chanting, a havana ritual and meditation classes. He outlined the necessary steps in organizing for the series, an easy to reach location that would accommodate several hundred people, publicity arrangements, facilities and funds for the printing and mailing of the *Yajña Prasāda*. Realizing that such an opportunity to hear this ancient philosophy expounded was indeed rare, everyone in the gathering were enthusiastic.

Leaving Delhi he then boarded a train for the twenty-four hour ride across the planes to Rishikesh. There he received a warm welcome from Swami Sivananda, who bubbled with joy as Chinmaya told him the details of the success of the yajña. Swami Sivananda said that he was particularly impressed with the idea of recording the lectures, compiling them into the *Yajña Prasāda,* and sending them out so that the message would go to a larger audience. "This kind of innovation is necessary if we are to succeed in bringing the truths of the Upaniṣads to the modern world where this wisdom is so urgently needed," he enthusiastically concluded. That evening a short film of one yajña class was shown.[1] Swami Sivananda was very pleased and encouraged by the success of the Poona discourses, but he did advise that one hundred days was too long. He felt that shorter doses at regular intervals would be more beneficial. People would need time to contemplate and assimilate the ideas of Vedānta, which were so new to them.

"There are many disciples here, but no one so daring and courageous as Chinmaya," he proclaimed to others with a smile and a deep thoughtful look in his eyes, as he watched Chinmaya fade into the distance as he hiked down to the village to board the bus for Uttarkashi.

Chinmaya had corresponded with Swami Tapovanam, so he knew that his Guru at least accepted the success of the yajña at Poona, even if he did not approve. The tension mounted around

[1] The present whereabouts of the film is unknown.

Tapovanam Kutir, for students knew that Chinmaya was arriving soon. They were curious to see the Master's reaction to this rebel disciple. His days of strenuous hiking over, the elderly Swami Tapovanam daily sat on his veranda and watched the world go by. Whoever came to his feet, he considered sent directly by the Lord and he treated the person with one hundred percent of his love and consideration. When Chinmaya arrived, the Guru sat quietly listening to the optimistic, bubbling report of his disciple, nodding with seeming approval, but he gave no opinion, nor advice. Later, he commented to others, "A little ambition is good, but this young man wants to carry the whole Himalaya."

Chinmaya continued to travel up to Uttarkashi each monsoon season (June-August) to be with his Guru. Swami Govindagiri, a fellow disciple who remained with Swami Tapovanam, commented of Chinmaya, "One thing that I can definitely say during the entire time I have known him, Chinmaya is fearless. Actually, when you have one quality totally developed, all other positive qualities come to you. And when that quality is dedicated to a higher ideal, then the whole universe comes to aid you."

As the rains slowed down in August, Chinmaya left the cool peaceful Himalayan valley for Madras via Delhi and Bombay. He also stopped in Poona en route to meet with and encourage the seekers there. Some had encountered obstacles in applying the spiritual ideals in their daily lives, or in practising meditation. With sincere and careful attention to each individual, he brought each one out of his particular confusion. Others arrived early in the morning to be initiated into the use of a mantra for meditation.

A happy, but tearful, crowd gathered at the Poona train station to send Swamiji off to Madras (now Chennai). He had several relatives there, so he had a place to stay while he organized a yajña. Once in Madras, he immediately met with some sincere folk, several of whom he had met in Poona. They willingly formed a committee and took on the responsibility of organizing a yajña. With a plan confirmed, Swamiji was free to look into other possibilities, such as a request from several families in Palghat to have a spiritual camp there. Swamiji wrote them to proceed with the plans and started the journey over to Kerala.

Once in Kerala, he stopped at his father's home. His father and stepmother called in their friends and neighbours for satsaṅga. Swami Chinmayananda might have renounced his connections in the world, but he would always be son to his father, who was beaming with pride as he listened to the clear, precise answers Swamiji gave to every question, both spiritual and mundane. His son had found his place in the world after all. Kurupath Menon was unusually peaceful and content after this visit, which those who knew him attributed to his satisfaction at seeing his eldest son happy and successful. He died soon after the visit.

Some fifty seekers attended the Palghat sādhanā camp. There were daily lectures from the scriptures, group meditations in the early morning, and lengthy sessions of questions and answers in the afternoon. These satsaṅgas were a principal part of the schedule everywhere Swamiji went, as the people were eager to understand the meaning of their religion and culture. Those who already knew the scriptures came to perceive the true meaning of the words, some of which they had heard for years without questioning. Many in Kerala were very devoted and started to idolize the Swami because of his great wisdom and charisma. He explained to them, "You must not surrender to a wandering Swami, for, it could result in a disaster or at least some despairing moments for the student if he should learn some negative news about the Teacher. Since the student had not been present, he could not make a correct assessment and might lose faith. You surrender to God only. He will always live up to your expectations!"

Then Swamiji returned to Madras. He had expected most of the organizing for the yajña there to have been completed, but when he arrived he found that hardly anything had been accomplished. The leader of the group was laid up with a broken leg; the others were awaiting transportation. The committee had decided that they needed a car to carry out all the logistics of the organization. "What! Buy a car! A Swami doesn't have the money, or interest, in buying a car!" Swamiji assured them emphatically. He then dismissed them from service and proceeded on his own.

In Madras he stayed with an uncle, Kuttikrishna Menon, who offered to help find a suitable place for the talks. Mr. Menon was not free from his duties as an attorney until mid-afternoon. Afterward, he and Swamiji would go out to look for a lecture hall, starting with the most logical places, particularly the temples. As it turned out, however, the Brāhmaṇa orthodox priests who presided over the temples were not receptive. From one end of Madras to the other, the response was the same. No priest would consider having a non-Brāhmaṇa talk on the scriptures, especially the difficult Upaniṣads; further, none would allow the sacred scriptures to be spoken in English.

Madras was a tradition conscious state. Its pride in its economic and cultural strength had been emphasized by the events of the previous several years. At the end of 1951, a nationwide election had been held in India. Yet the winner of the election, Jawaharlal Nehru, was not sworn in as the first Prime Minister of constitutional democracy until 13 May 1952. It had taken six months to retrieve all the votes and count them. The final results showed that Nehru's Congress party had won an overwhelming majority of seats in Parliament except in four states, one of which was Madras. Having the second largest port in India, the Madrasis knew that they could be economically independent.

The people of Madras also considered themselves culturally unique. At that time India contained thirteen major languages and innumerable dialects. After much protest and mediation, Tamil Nadu was made a separate state with the boundaries consistent with the speakers of Tamil. But this compensation had not been adequate, now there was a movement to purge the state of all aspects of foreign influence – Muslim, British and even the Hindu Āryan – to establish the nation of Draviḍasthāna (place of the

Dravidians), based on the ancient traditions of the area's original inhabitants.

And it might have happened if it had not been for an inexplicable and sudden attack by the Communist Chinese in 1957. They had crossed the Himalayas into Northern India, staying long enough to seize prisoners, then to retreat across the border. The defeat shocked the country into realising that freedom and nationhood could not be taken casually. The ideas of secession collapsed in the resulting surge of national patriotism.

But in 1953, the political unrest was in full force and could have contributed to the unyielding attitude of the Hindu Brāhmaṇa priests in Madras. Not considered to be Dravidians, these Brāhmaṇas seemed loathe to relinquish any authority during the embattled times.

Swamiji spent each day in his room, in study, contemplation and meditation, until his uncle returned from work. However, their evening forays, even to the surrounding villages, produced no results since any temple of adequate size for the yajña was lorded over by a Brāhmaṇa priest.

The only relief from this unfruitful searching came from a group of young students from the medical school who asked Swamiji to speak at their college. Then, just when it looked like Madras would have to be put on hold, a person who was an acquaintance of the Menon family and enthusiast of the yajña idea came forward with a suggestion – a Muslim friend had a large, vacant estate. He would be willing to allow the use of it for the forty-one days of the lecture series. There was just one problem – the palace was known to be haunted. "Well, I've never seen a ghost. This looks like a good opportunity," quipped the Swami, as he gratefully accepted the offer.

So it happened that the Hindu spiritual renaissance was continued through the generosity of a Muslim landlord. A group of ten relatives and their friends assembled at Arni Palace (now the Children's Hospital, Egmore) that first evening at 6:30 p.m. on April 26, 1953, a year after the completion of the Poona yajña. In his introductory talks, Swamiji gave an inspiring analysis of the evolution of life and the nature of experience as developed by Vedānta philosophy.

Afterwards, the disappointed look on the faces of his assistants was obvious to Swamiji. "Don't worry, others will come tomorrow night. You'll see!" Swamiji encouraged them. "You have done your part, now leave the rest on the Lord." The flickering kerosene lanterns did call up images of ghosts as the small group dissolved into the dark night to rest for the next day's activities.

The next two evenings Swamiji discussed the personality of man and the five sense organs through which he was able to perceive the world. Through ensuing days the Teacher slowly moved his analysis toward the subtler realms of man's nature. He interspersed the logic with practical examples of strategies to deal with the rebellious mind as it performs its eternal dance of likes and dislikes.

To assist with the secretarial work, Swamiji had been joined by Shusheela Mudliar and Devaki Naik from Poona and Śrī Shukali, who came from Delhi. He would be a loyal assistant to Swamiji at every yajña in the capacity of secretary-treasurer until his death in 1959. At noon and after the evening talk, one of the local families would bring a meal in for Swamiji and the three assistants.

After everyone had eaten, the family who contributed the food, along with others who had stayed after the talks, would gather around to ask their questions. However, when Swamiji uttered three loud Oms, it was the signal that satsaṅga was over. Then everyone would immediately rush off. As time went on, the crowd and the interest grew, so the satsaṅgas were lasting later and later. "Mahārāja", as Śrī Shukali was affectionately called by Swamiji, was concerned that Swamiji should have adequate rest, so he set an alarm clock for 11 p.m. as a signal for everyone to leave. Even then, someone in the group would manage to grab the clock when Mahārāja was not looking and set it back in order to gain additional precious time with Swamiji.

Among the group would always be some young college students from Madras University, determined to argue their materialistic point of view. Swamiji always encouraged the discussions. He would give them careful explanations with practical examples taken right from their own experience. They were quite surprised – how could a Swami know so much about their weaknesses?

One day a young man, who came to meet the Swami, took Swamiji completely by surprise. After boasting that "in my house we have been reading the *Bhagavad-gītā* everyday for the past twenty-eight years," he went on to say that he did not know a single line of the *Gītā* or anything of its contents. Of course, Swamiji was dumbfounded. In utter despair he asked, "Why. . . how is it?. . . Twenty-eight years?" Then came the explanation – It wasn't that he or any member of his family had read the *Gītā* or even listened to it. They had arranged for a Brāhmaṇa priest to come in daily for a small fee and read the *Gītā* in its original Sanskrit for the sake of their spiritual upliftment.

No doubt this 'convenient and comfortable Hinduism' was useful in the modern world – but only to priest who collected the fees – pointed out Swamiji. He added that all the Vaidika texts constantly declare that only one who has done worship for himself is considered fit for spiritual life. Scripture reading and rituals do have a place in spiritual practice. When performed with devotion and without any worldly desires – they have a unique capacity of integrating the personality of the seeker. However, for real results, continued Swamiji, one had to take the ideas of the scriptures and apply them in his life.

In an introductory letter of the Madras *Yajña Prasāda*, the editor, Śrī Keshavlal Thakharwadi, expressed the sentiments of the yajña participants at that time.

Many of us have, indeed, attended regularly many satsaṅgas. However, for the number of practical tips we are getting here, this yajña is an unprecedented opportunity for everyone of us. This is the general opinion expressed by the members of the audience. Every speech of Śrī Swamiji is an exhaustive treatment of the subject chosen for the day, replete with examples from everyday life, riveted with perfect logic and good sense. Ever practical and always scientific, Śrī Swamiji is proving himself to be the final answer to the materialists' turn to atheism!

Within a week the crowd had grown so large that the veranda of the palace had to be abandoned for a roomy canvas shelter, complete with platform and microphone, that was erected on the spacious palace grounds. Of the some fifty daily attendees, many were recruited by friends, but others were out for an evening stroll, as is common in tropical countries. While walking, they spotted something interesting going on and went over to investigate. A spiritual gathering with an orange clad speaker of regal bearing, punctuated with gales of laughter was a real attention getter. Passers-by stood entranced at the back of the canvas shelter as they watched the animated enthusiasm of the Swami as he explained the truths of life. Then they returned the next day with friends and family to get a front row seat.

Śrī V. Nagarajan expressed the feelings of many in the audience –

"Every evening at half past five, whether I was at home or in the office, I would have a great urge to run to my room, get out of my long pants, dress in the traditional Indian dhoti, and hasten to the palace. Never had I found, nor can I ever find elsewhere, the effect perfect silence and discipline can produce. Precisely at 6

> p.m. – one could set his watch accordingly – Swamiji would enter the platform. At his appearance a feeling arose in each one of us that was inexpressible and incomparable, a joy greater than when one meets a beloved family member after a long absence.
>
> ....

Two aspects of his discourses endeared him to all who listened. First, he was presenting the highest philosophy of the scriptures that had been entirely unknown to the general populace. Second, he was presenting it in such a way that they could understand the ideas and apply them to their own lives in the immediate circumstances, not sometime after retirement. His down to earth examples often would propel his audience into tears from laughter."

To introduce the commentary of the first verse of *Muṇḍaka-upaniṣad*, he told the following story –

> ....
>
> 'Gopal Iyer is a poor insignificant member of a big family. In his own house, he is a victim of the mischief of even his youngest son. Now Mr. Iyer earns his livelihood on a paltry pay that he gets as a police constable in the local precinct. Thus, he has, in fact, more than one personality operating through him – the anxious father, the unhappy husband and the mighty policeman!
>
> Now, when exactly does the ineffectual Gopal Iyer become the mighty 'hand of law' as a policemen, a dread to the mischief-makers, a phantom for our criminals, and an ever present threat to every rash driver? Certainly, the policeman in him is not there when he is wrapped in dhoti and shirt, lolling about on the veranda of his house, persecuted by the pranks of his son, or bullied by the demands of his wife. The moment Mr. Gopal Iyer gets into his khaki shorts

and puts on his red turban – out of that very same personality – the policeman appears. Thereafter, he is a potent power to be reckoned with by every citizen!'

Similarly, my friends, each one of us is not merely an ineffectual, fearful, ever sighing, limited creature, but has within himself a personality supremely omnipotent, fearless, unlimited, all blissful and godly. Just as Gopal Iyer becomes a policeman by process of self invocation, and thereafter the policeman forgets to act and live the weaknesses and limitations of the father and husband, so too can we, through meditation and prayer, invoke the Divine in us and come to transcend our own personality with its defects and limitations. Meditation and prayer are the techniques by which we tune ourselves to the highest perfection and thereby come to invoke in ourselves a greater perfection of both the mind and intellect.

After two weeks of classes, with the introduction complete, Swamiji began leading a meditation immediately after the lecture. Starting with the chanting of Om, the crowd would then be quietly guided into what he termed 'the most sacred vocation of mankind'. The first step was leaving the awareness of the gross body. Then japa (repetition of a mantra) with the use of the mālā beads was carefully explained. He forcefully challenged the group –

"Start today! Right now put this sacred practice into your daily routine! There is no moment more auspicious than here and now for spiritual practice. Japa is an easy method for people like us, kicked about and bullied by the world both within and without."

The practices of the havana ritual and continuous chanting for two weeks, used with success in Poona, were repeated here.

They were a success – with the exception of a small mishap. One evening after satsaṅga, no one showed up for the continual chanting. Shusheela and Devaki noticed and filled in for the hour, but still no one appeared for two more sessions. They would have been stuck there even longer, but Mahārāja awoke, recognized the girls' voices and went to awaken the person assigned to the 2 a.m. slot. The people on the night shift slept on the veranda to avoid the inconvenience of getting up and driving in the middle of the night.

The next day Swamiji expressed his concern in an angry tone that these two young girls were caused to be up so late, for, they had many responsibilities during the day and needed their sleep. Every morning they arose when they heard Swamiji's three hearty Om echoing down the veranda at 3 a.m. They would quickly jump up, bathe and dress, then spend the entire day helping him with his correspondence or working on the *Yajña Prasāda,* which was sent out daily, including to the prior yajña audience in Poona. In that evening class, after explaining the incident of the previous night, Swamiji challenged them, "Do you people in Madras want this japa or not. It is for your benefit. If this happens again, the japa will stop."

On the last day of the japa, there was a procession through the city with everyone chanting the mahā mantra together. Everyone marched in neat files with Swamiji walking along beside them, moving from front to back to make sure that everyone was giving attention to his own action. Every action could be considered a discipline if done with the correct attitude of conscious attention. By the time the procession wound its way through the narrow streets lined with whitewashed houses to the Arni Palace, the group had almost doubled in size as strangers were caught up by the joyful mood and joined the parade.

During his previous trip to Rishikesh, Swamiji had collected two large pots of water from the Ganga and had sealed them. These pots had sat beside the altar to be sanctified by the continuous chanting for the two weeks. Ten minutes before the close of the yajña, these pots were brought out and Swamiji walked up and down the aisles sprinkling the sacred water over the heads of the Hindus. Most of them had never seen the Ganga, but knew of her lore through the stories in the Purāṇas (epics).

To conclude the yajña in a special way, Swamiji came up with the idea of taking a pilgrimage during which the participants could practise the ideals of spiritual life. Realizing the difficulties of detaching from the world when surrounded by familiar objects and activities, Swamiji told the group that this trip would give them a taste of renunciation, so they could bring that spirit of surrender into their daily lives. They were to carry no toiletries – no perfumes, lotions or make-up – except for a toothbrush, comb and coconut oil for the hair. At 6 a.m. they boarded six buses for the 200-mile trip to Rameswaram Temple, a full day's journey. However, time appeared to stand still, as they merrily travelled down the bumpy roads chanting and singing bhajanas along the way. At an occasional stop, Swamiji would change buses and join in the singing, so he spent time with everyone. After spending the night in the sparse accommodations available for pilgrims near the temple, everyone rose early in the morning for a bath of purification in the sea. Afterwards Swamiji gave a talk about the importance of meditation in maintaining mental balance through the vicissitudes of life. Following the talk, he took advantage of the peaceful scenic spot. With a soft breeze blessing the devotees, he led them in meditation while they were seated on the seashore. After a light breakfast, they all visited the incredible temple, the largest in India.

A visit to the Rameswaram Temple is a visit back to ancient times. The original temple, situated on an island, is believed to have been built by the avatāra Rāma to expiate for the sin of killing a Brāhmaṇa when he vanquished the demon king, Rāvaṇa, who, in spite of his evil ways, was also a Brāhmaṇa. There are two principal deities in the sanctum sanctorum, one was formed out of the nearby sand by Sītā, Rāma's consort. Śrī Hanumāna brought the other from the sacred Kailash mountain.

Since Rāma's time, many great kings had commissioned the temple's enlargement and embellishment until it had reached its present proportions. Twelve-foot walls enclosed the temple grounds of thirteen acres. The spacious compound contained many ornately carved sanctuaries and twenty-two wells of holy water, as well as the dwellings of the priests, their families and cows, and the colourful stalls where one could purchase the coconuts and garlands, made of pink cabbage roses, to offer to the deities. The most outstanding feature in the principle temple was the long corridors lined with over one thousand ornately sculpted pillars, which gave the appearance of an orderly petrified forest. The stones for these pillars would have been transported over the sea. It was believed that a causeway from the mainland once existed, but even so it would have been quite an engineering feat to move such immense stones.

A pilgrimage between Rameswaram and Varanasi, a journey of some one thousand miles, is among the important injunctions for a Hindu. In ancient times kings and landowners built rest houses along the route to assist the pilgrims. However, this pilgrimage to Rameswaram was the first visit for most of the members of the group from nearby Madras.

Everyone spent the remainder of the day in singing bhajanas or in meditation. After the chanting of 'Om' in unison, the crowd quietly dispersed to board the buses to return home. They carried with them the seeds of an experience that would take root and manifest according to their individual personalities and talents in the service of their families and fellow humanity.

21

Development of the Yajña Plan

Test religion before condemning it! Try the spiritual life for two years, then you decide for yourself its benefits.
—Swami Chinmayananda, 1956.

It soon became clear that this yajña plan was not the will of an individual, but the individual was the means of the collective will of a population eager to connect with their religious roots and know the religious experiences of their forefathers. As word spread of the young Swami's spiritual brilliance and marvellous oratory, intellectual professors, agnostic scientists, incorrigible politicians, the young and the old, the rich and the poor, all gathered at the Upaniṣad jñāna-yajñas.

In 1956 the Delhi yajña was inaugurated by the President of India, Dr. Rajendra Prasad, who spoke in glowing terms of the work Swamiji was doing to restore India's cultural glory. Within a short span of five years, Swamiji had sowed the seeds of a better way of life in over 50,000 hearts during twenty-five jñāna-yajñas throughout the country. No doubt this technique of reviving Hinduism was working. Each year there had been more and more invitations – in 1952, one yajña; in 1953, two yajñas; in 1954, four yajñas; 1955, eight yajñas; 1956, ten yajñas. After the second yajña, the invitation was backed by a group of dedicated, selfless workers who organized all the activities. The largest assembly was consistently in Madras until 1956, when the first yajña in Bangalore drew 4,300 attendees. It is noteworthy that in the initial five years, with the exception of seven yajñas in Delhi and one in Calcutta, all of the first twenty-five yajñas were in Southern India.

At each yajña, Swamiji explained in an introductory talk that the nature of man is evolving from an emotional character – in which surrender and devotion to a Guru was paramount – to the kingdom of the higher mind, the intellect. The development of this sacred instrument is essential for the independent thought that is necessary for individual spiritual unfoldment. Humans are living in a modern world with many complex relationships among family, friends, co-workers and government officials, and we must develop within that environment. We can no longer rely on a Guru to take responsibility for our spiritual unfoldment. Swamiji elaborated –

> In the past, men had a larger share of the heart than the head, and consequently the quality of faith superseded that of the rational capacity. Even today it is noticeable that in any country or society where the intellect is not predominant, that society or nation lives on emotion or in tune with the heart. For example, in India it is well-known that those of the south are more intellectual than those from the north. I, as a sannyāsī, have been personally experiencing the difference in the attitudes of the northerners and southerners toward the sacred robe I wear. In the north, we experience that our brothers are ready to worship and respect a sannyāsī merely because the individual is clothed in the sacred saffron garb. It is to them a question of faith, a matter of the heart. But in the south, the Swami is looked on with suspicion until otherwise proved worthy by a careful intellectual inquiry into the Swami's character. Wherever the intellect is developed more than the heart, there critical acumen and severity of judgement become predominant.
>
> Our ancient generation seems to have had a more developed heart than head. To them any truth was absolute and fully acceptable just because the ancient sages said so. The days of the prophets are no longer with us. Today even if a prophet, or God himself, were

> to walk into our homes for a cup of tea and tell us about the Truth directly, we would accept neither him nor his words unless he produced for us experimental data based on logical reasoning. That is the spirit of the Age we live in. Man has grown away from his heart and has come to live with his intellect. Thus today if the youth of the world refuse to accept religion when it is based merely upon faith, it is not a thing to be condemned, but rather a great step in evolution at which the world is to be congratulated and the Age to be applauded.

And Swamiji had a large ration of both the head and the heart. In devotion to his Guru, he returned to Uttarkashi each year to spend the summer months of the rainy season with Swami Tapovanam. After his annual stay there in 1953, he arrived in New Delhi for the third yajña. He began by announcing the mistakes and problems of the previous yajñas, so this group would be alert to avoid them. Thus he continued with his task of shaping seekers into harmonised students of discipline. No doubt his choice for the text, the *Māṇḍūkya-upaniṣad*, must have shocked a good many. Publicly discussing the Upaniṣads was outrageous enough, but to deal with this formidable text among common businessmen and women was considered the ultimate folly. On the eve of the yajña, Swamiji wrote –

> 'Only twenty-four hours remain for me to find myself undertaking yet another great endeavour – a ninety-one day yajña with one of the toughest textbooks of Vedānta to explain. Mother Śruti's[1] grace alone is my wealth, my courage, my strength. If she fails me, why should I worry? She alone fails.'

Mother Śruti did not fail him. She lit his words with wisdom. The average daily attendance was 800. "Even the students of Delhi have accepted the Swami," he wrote a supporter in Madras.

[1] The Vedas, scriptures of divine revelation.

Since this yajña treated the subtlest of the Upaniṣads, Swamiji emphasized meditation to the audience. The first phase of the yajña was devoted to the explanation and practice of meditation, so that they could practise throughout the three months of the yajña.

When Swami Tapovanam read Chinmaya's discourses on the *Māṇḍūkya Kārikā* in the weekly *Yajña Prasāda* he received at Uttarkashi, he was very pleased. He smiled and commented to the disciples present, "Yes, this certainly was spoken by Chinmaya." He meant that the person Chinmaya had stepped aside for the wisdom of the true Chinmaya[1] to come through him. The ninety-one day yajña began on September 12, 1953; on October 26, the yajña committee received a message from Swami Tapovanam –

> Brahman is the only Reality. Nothing else is Real. All the universe, consisting of the ever shining sun, moon and stars, is a dream – a long, long dream. How can this everlasting universe that we perceive in the waking state be a dream? In the great *Māṇḍūkya Kārikā* the illustrious Seer and Teacher Śrī Gauḍapāda attempts to answer this question. The *Kārikā* explains clearly and proves with various methods of logic that this universe is nothing but a dream.
>
> Let this universe be a dream. Of what use is it to waste our time thinking about this? It is only by pondering this matter that we can come to the conclusion that this world and worldly objects are all impermanent, and therefore, not real. Such impermanent worldly objects cannot give us an eternal happiness. Eternal Bliss is Brahman, and not this dreamlike changing universe.
>
> Then we should try to realize that eternal, blissful Brahman and to become established in that imperishable Bliss. Śrī Gauḍapāda leads us to that

[1] Chinmaya - true knowledge that both supports, and is beyond nature.

eternal Bliss, the eternal Brahman, by the most direct shortcut – straight as an arrow flies, not by a serpentine, twisting path. That is the greatness and distinction of this wonderful work, *Kārikā*.

The English educated people of our capital city are very fortunate to have the opportunity of hearing the discourses on this *Kārikā* from the lips of Swami Chinmayananda, a modern sannyāsī of contemporary education. I believe that he will explain to you the subject of the text in the modern and scientific method rather than in the orthodox way of the Sanskrit paṇḍitas (priests).

Perhaps, by attending the lectures, you may understand intellectually the non-creation theory of the *Kārikā*. You may feel intellectually convinced that Brahman alone is Real and that the world of the three states of Consciousness – waking, dream and deep sleep – is not really created and, hence, life is a long, long dream. To realize the Reality of 'I am Brahman', to experience that Reality, and to get established in that Reality, is quite far, far away from a mere academic understanding.

Therefore, don't neglect God. By God's grace alone can his real nature, that fourth state[1] of existence, be realized. Practice love and devotion to God. Chant his name. Praise his glory, and always meditate upon his greatness. With this practice, in the course of time, the purity and concentration of your impure and wavering mind is acquired and you will be able to realize the eternal blissful Self, Brahman.

Perhaps it is with this idea in mind that along with the teaching of the non-creation theory, the

1 The fourth, or Turīya state is that Consciousness that underlies all other states of Consciousness.

akhaṇḍa kīrtana (continual chanting) of the personal God is also being conducted as an important item in the yajñaśālā (hall).

I hope the Delhi people will be highly benefitted by this jñāna-yajña ceremony, now being conducted by Śrī Swami Chinmayanandaji. May God bless you all for the successful completion of the jñāna-yajña, and for the successful practice of the knowledge which you attain from it.

....

Swami Govindagiri reported that the only time he ever heard Swami Tapovanam actually laugh was after Chinmaya was successful with his yajña plan. Afterwards, when Swami Chinmayananda went to Uttarkashi, he and Swami Tapovanam would sit out on the veranda of his hut, engrossed in discussions. By the peals of laughter and the looks on their faces, Swami Govindagiri could tell that the two were really enjoying each other's company. 'From that time onward, Swami Tapovanam always treated Swami Chinmayananda as a friend, no longer as a student. This means that Chinmaya had the total blessings of his Guru – which could only come from his own merit,' observed Swami Govindagiri.

In 1954, the second yajña at Madras was a special event as his second mother, Kouchi Amma, was present to hear her nephew. Everyone happily took on the task of caring for the tiny eighty-year old; they treated her with the reverence due to a saint. The Madras devotees arranged a pāda pūjā, or worship of the feet, for the Swami and his 'mother'. Although the ceremony of washing of the feet as a show of respect has been a custom in several tropical countries, it carries a special spiritual significance in India. The feet of a holy man are the physical support of the sage; therefore, they symbolise the spiritual truth that is his true foundation. It was a rare honour for Kouchi Amma, although the mothers of India's holy men have always received special reverence. The frail Kouchi Amma was humbly embarrassed, but she managed to abide the ceremony with grace. She was to live for another ten years, serving the Lord in whatever form he appeared, whether a beggar or a child. After her cremation and funeral ceremony, her son Achuthan immersed her ashes in the Ganga at Haridwar and, following in his cousin's footsteps, continued on a pilgrimage to Uttarkashi and Gangotri.

Several members of the Madras audience organized a dinner for the poor at the end of the havana ritual. The ceremony closed with a procession of seven truckloads of participants chanting all the way to Madras Beach from the yajña site at T-nagar to immerse ashes from the havana and take a sacred bath in the sea. Swamiji spoke in a small open tent that had been erected for the occasion. Then he led the group in meditation. During the last moments, several rowdy young men had joined the fringes of the curiosity seekers who had gathered round the tent to observe. Soon one interrupted and loudly accused the Swami of starting a cult. "Yes, you are quite correct! That is exactly what is going on here. I am starting a Cult of Goodness!" replied Swamiji in a serious tone of voice. "You are welcome to join us!"

Beginning with the thirteenth yajña, held in New Delhi in October 1955, Swamiji started unravelling the hidden gems of wisdom in the *Bhagavad-gītā*. The Sage Vyāsa had written the *Gītā* to preserve the message of the Upaniṣads in a more practical form that could be understood by persons living and acting in the world. The setting chosen for the message – a student facing a war at daybreak against his own beloved relatives – was a compelling example of the conflicts of loyalty one may encounter in life.

As Swamiji was giving the commentary on this scripture, several people in the audience saw his form change into that of Lord Kṛṣṇa playing his flute. At other lectures, some saw a divine being standing behind him on the platform and felt that the apparition was Śrī Vyāsa, the author of the *Gītā*. These type of visions experienced by diverse people have continued through Swamiji's many yajñas. Whenever Swamiji was told of these experiences, he always dismissed them as unimportant. He explained, "You must look to that Truth of which even Kṛṣṇa is a messenger. Even in your meditation if Lord Kṛṣṇa appears, you ask him to step aside. Tell him not to disturb your meditation. You are aiming for the Truth beyond all forms."

The enthusiasm, love and joy of the people around Swamiji were remarkable. The Hindus might have forgotten their scriptures, but they had not forgotten that to have a holy man in their homes was equivalent to a visit from the Lord. Bhikṣās were no longer roti and soupy dal of his student days in the Himalayas, but elaborate, gala affairs. All the family members, friends and neighbours were invited to the feast. Everyone accepted because the gathering was also an opportunity to ask the Swami questions and to receive the blessings of his wisdom. Wherever he travelled, he stayed with a family who took care of his transportation, correspondence, morning and afternoon tea, plus his laundry and other such necessities. Daily, in the sitting room of the home, people would wait for hours until he finished his daily correspondence, so that they could ask him a question or simply be in his presence, a presence overflowing with love.

At the Delhi yajña, Swamiji also began a formal morning class at his residence on the text, *Vivekacūḍāmaṇi* (Crown Jewel of Discrimination). The difficulty of personally lecturing in all of India's towns and cities was becoming very apparent. More people would receive the message and be able to study individually if the ideas were available in book form. Therefore, he was inspired to complete books of both the *Bhagavad-gītā* and Ādi Śaṅkarācārya's comprehensive text, *Vivekacūḍāmaṇi,* so that they could be printed and distributed publicly.

Also about this time, Swamiji began use of what he referred to as a visual aid, which later became known as the 'Om' chart. Although in the first stages of development there was no Om, but an 'X' at the top of the chart. This 'X' represented the source of the three worlds of human experience – the three states of Consciousness of sleep, dream and waking – and their substratum. With this chart and his long pointer, he illustrated how Vedānta was a scientific method of investigation to discover the route back to this very source.

To help the audience keep alert, he insisted that each person bring a copy of the textbook. Before each verse was discussed, it was chanted in unison by the group. He explained to the audience –

> There will be a dullness of the intellect after a period of silent attention. A quiet mind has a tendency to go to sleep because that is what it has been doing for years. Therefore, we have to restrain it from sleeping, while at the same time, we must sustain the quietude and keep it as alert as possible. In the talks I keep you awake with a joke, or by the chanting of the *Gītā*. That's why I insist that everyone has a *Gītā* in his hand to participate in the chanting.

From the beginning of his mission, Swamiji was continually working on programmes to interest the young people in their spiritual heritage, for, the future of India was in their hands. He hadn't completely forgotten the listlessness of his university days and wanted to help the students avoid the pitfalls he had encountered. Therefore, he was thrilled to receive an invitation in 1953 to speak for four consecutive evenings at the Fergusson College in Poona. Emphasizing that religion can stand the test of modern analysis, while at the same time attract the restless students' attention, Swamiji spoke on the 'creative power'. Bringing his message to the level of the students' interests, he introduced his topic that first evening.

The Creative Power under the Lens of Logic and Science

At the very outset, I must make it clear that I have not come tonight to talk to you upon a set of somber truths discovered by myself. I have come here to have the benefit of mutual discussion with you. I was once a student like you. Then by chance I came across some great living Masters of our philosophy who were not only well versed in the scriptural textbooks, but had made these truths the substance of their very lives. They have, I must admit, convinced me that the values that I used to live in my university days were not healthy or wise. These sages not only robbed me of these old values, but have given me a new set of values to live by, a new set of thoughts to draw inspiration from. In short, they have revolutionized my life.

At the same time, you may consider that I am not fully convinced; so I have come here seeking an opportunity to discuss with you the ideas in a spirit of equality. Please do not consider these talks as a usual lecture, for, I have not come to you to thrust upon you any original ideas of mine as a preacher would from his pulpit. I have no original truths to declare. I have only to repeat to you the words of the great Masters as they were taught to me and to the extent I have digested them.

This is to say that I am here tonight to act as an agent between the wise old Masters, who were born in an Age of belief in the great philosophical declarations of the ancient textbooks, and you, the modern generation brought up in an Age of science and logic.

To the delight of the organizer Jaybala Gujjar, herself a student at Fergusson, and Swamiji, the auditorium was packed with young students, listening with rapt attention in an atmosphere of divine silence. He encouraged them to raise questions and air their doubts. The following week, they gathered at his residence in the afternoons for lively discussions. "This will be one of the greatest experiences in my work to look back upon for all times," declared Swamiji afterwards.

He urged the young people to start thinking for themselves about the religious ideas presented in the yajña talks, as many students were attending with their parents. In the second *Gītā* jñāna-yajña in 1955, the students presented a short satire, based on the *Gītā* talks, that was set in modern life. He announced a student essay competition on the subject 'My Religion' based on the ideas in the third and fourth chapters of the *Gītā*. In Calcutta that same year, the yajña committee announced a student competition on the theme, 'More Light on My Religion', to be based on the classes of *Īśāvāsya-upaniṣad*. First prize was a generous 100 rupees, with 50 rupees for second place. Swamiji addressed students at various colleges at any opportunity. Once he rode in a car all night after the evening lecture to give a presentation at a college graduation ceremony in the morning, and returned that afternoon just in time for the evening *Gītā* class.

The book, *Meditation and Life*, compiled from the meditation classes at the 1955 Delhi yajña, was distributed to all graduates of Madras University and Delhi University through a non-profit trust. Activities were initiated for the revival of the many facets of Hindu culture. In spring of 1959, a Spiritual Arts Festival was held in Hyderabad to encourage the development of individual talent. The competitions included an exhibition of religious paintings, classical dance, musical performances and drama presentations.

In 1955 Swamiji tried a new method of reaching the public. He took his teaching to the air waves on All India Radio with a three part series. The first topic was an explanation of the symbolism of the various Hindu rituals and temple worship. Swamiji explained that in Hinduism art, dance and music, in fact all creative arts, served the function of glorifying God. The second topic was the 'Science of Life', which included a challenge of self-development through self-discipline. The third talk, 'Work as Worship', included the ideas of karma-yoga as explained in the *Gītā*.

At that time the yajñas were operating without any capital reserves, so the cost of publication of the *Yajña Prasāda* was a prohibitive burden on some of the smaller towns. These devotees would have liked to invite Swamiji for a yajña, but lacked funds for the publishing and mailing of the 12,000 name list. To alleviate the problem, a group in Madras initiated a new publication. From September 1955, Swamiji's lectures on the scriptures were published in a fortnightly magazine named *Tyagi*, available by subscription at a nominal cost. In addition to Swamiji's lectures, it would include articles by such great saints as Swami Sivananda, Śrī Aurobindo, Swami Vivekananda and European thinkers as diverse as Aldous

Huxley and St. Francis. Swamiji was grateful that his supporters were taking on the projects and encouraged the editor to provide 'a forum in which all thinkers of every creed can ventilate their ideas; so that, as a result of our cooperative effort, we may discover a way of better living by which we can make a spiritual life practical for every man of imagination and courage.' Swami Tapovanam sent his blessings upon the receipt of the first issue of *Tyagi*, commenting on the simple format, 'No waste on frills.'

Throughout the early development of his mission, Swami Chinmayananda remained loyal to and respectful of both his Teachers, Swami Tapovanam and Swami Sivananda. He always stopped over at Ananda Kutir and met with Swami Sivananda on his trips back to the Himalayas. On one of these visits, he invited several Swamis to go on a trek up to Bada. En route they saw a dirty, miserable looking Swami. "Look at that poor fellow. How can this sad dejected creature be called spiritual? Look at our Guruji. Dynamism oozes from every pore," Chinmaya exclaimed.

But unfortunately the jealousies at Ananda Kutir were growing. Swamiji was even being accused of attempting to take Swami Sivananda's supporters away from him. While it was true that in Poona and Delhi several of Swami Sivananda's devotees were indispensable in their service to the yajña organization, they considered their service was to the Truth, not to a man. Nevertheless, as Chinmaya's success grew, so did the criticism.

For example, the Swamis at Ananda Kutir were particularly irked at the frontispiece on the Poona *Yajña Prasāda* that hinted of Swamiji's enlightenment. They proclaimed it 'egotistical' and went over every word of every *Yajña Prasāda*, not for knowledge, but to find something that they could use to accuse him. In one of his talks he had criticized 'weekend devotees'. The Swamis insisted that this was direct insult to Swami Sivananda's householder supporters.

In a prior incident, shortly after he had taken sannyāsa, Swami Chinmayananda had been asked by Swami Sivananda to accompany an American couple to Dehradun. The wife had been ailing and the Guru had hoped that the fresh mountain air would rejuvenate her. Swami Chinmayananda and another Swami from Ananda Kutir accompanied the couple. Although it was a small town, they distributed some spiritual literature written by Swami Sivananda. Even back then, the action had brought accusations that he was using Swami Sivananda's name to make his fame.

However, Swami Shivananda continued to remain complimentary of the work of his disciple. "Chinmaya is doing good work, he has thrilled the whole of India!" he commented when he was brought a newspaper clipping about one of the yajñas.

"No, Chinmaya is only after name and fame," his disciples asserted.

"So who doesn't want name and fame? I want it; he wants it. But the point is to what percent is that desire – some eighty percent, some twenty percent? He has dedicated that twenty percent desire to a higher goal. Look at the way he is working! If he just wanted name and fame, surely there would be an easier way for him to get it! He's very clever!"

But Swami Sivananda's opinion seemed to make no difference, the discord and criticism continued among the Swamis. According to one of the disciples at Ananda Kutir, it was for the sake of peace in the āśrama that Swami Sivananda at last wrote to his disciple, Chinmaya, "From this moment, let us worship each other in our hearts."

During this period, Swami Tapovanam had taken on the image of the wise old man for Swamiji's audiences. Many seekers made pilgrimages up to his kuṭira where they were all welcomed equally. In early 1956, Swamiji took a group of devotees with him to Uttarkashi. Everyone who trooped up to the veranda of Tapovanam Kutir found that Swami Tapovanam had lost weight and was looking quite pale. He greeted everyone, recollecting the ones he had met the previous year in Rishikesh where there had been a spiritual pilgrimage after a Delhi yajña. He inquired whether the accommodations at the dharmaśālā there in Uttarkashi were comfortable. Gradually, the conversation moved to more serious spiritual subjects.

Swami Tapovanam loved and revered the holy Ganga. He had composed a lengthy, devotional poem in Sanskrit describing her glories. He related that the changing life of the river was a personification of the changing nature of the human life. He described her many moods – often, the sound of innumerable bells ringing together could be heard, other times the thumping roar of laughter, sometimes, she resounded with the rolling of drums as she tumbled over the huge boulders of her river bed. He then added, "She is all of these things, but above all she is a river of the eternal sound of an endless Om, rising from a million mouths in perfect unison."

The group of guests who were householders wanted to contribute some worthwhile service while they were there, so Swamiji assisted in organizing a feast for the nearly 150 sannyāsīs living in and around Uttarkashi. The evening before, like a true host, Swamiji went with the group to each āśrama and each hut. With folded hands, they asked each Swami to come to the bhikṣā.

While making the rounds, they came to a hut of a rather robust Swami, one of the types who could quote a scripture for even the most insignificant incident. Before long, like a gurgling spring, he started quoting passage after passage, while making indirect allusions that he considered himself to be a great Enlightened Master. The lonesome soul very rarely had an audience and was taking advantage of the opportunity of having one. Only warming up after twenty minutes of monologue, he began to recount a tale of his great fearlessness during his younger days of tapas (austerities) while wandering in the Himalayas. With this opening, he started in on his great 'tiger story'.

It occurred that one evening he saw a tiger approaching him, stealthily and majestically, with his tongue hanging out. This self-proclaimed master declared that he just sat down in the path, right in front of the beast, with his legs sprawled out and refused to give way even an inch for the beast. "For I was sitting in my own Svarūpa (true nature)," he explained. He said the two of them continued to sit there staring in each other's eyes for some time, until the tiger finally decided to retreat. Everyone was surprised that Swamiji patiently listened to, and even encouraged, this boastful man. As soon as the group was out of sight of the hut, Swamiji turned to them with a smile, "Note, I am showing you many different types of Swamis. Now this example is a rare type indeed."

The next morning the little veranda at Tapovanam Kutir was astir with preparations for the feast. The ladies were cleaning the dal and rice and cutting the vegetables, while Swamiji was overseeing the process. They were laughing among themselves about the tiger Swami, when Swamiji countered with his own story. "Why, didn't you know that I too met a tiger when I was on a trek in the Himalayas. Yes, there was the tiger right on my path! Directly in front of me. Another ten metres and I would have been on top of him," he detailed with appropriate gestures. "And what did I do? I turned around and ran like hell!" he rolled with laughter.

In March, only days after Swamiji had left Uttarkashi, he received word that Swami Tapovanam had fallen ill. Swamiji took a month off from his yajña schedule to be with his Guru. He was accompanied by Śrī Natarajan Iyer[1*] from Madras and a few other devotees. Swami Tapovanam told this group that he commended the idea of Chinmaya's jñāna-yajña. He said that the mission of taking the teachings of Vedānta to the hearts of the people was "the highest service one can do for his fellow men." He continued by praising Chinmaya's methods and interpretations of the scriptural texts. He added that it was an advantage that Chinmaya was giving all the classes in English because the message of Vedānta was to be taken to the spiritually starved people of Europe and America.

During this month Swamiji took up the long arduous task of dictating the commentaries on the *Bhagavad-gītā*. He had taught up to chapter 11 in the jñāna-yajñas, but whenever time

[1] The future Swami Dayananda.

permitted, he preferred to dictate original material. He used a less formal language in his talks, and he often took examples from the lives of people in the audience, which became meaningless, out of context. Also he gave careful attention that each verse should have a completeness in itself, so if one picked up the book and read just a couple of verses, one would not be misled.

For this project Swami Sivananda had volunteered the use of the Sanskrit translations from his published *Bhagavad-gītā*, a donation that would save hours of work. They had been composed by accomplished Sanskrit scholars with exacting accuracy. So with books, notes and Sanskrit verses, Swamiji sat down to dictate – verse by verse – to Śrī Natarajan Iyer, who had to squeeze in time to type out the chapters of the thick text while everyone else was napping or taking a stroll alongside the Ganga. Natarajan had met Swamiji at the first Madras yajña and was now a full time worker. Along with assisting in the editing of *Tyagi*, he travelled to the various cities in advance to help with the arrangements for the yajñas and the spiritual pilgrimages afterwards. His profession as a secretary made his service viable to all the publishing projects. Even though Natarajan borrowed lanterns so that he and Swamiji could continue working long into the night, they were unable to complete the *Gītā* commentaries during this month. Swamiji had to interrupt the work for a scheduled yajña. However, they were able to finish the bulk of the work.

Later that year word was received that Swami Tapovanam's health was much worse. Immediately, several of the devotees in Delhi drove up to Uttarkashi to bring him back for an accurate diagnosis and proper medical treatment. One person even wanted to send him to London; another was sure New York would offer the best medical care. But Swami Tapovanam had his own opinions –

> "So according to your arguments, one, having gone down to Delhi to the medical facilities for his physical ailment, must finish off with a round the world trip in search of the best diagnosis – and all for the sake of

> this perishable body. (He paused for a few minutes, then continued) And where is the guarantee that I will live? Are there not people dying in London, in New York, and in Delhi with all these 'best' facilities for diagnosis and treatment? Then why should I not end my life here in peace amidst these Himalayas where I have lived for these many years as a Yogī?

....

Later that year, when Swami Chinmayananda completed the yajña in New Delhi, he again travelled to Uttarkashi to be with his Guru. He later wrote of that last meeting –

....

> During my last visit to Tapovanam Kutir in early December 1956, I broke down suddenly and burst into tears. Swamiji saw the tears and said softly, 'Chinmaya, it is easy to learn Vedānta, easier to preach Vedānta – hard indeed to live the Knowledge. When we are born, death is born with us. The Lord gave me so long an opportunity to live and experience. Now He, who was waiting so long, is coming to meet me. You say I must now run to escape him? How? Here quietly I have lived; now cannot I quietly die, hearing the eternal music of my Mother Ganga? Don't weep. You go and continue the work. . . Come now!

....

When they bid each other farewell, they both must have known it would be their last meeting. Swami Tapovanam's condition continued to deteriorate. It was only one month later that he departed from his physical body.

On a cold night in January, the winter sun had long since disappeared behind the mountain peaks. Seven devotees, including four sādhus, had fallen asleep on the small veranda of Swami Tapovanam's hut. All through the day, they had been urging their Guru to take an Ayurvedic medicine, but he had refused. His difficulty was that he could not digest food, which is a common malady among the sādhus who take arduous pilgrimage and practise severe austerities. The digestive system is damaged from lack of regular food through the years, so it eventually atrophies and finally shuts down.

Only his personal attendant, the young Swami Sunderananda, remained with him through the night. Later, he described Swami Tapovanam's passing.

That night at about 3 a.m., Swami Mahārāja asked me to help him sit up. Gently I helped into a sitting position with his legs out straight. This was the posture that he had always slept in, so it was unusual for him to be lying flat. After I helped him up, I started pressing his legs to aid him in feeling more comfortable. Some time later, maybe after an hour or so, he asked me to make him a little coffee with Ganga water and milk.

> Of course, I had to go down to the river at night to get fresh water, so that trip took some fifteen minutes. Also, heating the water and milk was time consuming since I had to make a fire with wood. When I brought the hot coffee to him, he told me, 'Now you put it in my mouth.' Carefully, I put one spoonful in his open mouth, then another – a total of three spoonfuls. Then he signaled me with his hand that he had had enough.
>
> As he sat there peacefully, suddenly he uttered the words, 'Thank you, God. Now I take rest.' He expressed these words with such an expression of gratitude that I could see a bright glow in his eyes. Actually, a crystal-clear light radiated from his eyes. Then he slumped over and was gone.

Swami Chinmayananda was conducting a yajña in Palghat, Kerala when he received word that Swami Tapovanam had breathed his last breath on the day of the full moon (pūrṇimā) in January. Upon hearing the news, Swamiji's eyes filled with tears.

"Swamiji, are you crying?" ventured one of the ladies.

"Yes, of course. Do not think that because a man is a renunciate that he is devoid of feelings? I have emotions just like everyone."

Swamiji journeyed up to Rishikesh to stay alone for a few days in meditation. A sage is not attached to the physical world because he knows the Reality beyond it; therefore, for him there is no funeral, no ritual, nor cremation. Immediately after the death, the body of Swami Tapovanam was carried to the holy Ganga he had loved so dearly and immersed into her icy waters.

On Dīpāvalī in 1957, Swamiji announced that the *Gītā* commentary, 2085 pages of manuscript, was complete. Dīpāvalī, or festival of lights, is the Hindu New Year (on most Indian calendars) and falls in the month of Kārtika (October-November). To celebrate the much loved and enjoyed festival, everyone dons their best clothes and goes out in the evening to distribute sweets, which are made of thickened milk, cooked with sugar and decorated with pure silver or gold leaf, among their friends. Then everyone strolls about to view the lighted city, as tiny earthenware oil lamps not only outline the rooftops, but also flicker on every ledge and window sill of the houses.

Swamiji commented that the lighting of the lamps of Dīpāvalī had a symbolic meaning for each level of the personality and then explained their significance. For the spiritual self, the lighting of the lamp represents the dawning of true knowledge. For the intellect, the flame represents the light of intellectual understanding. For the emotional personality, the light symbolises love of an ideal.

Also in 1957, Swamiji was finally invited for a yajña in his own hometown of Ernakulam and Trichur. Even though he had given yajñas throughout Kerala, it had seemed as though he was not going to be accepted in his home territory, for, there too many remembered him as the worldly Balakrishnan Menon. His reception in Ernakulam was quiet, in contrast to the response he drew elsewhere in Kerala. Ordinarily, even when he was just passing through a town, people would be gathered on the platform, singing bhajanas and patiently awaiting the inevitably late train, to greet him with a flower garland.

At yajñas in South India, his welcoming was especially elaborate. After garlanding him with ropes of jasmine flowers, they would drive him to the lecture site in a jeep decorated with flowers. There he was greeted by a beautifully ornamented temple elephant, a band of brass horns, and a display of fireworks. However, in Ernakulam only a handful of people came to hear their native son on the first day, even though the Mahārājā of Cochin inaugurated the yajña. But word spread of the quality of his discourses, and the crowd grew to one thousand. During those two weeks, it was apparent that Balakrishnan Menon's past was being forgiven and forgotten. Swami Chinmayananda was accepted in the place of his birth.

As Swamiji went from city to city, town to town, new ideas to incorporate into the yajñas were continually dawning on him. Also, as time went on and the crowd grew, some programmes had to be eliminated. It was impractical to attempt to carry enough pots of Ganga water for the symbolic baptism at the end of the yajña. It was impossible to find accommodations in temples for such large groups to take the spiritual pilgrimages. The havana ritual was changed to chanting of the one thousand names of Lord Viṣṇu, while giving an offering of a flower petal with each name – the same one thousand names that had bored Balakrishnan as a youngster.

Swami Chinmayananda had forgiven and accepted some of his past too, now that he understood the purifying power of ritual on the mind. Also, the length of the yajña was gradually shortened to ten days to enable him to be in contact with the principal cities at least once a year, as well as include several new ones. Visiting cities regularly seemed to be necessary to keep the enthusiasm going and to clear the accumulated doubts of the devotees. Keeping up the momentum for leading a spiritual renaissance in 'spiritual' India was turning out to be quite a mission.

22

The Chinmaya Mission

Maximum happiness for the maximum number of people – that is our goal!

—Swami Chinmayananda, 1956.

In Madras on August 8, 1953, a handful of people who had attended the first yajña there, including the Rangaswami Iyer family, Śrī Kanti Iyer and Śrī Natarajan Iyer, got together to create a forum for study and discussions of the scriptures. They wanted an ongoing programme to clarify the understanding of Vedānta and to keep up the inspiration of the 100 days spent with Swamiji during the yajñas. This group was composed of educated Brāhmaṇas who had been brought up studying the ritual section of Vedas, and in some cases the *Bhagavad-gītā*, but not the Upaniṣads. The message of these ancient treatises was a revelation to them, and they wanted the opportunity to study them more thoroughly. They enthusiastically wrote to Swamiji about their plan, plus their intention to call their new organization 'Chinmaya Mission'. His reply arrived from Tapovanam Kutir in the Himalayas –

> Don't start any organization in my name. I've not come here to be institutionalized. I've come here to give the message of our ancient sages, which has benefitted me. If it has benefitted you, pass it on.

These dozen people were convinced that the best way to 'pass it on' was through the support of a group. They wrote back stating that the word 'Chinmaya', did not have to indicate

Swamiji's name, since the word itself meant 'the true knowledge' that they were seeking. "As seekers of the Truth, we are calling ourselves the Chinmaya Mission," they concluded. Therefore, Swamiji had no actual decision in the initiation of what has developed into a many armed cultural and service organization that has provided an arena for the practical manifestation of the spiritual ideals. "If you are going to do it, of course, I will help you in an advisory capacity," he conceded in his reply.

After two years the Mission had six branches in Madras, each with a small library of spiritual books and a weekly programme of discussions, singing of devotional hymns, chanting of the scriptures and group meditations. In March of 1956, in a meeting with new members after a Delhi yajña, Swamiji emphasized the necessity for meeting regularly with a definite venue for the study of the intricate logic of Vedānta. Mutual discussions and exchange of ideas in small groups were an excellent means for individual self-development, he advised. Along with the Study Groups, cultural activities were initiated independently in the various cities for the support and revival of the traditional creative arts of dance, drama, music and painting.

Of course, when you get humans together, there is always learning in the dynamics of the group. On the occasion of the celebration of the third year anniversary of the Mission, his letter to the Madras Mission reflected that personal interests of various members had begun to surface.

> Don't forget that the Mission is a family. No one needs to harbour any ill will toward anyone. Act as missionaries, keeping the great goal as your pole star. Remember that our work is too sacred, urgent, imperative and divine to be hampered at any cost.

Among the devotees who came to hear Swamiji were many talented and energetic women. The struggle for India's independence had forced many women into women's liberation long before their Western counterparts. The women had taken up the political and business affairs of their husbands who were often imprisoned[1] or involved in political conventions, protests or strikes. Some women even spent time in prison themselves. However, in spite of their liberation and education, according to the modern male Brāhmaṇa priest, the Hindu religion was not for women; therefore, the universality of Vedānta was especially appealing to them. As early as 1954 in Delhi, there was an all female committee to organize the Upaniṣad yajña; in 1962, the women of Madras organized the 100th yajña lecture series.

In particular, women have continued to be a noteworthy source of creative initiative for the many cultural and service projects of the Chinmaya Mission. In 1958 in Madras, Ma Sundaran started a ladies' group from a number of Chinmaya Mission members after they had gone together to hear a Bengali singer of classical music. They wanted to keep in contact and decided to meet weekly to discuss the scriptures and how the concepts could be applied to specific problems in their homes. When they approached Swamiji with the news of the latest Chinmaya Mission activity, he encouraged them in their endeavour and named them the Chinmaya Devi (Goddess) Group.

The momentum of the women's activities was given a real boost when in January 1960, several hundred women delegates from twenty-three towns gathered at the Kollengode Palace, Kerala for a Chinmaya Devi Conference. The Raja of Kollengode personally saw to the comfort of every person. Each day was filled with classes on the scriptures, instruction and practice in bhajanas, followed by satsaṅga with Swamiji. In the evening, the local people presented a cultural programme of songs and folk dances. The convention concluded with a talent show in which each participant gave a talk on a religious subject, enacted a short drama, or sang either a classical or devotional bhajana.

[1] For example, Gandhi spent nearly six years in prison in India. J. Nehru spent nine years in nine different prisons.

Swamiji's message to these women centred on the importance of the woman in the family. When the mother is a true sādhaka (seeker), the whole environment of the household changes. "Your family does not have to go out to hear a Swami. You change and your environment will follow suit," he assured them. "You are the mother, the model and the Guru." He instructed them in guiding their children, answering their spiritual questions with small hints instead of elaborate details, telling them simple stories to illustrate the greater values of life, and explaining how to perform a daily pūjā (worship) service in their homes.

Swamiji considered the training of the children the most tangible step in the revival of the values of Hinduism in the society. "The spiritual seed must be sown to germinate," he often repeated when he had an audience of mothers or teachers.

> Children are the architects of the future world. They are the builders of humanity. The most sacred task of the parents as well as teachers is to mould their lives in accordance with the sublime Indian tradition. The seed of spiritual values should be sown in the young hearts, and conditions should be made favourable for its sprouting and steady growth by the exercise of proper control and discipline. When cared for with warmth of love and affection, a tree will blossom forth with the flowers of brotherhood, universal love, peace, bliss, beauty and perfection.

One of the first programmes specifically for children was organized by Mrs. Janaki Seth in Delhi in 1955. She gathered thirty-five children, the youngest three years old, to begin the Children's Well-Being Mission. Soon others wanted to join, but there was no building available to hold more children. This did not deter Janaki; she moved her expanding group to a public park. The surrounding nature provided a learning environment to point out the beauty and wonder of the play of God surrounding them.

She told stories with an emphasis on making the children self-reliant and organized in their daily habits. They would often act out these stories in short skits to reinforce the ideas. Parents began to see the results, their children studying regularly, getting along with the family, and voluntarily saying their daily prayers. That Spring, the children gave a performance of the Rādhā-Kṛṣṇa dance depicting Holī, the divine play of the Lord Kṛṣṇa with his consort. Two hundred parents and family members were invited; a crowd of three thousand arrived. The citizens of Delhi enthusiastically welcomed this opportunity to honour their past culture.

In Ernakulam, Miss Janaki Menon started the second Well-Being Centre. Children came to her home weekly to learn bhajanas, prayers and story telling. At the Mylapore yajña, children met to practise for weeks in advance to prepare to lead the chanting of the *Gītā* verses during Swamiji's lectures. In several other towns, the youngsters also led the bhajana singing to begin each yajña.

In 1956, the Madras group organized a children's excursion to Guruvayur. Enthusiastic children filled one entire train car for the long trip across Southern India to Trichur. After twenty-four hours, they reached their destination where everyone packed onto a bus to finish the remaining twenty miles. As they bumped along the rough, dusty road, the melodious chant of 'Hare Kṛṣṇa, Hare Rāma' resounded through the coconut groves.

Guruvayur is considered a special temple for children because the idol is the child Kṛṣṇa. It is believed that Devakī, the mother of Kṛṣṇa, used this very idol in her daily worship service in her home at Dwarka. Later when this town was sinking into the Arabian Sea at the termination of the Kṛṣṇa's Yadav dynasty, Guru Bṛhaspati, the presiding deity of the intellect and Guru to the gods; and Vāyu, the powerful deity of the wind, determined to save the holy shrine. Together they carried it to a safe spot in a small village on the Malabar Coast in the area now called Kerala. Hence, the place where the temple was established has long been called Guruvayur, the place of Guru and Vāyu (Guru + Vāyu + ur [village]).

At the temple, the children marched in pairs down the palm decorated corridor to the entrance gates, chanting in unison. They were followed by Chinmaya Mission members from all over India who took the opportunity of this auspicious occasion to visit the temple. The entire parade, headed by Swamiji, was received with temple honours – the temple elephant was brought out to greet them to the accompaniment of the traditional horns and drums. Everyone circled the sanctum sanctorum three times, symbolizing the surrender of the three physical spheres of experience – body, mind and intellect. With serenity, each one looked directly at the Child Kṛṣṇa to perceive a vision of the Truth through the vision of this divine avatāra. Afterward, Swamiji suggested to the temple priests that they begin a Sanskrit school to teach the *Bhagavad-gītā* and the epics of Kṛṣṇa to the children in the evenings after school.

These various projects were the impetus for the beginning of a children's section of the Chinmaya Mission for weekly study, singing and story telling. In each city, one or two women took the responsibility for a Bala Vihar club of eight to ten children who met in the leader's home. Soon there were twenty to thirty clubs in each of the large cities and at least one group in dozens of small towns.

In the spring of 1959, a national Spiritual Arts Festival was held in Hyderabad. The competitions and exhibitions were to encourage development of individual talent, and included religious paintings, classical dances and several drama presentations. All the artisans – children and teenagers up to nineteen years of age – went home with inspiration and enthusiasm from the exchange of creative ideas.

In the fall of 1959, the Chinmaya Mission sponsored an All India Children's Conference to highlight the results of two years of Bala Vihar activities and to stimulate the exchange of ideas among the leaders. Prizes were given for competitions in story telling with the subjects ranging from the Purāṇas to the lives of India's recent saints such as Ramakrishna and Gandhi.

Each evening a group from the various centres gave a cultural programme of dance, poetry recitation and drama. To the delight of the audience, especially Swamiji, one skit included a satsaṅga during which an eight-year old Swami Chinmayananda, complete with orange robe and gray beard, gave out words of wisdom to his six-year old students.

Swamiji loved children and that love was wholeheartedly reciprocated by the wide-eyed, self-assured Hindu children. Thousands of adults in India today happily claim the honour of having sat on Swamiji's knee when they were toddlers. He never turned down an opportunity to talk to the children. Often, he would start his presentation at a school with the question – "Everyone tells you that you must be good, but did anyone ever tell you how to be good?" When he had gotten their attention with these words, he continued.

> Of course, you all want to be good. You don't need Mommy and Pappy to tell you to be good because you all want to be good. But then something happens and we don't act like we want to act. Why?
>
> A bad action means that at that moment we had a bad thought. Think about it. It's true, isn't it? I must have had a kicking thought before I kicked my little brother. So here we have our clue. If bad thoughts mean bad actions, then good thoughts must mean good actions. So we must change our thoughts.
>
> So how do we get good thoughts? First, we can think of someone who is very good. It could be someone you have heard about from the scriptures like Rāma or Sītā, or it could be a person you know whom you feel is very good. You remember them and think how they would behave if they were in your situation. If I am thinking that I am as good and kind as Rāma, I will not have a kicking thought when

my little brother takes my toy truck. If I do not have a kicking thought, then I will not kick my dear little brother who only wanted to play with the toy.

It is the same as when we call a pot by what it contains – a pot with honey is called a 'honey pot', a pot with milk is called a 'milk pot', and a pot with ink is called. . . what? (The children shouted, 'ink pot'.) Yes, an ink pot! In the same way, your mind is called by the thoughts that it contains. Bully thoughts mean a bully mind, so the actions will be those of a bully. Good thoughts mean a good mind, so the actions will be . . .? (The children shout 'good'.) Yes, so now you know how to be good. Good thoughts – good actions.

The first of many teachers' conferences sponsored by the Chinmaya Mission was held in Bombay (now Mumbai) for the teachers of fifth standard. This training was for teachers already employed in the public schools to give them a background in their religious heritage to enable them to share it with their students. The one week course was tuition free to all participants, but they did have to give up a week of their vacation time.

Swamiji inaugurated the course with a lecture on the difference between instructors and teachers. He stated that it was unfortunate that India had patterned its modern education after the style of the West, which was based on stuffing facts and figures into the children's minds where they remained just long enough to be vomited back at exam time. "This is not education!" he emphatically declared. Then he gave his definition.

Real education means the transformation of knowledge into wisdom, which is then used to carve out a strong character. In the educational process, the character and personality of the teacher is most important. The teacher must be able to command, not just the mere respect or love of the children, but a true reverence which can only result from emotional harmony with and intellectual appreciation of the teacher. Without this reverence none of the teaching will have a lasting effect on the children.

Example and precept go together. The children must start looking up to the teacher as a friend, a guide and a philosopher. Sincerity is an important factor, since all children learn more quickly by seeing than by hearing. For this reason, during the ancient days in India, education was only entrusted to persons devoted to a religious life. Such sincere people were totally dedicated to the cause of moulding character in the youth.

....

Swamiji concluded the talk with words to inspire all the attendees to work and live such a moral life that they would become known as ideal teachers. During the following week, the teachers attended classes on the content and meaning of the stories from the Purāṇas and other epics such as the *Rāmāyaṇa* (history of Rāma) and *Bhāgavatam* (stories of Kṛṣṇa), plus the lives of various saints. Although the Purāṇas are full of ethical and moral heroes to act as role models for the children, they also contain the basic truths given in the Upaniṣads. The teachers studied how the characters symbolise aspects of the human personality in the universal struggle to overcome the material dream of the ego and thereby contact the divine Self. Explanations were also given of the deeper philosophical significance of several of the most commonly known gods – Śiva, Gaṇeśa and Pārvatī – with whom the children were already familiar.

Swamiji concluded the week with a reminder that self-development is a long process. The teachers were to keep in mind that their attempts at religious education would not necessarily alter the students' attitudes immediately. But he noted that once the seed had been planted the potential remained. Even though the students might spend four years of sensuous living in the university, experimenting with the tasting and testing of life, they could return to the teaching of an earlier time to help them when they began to face the pressures and competition in their careers. The early glimpses of a basic philosophy of life would have taken root and its blossoming forth would make them better persons and citizens.

Again and again, Swamiji emphasized that the improvement of one's own life and attitudes should be each one's primary concern. In an address to the members in Madras during the celebration of the 10th year anniversary of the Chinmaya Mission, he cautioned the audience –

> "Others will not accept your ideas unless you are improving day by day. If they see your improvement, naturally they will begin asking you, 'How is it that you have totally changed?' Then you give them a few ideas. Don't flood them with dozens of quotes from the Upaniṣads. Give them your own views, those you have digested. Offer your thoughts to them in cupfuls, not by the tub full. They are not elephants."
>
> Before we are concerned with others – whether they are coming to the yajña, whether they are coming to a Study Group – we have to make an annual report of our own improvements. How much have you progressed in these ten years? The only thing to be considered at this moment is how much you and I have improved ourselves.
>
> In five years, an ordinary Narendra became a Vivekananda. Have you at least become a vivekī (one who discriminates between the unreal and Real)?

When the third national Chinmaya Mission conference convened in 1964, there were more than one hundred centres with Study Groups, children's and women's groups, and numerous cultural activities. At this time the officers from the various cities decided that a centralized organization was needed to coordinate the various activities of the Mission – national conferences, spiritual retreats, yajña organization in new towns, projected schools and later the coordination of students-teachers in the various cities. Swamiji suggested that the central committee serves as a bridge, not an authority, to provide a connection for the extended Chinmaya family. The individual centres were to retain their autonomy and remain the backbone of the Mission.

Several of the centres had managed, usually with donations from wealthy devotees, to own a building to serve as a centre to coordinate the various groups in that city, as well as to furnish space for meetings and classes. Others were enthusiastic about acquiring a similar centre, but they were not financially able. Swamiji reminded them that sincerity and ardent desire were their true assets. "If you use these assets properly in the work of the Lord, then Lakṣmī Devī (Goddess of wealth) will come. Because where the Lord is, there she will be."

The symbol of the Mission was designed with an artistic integration of books, a burning oil lamp, a haṁsa (swanlike bird) and a lotus blossom. The books represented the Prasthāna Trayī – the Upaniṣads, the *Brahmasūtras* and the *Bhagavad-gītā*. The oil lamp is the symbol of the moral and ethical life necessary to develop the discriminating power to bring forth the light within. The haṁsa, a sacred bird in Hindu mythology, was said to be capable of drinking only the milk, the sustenance, even though it had been mixed with water, the dross. Such a capacity to discriminate was the goal of the spiritual student. The lovely lotus, also the national flower of India, symbolized the final goal of human life – the flowering and unfolding of the innate inner beauty even while remaining physically rooted in the mud of the earth.

At the conference Swamiji encouraged the Mission members to start doing some project to express their own concerns and talents. Everyone had been soaking up the ideals of the Sanātana-dharma for some ten years, so now was the season to start giving out to others; even if they had to go to the village to find a field of service. He commended one lady who started classes for the harijan (outcaste) children, including furnishing all the necessary supplies out of her pocket. He also mentioned another member, a professional builder, who had constructed two large housing colonies for the lowest income level.

The organizational skills that until now had been used to plan Swamiji's annual yajña in each city, the publishing of his books, and various activities centred around cultural and scriptural study were now to be applied to other fields of service. Some of the Chinmaya Mission workers took to heart Swamiji's words that the most important task in India was to give the children the very best preparation for the demands of an ominous future – a preparation that aimed at the cultivation of their innate talents and spiritual potential. The first nursery school was opened in 1965 in Kollengode, principally due to the generous donations and inexhaustible energy of the regent of that district and her sister who continued to manage it and cover all operating expenses.

Each year thereafter, one nursery school was opened in different areas of India – Kurnool, Mysore, Madras, Calicut, and Bombay (now Mumbai). To assist with this undertaking, Swamini[1] Vidyananda, a retired principal of the women's college in Kurnool, went from town to town to work with the teachers. They would organize their programmes according to the Education Department's guidelines, while incorporating Indian culture and history through story telling and celebration of the numerous religious festivals. The goal was to create schools that would give the latest secular education, but not be divorced from the Hindu cultural moorings of moral values, religious ideals and philosophy of life. In traditional

[1] Swamini is the feminine form of Swami.

Bhārata, it was impossible to separate education and religion, for, religion was a way of life. As soon as the nursery school programme was stabilized, a new grade was added each year, so that the children could complete studies through the sixth standard in the Chinmaya Schools. Then high schools were added in several places as the enthusiasm for the plan and resources grew. The schools were supported by student tuition fees, individual donations and funds from the local Chinmaya Mission chapter.

Swamiji continually emphasized that the Chinmaya Mission was for anyone who was working for the upliftment of the people of Bhārata. In 1963, on behalf of the Chinmaya Mission centres, Swamiji donated an offering of 10,000 rupees to the Swami Vivekananda Rock Memorial Committee at a celebration held in Madras commemorating the centennial birthday of the Swami. The memorial was to be built on the rock at the southern tip of India where Swami Vivekananda had vowed that Bhārata would be free from the foreign rulers and their foreign capitalism and their foreign religion. From that moment onward, he was the motivating force behind the concentrated, although erratic, struggle for freedom of the Indians from the British economic tyranny. At one point, he even recommended that the Hindus should put their spiritual life second to their fight for freedom. Swami Chinmayananda was an appropriate guest speaker for the occasion as he had often expressed respect and admiration for Swami Vivekananda, certainly because of his extensive work for India and Hinduism, and possibly because he was as much of an innovator, rebel and individual as Swami Chinmayananda.

In 1965, when Pakistan attacked India over the old partition feud, the Chinmaya Mission collected money, gold and clothes for the war effort. Swamiji went to the yajña lecture auditorium in Bombay one hour early to personally attend to the collections being made there. Bhāratīyas were no longer willing to sit quietly while invaders slaughtered and looted. This was the attitude throughout India. The Indian soldiers caught the spirit of their countrymen and the war was terminated successfully within a year.

Service projects began in response to the needs in one area, then that project would serve as an inspiration and model to other Chinmaya Mission groups. Soon there were food distribution centres for the poor, free medical diagnostic clinics, hostels for students and places for spiritual retreats scattered around the country.

Seeing the Hindus working together for the improvement of their society and future generations, Swamiji must have felt it was sufficient reward for his efforts. However, in spite of the high ideals, wherever Swamiji went there was some bickering among a small, but often visible, minority of the Mission members. In a reception in Bangalore after his world tour in 1978, Swamiji was confronted with the most common complaint, a member was trying to dominate a committee or a Study Group.

Swamiji cleared his throat and shook his head, "Vedānta has changed me from such a useless fellow – I cannot understand why you all don't change too. Here we are together again, year after year, for some 20 years. The same faces – you've grown old listening. . . and I suppose I've grown old talking. I just can't understand it. If it is too difficult for you to do any sādhanā, why can't you at least bring some kindness and goodness into your treatment of others."

Nevertheless, without a doubt the Chinmaya Mission has created an organized, conscious group of people who are capable of carrying out projects in an orderly, timely, responsible manner. This training has been applied to many areas – from serving one's own family to organizing village craft schools – according to each individual's talents and situation. This quality of integrity of character of the individual citizen is a must if modern Bhārata is going to solve its numerous problems and become once again the true Bhāratvarṣam – home of the sons of light.

23

Sandeepany Sadhanalaya

A new type of Swami is emerging in this country who will serve as a missionary to his or her own people. At this crucial time in our history, we do not need those who live in a cave and meditate.

—Swami Chinmayananda, 1962.

The first stage of the Hindu Renaissance had been the jñāna-yajñas on the major Upaniṣads and the *Bhagavad-gītā*, plus the publication of their commentaries. Swami Chinmayananda had brought respect to the spiritual traditions and had started a spiritual reawakening in India. The second phase would be the training of young people to serve as teachers in future India. As early as June 1955, in an inauguration address of a Madras yajña, Swamiji mentioned that he had an idea of founding a school to teach and train young men and women, so that they could dedicate their lives to the noble cause. As Swamiji put it, "The message of the Upaniṣads is to be interpreted, taught and broadcast – carried from door to door."

He later spoke of this idea to a group in Bombay.

A nation has no future without its connection with its past. We can draw our inspiration, our necessary strength, vitality and beauty only from our traditions. Therefore, the awakening of the consciousness of the populace to the sacred past is to be accomplished now. It is not such a difficult task at all, even though alien missionaries and governments have been trying for

> the past 200 years to break us away from our culture. Now the independent country is atheist and anxious for an ideal. Indeed, the people are very receptive. What we need is more spiritual Teachers.

Swamiji wanted full-time servants of the divine Mission, without worldly ties or vested interests, brave and courageous like himself, who were willing to leave personal ties and concerns for a life of service of the Divine through service to mankind. The training of the young people would be twofold. First, in an āśrama setting, the major scriptures would be studied. Then the graduates would be able to give discourses on the scriptures in their respective communities.

The inspiration, and scriptural authority, for this plan came from the eighteenth chapter of the *Bhagavad-gītā.* After having stated an injunction concerning imparting the divine Knowledge to others, Lord Kṛṣṇa states the benefits to both the one who teaches and the one who studies the scriptures –

> "This (Knowledge) is never to be spoken by you to one who is devoid of austerities or devotion, nor one who does not render service, nor one who desires not to listen, nor to one who mocks Me.
>
> But he who, with supreme devotion to Me, teaches this supreme secret to My devotees shall doubtless know Me.
>
> Nor is there any among men who does dearer service to Me, nor shall there be another on earth dearer to Me than he.
>
> And he who will study this sacred dialogue of ours, by him I shall have been worshipped by the jñāna-yajña, such is My conviction.[1]"

[1] *Bhagavad-gītā* – 18.67-70

Thus the construction of Sandeepany Sadhanalaya, an āśrama school, was the fulfilment of a long cherished dream. Begun early in 1961, it was built entirely through yajña collections and private donations offered by the numerous supporters of Swamiji's mission. Situated in a natural setting beside the lovely Powai lake thirty kilometers north of Bombay, the school was named after the Guru of Śrī Kṛṣṇa, Ṛṣi Sāndīpanī. In a thorough training for three years, free of any personal expense, young men and women would gain knowledge of the basic Hindu scriptures. All of Swamiji's lectures would be cancelled for the three-year period, so that he would be able to teach.

Swamiji took up residence at Sandeepany in mid November, 1962, his first home in many years. At that time, a team of volunteer staff members met and divided the various tasks among themselves, including the supervision of the completion of the buildings for classes, hostels and the combined kitchen and dining hall.

On January 9, 1963, the sixth anniversary of the Mahāsamādhi of Swami Tapovanam, the training course was begun with appropriate rites. Two days earlier, the students had been initiated into the brahmacarya āśrama in preparation for the inauguration. The students received a mantra and the yellow robes from the presiding paṇḍita along with blessings of their Guru, Swami Chinmayananda.

The actual inauguration was a simple function. After chanting the peace prayer and the '*Guru Stotram*' (Hymn to the Guru), Swamiji, in his role as Chief Ācārya (Teacher), gave the first class. Then he turned the students over to Śrī Raja Raja Varma, the Sanskrit teacher, and requested that they gain a working knowledge of Sanskrit as soon as possible. He expressed his desire that they would be able to study the Upaniṣads in the beauty of their original language. Swami Govindagiri, Swamiji's brother disciple from Uttarkashi, and Shusheela Mudliar, who had assisted Swamiji since his first Poona yajña, were among the guests.

A few months later on the 11th of April, with the sun shining overhead, the official opening ceremony was celebrated. The brahmacārīs hoisted the flag on a 60-foot pole amidst chanting of the Vedas, ringing bells and blowing of a conch. Turning to the young men, Swamiji said, "Look! I have not hoisted the flag. You have done it. Now it is up to you to keep the flag flying."

Swamiji never expressed any discouragement about the number of students, although it was fewer than he had anticipated, and considerably less than had originally expressed interest in taking the course. Construction of the school had taken three years longer than planned. In the interim, many potential students had become involved in other pursuits and were no longer available for such a commitment.

Some years later, on March 27, 1978, another ceremony was performed with the installation of a statue of Swami Tapovanam. The image of black stone was placed under an elaborate dome, which was carved of red stone, near the main gate of Sandeepany. Swamiji desired that his Guru, a paragon of spiritual understanding, should be present as a guardian angel to shower his blessings over the entire activities of the school and students. After an elegant unveiling ceremony, Swamiji explained to the devotees that the true unveiling of Swami Tapovanam was the revealing of the Truth in all their hearts.

Before being accepted for the course, each prospective student had to have a preliminary interview with Swamiji. Swami Purushottamananda remembers his first interview with Swamiji – "I will watch you; you will watch me," Swamiji wound up the interview. After watching the teacher for three years, the student concluded, "He has the discipline of a father and the love of a mother."

This student also remembered well the day he interrupted Swamiji during the class to ask – "Swamiji, this ignorance that Vedānta is always pointing out, where did it come from?"

"Are you here to learn about knowledge or ignorance? I think you all are already masters of ignorance without studying it!" Swamiji wisecracked as the class exploded into laughter.

The students were to find out that learning about knowledge was an arduous endeavour. At 4 a.m. a bell rang to announce the beginning of the day. Their first duty was to clean the classroom and prepare it for the day, which meant that the students already had to be up, bathed and dressed before they heard the bell. From 4:30 to 5 a.m. daily, there was a period of chanting the scriptures, then the class began promptly at 5 a.m. However, sometimes Swamiji would show up at 4 a.m. to address the class because he had some function to attend in Bombay or a meeting before noon; the students knew they had better be in the classroom at the first bell, just in case. It was also the hour that tea was served, an impetus to be on time as the tea was beneficial for staying awake for the two hour – or longer – class. Swamiji would watch the students, as long as their faces remained alert and interested, he would continue talking.

After class, each student had been assigned a task around the āśrama. Some cleaned the rice, dal or wheat, which would be ground into flour for rotis; the women washed and cut the vegetables for the meals; the men did gardening or general clean up. Others worked on the production of *Tapovan Prasad* magazine, which was a magazine focussing on the Chinmaya Mission activities, rather than transcripts of Swamiji's teaching as the previous publications had done. For the remainder of their free time, the students were expected to be studying and reflecting on the ideas from their scriptural studies.

During the first year Swamiji lived in the men's hostel, insisting that his cottage should not be built until all the school facilities were completed. He organized his daily schedule carefully with precise arrangements for every appointment after the morning class. Satsaṅga with the students was fitted into the day only after he had finished all of his duties overseeing the āśrama and his daily stack of correspondence was answered. Sundays were exceptions, for some one hundred people drove out to the āśrama from Bombay to spend the day. It was like a holiday, for, his satsaṅgas lasted for hours.

He always insisted that the many devotees who gathered around him wherever he travelled were to worship God – not the Guru. "If the Guru does something that you don't like or understand, then your faith will be shaken. You worship the Lord. He is the only one who will never disappoint you," he instructed repeatedly.

For years, he refused to let anyone give the traditional prostration at his feet. One Sunday, an old, crippled lady came out to see the Swami; of course, she wanted to bow at his feet. Swamiji kindly told her, "You don't need to touch my feet. Anyway, it is too difficult for you to bend over." But when she would not be dissuaded, he said, "Here, I'll make it easy for you," as he lifted his foot up to the lady's hand to save her from stooping.

The students would always arrange a celebration for Swamiji's birthday. A caravan of devotees would come up from Bombay for the special celebration. He would tease them, saying, "I am just allowing you to play; as an affectionate father, out of his infinite love for his child, may temporarily get down on all fours and pretend he's an elephant, so his small boy can climb up on his back and beat him. Similarly, I'm allowing you to play and think that I have a birthday. How can the unborn ever have a birth date? The man living in that Consciousness is identified only with the eternally unborn."

Whatever Swamiji did, he did with undivided attention. When the students told him he should rest more, for, the light in his cottage was often on until after midnight, he reminded them that work done with total attention and confidence was executed in such a manner that there would be no anxieties produced and no residue of thought left over; therefore, the mind remained peaceful. It was the anxiety and residual thoughts that sap the energy. One who retains a clear, calm attitude throughout his work does not require relaxation time and will need much less sleep, he assured them.

Each afternoon, walking tall and straight with his measured pace, Swamiji would take a round of the āśrama to check the ongoing construction. His astute mind was quick to see a better way to do a job; he had not lost his flair for mechanics. Since Sandeepany is located on a hill, a question arose as to whether they would reach the water necessary for the operation of an āśrama. "Dig until you strike," he instructed the men as he pointed out the spot to dig. Water was encountered at four hundred feet.

He began to tease the students that they should use this slogan for their spiritual quest. "Dig until you strike!" he would throw out at them as he passed them on the walkway sometimes in a loud voice, sometimes in a soft tone, or other times with laughter and a wink.

As often occurred in Swamiji's Mission, whenever a need arose, a reliable, dedicated person appeared to fill the position. Śrī A. Parthasarathy gave up his career to serve Swamiji as the āśrama manager to administer the organization and finances. He had already been spending his spare hours working for the Mission, including organizing yajñas and Study Groups in Bombay, as well as compiling ideas and examples from Swamiji's lectures into a one year correspondence course. He supervised the construction of a library and a temple.

The Śrī Śankarācārya at Kavir Maṭha laid the foundation stone for the temple at Sandeepany on April 10, 1964. Amidst a crowd of students and Chinmaya Mission members, the ninety-nine year old Swami blessed the auspicious occasion with his holy presence and prayers. He praised the institution and said he was glad to see the work being done by Swami Chinmayananda, for Sandeepany was exactly the type of institution that he had been contemplating establishing. He added that this cherished desire had found its fulfilment in Sandeepany Sadhanalaya and he prayed for its success.

This year at Sandeepany, which was free from travel, gave Swamiji the time to finalise an idea that had been in the back of his mind and bring it into manifestation. In November 1963, he announced an idea to convene a Hindu Council, inviting delegates from all over the world to meet, discuss and discover the needs and difficulties for the maintenance and revitalization of Hindu culture. "In this council we shall try to hammer out the plans and means to hold our spiritual family together," Swamiji vowed.

In August 1964, sixty delegates assembled at Sandeepany, representing the many different sects of the Hindu society – the Vaiṣṇavites, Śaivites, Liṅgāyatas, Advaitins, Dvaitins, Sikhs and representatives of other small groups. Many of these factions were founded on an allegiance to a particular Master in the past. While the Master had considered himself only a Teacher of spiritual truths and interpreted the practical part of the Hindu scriptures according to the temperament and needs of the people of his generation, those who followed often made his words into dogma. This tendency was aided by the lack of communication between the many areas of Bhārata until the mid twentieth century. The majority of these sects only exist in small regions.

In his introductory remarks, Swamiji stated that it was essential for all the different factions of Hinduism to rub off their harsh corners and become pliable, so that everyone could work together to consolidate Hindu culture. This conference was the initiation of a yearly Vishwa Hindu Parishad, or World Hindu Conference, with specific aims – (1) To take steps to consolidate and strengthen the Hindu society, (2) To protect, develop and spread the Hindu values, both ethical and spiritual, in the context of modern times, (3) To establish and strengthen contacts with Hindus living abroad.

By the end of the first year of classes, it was apparent that to financially sustain the operating funds for the āśrama, Swamiji would have to continue with the yajñas. So with his 'one square inch of assets,' as he referred to his tongue, he would be gone for ten days at a time. "Do not waste a single minute!" he challenged the students on his way out of the āśrama gates.

When he returned to the āśrama, usually for some four or five days, he would be met at the Bombay airport, whisked to the āśrama where he walked straight into the classroom. The students knew when he was arriving, so they would be assembled ready for his instructions. Swamiji always pointed out to them – "After listening to the Teacher, you must do your own contemplation. This time when I am away is a God given opportunity for you."

The āśrama kept strict rules. Every departure by a student had to be approved in advance. Visits from outsiders had to be approved also. No letters to or from the family were allowed during the first year. On one occasion Swamiji was away when J. Krishnamurthi was speaking in the nearby town of Andheri. Several of the boys went to hear him without obtaining prior permission. When Swamiji returned, the infraction of the rules was reported to him. He listened and made no comment. Everyone was in suspense; they couldn't believe that he was going to forget the incident, but a week or so went by while he remained silent on the matter.

The next week, the students were going to join him for the upcoming yajña in Ahmedabad. Packed and ready, they were standing at the āśrama gate waiting for the transportation to arrive. "Okay, who were the ones who left the āśrama without permission?" his stern voice boomed out. "You'll be staying here while the rest of us go to Ahmedabad." It was a tough punishment for a few hours away from the āśrama, but he was tough. He would tell the students, "You have to have self-discipline to back your desire for Liberation. If you can't take these few āśrama rules, how will you ever learn to control your mind when you return to the world?"

When he saw the long looks on their faces when he announced some task or discipline, he would remind them – "You are here to learn, and I am teaching you in the best way I know. The gate is always open. But once you walk out, there is no coming back." Those who took the disciplines in the spirit that they were intended – preparation for an important task out in the world where temptations would be many – remained. Others left because they had come with a traditional conception of life with a Guru, and life with Swamiji did not fit the description. They wanted more personal attention from him than he was able to give them with the many yajñas away from the āśrama and the numerous responsibilities when he returned.

In times past, the student, desiring Liberation, searched for a Guru in the remote areas of the mountains. The student who arrived at the Master's feet had already reaped his harvest of experiences in the world. Now he had only one desire remaining in his heart – to know the Truth behind all this world of change that he had daily observed and interacted with. As the students served the Guru, he put them through various tests. Continually, the Guru watched to ascertain the student's mental peace. When his mind was perceived to be balanced and calm, the Guru would then allow the student to ask his spiritual questions. Ideally, a simple statement of Truth by the Guru was all that was necessary for the dawning of the divine Truth in such a purified mind.

Enlightenment is not an experience of the physical, emotional or intellectual apparatus of man, but a falling back into the being of which these instruments of body, mind and intellect are becomings. Without these instruments there is no external world, therefore, no experience or experiencer. 'An experience beyond all experiences,' the sages say for the purpose of communication.

To reach such a purity or stillness of mind is the purpose of spiritual discipline. But instead of retirement to the Himalayas to live with a Teacher, Swamiji was attempting a new means to achieve the same result. With the training at Sandeepany, he intended to bring the students to a certain intellectual understanding of life's processes, as well as a capacity for the discipline necessary for insight into their divine nature. Then for spiritual refinement, they would go out to teach the scriptures and work on uplifting projects for society as a means to complete the purification. After some twenty years of working they could retire to a Chinmaya Mission retreat for a period of sustained meditation.

There were also opportunities for those who were not to be full-time teachers to take advantage of the classes at Sandeepany. During the summer after the opening of the āśrama there was a one week sādhanā camp for the Chinmaya Mission Study Group members. This type of camp was repeated regularly, so that the members could spend time with Swamiji and have a retreat in a peaceful setting away from the responsibilities of home and office. The āśrama was also available to the Chinmaya Mission workers for a spiritual retreat during their vacation time. All visitors were expected to follow the same disciplines as the students.

Swamiji would not miss an opportunity to give his students experience in teaching also. Periodically, he would ask them to speak a few words on a text in front of the class, more often if there were guests present. Their delivery had to be original. If the student dared to repeat the words or examples that Swamiji had used in his discussion, he would roar, "Stop! If I wanted to hear the exact words I had said, I could have bought myself a dozen tape recorders and taped it. I would not have the expense of feeding and clothing the tape recorders. Don't vomit back my words! What have you thought of these verses for yourself? What mananam (contemplation) have you done? You must reflect on the verses and reach your own insights. You must discuss only what you have assimilated yourself."

One of the visitors, with the innate capacity of the Indians to tell everything they know, came to Swamiji with the accusation that one of the students was smoking in the bathroom of the men's hostel. "These boys aren't perfect; perfect people never come to an āśrama. Religion is for the wicked and the vulgar, just as a hospital is for the ill. Will the doctor complain because only sick people are coming to his office? The boy is here attempting to improve, that is all that matters."

The āśrama also served as a temporary home for Swamis from the Himalayas who needed medical care. Even his cousin, Swami Jnanananda, who had become a strict recluse, came here when it was absolutely necessary to have his body repaired. Then as soon as possible, he ran back to his simple hut on the Ganga banks. He had no interest in living in an āśrama. Soon after his pilgrimage through the Himalayas with Balakrishnan Menon, Swami Jnanananda had packed his small box of belongings and moved to the higher altitudes of Badarinath where the weather is so extreme that even the temple is closed for six months of winter. Even so, he remained there year round in contemplation and meditation without proper food and giving no attention to the general needs of his body except the daily bath in the icy Ganga waters – when they were unfrozen. Although he loved nature and was a devotee of the Lord, he had no patience with man. He was quite content when Swamiji was away at a yajña, but as soon as he returned Swami Jnanananda fussed and fumed. "You bring a storm into this place. How do you live in the middle of a such a storm all the year round?" Swamiji would smile and accept the criticism in silence, for, all remained peaceful in the eye of the storm.

Since he had only three or four days in the āśrama, Swamiji would extend the morning class to three hours or longer. Or just at lunchtime he would call the students over to the classroom. "I have some extra time now, let's continue with the Upaniṣad." With their stomachs growling from their light breakfast of a cup of tea, and with the odours of the kitchen next door wafting into the windows, they trooped into the classroom, hoping that the lecture would be a short one. But he would talk without any signs of fatigue or hunger for one and half hours. "Well, we could not have had the Upaniṣad class after lunch," he explained as they left the hall. "With full stomachs, you would have all slept off on me. Eat your food, take a rest, and meet me back here at 4 p.m. so we can continue."

In the third year of classes, he announced, "Tomorrow we will begin *Māṇḍūkya-upaniṣad.* You can't understand *Māṇḍūkya* if you eat two meals a day – so now you'll have only one meal a day, at noon."

By the third year, over half of the original thirty students had gone and another five or six had begun the course. As the years rolled on, Swamiji's responsibilities to the many Chinmaya Mission centres, in addition to his daily correspondence and visitors, continued to multiply. "We're never going to get any peace here in Bombay. Let's pack up and go to the Himalayas, so we can really get down to serious study," he instructed his students. It was the monsoon season, so no yajñas had been scheduled for three months.

Life was more leisurely, yet more intense in the clear, clean, quiet atmosphere of the Himalayan valley. Sitting in the environment where sages had dwelled, the students begin to glimpse the profound nature of the Hindu tradition. After the first month of classes at Tapovanam Kutir, Swamiji happily announced while rubbing his palms together with a broad grin, "Now it's your turn to start talking."

Each day several of the students were to explain the *Bhagavad-gītā*, taking it verse by verse, each one speaking for ten to fifteen minutes on each verse. After they completed that exercise successfully, he expanded the time to thirty minutes per person. "Now, you know how to talk. . . It's time to listen," he beamed as he brought out a tape recorder. About that same time, he pulled the plug on their rotation system. After several days they had been able to figure which verse would fall at their turn, so naturally they had prepared exclusively for that specific verse. But under the new system, the selection would be by pulling straws – and the speaking time extended to one hour each. Oh, how they suffered listening to their 'ands', 'aahs', and long pauses on the tape recorder, not to speak of the lack of content of their talks. Would they ever be prepared for the great mission, they wondered.

When they returned to Uttarkashi the following summer during the rainy season, he informed them – "Okay, now you can explain the *Gītā*, but you cannot talk to an audience." He would give them a hypothetical case of a certain type of audience that they were to address, so they would learn to speak on the level of any specific person or organization. Giggling college girls, an old folks' retirement home, a businessmen's club, a sick friend, a bereaved mother – Swamiji's imagination ran rampant as he challenged their flexibility. After they spoke, Swamiji would criticize their approach and give them suggestions. Then one day he hit Kutty with the impossible – a night club. Neither Kutty nor any of his fellow students had ever entered a night club. Nevertheless, he forged ahead with a lengthy discussion on the three states of Consciousness. "Look", Swamiji interrupted him. "You are surrounded by dancing girls and a drunk manager. You only have three minutes before the beer bottles start to fly. Now, what will you have to say?"

Next he gave them further instructions. "You know now to sit and talk; now you must learn to stand and talk." He would observe them during their discourses and make comments, sometimes imitating them, their shifting feet and wringing hands. He then demonstrated how to stand by planting the feet squarely for a good base. Thus he proceeded, moulding and shaping them into teachers by making them aware of every aspect of their delivery, both physical and intellectual. With this intense training, when they actually became Teachers, they could forego their self-conscious preoccupations with the physical aspects of the delivery. They would remain relaxed and focused, so that the message of the eternal Truth could flow through them without obstruction.

The students had been chanting the *'Gaṅgā Stotram'* (Hymn to the Ganga) during their first stay, but somehow they had not gotten around to chanting it this second trip. One morning Swamiji noticed and questioned them, "Why aren't you singing the *'Gaṅgā Stotram'* in the evening? Everyone fasts today." When he was brought his lunch, he would not eat it. "When I said everyone, I meant everyone. If my students don't eat, I don't eat either." The following day, he accused them of being dry intellectuals and made them sing bhajanas for four days straight without any breaks for classes. "The spiritual ideas of the intellect must trickle down and melt the heart," he admonished them.

His model of conscious action in his daily life was their greatest Teacher. As a service project, the students had made up a small booklet on simple daily spiritual practices to be passed out to the local villagers. After distributing a bundle, Brahmacāriṇī[1] Sharada returned with a couple of the booklets that the printer had put together with some of the pages turned upside down. She handed Swamiji the books, commenting, "I passed them all out except these two because they were defective." Swamiji took the books, carefully removed the staples in the spine, righted the pages, and then re-stapled them. "There, now you can pass these out too," he commented, returning the books to the brahmacāriṇī.

One day after their return to Sandeepany in Bombay, Swamiji ordered the students – "Go out to sweat and work! You've been hanging around here too long now. Let's see what you lazy ones can do out there in the world!"

Working out in the world brought some real challenges for the students. The disciplines of the āśrama suddenly seemed almost easy in comparison to managing people and classes for the Chinmaya Mission. Brahmacārī Hari Das recalled his first five years of teaching –

[1] Brahmacāriṇī is the feminine form of brahmacārī.

"I remember how some of us would complain that there were not enough people at our talks. Swamiji would just laugh at us and say, 'What do you expect? A thousand people to come and listen to you?' We would try to get him to come inaugurate our lecture series because we know his presence would draw a crowd and at least get us off to a good start, but he would refuse. We were on our own. When I think of how at his first yajña the audience swelled to nine hundred, I know that there must have been a divine purpose behind the work. In spite of the fact that we have hundreds of Mission members helping us with organizing and advertising, so few come to hear us. If ten people came to hear me in Calcutta, I had to be satisfied."

The young men and women who trained at Sandeepany through the years encountered many challenges in their attempts to live up to Swamiji's ideal. Perhaps, they grew too dependent on the protection of an āśrama environment to be able to be disciplined in their spiritual practices. Or they became too accustomed to being cared for and now expected it from the Chinmaya Mission members, for, most of the students had not been on their own before. Cut off from the safe harbour of both āśrama and family, some were tested beyond their capacity. Complaints would crop up regularly, but Swamiji considered the brahmacārīs his children and would always take their side. One member reported that the brahmacārī in his city was not living up to what he was teaching. "Of course, he is not!" retorted Swamiji. "No one can! He is teaching the goal that each of us is striving for. I've sent these young people out into the world to be polished up; they are learning. They are so young; you are older, more mature. What example are you setting for them?"

Another complained that some of the brahmacārīs were not staying to work in the Chinmaya Mission, but were drifting away after finishing the course. Swamiji looked into the situation and found those who were not involved in the Mission were finding success in their own fields of endeavour. "We do not need them to hang on to the organization. We wanted to give them the knowledge and courage to face life, whether it be a spiritual or material endeavour. The Mission only provides one field of many possibilities in which the individual can purify his mind through service to others," Swamiji explained.

When someone wrote him inquiring how the brahmacārīs were doing, as he never heard anything notable about them, Swamiji replied –

"All of them are doing really well, and they are improving; they are all in different stages of unfoldment. Some take longer to shed their ego and so for a length of time they suffer under its inner entanglements and inhibitions. Some surrender their personal ego too quickly, explode into blinding brilliance, and then again recrystallize for themselves a new ego built labouriously on their own little successes. To break it, they need constant help from us, perhaps for years.

As the ancient Masters have said, disciples fall characteristically into three prototypes – (1) those who impart Vedānta-śāstra (scriptural) knowledge to others, efficiently and eloquently; (2) those who maintain and administer our various organizational activities; and (3) those who are but dreary rice bags and hapless clothes hangers. We also have our share of the third category. They are in every institution the world over, especially, I must admit, in spiritual and religious organizations. We can't avoid it. We can only weed them out and attempt to keep them at a minimum within the organization.

In fact, it is almost axiomatic to declare that every teacher must recognize that his disciples are a mixture of the poor, the fair and the good. The poor disciple utilises and benefits by the teacher's influence; the fair disciple admires and reveres the teacher's kindness; the good disciple alone can thrive under the teacher's strict discipline and grow to become a teacher.

I have replied to you exhaustively. If you have written to discourage me, you have certainly failed. I am closely observing and anxiously reviewing the performance of my boys and girls who have completed the course and those who are now with us in the Sandeepany Sadhanalaya. There is no point in hurrying anyone. Growth is effective and enduring, beautiful and enchanting, only when it takes place at its own leisurely stride and natural rhythm. Watch a flower opening! Look at the dawn and the sunrise, the dusk and the sunset! No hurry. Let it happen in His gracious pace!"

Repeatedly, he explained to the students that one who renounces the world would build up a mental energy from his meditation because his energy is no longer being dissipated in the world of objects. This energy can become like a dam without any channels to handle the overflow; inevitably, the dam will break. To avoid this problem, the students were to put energy into study and meditation, and also into performing physical actions by teaching and serving others. This channeling of the conserved energy into some project was necessary to avoid the breaking of the mind.

He also cautioned them about the development of an ego that could grow from their teaching of the scriptures. "Teaching is also thinking of the Lord. You are doing your own mananam (contemplation) aloud. If others benefit, fine; if not, fine. Your only interest is that you yourself benefit from the words," Swamiji reminded them again and again.

In that first group of students were Swami Purushottamananda, Swamini Saradapriyananda and Swami Jyotirmayananda, who have faithfully served the Mission since their training in the āśrama, along with Swami Harinamananda who served the Mission for twenty years. Many other students including Swamini Gangananda and Swami Sarvananda, although they did not immediately become full-time Mission workers, helped with organization of yajñas and Study Groups in their hometowns. Swamiji never exacted any obligation that the students owed him or the Mission anything. He was confident that with the knowledge of their heritage and insight into their spiritual nature that the students would bring a special quality to whatever work they found to do in the world; thereby they would mature spiritually. All beneficial work was the Lord's work, not just teaching the scriptures.

24

Around the World

I am not coming to the West to teach you; it is also to learn from you.

—Swami Chinmayananda, 1964.

Wishing to share the wisdom of the ancient Hindu sages with others, Swamiji at last agreed to carry the message to distant lands. Mr. B. V. Reddy had been quite taken with Swamiji's unique presentation of the Hindu scriptures when he met him in 1962. A successful businessman, Mr. Reddy had plans for establishing an international yoga school. Full of enthusiasm, his head spinning with ideas, he remarked to Swamiji at the train station as he was leaving Madras, "Swamiji, why don't you go overseas? I want ammunition to export yoga to America." Reddy was not the first person to suggest that Swamiji travel outside of India; several Americans and Europeans who had visited Sandeepany had invited him abroad. He had always replied it would happen at the appropriate time. But on this occasion, Swamiji replied, "Go on, arrange it," as he disappeared into the train.

Arrange it B.V. Reddy did. Two years and fifteen hundred letters later, Swamiji was on his way. The itinerary included twelve countries as diverse as Thailand and Switzerland. Every detail of every stop had been arranged – reception committee formed, car rented, press releases and advertising handled, and auditoriums rented.

Before leaving on his first world tour, Swamiji made a trip to the Himalayas to visit Ananda Kutir at Rishikesh. He paid his respects at the place of interment[1] of Swami Sivananda, the man who had instilled in him twenty years earlier the idea to take the message of the Sanātana-dharma of the Vedas to foreign lands. After returning to Delhi, Swamiji and B.V. Reddy boarded the plane on the 6th of March 1965, bound for their first stop – Bangkok.

During this first tour, Swamiji introduced the ideas of Vedānta in one or two day talks on the logic of a spiritual life. Persons who had met Swamiji previously in India had arranged some of the talks. He spoke at such places as the Asia Society in San Francisco and the Vedānta Society in Los Angeles.

He was genuinely inquisitive about the young Americans. He wanted to understand what the American culture was about and what was causing the young people of the 1960s to reject their parents' values. In San Francisco, he walked through Haight-Ashbury and Golden Gate Park, the heavens of the hippie generation. When a group gathered, he would discuss whatever questions were asked him. If there were no questions from the onlookers, he would ask them questions about their outlook on life, their dreams and aspirations. He even stood inconspicuously in the back of a bar one evening watching this typical American scene.

In his discussions, Swamiji found that wherever he went the people asked the same questions as the Indians back home – "Why did God create this world?" "What is God's grace?" "What is the difference in self-hypnosis and Self-realization?" But there was one new one – "Why do you think Christianity has failed the young people here in America?" He replied –

"It is true that Christianity has failed to satisfy the youth here. They feel that there is something lacking in their religion and they tell you this straight and openly. Naturally, they are trying to understand the Eastern philosophy to see if it can fill up the vacuum. They make an honest attempt, and, in fact, many

[1] Swami Sivananda had died on July 17, 1963. Mahātmās are not cremated since there is no attachment to the body.

American universities now have a department teaching Indian and other Asian religions.

It is not that the Christian religion has nothing to offer. It is simply that the Church is not able to satisfy the rational demand of modern youth looking for explanations about life. It is not Christ and the *Bible* that have failed, but the priests and preachers and their sermons have disillusioned the youth. Even in India the students are not inclined to discuss the (philosophical) truths of life unless it is interpreted to them in a language they can understand.

> Hinduism includes a logical science to explain our divine essence as well as practices to guide its followers to recast their personalities. Therefore, it is at once a science and an art. In learning science, freedom is necessary. In practising the art of self-development, freedom is the very atmosphere required. So in Hinduism, there is a greater freedom and elasticity. These are at once the very beauty and the bane of Hinduism.
>
> Christianity gives no logic nor positive practices for improvement, but rather a list of don'ts. Decadence in culture and religion generally bring about an era wherein the negative aspects of the spiritual disciplines are over-emphasized. This is the problem with the priests, parents and scriptures today – and not only in America. On the other hand, the moment the positive side of religion is taken up for serious study and practice, a spiritual renaissance is ushered in."

The tour included stops in the West Indies, South Africa, Mauritius and Malaysia, areas with large Hindu populations. These people remain a reminder of the British Raj when thousands of Indians, mostly from Tamil Nadu and Northern

Bengal, were rounded up and packed into ships – many to die from the conditions en route – to be taken to areas where cheap agricultural labour was needed. After satisfying their obligation of ten years' indentured labour, they often exchanged their fare to return home for a plot of land. Those who had become permanent property of the landowners because of the labourers' debts were freed by the Reform Bill of 1833 when British Parliament abolished slavery throughout the Empire.

These Hindus had clung to their religion even though they were away from India. As there had not been proper guidance and little contact with their homeland for a century, many misconceptions about the scriptures and rituals were prevalent. The people from these countries welcomed Swamiji and became serious students of Vedānta. It was a time when people everywhere were interested in the Indian Gurus. Wherever he travelled, people from other religions came to listen to him. A black Christian minister from Trinidad, Dr. George Baldwin, left Trinidad to attend the course at Sandeepany in Bombay.

Swamiji was welcomed in the Buddhist countries. India was the source of their religion; therefore, Buddhists everywhere have an admiration for the homeland of their religion. Most of the descriptions of India in the early centuries are accounts written by Chinese Buddhist monks on pilgrimage to the monasteries and holy places in Buddhist India.

Mr. Reddy described their three month tour –

> "It was a divine song. Everything went perfectly. Everywhere there was such love, as if old friends, as if old lovers, were meeting again – and all of these people had never heard of Swamiji before."

From Athens, Greece, Swamiji wrote a letter, dated June 15, 1965, to all the Mission members for publication in *Tapovan Prasad*.

"I am now almost on the shores of India. I can almost hug her from here. From March 7th when I left, till today, never was a day spent in rest or idleness. There were two to three meetings everyday, besides group discussions, newspaper and radio interviews, and television appearances. I met politicians, economists, historians, poets, writers, publishers, professors and teachers. We visited museums, schools, colleges, clubs, hotels, restaurants, supermarkets and hospitals. In between all these activities, we had to pack and unpack, travel and catch the next plane. There were no invitations for bhikṣā, so we had to hunt for vegetarian food. There were reports to be prepared, letters to be answered and instructions to be given to the students at Sandeepany Sadhanalaya and the directors of the Central Chinmaya Mission Trust.

Altogether, there was no time to worry or to feel the fatigue. No, in fact, there was no time even to assimilate what I have gone through. Everything seems to be a maze of misty memories and marching experiences.

Now we have to cover only Lebanon and Jordan, then on the 27th I will touch the sacred land of India. I can already smell her mangoes, her rain soaked earth, her fragrant peace and sweet tenderness. There is no place on the face of the earth like my country."

On his second trip to America, he conducted a series of lectures of four or five days on specific topics. The 1960s had brought a regular troupe of Gurus with their yoga postures, meditation techniques and promises of cosmic Consciousness, particularly in the large cities of the east and west coasts, but none had taught the actual scriptures. It was not difficult to draw a crowd because there was a habitual group who were going out to hear the Gurus – any Indian Guru – who passed through the country. But they found Swami Chinmayananda to be different.

First, in spite of his Indian accent, he spoke English quite well. This meant that they could go to him directly with a question. As he travelled, Swamiji investigated and observed life of the American, so when he answered their questions it was in their everyday language embellished with examples from their experiences. Then too, he was so practical; he seemed to have a sensible answer to every aspect of life, whether material or spiritual. People who had already heard other Indian Gurus were surprised, and pleased, by the fact that there was no fee for any of the discourses, only an opportunity to drop a donation in a basket at the exit at the end of the lecture series, which is the true Indian tradition.

Students of Vedānta carried their sleeping bags and followed him from city to city. In several towns, a small house was available for Swamiji to stay in, so everyone else camped out in the backyard. They cooked American style vegetarian meals. Occasionally, Swamiji would join in to show them how to make an Indian dish.

A group of sincere American students formed in San Francisco for weekly meetings to read and study the *Bhagavad-gītā*. They waited for Swamiji's annual return to the United States and began to help organize his tour schedule. Once, it included an outdoor talk on a Sunday afternoon in Golden Gate Park. Swamiji seemed to be more inspired in the outdoor setting, similar to the set-up in India. The discourses were light with a lot of stories, but he always challenged the audience to look towards a deeper reality.

The Americans knew they could not ignore or change their heritage, but they asked themselves how they could integrate East and West. Several had set an ideal of somehow combining the materialism of America with the spiritual wisdom of India for the best of all possible worlds. When Robert Holbin wrote Swamiji of this idea in June of 1968, Swamiji replied with detailed comments on the priorities for the Americans if they were to succeed in their spiritual ideals.

Letter to American Student

Dear Robert,

I received your letter yesterday. It was a joy to hear from you in this quiet mountain retreat. I heard from Bombay that they have sent extra copies of the preview of our correspondence lessons to Nalini Browning, and therefore, you must have received it by now.

To serve as a bridge between the East and the West, the individual must have an inconceivable height, and his arms must have the widest imaginable embrace. Remember your geography, he will have to stand in the middle of the Pacific Ocean to hold California and Madras (now Chennai) together or stand in the mid-Atlantic to hold New York and Bombay in one embrace... Supposing Mr. Holbin acquires the necessary height to stand safely in the Atlantic, and let us hope that he has cultivated an embrace sufficient to hug both Boston and Badarinath – still, remember, Mr. Holbin, that the entire traffic has to run over the crossroads of your shoulders.

When an individual has grown to such a height and such an arm's length and has lost his head in the heights of meditation, he becomes that All-pervading. Because where the ego has ended, Spirit alone exists. The Spirit needs neither the Eastern spirituality and its values of life, nor the Western materialism and its all annihilating missiles of death and disaster. In the Eternal Heart, there are no continents; there are no people – there is only love. Cultivate such an all embracing love which seeks no distinction, sees no difference, knows no East and West – and you will bring the whole universe into your palm.

Complete the study course, sincerely and seriously. Absorb the lessons until they become the very essence of your spiritual existence. Live every word conscientiously. Even though some ideas may look impractical and absurd, live them all. Live the ideas without any compromise. You can. And you must.

It is urgent. Perhaps you don't see how urgent it is. A wonderful civilization is slipping into a devastating destruction. The symptoms are obvious. You are a people who have no control over your passions, who live in an atmosphere of hatred and mutual incrimination, who are sinking into tribal levels, despoiling your culture and shattering your civilization. This destruction is a tragedy. In the psychological cataclysm that is taking place in America, saner islands of quiet and peace are to be discovered, so that some can hold their hands together and form at least a Noah's Ark!

Life survives. It has a tenacity and a larger purpose than modern man has ever even suspected. The Roman and the Greek civilizations were wiped out because of their own excesses. Yet, life did not cease. India may rot, America may decay, Europe may be blasted, Asia may be wiped out, but life will survive. The world and its continents are only platforms on which mere individuals for a few hours flicker, dance and jump about making what they call 'history'. But if this good old globe of ours, so consistently moving around its own axis once a day – moving now at an angle to the vertical – if it were to take into its head to straighten itself, the existing continents would get submerged and equal amounts of new land would rise from the ooze of the sea. Thus, life will continue.

Man, as he is today, has no control over himself. He has been given a freedom to evolve and, in this attempted evolution, he is also allowed to do some mischief. A very considerate, old, generous heavenly Father loves all these childish pranks of man, and apparently even allows man to spread his chest in his empty vanity!

But let us not, at least in our saner moments, forget that at our level of consciousness today we are not masters, neither over ourselves nor over our world. Vedānta points the way to self-mastery – a great grand path, an expressway to the higher Consciousness.

Ardently wish to embrace the whole universe. Never plan to make a crazy quilt of the world by bringing together the spiritual experience of the East and the material wealth of the West. This cannot be done. Where one is, the other cannot be.

Study the lessons. Study yourself.
Start the pilgrimage. Reach the goal.

s/Swami Chinmayananda

After several trips to the U.S. he decided that the introductory phase was over and it was time for serious business. He began an intensive schedule similar to the yajñas in India. In the morning, he gave a text such as Ādi Śaṅkarācārya's *Bhaja Govindam*, in the evening, a one and one-half hour's class from the *Bhagavad-gītā*; then after a ten-minute break, a class on an Upaniṣad began. Afterwards, there was a period of meditation. He soon discovered that the participants' minds were not settled enough for meditation, for, they still needed some cleansing. Therefore, he discontinued the meditation classes for a few years.

The Study Group that had formed in San Francisco wanted to continue the camaraderie created by their common interest in the study of Vedānta. When an opportunity came to join together to build a small commune near Yosemite, everyone sold their properties, packed up and headed for the mountains. One couple of the Quaker faith had offered them land for the endeavour. However, the local zoning authorities did not agree with the plan of each family building its own cottage. In addition, there were other problems with installation of utilities. The distraught group wrote Swamiji for encouragement. To their amazement, he ordered them back to society. "Americans have the misconception that they have to give up the family and job for the spiritual life," he admonished them.

In his talks in the West, he emphasized that all Truth is one. Christians were not to become Hindus, but by study of Hindu philosophy they would become better Christians. Their own understanding of Christianity would be enhanced, and their own personal relationship with Christ and his teachings would deepen.

In 1972, the Vedānta talks were arranged at universities with the assistance of the professors and staff of the Department of

Philosophy or Religious Studies, including University of Hawaii, University of California at Berkeley, M.I.T. and Cornell. Of this fifth world tour, Swamiji wrote to the Indians in *Tapovan Prasad* –

"My Gurudev often used to tell me, 'Go and sit near the Ganga. She alone can teach you the deepest knowledge in the Vedas. Learn to listen with a still mind. Stop your mental chatter and then listen with an alert and patient attention; without passions and desires, listen without straining to form judgements, without struggling to form opinions.' This I practiced for many an hour and I think I have learned to listen. Often I felt moments of ecstatic harmony with Mother Ganga. As she flowed on – ever recreating herself afresh, never the same, yet she is She all the time – ever the same!

It is in this passionless attitude of alert listening that I had, this trip, roamed around the world, speaking about the glory of our divine nature, the beauty of Truth, the magnificent essence of God that lies unattended and, therefore, unlit in the bosom of all creatures and things of the universe. The world of happenings – the realm of clamorous objects and confused beings – have flowed by me all these six months; frisking and skipping, jumping and dashing, variegated in a thousand hues of individual behaviours, characters and ideals. They all heard me, and some of them did truly listen. To listen to those who listened was in itself a reward totally fulfilling.

Round the world on this trip I passed through eleven universities, addressed the young students of some eight nations, held twenty-one lecture series in which the ideas of the *Bhagavad-gītā* were discussed, and at some centres we had an exhaustive study of one of the Upaniṣads.

This tour of service around the world could never have been such a satisfying success but for the honest and dedicated work of hundreds of volunteers, patrons and sympathizers everywhere, and with the sympathy of many forward-looking university authorities and the

> enlightened enthusiasm of many department heads therein. I am grateful to them all. All of our Chinmaya family must realize that we are now gaining the support of thinking people everywhere. And our ardent pursuit of the path divine alone can express our gratitude to the supreme Lord. Let Him make each one of us a better instrument to serve His cause more effectively."

....

The first Chinmaya Spiritual Camp outside of India was held in 1973 at California State College, Sonoma. The Americans had read about such camps in India and had questioned – "Why not in the West too?" They thought it would be wonderful to live, even for only a short time, an intense āśrama life with the Teacher. At this camp, the idea became a reality. When the camp was over Swamiji sent the organizers a letter: "Only in the future will you come to recognize the significance of this event."

In 1975 he arrived in San Francisco just in time to be driven straight from the airport to the Civic Centre to participate in an open forum of all religions, organized by the Sufi Master, Pir Vilayat Khan. Swamiji's insightful answers to all questions put to him, including one on sex, impressed many members of the young audience. A sizeable group of 'Guru seekers' drove forty miles south to Stanford University in Palo Alto for the first talk of Swamiji's lecture series that evening. However, Swamiji made his no-nonsense attitude quite clear when, after the discourse, they asked him to describe his technique.

"What is my technique? My technique is to stand on my nose and meditate. But I only practise it in private." He laughed his impish laughter, then thundered seriously, "If you are looking for shortcuts to spirituality or instant psychedelic happenings, you have made a mistake today. But don't repeat it – Don't come tomorrow!" They got the message, as they returned everyday for the following week to hear the discourses on the twelfth chapter of the *Gītā* in the evenings and *Kenopaniṣad* in the mornings.

After the 1975 camp at Humboldt State University, the Chinmaya Mission West was incorporated. The principal goal of the organization was to broadcast Swamiji's vision to be ever awake to the creative possibilities for reaching people of all ages, faiths and social status with a philosophy which is neither Eastern nor Western, but simply Truth.

The Chinmaya Mission West included the United States, Canada, Trinidad, Mexico, Central and South America, and the West Indies. The regional centres sponsor Study Groups, classes, minicamps, Bala Vihar for children, and had the responsibility for organizing Swamiji's lectures. For years, the central office was in Napa, California in the home of Nalini and Bill Browning, who, on a voluntary basis, took on the entire responsibility of the publishing of all the newsletters and books that held the Mission together in the West for almost twenty years. In 1989 property was purchased in San Jose, California to expand the activities of the Mission, as well as have space for classes. Swami Tejomayananda came from India to head the organization and teach in the centre, and in other Mission centres that had been created in many of the large cities, including Washington D.C., Flint, Michigan, Houston and Texas. However, the Brownings continued to have responsibility for the publishing and distribution of Chinmaya books, tapes, a newsletter and *Mananam*, a quarterly journal.

Swamiji continued to return to the U.S. each year to speak at universities in a half-dozen major cities, with the exception of 1977 when his passport renewal was mysteriously delayed after he had publicly criticized Indira Gandhi's emergency programme. In 1979 an eight-acre parcel of land in the redwood country of Northern California was purchased for an āśrama school in the style of Sandeepany Sadhanalaya. The pre freeway era motel on the property served as a dormitory for the fifty students. The motel restaurant was divided into a classroom and a dining area. Swami Dayananda[1] left his position at Sandeepany in Bombay to serve as

[1] The former Śrī Natarajan Iyer.

the director and teacher of the three year course. On the first day of classes, Swami Chinmayananda addressed the students.

Swamiji's Inaugural Address

A great dream is coming true on this auspicious day. Twenty-five years ago the idea sprang up that we must have an up to date, modern, organized institute where the young people of the technological Age could be intelligently introduced to the in depth significance of life itself. This subjective science of Vedānta was our true birthright, but in the march of society under the propulsion of history, we were exiled from this inherent self-mastery and have come to roam about in sorrow and dejection in the forest of shameless sensuality.

Twenty-five years ago when the idea exploded in me, nobody took me seriously. Even the priests looked at me aghast, with silent sympathy, wondering how such a bright, intelligent young man could, so early in life, go so totally crazy!

These have been years of struggle, of uphill climb, of meeting objections, of bulldozing opposition, then fearlessly marching ahead against insufferable odds and painful inertia. It is incomprehensible even to the faithful and religious how barriers have broken down due to our spectacular success in India. An immeasurable flood of dynamic devotion has gushed out from the Hindu community in India. It is on the crest of that wave that Chinmaya Mission reached America to be born as Chinmaya Mission West.

We expect from you hard and sincere work, selfless dedication, total surrender, admirable discipline, and industrious sādhanā. We are not asking you to change, but we shall ask you to watch the transmutation of your outer lifestyle taking place as a result of your inner unfoldment.

Perfect yourself, so that you can help others in perfecting themselves.

25

The Later Years

World perfection through individual perfection! The world can only be changed by the spiritual unfoldment of each individual – not by political revolution, but by spiritual evolution.

—Swami Chinmayananda, 1972.

By 1970, India had managed to defy all predictions that she would not be able to feed her people. Partially motivated by the political blackmail of the Americans, who insisted on alignment[1] with American policy in exchange for assistance, India chose not to make any international political commitments. The memory of the Empire was too close. Then too, America's record with the neighbouring country of the Philippines was not to be dismissed. India was not interested in alignment or non-alignment; Russia bordered India on the north, and India was not willing to disturb the centuries old equilibrium for the sake of getting wheat from America. India set out to raise enough grain for her countrymen and succeeded.

However, the agricultural emphasis had left her short in other areas, particularly in industry. Since the government has attempted a socialistic orientation toward business, regulations and taxes on industry have thwarted investments and crippled

[1] It was after Indira Gandhi openly criticized the bombing of Hanoi that the Americans withdrew their promise of wheat during the famine of 1965. When the embarrassed Indian Ambassador reminded the Johnson Administration officials that Mrs. Gandhi had not said anything that the Pope and U Thant had not already said, he received the official rebuke: "The Pope and U Thant do not need our wheat."

economic growth. The income tax system represses individual and corporate enterprise while stimulating dishonest currency manipulation and black market activities.[1] The black market had its roots in the colonial regime. The British Raj had been alien to the people; therefore, embezzling from it was the same as stealing from a foreign thief. The new government had failed to instil – or perhaps to earn – the trust needed to break the pattern.

The crisis of society at large, as well as the needs of individuals, created the impetus that kept Swamiji constantly at work. He had an inexhaustible energy that seemed to be continually replenished by the crowds of people who came to listen to him. By 1970, progress had been made for a spiritual renaissance. All the principal scriptures of Vedānta had been taught in the larger cities. They had been translated and published in many Indian languages. A dozen brahmacārīs were scattered in the major cities to teach classes.

With his students now Teachers, Swamiji mentioned that he would be able to slow down and spend more time advising and encouraging others with their own plans and with the many Chinmaya Mission projects. Illness had slowed his activities more than once; he took it as a warning that his physical body would not be able to continue at its usual pace. As early as 1957 he had had to cancel four days of the Delhi yajña because of a sore throat and high fever. Later that year he was laid up for several days with a high fever in Ernakulam where Kouchi Amma was able to care for him. In 1960 he suffered another severe attack of high fever. In their anxiety to serve him, the Mission members overdid their care, failing to give him a moment's peace. When the doctor came to check on him, Swamiji told him with dignified seriousness, "Is there a nursing home available where I can get some rest. These people won't leave me alone a minute!"

---

[1] Commercial exchanges made with no official records for the purpose of avoiding taxes.

This pattern of an exhaustive work schedule interspersed with short, minor illnesses of high fever, sore throat and coughs continued through the sixties. Then on March 21, 1970, just five days into a yajña in Mysore, Swamiji suffered a heart attack. On the previous day he had announced that he would be unable to finish the text in the time allotted, so everyone should come for a marathon class on the following day. Since it was a Sunday, everyone would be free to attend. Thus it had been a long day, although he appeared his usual energetic self as he gleefully told his stories and examples to illustrate the scriptures.

That night, about an hour after retiring, he got up and called out to his host, who was sleeping in a nearby room. Swamiji reported that he was having severe chest pain. A heart specialist was called immediately. After a short examination, he recommended that Swamiji be taken to the hospital. As he was carried away on an ambulance stretcher, he calmly and peacefully reassured the family members who were huddled around him, "There is no cause for worry. This physical structure has been put to a lot of strain, so it requires some repair and rest. That's all."

At the hospital, the electrocardiogram confirmed Dr. Das's suspicions. Swamiji's heart was showing signs of stress. Since the hospital was full, without a single vacant bed, a temporary ward was set up on the hospital veranda for him. Mission members brought in everything necessary to make him comfortable – from bed to curtains. Everyone waited in suspense for signs of improvement as experts in cardiology came from all over India to be of service to their Guru.

After three days, there were signs of improvement. Fortunately, two days later there was a room available in the hospital. With the exception of a couple of minor relapses during the following month, Swamiji continued to improve. On May 10, he was discharged so he could travel to Bangalore. Devotees awaited him at the new Chinmaya Hospital; Swamiji would be the first patient. He greeted everyone with his usual sense of humour – "I inaugurated the out patient ward in Mysore, and today I inaugurate the in patient ward here!"

Since the kitchen was not yet in operation, Shivaram, who would become his personal attendant, came from Uttarkashi to prepare the special diet that Swamiji's condition required. The Bangalore Hospital had been conceived as an arena of service for the local Mission members. Funded by many generous contributions from Chinmaya Mission members, it was directed by Mr. and Mrs. Ramakrishnan Reddy and the Dr. Purushottams. However, with the exception of the Purushottams, who had planned and overseen the project, not any medical personnel from the Chinmaya Mission was available for working in it, as had been hoped and projected. Without any volunteer support, the operating costs were high and start up was delayed.

Since the first yajña there in 1956, Bangalore had been a stronghold of Mission activities. The audience at the annual yajña regularly numbered over ten thousand persons. So everyday while Swamiji was in the hospital, many people continually trooped in and out of his room. He always remained in his usual jovial mood, making a joke of the slightest inconvenience. Someone noticed a bug in his bed and flicked it away. "Isn't that my luck. Lord Viṣṇu is sleeping on that wonderful snake in the Milky Ocean, and all I get is a few stray bugs!" Swamiji jested.

Brahmacārī Hari Das came from Calcutta to visit him. He remarked that now because of his bad health one of the brahmacārīs should travel with Swamiji to take care of him. "Huh! To take care of me!? What do I need? An occasional cup of tea? There are hundreds of ladies all over India fighting to serve me a cup of tea. No, you brahmacārīs will continue with your work. You are needed more than ever now."

At the invitation of several of the Mission members, Satya Sai Baba, India's renowned miracle man, came to visit Swamiji at the hospital. He offered Swamiji the sacred ash, which often heals spontaneously, but it was refused, for, Swamiji knew that he was in the Lord's hands – all was in a divine plan. He had no fear of illness or pain.

Even the purest sage is a combination of God and man on the physical plane. The physical element is subject to the laws of nature – birth, growth, decay, death. For a natural phenomenon like an illness, no supra phenomenal explanation is necessary. As Swamiji expressed it –

> "Illness and pain are the nature of the body. Whoever has a body will experience them. We must have the courage to suffer them with peaceful joy. Never pray for a cure. The Lord will never give anyone – even His enemy – more pain than he deserves. Pray for the strength and courage to suffer, and pray ardently to the Lord for His love. Keep on smiling, always, at all times, under all conditions."

Upon the insistence of his doctors, Swamiji spent the following year in recuperation, although he would become restless when he thought of all the things waiting to be accomplished in the spiritual renaissance of India. Gradually, he began to turn over responsibilities to others. Swami Chinmayananda had initiated the former Śrī Natarajan Iyer of Madras into sannyāsa in 1962. Swamiji maintained strict rules for anyone he initiated into sannyāsa, so such a ceremony was a rare occasion. However, an exception was justified as Natarajan had served the Chinmaya Mission faithfully as Swamiji's right-hand man and troubleshooter for a decade. At that time, Natarajan had a health problem and wanted to take the sannyāsa vows before his surgery. For this reason, the initiation took place in the Bedford Villa of Mr. M. C. Petachi in Madras instead of the usual Himalayan venue. After his recuperation, Swami Dayananda left for a long period of study and austerities at Rishikesh.

At this time (1971), Swamiji wrote him that it was time for him to come back and put his knowledge to use. Swamiji appointed him the Head Teacher at Sandeepany Sadhanalaya. Swami Dayananda had become an ardent scholar of Sanskrit and the scriptures; therefore, he was a perfect choice. His presence meant there would be a permanent Teacher at Sandeepany; the Teacher would no longer have to go out and collect finances. Therefore, the āśrama atmosphere would be more in the traditional style of the close relationship between student and Guru. Swamiji also called two very capable retired businessmen, Jagdish Prasad and Hanumanthan Rao to Bombay to head the operation of the Central Chinmaya Mission and the Sandeepany Sadhanalaya Trust, respectively. He then had a viable team to take care of the operations and finances.

After a retreat at Tapovanam Kutir in the spring of 1972, Swamiji was again going full pace, scheduling yajñas both in India and abroad. In the succeeding years, he received two awards that showed that the philosopher had been accepted in his birthplace of Kerala. In January of 1973, he was invited as an honoured guest to the All-India Ramayana Conference in Trivandrum. There he was named one of the Sapta ṛṣis, that is, one of the seven immortal ṛṣis who continue to come to the earth to serve humanity. In recent decades, great sages, such as the Śaṅkarācārya of Kanchipuram, Swami Abhedananda and Śrī Nataraja Guru, have received this award in recognition for the spiritual work that they were doing for the evolution of mankind.

In 1975 Swamiji travelled to the Sringeri Matha to pay his respects to the presiding Śrī Śaṅkarācārya, Abhinava Vidyatirtha Mahaswamigal. The Śaṅkarācārya presented Swami Chinmayananda with a double rudrākṣa seed, encased in gold. The seed of the rudrākṣa tree is the favoured bead of the mālā (meditation beads). A double rudrākṣa seed is quite rare and is considered of a special significance as it symbolises the wedding of Śaṅkara and Gaurī (Śiva and Pārvatī), Spirit and matter; the two pillars of creation joined into one. The Śrī Gaurī-Śaṅkara pendant was presented to Swamiji in recognition of his service to mankind in propagating Sanātana-dharma, the most ancient knowledge.

With his great compassion and universal understanding, Swamiji perceived all aspects of Hindu religion and culture as one harmony. In 1973, he personally invited Satya Sai Baba to preside over the opening ceremony of the national yajña held in Bangalore. At the end of the programme many of the workers approached Swamiji at his host's residence. Swamiji knew what was on their minds. As always he dealt directly with their question. "I know that you have been asking why the Chinmaya Mission has invited a Swami here for the opening ceremony who is not a pure Vedāntin. Satya Sai Baba is teaching the one Truth; besides, look at how much love he has given to the people. The Chinmaya Mission is not a personality cult; it is for renaissance of the Hindu culture. Whoever is working for the upliftment and propagation of our culture in whatever form, we are with them!"

Many of Swamiji's activities supported this open-minded view. As early as 1956, he had been invited to attend and address the All-Indian Vedānta Sammelan (conference) organized by Swami Nirmal Mahārāja in Amritsar. Leaving at midnight, he travelled three hundred miles by car to address the assembly in the morning, then travelled all day to return for the 6 p.m. yajña in Delhi. In December of that year he interrupted his yajña programme to preside over the Hindu Sammelan in Kerala, arranged by the Nair Service Society (NSS).

In 1978 Swamiji visited Dharmashala to view a proposed building site of the future Himalayan āśrama where Swamiji planned to retire in 1980. While he was there he met with the Tibetan Buddhist leader, the Dalai Lama.

Swamiji immediately started up the conversation, "Why don't you come down to the planes of India with the great

Buddhist ideas, so unknown in this country. You are a repository of the whole Buddhist culture and teaching. Spiritual knowledge is needed; people are anxious for it."

"We always wait for students to come to us," replied the Dalai Lama with a shy grin.

"Yes. Yes. I know. . . but they're not coming. So we Teachers have to go to them," Swamiji retorted with a chuckle.

The Dalai Lama gave a nod in agreement, as he replied, "I will think it over." Then he added with a wide smile, "I think you are an impatient one."

"Yes, yes. I am very impatient to arouse everyone to their own divine nature!" Swamiji demonstrated by throwing out his arms.

The Dalai Lama then took the opportunity to ask Swamiji some clarifications of Sanskrit terms as used in Hinduism. He then asked Swamiji if he knew of the Teacher, J. Krishnamurthi.

Swamiji replied, "Yes, he is a great Buddhist, and a great Vedāntin. However, he speaks from the highest level where there is no practice, or teacher, necessary. But there are very few people who have the quiet, prepared mind to understand what he is saying. The spiritual disciplines are necessary for people in today's world."

To the Dalai Lama's inquiry as to what method of meditation he taught, Swamiji succinctly replied, "Repetition of the name of the Lord to remove all other thoughts until one merges into the object of meditation."

After some general discussion about Buddhism, accompanied by the serving of tea, the Dalai Lama announced – "Okay. If you plan something, I will go down and talk." At Swamiji's invitation, on January 25, 1979, the Dalai Lama came to Prayag to inaugurate the Vishwa Hindu Parishad Sammelan (All World Hindu Conference) attended by over a thousand Hindus from over two dozen countries.

In the spring of 1979, Swamiji was among a group of distinguished Swamis who were invited to speak at the 83rd birthday celebration of Anandamayi Ma, which was held in Bangalore. At that time he expressed great affection and reverence for her, and it was reciprocated. They had met previously; she had been a guest at Sandeepany Sadhanalaya in 1975. Although the circumstances of their first meeting is unknown, there was a persistent, but unverified, rumour that at Ananda Kutir before he was a student of Vedānta, he developed a problem in his practice of prāṇāyāma (exercises of breath control). It was reported that at that time, Swami Sivananda sent him to Anandamayi Ma to assist him.

There were also instances of his interaction with Christians. In 1963, Swamiji had visited the Christian area of Goa, which had remained a Portuguese territory until 1950. This was an unprecedented event for the people of Goa. A Hindu missionary had come to remind them of their ancient cultural and spiritual heritage. Nevertheless, the inauguration speech by the Chief Secretary of the state of Goa indicated that there was at least one government official who was well versed in religious thought. After declaring that God had created all the races of man from the same clay, he continued.

> Even your own *Bible* says so. This creation of man from clay in the Bible is to bring home to us the irrevocable fact that we are all children of one God. Forgetting this we are making too much fuss about our castes and religions. We quarrel and fight among ourselves for petty reasons. Jesus and Kṛṣṇa, Buddha and Mohammed – all delivered their messages to humanity showing different paths to the Infinite. We are running after the shadow while casting aside the substance. Our morality is steadily eroding. In our blind dash toward doom, we are being aided by the discoveries of science. We do not have the good sense to make use of this

> scientific knowledge for the advancement of mankind. The atheists are all united under one belief; let those who believe in God unite and work together!

....

Goa was not the only place that Swamiji was to address Christians. Out of curiosity, missionaries came to hear him wherever he went. Unfortunately, some were not open-minded about the Hindu practices. In Hyderabad there was a Catholic priest present on the last day of the yajña, the day of the sprinkling of the Ganga water. As Swamiji approached the priest's row, he got up and scurried out to avoid any drops of the Hindu holy water. Undaunted, Swamiji noted his intended escape and chased him down the aisle to give him a good sprinkle.

There were many Christian priests who, recognizing the intention for the upliftment of the society – both economic and spiritual – accepted Swamiji and the Chinmaya Mission. The 137th Gītā yajña in Bombay was inaugurated by Valerian Cardinal Gracias, who called for a revitalization of all religions to meet new challenges of the changing times. He paid tribute to Swamiji for his work in the philosophical field and the interpretation of true religion. In Kerala where Christianity had long been integrated into the cultural life of the Indians, Christian priests were often present at the various yajñas and Mission activities.

On the occasion of an International Catholic Conference in Bombay, Swamiji explained to some complaining Hindus that there was no cause for worry about Christian activities in India because all attempts of Christianity to conquer Hinduism had failed, "... even though they have the strength of organization, and the Hindus the weakness of disorganization."

This is not to say that he did not criticize the Christian hierarchy, just as judiciously as he did the Hindu priests. When the Pope visited India with a security deployment of some one hundred men, Swamiji did not resist the opportunity for a tirade.

"Outrageous", he chided. "The Indian holy man goes with his simple cotton cloth and never encounters any harm, but this man with his velvet robes covered with gold and jewels has to have machine guns for protection. Christians carrying machine guns. Don't you see the irony of it. Is this a model of the Christian ideal that love conquers all?"

While touring outside of India, Swamiji always encouraged those of other beliefs to stick to their own religion, for Vedānta is a universal philosophy that can enhance any religious system. However, in India he was a relentless critic of the Christian missionaries who paid out ten rupees to a peasant to buy a conversion in order to show large numbers on their reports that were sent back home.

The teaching of Christianity itself was not the problem; difficulties arose when Christianity contributed to the break-up of traditional Hindu cultural life that is based on mutual cooperation of the family unit, as opposed to independence of the individual. This seemingly small distinction has had an unforeseen impact on Indian society. In traditional India there had never been any need for orphanages, welfare programmes or social security. Even the temples were not involved in social endeavours because their assistance had not been needed.

However, things changed drastically in the twentieth century with the superimposition of the Western/Christian individual oriented culture, accompanied by a tremendous population explosion, and the resulting need for orphanages, welfare programmes, medical care, famine relief and education. These expenses were devastating for the economy of the new nation.

The inclination of the leaders of the new nation state had been to imitate their former ruler – the rule of many by the few. A 'get rich quick' mentality and an appetite for Western goods ruled those few. Swamiji was never timid in expressing his views on the state of the nation publicly –

"Wedded as I am to the socialistic viewpoint, I do believe in the idea of the present necessity of redistribution of wealth – but it should originate in the producers themselves, spontaneously. They should not be forced to part with their profits, but should be educated morally to appreciate the glory of distribution, the joy of sharing, the philosophy of oneness. They should be made to feel they belong to one family, bound together with a common culture, with a common religion, with a common scripture. Then alone will there be a spontaneous response that is more fundamental and deep – one not subject to corruption and the other malpractices that go along with it.

In the modern world, material success was indeed necessary. The Hindu scriptures never opposed prosperity. Activity in the world aimed at success has the potential to sharpen and focus the mind to render it capable of understanding the subtler truths of life. With birth, an individual brings into the world a particular set of experiences to be gained in life. The fulfilment of these tendencies will lead him into certain activities. Actions that are done with the right frame of mind liquidate the layers of impressions (vāsanās) that the individual was born with and those that continue to accumulate from birth. Only then is the individual a qualified candidate to experience the Truth reflected in the purified mind. Anyone who came to Swamiji with spiritual questions was answered with spiritual insight; anyone who came to him asking about business matters got advice of a temporal nature, often backed with concrete suggestions of potential contacts for their business."

In addition, Swamiji gave many talks on 'efficiency in action' as it pertained to success –

"To be successful in any endeavour one must first have proficiency – knowledge of the subject, the proper tools and the skill to put them to use. With this preparation, you will be able to act efficiently. Efficiency is the ability to focus your total attention on the action you are performing. This ability is not easily won. Each moment our attention is diverted because we have not properly prepared ourselves for our assignment and are afraid the boss will find out. We have anxieties about our income and future expenses, for, we are not sure the paychecks will cover the cost of the children's education or the daughter's wedding. Then we worry over memories of the past and its failures. You say you have failed four times? Good! Now you know how to fail, so you are sure to succeed next time!

So you have the necessary proficiency, but your mind is filled with a multitude of distractions. It is like an overhead tank for water storage, located on the roof of your home. The tank is full, but you are not getting water in the faucet on the ground floor. The defect must be due to a blockage in the pipes, so it has to be cleared. Likewise, you may have plenty of good ideas – but unless the ideas are efficiently executed, of what avail is all your knowledge? Success depends on execution, not on ideas. In India, we are not lacking the proficiency, but we suffer from the lack of efficiency. So ideas create proficiency, while execution makes efficiency."

Although Swamiji was a renunciate, having vowed to take only what came to him unasked, whether material objects or situations of life, his capacity for enjoyment of both was immense. Since he had no expectations or appointments with the future, he remained free to enjoy what every moment brought. The Vedas extolled the continuous fullness of life. The *Yajur-veda* included the prayer –

'May we hear, speak well, hold our heads high;
Even beyond one hundred autumns.'

Swamiji appreciates anyone actively participating in life, no matter the field of endeavour. He would often lament that the problem in India is to get the people moving because only then could they be pointed in the right direction.

The attitude was spelled out in Swamiji's remarks at a dinner given by the Bombay Mission members to celebrate the election of the Chinmaya Mission Board President, Ram Batra, to the civil position of Sheriff of Bombay. Swamiji attended and was prodded into saying a few words for the occasion. "Actually, there's nothing to commend when a person does his duty in his country. Such a thing is only noticed in a country like ours because it is so rare." Another time in a satsaṅga in Hyderabad he berated the group in jest, with saying, "We Indians cannot even do a successful job of cheating. You all spend your time constantly worrying over how to make a dishonest nickel or dime. In the West, they at least know how to cheat. One big $100,000 embezzlement and it's over and done with. He can forget crime and go on with his life. But daily you keep your mind on this petty cheating. Petty... Petty... We must think BIG, whatever we do."

Wherever he went, he supported all the social programmes done by any group, spiritual or secular. The directors of many projects came to him for consultation and ideas. He always had useful advice drawn from his experiences and observations travelling around the country. Whenever possible, he would inspire them to form a broader vision of their project. For example, he complimented a flood relief organization for their capable work, then told them, "But don't just sit around waiting for a flood to have some service to do. Your goal must be to eliminate the need for your organization. Now you are sitting idle because there are no floods. You must take up the project of reforestation. With trees planted on the hillsides, in ten years there will be no floods."

The ideals of Vedānta have brought together many capable workers, who proceeded with their own ventures and projects. Nevertheless, there were a number who depended on Swamiji's leadership and inspiration for any Mission endeavour and he did not discourage them. He carefully considered each situation and, tapping his knowledge acquired from the other Mission centres, he was able to give them new ideas or further suggestions. This assistance led to further dependence on him. Mission centres often delayed projects until they could consult him when he came for the annual yajña in their hometown. Because of the year of convalescence in 1970-71, more time was available to directly administer the Chinmaya Mission organization. Gradually, a band of Chinmayers – people who could not do anything without consulting Swamiji – mushroomed. Continually, he had to answer every complaint throughout the Mission. In 1978, he received several personal letters about absenteeism in the Study Groups. He took his pen to hand, and wrote to the complaining leaders.

Regarding Study Class Absenteeism

Two or three centres in India have written for advice on what they can do to reduce, if not totally eliminate, absenteeism from our weekly study classes. The following instructions are suggested as our rules.

Sickness – No excuses based on sickness are acceptable to Chinmaya Mission Study Centres. We will no longer accept your doctor's certificate as proof of illness since we firmly believe that, if you are able to go to a doctor for consultation, you are surely fit to come to our classes. If you received the medical certificate through a phone call or through an agent, please send us the doctor's name and address, along with your apology for your absence.

Death (other than your own) – Death of friends or relations cannot be a sufficiently valid reason, as it is then too late to do anything for those concerned. We are sure someone else can take care of the necessary arrangements. You may be so kind as to come to the study class and let us pray for the departed. This will be a more fitting service to the beloved one who has left, than your following the food sheath (physical body) to the cremation ground.

Death (your own) – This will be accepted as a very reasonable and valid excuse, but we would like to have at least a week's notice to check whether you have paid all dues and subscriptions. You who are group leaders should give a week's notice, and, during that week, train another member of the group to take up your work.

Interruptions – During the study class we would like to discourage people from running to the bathroom too often. We shall, in the future, decide to go to the washroom in alphabetical order. For instance, those whose names start with 'A' will go in the first 15 minutes and so on. If you are unable to go at your appointed time, it will be necessary for you to wait until the next study session when your turn will surely come round.

If the above rules are accepted and openly circulated, by letter if necessary, to all our serious Study Group members, I am sure absenteeism will be totally eliminated.

The Study Group leaders got the message, inscribed with wit, and realized their mistake of worrying over such petty considerations, instead of focusing on the purpose of the Study Groups. "If you improve, they'll improve," Swamiji always reminded the leaders.

In the late 1970s, the high fever, sore throat and cough were again occurring regularly. Swamiji declared that the time had come to conclude his work and retire. A spot for an āśrama complex had been selected in the Western Himalayas at Sidhabari in the Kangra Valley. It was to serve as a retirement place for

Swamiji and other Mission workers. The grounds would also contain a school styled after Sandeepany Sadhanalaya, taught by a graduate, Brahmacārī Vivek Chaitanya.

This course would be distinct, for, Hindi instead of English, would be used in the classes. The principal text would be the *Rāmāyaṇa.* Rāma, hero of the *Rāmāyaṇa,* had lived in the Himalayas and has continued to be loved and emulated as the model king, father, brother and husband by the mountain folk. Even today it is not unusual to find persons in the area, young and old alike, who can recite long portions of the lengthy epic poem from memory. The school was to produce Hindi speaking Teachers, versed in a curriculum compatible with their own cultural roots, to teach the people of Northern India.

In 1980 while Swamiji was in the United States for a series of yajñas, he was diagnosed with a heart condition that required surgery. In Detroit, several of the Indian doctors, who were always around trying to check-up on his health, noted that both his blood sugar and pulse were erratic. He laughed it off, informing them that their job was to give check-ups and his job was to teach classes; they had done their check-up and he was going to continue with his teaching. He was finally persuaded to go to a hospital to have his heart function tested. Cardiac catherization revealed a blockage of more than eighty percent in all of the four main arteries supplying blood to the heart. The examining doctors insisted that he cancel his lecture schedule. They then contacted Dr. Denton Cooley at the Medical Centre in Houston, Texas, who performed bypass surgery on August 26, 1980, following a three-day diagnostic period.

Subsequent to two months' recuperation in Houston and Detroit, Swamiji pushed up his sleeves, rubbed his palms together, and declared – "Okay, now I have ten more years, let's see what I can do!" Twenty-four hours later he was en route to India with a full itinerary for 1981. Upon arriving in Bombay, he met with all the Chinmaya Mission Board members and put forth a plan making the Mission centres in each city independent. A new group of brahmacārīs were just completing the two and half year course in Bombay. Up until this point all the brahmacārīs had been responsible to the central office at Sandeepany for the coordination of activities, expense accounts and ironing out of any problems. Now the Mission centres would be entirely independent and responsible for organizing and coordinating all activities according to the needs they perceived in their communities. This would seem as if the brahmacārīs were also independent, but, to the contrary, the householders who ran the Mission would also manage the brahmacārīs. The system imposed a great challenge and opportunity for the householders. Would they have the depth of insight to run a spiritual organization for the greatest benefit of all?

After his surgery, Swamiji's retirement at Sidhabari was postponed indefinitely. In fact, circumstances other than health dictated his decision. He had lost a pillar of his support, for, Swami Dayananda decided he had garnered sufficient resources to leave his teaching position and form his own organization. Losing the principal Teacher was difficult enough, but Swami Dayananda also inducted many of the brahmacārīs whom he had taught at Sandeepany into his organization. It would take another Vedānta course to replace the coordinators at the Mission centres in several cities.

However, the activities continued as usual at the Himalayan, Hindi medium āśrama. Swamiji would continue to conduct an annual spiritual camp there each summer. In addition to these retreats and the Vedānta course, social endeavours continued to flourish in the area. A free clinic for the local villagers was incorporated into the complex. In April of 1985, thirty bright, cheerful young women of about twenty years of age began a one and half year course aimed at making them proficient in the treatment of the common medical problems in the region. In addition, they would attend the morning class on the *Rāmāyaṇa* in order to study the basic concepts of its spiritual teaching. Each young woman could then act as both counsellor and nurse among the Himalayan villagers. This was the first time the Government of India participated in a Chinmaya Mission project by furnishing the necessary laboratory equipment.

In autumn of 1986, the initial group of brahmacārīs had completed the course at Sidhabari. At a ceremony presided over by Swamiji, they were presented with the yellow robe of the brahmacārīs and a new name. With these words of encouragement, Swamiji guided them –

Graduation Address at Himalayan Sandeepany

"This yellow cloth is bestowed so that your path will be easier. The uniform does not make you a brahmacārī. This uniform is fencing. The flowers and the fruits come from the tree itself, but to protect the tree we put up a fence. Don't expect the fence to bring forth fruits. The uniform is given so that you will be protected in the community, and the community will be protected from you!

Your duty now is to remember, again and again, what has been pumped into you for these two-and-a-half years. Here, in the class, it is one-way traffic – merely pumping ideas into you. Out in the world you will need to find quiet moments to contemplate and reflect upon these ideas and make them your own. When you have not thought the concepts over completely for yourself, however great a scholar you may be, your expressions will not communicate the ideas, though you have said the correct words. A great deal of reflection is needed before the Truth of the scriptures will be clear to you. When it becomes clear to you, then, through your words, it becomes clear to others.

During the past two-and-a-half years you have just studied, that is all. You gazed through the textbooks. You can repeat certain portions because you have memorised them. That is merely chanting! The ability to chant is not going to help others. What we are attempting is missionary work – pracāra[1], and pracāra will not be possible unless you have ācāra[2].

So do your sādhanā regularly. If you miss your meditation one day, your words will have no value on that day... Four or five of the brahmacārīs who have not done their own sādhanā have not succeeded in teaching others. In contrast, several students who seemed hopeless cases have performed so beautifully – because of their regular practice. It is not only written in the śāstras (scriptures), but it is my experience in the last twenty-eight years – people who are doing regular sādhanā certainly do excel in teaching. So meditate, study daily, reflect on what you have studied, then serve. When one continually thinks only of the higher Reality, the mind becomes one with that highest thought at all times. This is true practice.

This work is a wonderful opportunity for your sādhanā. Our society will respect you as a sādhu (spiritual practitioner) because that is the tradition of our country. But that does not mean you do not have to improve by your own effort. Struggle hard to be regular in your practice and to live this great Truth to the extent that you can. The householders may not be able to live the Truth as fully as you because they will have to compromise in living with day-to-day demands in society. You do not have such limitations.

Brahmacārīs, living without compromise, develop into real servants of the society. India needs your services very badly. In the last thirty years much has been accomplished, for, today the people are demanding to hear their scriptures. When I started this work there was no such desire. Now they are writing, 'Swamiji, send us one brahmacārī. We desperately need the services of one brahmacārī.' We have not been able to produce as many workers as they require.

1 Wanderer in the sense of a wandering monk who has faith that his needs will be provided.

2 Spiritual practice and formal code of conduct.

So here is your chance. Live it. Come to realize that which is here and now.

In 1987 at Sandeepany in Bombay in an address to the graduating class taught by Swami Tejomayananda, Swamiji told the new brahmacārī –

> "The old idea of a brahmacārī is one who goes and brings food for the Guru and then eats and sleeps. In this way, Hinduism has reached a state of decadence and disaster. Now you are carrying the same name, but not the same form. We are creating an army of workers for the protection of Hinduism and for its further development – to rediscover the true heart of Mother India for the people.
>
> I don't want you to have any rest in this regard. No sympathy about your overworking! Nobody sympathizes when I am working. And now suddenly they tell me that I am seventy years old! I did not know that I was growing old because I had not a moment to think about it. So that is the way I expect everyone of the brahmacārī to work.

By 1987, there were fifty brahmacārīs dispersed in the major cities and towns. They were teaching classes, organizing Mission projects, administering schools and participating in any number of service projects according to their own talents and the needs and circumstances of the community. Several of the students created their own circumstances and were carrying out their own unique plans.

In the Cuddapah (now Kadapa) district of Andhra Pradesh on twenty-two acres of land, donated by the local villagers – land so barren that it contained no tree, and so isolated, an ox cart picked up visitors on a road one mile away – Swamini Saradapriyananda established a rural service oriented āśrama. Within a five year period, wells had been drilled, trees planted, land cultivated and buildings constructed around a large courtyard. Except for the kitchen and dining hall, all the buildings were made with local materials in the regional style of mud walls, reinforced with bamboo, and topped with a straw roof. The complex contained an assembly hall for classes, a lecture hall, a home for the aged (composed of individual huts), and an elementary school with two hostels for students. In addition, the āśrama offered several services directed to the needs of the local villagers, including a dispensary where they could obtain free homeopathic medicine, a school for harijana (outcaste) children to provide them with a basic education, as well as teach them a craft or trade, and an orphanage of six small children. An eighty-five year old grand granny, Śrīmatī Anantarama Mama, cared for all the children. Old and crippled harijanas received a free lunch daily. Every Sunday the āśrama students distributed a week's ration of rice and dal, as well as any vegetables and clothing that had been donated, in the surrounding villages. Swamini's relentless energy, bubbling enthusiasm and inspiration attracted both state and central government funds. In 1988, she supervised the construction of a branch of the Chinmaya Aranyam (Forest) āśrama on four acres of land in Guntur.

On one hundred acres near Coimbatore, Swami Sahajananda established Chinmaya Gardens, a large āśrama complex, offering classes to train brahmacārīs, a home for the elderly, and a clinic based on herbal and natural healing methods. In order to educate the local children, he initiated a school for harijanas and a rural development programme to assist ten schools that already existed in the area. Although the site originally had an intrinsic beauty, including a river with tumbling waterfalls, the students enhanced it with many gardens and the construction of buildings with bricks produced at their own brick factory. Swami Sahajananda was as relaxed and calm as Swamini Saradapriyananda was energetic and dynamic; even so, both were successful in their similar endeavours.

The two have incorporated Swamiji's idea for developing Hari Har schools for peasant children in rural areas. The youngest children were taught the essentials of reading, writing and simple arithmetic. At ten or twelve years of age, they started learning a trade or craft, determined by their ability and family tradition. This practical training was intended to enable them to become self-sufficient citizens of their community. Besides the secular education, the children were given a foundation in religious and moral instruction to develop their self-respect and appreciation of their culture.

Some of Swamiji's students were very independent, others more dependent. Students were at dissimilar levels of their spiritual evolution and viewed Swamiji according to their perceptions. He responded to each one in the spirit in which they approached him. He maintained a personal relationship with hundreds of students, but gave all equal time, consideration and advice with an impartiality that managed to avoid the usual jealousies that surround spiritual Teachers.

Swami Chinmayananda had never appeared to notice that he was a unique manifestation of the Divine. He saw himself as no different from his students. Due to this ideal, he experienced disappointments when some of them proved to be unequal to tackling life with its problems and temptations in the same manner he, the Teacher, had done. The Divine manifests in many ways, sometimes as a forest fire and sometimes as a candle flame. That is the nature of creation.

Swamiji's teaching was never affected by the progress of his audience. He continued to sing the song of Truth and those who benefitted, benefitted, and those who didn't benefit, sometimes criticized. Occasionally, when someone commented that one of the organizers was a crook in his business practices, Swamiji would nod and smile, saying, "Of course, only those who are dishonest need religion. That's why I have you here with me. Let's see if you both improve."

It is not that Swamiji had not faced tragedies in his life. One of the prominent Mission organizers in Delhi was murdered by his own son. An American who served as Swamiji's secretary succumbed to hepatitis while in India. His half-brother died prematurely from alcoholism. Some of his students felt that they had become greater than their Guru and started criticizing him publicly. And he just continued singing his song of freedom for those who would listen. "Doesn't matter whether you win or lose," he told everyone, and practised what he taught.

Throughout the years of his teaching, Swamiji maintained the single pointed goal to give each person with whom he came in contact the knowledge, understanding and courage for their personal, individual unfoldment. By one's own efforts, one would develop until he or she attained a personal contact with the true divinity, the God within. Swamiji never sidetracked, for even one day, not even one hour, from this goal of guiding others along the path.

Swamiji believed that a master of life was a master in the world itself – how else was he tested? Retirement to a Himalayan āśrama was a hospitalization that might be needed to cure the diseased mind, but even so he felt that it was not essential for everyone. "This box of matter is intended for acting in the world. The real Master is free to move at will at any level of Consciousness of any time, at any place – a diplomatic passport."

He criticized Swamis and holy men who were not serving mankind. "They are taking – eating from the national food supply – and not giving. Our economy cannot afford it. How can they be enlightened if there's a fear of coming down here to the planes and contributing to the world?" In the third chapter of the *Bhagavad-*

gītā, Lord Kṛṣṇa termed everyone who eats from the food supply without working a 'thief'. Gandhi had applied this verse as an argument to advocate spinning for the peasant farmers during their free time during the winter and monsoon seasons.

The members of the Chinmaya Mission often lamented that there would be no one to fill Swami Chinmayananda's sandals. And they were correct, there would not be another Swami Chinmayananda. But there would be many brahmacārīs who have and will continue to come forth to serve with their unique talents and their individual inspirations. The seeds have been planted with great care; the trees will bear fruit in their own time.

In 1974 Swami Govindagiri had come from Tapovanam Kutir to Madras for medical care. After his recovery, he attended a yajña conducted by his brother disciple. He succinctly summed up Swamiji's teaching –

"Swami Chinmayananda, as well as Swami Tapovanam, have been Guru to me. Yes, I have learned a lot from Swami Chinmayananda. He has the capacity to enable one to see the Truth. When you listen to him speak, you walk away thinking you know everything there is to know. Where we have failed is in our inability to keep the brightness of that Knowledge in our minds to blind out all doubts. We allow the clouds of our old tendencies to come back and settle in."

Each sage of God serves as an instrument of the divine symphony. Having surrendered to the Cosmic Intelligence, he or she does not ask for his particular manifestation to be one way or the other. He is content with himself and he is content with his world, wherever he finds himself. This is the uniqueness of a Master. Can Vedānta, the eternal philosophy of life, do all it promises an individual? There is one living proof of its validity – Swami Chinmayananda, his life and his Mission.

26

The Final Journey

I have been teaching you all these years that I am not the body. Even now you are trying to be my teachers and convince me that I am the body.

—Swami Chinmayananda
at his 72nd birthday celebration.

Swami Chinmaynanda's 'Divine Mission' passed through many phases. In the 1950s, he personally gave yajñas throughout India – in all the major towns and cities. In the 1960s, his emphasis was on creating an Institute of Vedānta to train others to teach the scriptures. In the 1970s, his work in foreign countries expanded and consolidated, while the Mission centres in India exploded with many cultural and service projects.

As he observed his audience through the years, he continued to modify his format. During his first yajñas, he found that householders were not up to the rigor of a one-hundred day period of teaching and sādhanā, so he cut the length. Although he taught only the Upaniṣads during the first five years, he found that the *Bhagavad-gītā* was the appropriate text for living and serving in today's world. In the first training course at Sandeepany, he initiated the students into brahmacarya immediately. Again he found this practice was not appropriate, so the initiation was given on completion of the training at the individual student's discretion. Throughout the 1960s and 1970s, the yajña length settled into a comfortable ten days, which allowed him to visit more towns. During the 1980s, although he taught continuously, much of his time was spent in coordinating and advising the many projects of the various Mission centres.

He never missed an opportunity to encourage the members to improve themselves. On the occasion of the North Indian New Year, he gave the following message –

> "Dīpāvalī is a day dedicated to inner purity and noble character. Cultivation of character is the premise for the national resurgence. Political awakening, economic growth, social reforms and educational programmes are all wonderful plans, but let us remember that all of these depend upon the character of the people.
>
> Dīpāvalī is a happy day dedicated to the opening of our individual hearts. Let everyone meet their friends and neighbours at the same table and partake of bread. Let all misgivings be forgotten; all grievances be forgiven. Let us remind ourselves, at least on this great day, that we can be victorious over our lower impulses and come to illumine the world around us with the lamp of spiritual light."

Wherever he went, Swamiji always found time to encourage the young people. Throughout the country, hundreds of Bala Vihar groups for children were meeting weekly. Chinmaya Vidyalayas, schools founded for the purpose of adding the knowledge of Hindu religion and culture to the curriculum, were opened in all the major cities. The CHYK clubs for the college students were expanding. In many states, these young people were creating service projects and holding conventions.

Naturally, the adult activities continued to expand. The number of dedicated brahmacārīs continued to grow. Wherever they were sent, the Mission centres flourished. The Study Groups were as popular as ever. The correspondence course continued to be a viable channel to introduce new seekers to the logic of Vedānta. Homes for the aged were built in āśrama settings to enable the elderly to have a meaningful retirement.

Each Mission centre was growing with projects suitable to the talents of its members. The active Bangalore centre, under the inspired guidance of Swami Brahmananda, developed by leaps and bounds. The services of the hospital expanded, including the addition of a training centre for nurses and a rural clinic to serve the poor. The Deenabandhu Devasthanam was enlarged; an Institute of Management was inaugurated; two primary schools were opened. The active Madras centre continued to be a leader in education under the guidance of Smt. Leela Nambiar. Outside of Madras, a Śiva temple was inaugurated with an āśrama for a Vedānta course in the Tamil language, as well as a rural medical dispensary. In Delhi, Swami Jyotirmayananda coordinated and managed the construction of a large school and Mission centre. All the projects were possible because of the many selfless workers, many of whom were volunteers.

Swamiji began to hold spiritual camps, as did other Swamis of the Mission, in retreat centres from Uttarkashi and Sidhabari in the Himalayas to Madurai and Cochin in South India. International spiritual conventions were held in 1983 in Bombay, in 1987 in Michigan, U.S.A., and in 1988 in Cochin. These camps enabled the Chinmaya Mission family to meet to share ideas and inspirations. At the same time, everyone was able to imbibe the wisdom of the *Bhagavad-gītā* and the Upaniṣads as expounded by Swamiji.

The Chinmaya International Foundation was established in Cochin to promote in-depth academic spiritual studies. The research centre and extensive library would bring together all the various philosophies of the world to search out, then publicise, universal themes that would encourage global understanding of peace. The research would include investigations into the various branches of India's spiritual wisdom, as well as analysis in comparative religions and philosophy. A college for the study of Sanskrit was included.

In April 1989, the Chinmaya International Foundation acquired the ancestral home of Ādi Śaṅkarācārya near Cochin. Although it was in a state of dilapidation, the original house still stood on an eight acre compound. Built in the architectural style of old Kerala, with extensive use of beautiful hardwood, the basic structure was still solid. Even some of the carved wooden panels, over one thousand years old, were still intact. The purchase definitely saved the structure from the bulldozer.

In 1978, Swamiji had selected property in the Western Himalayan peaks at Sidhabari as a place for retirement for himself and for his devotees, who could build their own cottages there. He announced that, due to his failing health, he planned to slow down. However, his heart surgery in Houston, Texas in 1980 had intervened. After a short recuperation time, he had renewed energy. Thereafter, he would spend several months each year in Sidhabari giving sādhanā camps. These camps gave the devotees the wonderful opportunity to spend optimum time – from one week to three months – with Swamiji in a peaceful setting, far away from the demands of their daily lives.

In order to use the āśrama space when he was not there, he had an idea of teaching an abbreviated course in Vedānta to a group of young people, who would be selected from the nearby villages. The course would emphasize the *Rāmāyaṇa*, authored by Tulasīdāsa that was loved by all the mountain folk. In addition, they would learn some practical skills, including homeopathy and some modern agricultural skills. After the course, the students would return to their own villages as all round counsellors. At that time, he told Vivek Chaitanya[1] of this idea and asked the brahmacārī to visit the surrounding villages to inquire as to the feasibility of such a plan. However, Vivek Chaitanya found that

[1] The future Swami Tejomayananda.

the young people were not interested in any course that was not specifically geared to producing an income.

He notified Swamiji of the indifferent response to his survey. At about that time, Vivek Chaitanya remarked to a Mission member, "Perhaps we could have a full Vedānta course in Hindi." Through the infallible Indian grapevine, Swamiji heard of the comment and wrote Vivek Chaitanya to proceed with this plan. Therefore, in 1981, the first Vedānta course in an Indian language, Hindi, was inaugurated at Sidhabari.

Not a year went by without a major service project being inaugurated in the many Mission centres, thereby giving aid to others throughout the country. Yet it seemed that Swamiji was not totally satisfied with the number of projects that served the lowest stratum of the society. In his annual New Year's message to the members published in a 1983 issue of *Tapovan Prasad* magazine, he included the following appeal –

> "The Hari Har Schools, to serve the Harijana (outcastes) people and the neglected and long oppressed members of our community, are still in a stage of mere discussion among our Mission members. Now and then I get a report, as if they are reminding me that they have not given up this programme, that they are still collecting data. This is a very sad situation. It clearly shows that our Chinmaya Mission members, who are living by a sheer accident in a comparatively happy condition, have not given serious thought to the sad, tragic travail in which these unfortunate members of our land are surviving. They are consigned to a most undignified condition of dire helplessness, poverty and ignorance. To serve them is the greatest charity and spiritual service to our community. All that I need from the Mission members is their legwork

and organizational ability. The providing of any required funds is my responsibility. Yet, nothing has happened so far – but I have great hopes that in 1983, the attitude will change and the work will start.

I am sure I will have the patience to wait yet another three months. If at the end of the three months my workers are still not capable of organizing it, I may have to cancel all my other programmes and go to the villages myself to start these schools. The work is to be done. With you or without you – it will be done."

Swami Chinmayananda

....

In April 1985, Swamiji's inspiration of providing service to the many village communities surrounding Sidhabari came to fruition. Inspired by Swamiji, Dr. Kshama Metre left her lucrative medical practice in Delhi and moved to Sidhabari. Her leadership in the improvement of life in the local villages has earned her international acclaim. Under her guidance, the midwives' training was expanded to a certified Nursing Training Course geared to serving the rural population. These projects were financed by grants from the U. S. Government and the Ford Foundation. Gradually, programmes were expanded to include assistance to over one hundred villages. These services included educating the populace, particularly widows and handicapped, of avenues of government relief available to them. They even needed assistance in applying for government pensions and following up until the money was received. Literacy programmes and micro banking were made available. In conjunction with these programmes, the Norwegian Government gave a grant to run a textile factory that would employ only destitute women – orphans, widows and women whose husbands had deserted the family.

To honour the occasion of Swamiji's 70th birthday on April 19, 1987 (Indian lunar calendar) the Bangalore Mission centre organized an elaborate ten-day celebration. Thousands gathered from all over India to express their love and affection to Swamiji. Every evening, a guest speaker from one of the many spiritual organizations spoke on one of the many great saints of India.

As an offering to their beloved Guru, on the tenth day of celebrations, the devotees were to gift Swamiji with his weight in silver. A custom in Kerala, the Tulābhāram ceremony, is a special offering made to God to express gratitude for a special blessing. For example, if a child were ill, the mother would pray to God, "If you heal my child then I will make an offering to you. I will give you my child's weight in coconuts" (or another offering). Amid bells ringing, conches blowing and ecstatic devotees, Swamiji ascended one side of the Tulābhāram scale with all solemnity. Surely all the devotees were holding only gratitude to God for their good fortune to have contact with a living Mahātmā, whose love for his devotees was boundless.

Swamiji's messages for the occasion was entitled – 'Role of the Mahātmās in National Integration.' In the address he emphasized that national integration, that is, a sense of brotherhood and love among people living in different Indian provinces, cannot be achieved by modifications or refinement in the external environment. Since love or hatred, violence or peace, understanding or misunderstanding, all arise in the mind, citizens can create only national, or world integration by bringing about a change in the texture of their thoughts, attitudes and values. Throughout the ages, in every country, the saints and Mahātmās have deeply influenced the collective mind of the people toward noble ideals by their own example of dispassion, selfless love and service to all living beings. Only when the mass of people have feelings of love, brotherhood and desire for the general welfare of the world can there be a family of nations dedicated to peace and human progress.

After his heart surgery in 1980 in Houston, Texas, Swamiji had proclaimed that he had ten more years to work. Eleven years later while giving a retreat at the Sidhabari Sandeepany āśrama in the Himalayas, Swamiji became so ill that an ambulance had to be called. The attendants wanted to carry him on a stretcher, but he refused. "I'll die with my boots on," he roared in his husky, though weak voice. On 17th October 1991, he was admitted to the hospital with acute respiratory distress and cardiac decompensation due to left ventricular failure, which caused acute pulmonary edema. The doctor ordered adequate rest, minimum physical exertion, a restricted diet and minimum travel; specifically, he was to limit travel by train and plane.

From his hospital bed, he made plans to distribute the responsibility of the Mission activities. On October 30, he issued a letter to all Chinmaya Mission centres. During the previous year, Swami Brahmananda and Swami Vedananda had been given the responsibility to coordinate the Mission activities and brahmacārīs stationed in Karnataka and Kerala, respectively. Then he divided the remainder of India into three additional districts to be administered by Swami Saradapriyananda (Andhra Pradesh and Tamil Nadu); Swami Jyotirmayananda (Delhi and Haridwar); Swami Subodhananda (Uttar Pradesh, Himachal Pradesh, Rajasthan, Punjab, Haryana).

After two months of rest, he had recovered his health sufficiently to travel to Bombay (now Mumbai) to participate in the celebration of his 75th birthday, which is considered the Platinum Jubilee Year. Again the members of Chinmaya Mission wished to give an offering to their divine Guru in the form of a Tulābhāram. However, this offering would be in gold to ensure the financial stability of the divine work without the continual strain on Swamiji's health. He used to joke that money only came in to support his growing 'family' of brahmacārīs and sannyāsīs when he was out in the public doing his dance. The ceremony was planned during the Christmas holidays in order to make it easy for foreign devotees to participate. The 75 kilograms of gold, the equivalent of 3.40 crores of rupees, would form a Corpus Trust for Central Chinmaya Mission Trust. The annual interest would be distributed to the two hundred Mission centres in India according to their needs.

Returning to Sidhabari after the birthday celebration, Swamiji remained there for a total of three and half months. Two hundred visitors and āśramites participated in the sacred ceremony for Śivarātrī in late February. For days Swamiji personally supervised every detail of the preparations, including making a daily trip to the temple to give instruction for the decorations, the installation of a Śiva Liṅga, and the erecting of shelters for the crowd of worshippers. Everyone remained in awe at the dynamic silence that he emanated wherever he went.

In spite of his many activities, the rest from his usual routine did prove beneficial. Dr. Rajgopal from the Yol Military Cantonment Hospital declared that Swamiji's health had stabilized; however, he cautioned the patient to abstain from any exertion that would put stress on his heart. With this bit of encouragement, the first week in April, Swamiji flew off for a yajña in Singapore, then back to India for a spiritual camp and yajña in Kerala. Again, he flew to the United States for his usual foreign tour, ending with the first world spiritual camp at Port Blair, Andamans Islands.

The highlight of the weeklong camp was a small cultural programme given every evening by children from different primary schools in Port Blair, including a presentation by the Chinmaya Bala Vihar group. Swamiji was delighted to see the talents of the youngsters, for, he truly loved and encouraged all children everywhere. There was certainly no evidence that he was curtailing his activities.

Neither had he lost his humour. The following was Swamiji's message in the April, 1992 issue of *Tapovan Prasad* –

"There are four people named Everybody, Somebody, Anybody and Nobody. They are bosom friends. An important project came up and the Swami asked everybody to do it efficiently.

> Everybody was sure somebody would do it. Anybody could have done it, but nobody did it. Somebody got angry because it was everybody's job. Everybody thought anybody could do it, but nobody realized that everybody wouldn't do it.
>
> It ended up that everybody blamed somebody when nobody did what anybody could have done.
>
> This happens in some Missions. Never in the Chinmaya Mission, I hope!"
>
> Swami Chinmayananda

....

On December 2, 1992, Swamiji addressed a gathering of distinguished persons at the United Nations in New York City. In his speech, he indicated that the UN – established over four decades previously for the purpose of bringing a New World order of peace to humankind – had at best become a firefighting organization. The moment the organization addressed itself to one problem area, strife and turbulence burst out in another area. Thus the UN's main preoccupation had been intervening in the regions of political unrest, while little had been done to root out the cause of these problems.

Further, he analysed that humanity was in the birth pangs of a new evolutionary state. Organizations like the UN had to recognize this thrust for a new order and ensure that they act as a catalyst to bring about this healthy and essential change. Although mankind had developed technologically and materialistically to great peaks, the powers that be had not been able to remove poverty, pestilence and misery among humankind. He continued to emphasize that the problem was not in the outer world of objects and their arrangements, but the problem lay in the mind and intellect of individuals. A new economic order or legislation was not a viable means to make the world a better and safer place.

A true metamorphosis could only be achieved when each individual improved his inner personality and joyously attempted to be of service to the entire universe. Nature constantly demonstrated to us that we should live to serve the society and not plunder it. To achieve this end, it would be necessary to remould our education system, he asserted. This younger generation had to learn to know their inner divinity. With this spiritual understanding, they would be able to lead peaceful, serene and happy lives.

At the year's end, *Hinduism Today,* the distinguished newspaper dedicated to the upholding of Hindu dharma, announced the presentation of its Hindu Renaissance Award for the year 1992 to His Holiness Swami Chinmayananda. This 'Hindu of the Year Award' is given to recognize those 'who make the strongest impact on all Hindus of the world and teach Hinduism's vastness, tolerance, compassion and spiritual depth.' Certainly, this statement was a concise, but meaningful, description of the Mission that Swami Chinmayananda had been sustaining for over forty years.

Swamiji's 1993 itinerary was finalised and printed – every day was packed right up until January 20, 1994. However, the ominous words – 'If Health permits!!' – were lettered on the cover. The schedule included his usual foreign tour, even though he had to be carried from the plane on a stretcher on his return from his 1992 trip abroad.

In early 1993, he gave introductory talks at various universities in the U.S.A. At the same time, he took the opportunity to address the Professors of Indology, Sanskrit, Philosophy, Religion and South Asian studies in informal meetings. He gave them a bird's eye view of the goals of Chinmaya International Foundation, the institute for spiritual and philosophical research in Cochin, Kerala. He invited the professors to help him with the task by giving their valuable ideas as to infrastructure, setting up the library, and the establishment of communication between the East and West. The professors pledged their support in the worthy endeavour. Clearly, the work of this institute was a project dear to his heart.

In July 1993, Swamiji had completed spiritual camps in Piercy, California and Washington, D.C. He then flew to San Diego, California on the 1st of August. Just a week earlier, he had made the ominous comment, "The Lord has been calling me, but all these people won't let me go. I feel like a rope being pulled on both ends."

As the message went out via telephones that Swamiji had been hospitalised and was in critical condition, the world shivered; then groaned, with the news that he had breathed his final breath. On August 4, 1993, with quiet prayers, devotees from around the world, including his brother disciple from the Divine Life Society, Swami Chidananda, gathered in San Diego. Swamiji had undergone emergency procedures and heart surgery. However, the moment had been ordained for 'the foot soldier of *Gītā*' to disappear from the physical earth and Chinmaya to return unto Itself. Swami Chidananda commented, "The combination of the lives of ten ṛṣis is Swami Chinmayanandaji. To perform all that he has done during his life will take the lives of ten."

With sombre hearts, several hundred devotees received the British Airways flight in Delhi on August 7th. Gurudev's physical body had been embalmed in a lotus position, so that it could be set in a chair and garlanded with masses of fragrant tropical flowers. Thousands of people filed by to say their farewells – a last farewell to the dear one who had served humanity with such infinite love and enthusiasm. During a six-hour ceremony, devotees and the general public, including many Indian political leaders, filed past the form that had played in the world as Swami Chinmayananda. Throughout the day, Indian T.V. channels broadcast news bulletins of the public darśana.

Early in the morning, the casket was loaded onto a large air-conditioned jeep for the final destination – the rose garden behind Swamiji's cottage in the Himalayan peaks. The skies streamed buckets of tears as the procession of automobiles wound its way through the foothills of the Western Himalayas toward Sidhabari. In spite of the heavy rains, crowds of devotees, peasants and children lined the road as it entered Kangra valley.

Fortunately, the rains cleared shortly after their arrival, so several thousand devotees were able to have a final darśana of their dear Swamiji. This procession of loving and weeping ones lasted until well into the night. At 5 a.m. on the following morning, August 9, the traditional burial rites for a sannyāsī were performed by a South Indian priest. With the devotees quietly chanting "Om Namaḥ Śivāya," the mortal coil was laid to rest in the holy atmosphere of the magnificent Himalayas. Arranged in the lotus position, the body was carefully lowered into a five-foot by five-foot cement vault with the head facing toward the east. Following a two-hour ceremony of mantras and offerings in strict accordance with the scriptures for interring a Mahāpuruṣa (Realized Soul), the physical form of the Swami was then packed with salt, and the tomb was sealed with cement blocks. The samādhi (final resting place) of a Jīvanmukta, a Liberated soul, was considered sacred and would remain a place of worship.

Surely, Mother Earth smiled as she received the mortal remains of this son back into her arms. This divine son, who realizing his divinity, had realized the divinity in all. Thereafter, he served the world faithfully and tirelessly for forty-two years – a model to everyone of what man can achieve when he turns his mind, intelligence and physical activities to a divine purpose.

The ṣodaśa, Sixteenth Day Ceremony, connected with Gurudev's samādhi was reverentially performed on August 19th at Sidhabari Ashram by devotees with all prescribed rituals including the giving of food and gifts to sixteen sannyāsīs. A huge bhaṇḍārā, or community feast, was given for some ten thousand peasants from all the surrounding villages. In order to accommodate everyone, food was served from 12 noon to 8 p.m. Similar ceremonies and bhaṇḍārā, though on a smaller scale, were performed in all the major Mission centres throughout India.

Swami Chinmayananda had made plans for the continuing leadership of the Mission. He had said many times that Swami Tejomayananda would be his successor. Early that year, he had written to Swami Tejomayananda in California to inform him that, when Swami Chidananda completed the current training of the brahmacārīs at Sandeepany, he should be posted to California. At that time, Swamiji instructed that Swami Tejomayananda would return to Bombay. Later when Swami Tejomayananda questioned Swamiji as to what would be his role in Bombay, Swamiji told him that he would start doing the Central Mission Trust work. Swamiji added that he should visit the various Mission centres to become familiar with their programmes and problems.

Swami Tejomayananda was the logical choice. He was a 'make things happen' person who had followed his inspiration to create the āśrama for the Hindi speaking populace of Northern India at Sidhabari. After taking the sannyāsa vows to become a Swami, he had been the Teacher at Sandeepany Sadhanalaya in Bombay. In addition, he had spent several years establishing the California centre in San Jose, so he was familiar also with the Mission activities abroad.

In a letter to all the Mission centres, Narain Bhatia, the Chief Executive of C.C.M.T., announced the appointment of Swami Tejomayananda as the Chairman of C.C.M.T. and the spiritual head of the Chinmaya Mission throughout the world. In addition, Swami Purushottamananda was appointed to the board and designated to act as the Chairman in the absence of Swami Tejomayananda.

In a letter dated 23 September 1993, Swami Tejomayananda addressed the bereaved Chinmaya Mission members.

Swami Tejomayananda's Letter to Mission Members

Parama Pūjya (supreme worshipful) Gurudev has attained mahāsamādhi, thus fulfilling his own life. However, the lives of all those who came in his contact will not be the same in his physical absence. It is only in the course of time that we may fully realize how deeply he has touched our lives, giving them purpose and direction. Indeed our lives have been blessed because of our association with him.

It is needless to recount here Pūjya Gurudev's achievements in various walks of life, for, they are all well-known. What is important, however, is for us to know that his work has provided us a variety of fields to serve the society, according to our aptitude and ability. Such work, in a spirit of devoted worship of God, is the only means of purifying our minds. Let us remember this at all times while working in our own endeavours.

It may be that once in a century a person like Pūjya Gurudev is born in this world. Like him, there is none and there will not be another in the future. None of us can take his place in the organization. Nevertheless, all of us can be his devoted and dedicated sevakas (servants) serving his Mission with the vision imparted by him in a way that would make him proud of us all. It is natural to have differences of opinion among ourselves on various issues, but let it not become a cause of division between us. We may doubt the merit of our brother or sister devotee's particular opinion, but may we not doubt his or her loyalty to, and devotion for, Pūjya Gurudev. Think and feel that the other member has more devotion than you do. Such an attitude will certainly bring greater mutual love and harmony among the Chinmaya family members. Love brings peace and bliss in the family.

We all shall work together and achieve together for the welfare of all. May God's grace and Pūjya Gurudev's blessings be with us ever!

In the Service of the Lord,
Swami Tejomayananda

27

The Vision

Where there is a vision – when even a single person has developed and cultivated the courage and heroism to live up to the vision – the Mission cannot die.

—Swami Chinmayananda, 1993.

The continuing journey of the Chinmaya Mission is a network originated and regenerated by Swami Chinmayananda's vision of a harmonious society, living a life based on sound ethical values and spiritual ideals. The network is made up of individuals who hold his vision. The vision empowers the individuals to work together to contribute to the society.

In Swamiji's own words –

Swami Chinmayananda's Vision for the Chinmaya Family

We, the Chinmaya Mission members, demand only the chance to do our duties towards our nation, our society and our family. Duties generate rights – Our eyes are upon our duties and our entire attention is observing the quality of our actions in fulfilling our duties. We strive ever to inspire the texture of our actions, the significance of our work, the content of our efforts. We demand that our life must have an overall heroic meaning and triumphant purpose.

To live thus – serving all – is in itself the essence of Vedānta. The Upaniṣads glorify it; the ṛṣis grow hoarse repeating it. All through the thousands of years of the unbroken spiritual culture of India's history, all our teachers have constantly pointed this truth out to us. In thus living our essential spiritual life, no force can challenge us – no obstacle can stop us – no threat shall halt us. We shall march along, silently and heroically doing our duties to all – demanding no rights or reward. Such mighty hearted, self-sacrificing, faith clad soldiers of the Lord are our Mission members.

Our services to the nation, society and home, our untold sacrifices, our joyous kindliness – we shall give out to encourage, to raise and to help revive others around us. This service is our spiritual sādhanā. We serve the Lord through service of the people around us. Every act in life is an act of worship of the ever present Sadāśiva (divine purity) everywhere.

In our vision we shall not limit our field to the Hindus only, nor to India only. Our vision shall comprehend all mankind, all nations, societies and communities. Mankind is the theme of our devotion; he is our field of worship. We expect nothing to happen, desire to gain nothing, hope to accomplish nothing more than our own inner spiritual unfoldment through our steady, faithful love for humanity. We believe that our religion is the 'Cult of Creative Goodness'. The Chinmaya Mission members are the servants of the Lord – serving His plans here among our fellowmen. As we do so, we continuously dedicate our sincere activities to the Lord.

In this grand new vision, the Hindu culture will revive, grow and flourish.

Swamiji loved children and saw in them the hope of a better future for India. "Children are the cleanest canvas on which to paint," he used to say. He never missed an opportunity to meet with them for informal talks.

From the 1950s, Bala Vihar groups were established at all the Mission centres to help children imbibe Indian religion and culture and have the opportunity to unfold their innate talents. In weekly meetings, the children were encouraged to sing bhajanas, tell stories of India's saints and perform in dramas portraying moral or spiritual themes. In 1959, a magazine was started to act as a vehicle for giving all children enriching ideas for their daily living. By the early 1960s, camps for children were being held in every province in India. Swami Chinmayananda would always manage to take time from his busy schedule to speak at these camps, as well as present the prizes for the various competitions.

In Swamiji's own words –

Vision for the Children

From the Lord when we come into this world, we arrive as good children of light. But as we live among others, the animal instincts in us rise up; we become bad children. To avoid this fall, we must always remember God. Bala Vihar is meant to help us remember Him. Keeping the songs of the glorious Lord in your heart, grow to be great men and women of Bhārata. As you grow, you will have to serve our country and look after the welfare of our people. All these duties need ability, character, strength and God's grace. Cultivate them all. Develop all these qualities through daily prayer and meditation. Each day as you go to sleep and when you leave your bed in the morning, remember the Lord's glories and beauty. Then your actions will reflect your own inner beauty.

With his interest in children, he also encouraged the Mission members who were establishing Chinmaya Vidyalayas around India. These schools, with a curriculum that emphasized the children's culture and spiritual heritage, were an important foundation for the revival of essential values in the country.

In Swamiji's own words –

Vision of Education

Education based on our culture is necessary. Then only it becomes true education. What is given out in schools today is not education, only instruction. Schools and colleges are only institutes; teachers and professors are only instructors. Instructors in institutes 'instruct' how to do things and how to earn a living. Today all we want is to earn our livelihood. Noble virtues are ignored; character is at a disgraceful level. We only want a comfortable job – minimum work with maximum pay.

Teachers in our schools have been trained with ideals of shaping the students into noble citizens. In addition to the normal academic syllabus required by government, they give importance to a moral education. The idea is to ensure that the schools not only produce academically brilliant students, but also turn out ideal citizens of the future. Character formation, respect for elders, devotion to God, truthfulness, along with a good sense of discipline – all these virtues are emphasized.

In Swamiji's own words –

Vision for the Teachers

Our Vidyalayas were started with the idea of giving the youngsters the traditional values of our dharma and to mould them into a productive force in society. Shouting slogans and burning buses is not socialism. Sitting down to rant and rave cannot remove poverty. Only strength can remove weakness. Traditional values must guide our youth.

Such values can only be practised by an efficient and poised mind. Our objective should be to inculcate values into the lives of our youngsters. We intend to educate with nobler motives in mind. We may not be applauded if we succeed, but we shall have all the mental satisfaction of having done our duty. We may be harassed, kicked around and laughed at, but we should develop the inner strength to bear it all and carry on undaunted. I myself have no formal experience in academic teaching, so I depend on all of you teachers, who know the situation clearly, to work on these ideas and formulate a viable plan for our schools.

In addition to the chanting of hymns, storytelling and other activities that make our institutions unique, I suggest an active parent-teacher association. You teachers can request the mothers to walk down the corridors of the classrooms to develop an intimacy with the classroom situation. The school becomes a backyard, an extension of the home.

This intimate atmosphere is very conducive to personality development. To avoid any inferiority complex in the child, you must try to eliminate any negative criticism. Instead, pump up his plus points and little achievements; thereby, you will earn his love and respect. Ideas picked up at this early stage will always come out later.

You must carry out this great mission to restore our glorious culture to its pristine splendour. If you are able to fulfil a fraction of this vision, you must consider yourselves blessed. As you communicate these noble ideas in all your secular teachings in schools, you will surely grow in stature yourself, glowing with the perfection of one who has served in the best tradition.

The Chinmaya Yuva Kendra (CHYK) was founded in May 1975 as the result of a weeklong camp for teenagers organized by Chinmaya Mission in Bangalore during Swamiji's yajña there. Within ten years, there were thirty centres, particularly in the larger cities of Madras, Bangalore and Bombay – with over 30,000 members.

Swamiji believed that the youth in the country were not 'useless', but 'used less'. They were not 'careless', but 'cared (for) less'. The final destiny of a nation is always in the hands of its youth. Through CHYK, he wanted to give the young adults a clear vision of the goal in life and exercises for the cultivation of right values to enable them to mould their personality and harness their inner resources along constructive lines.

In Swamiji's own words –

Vision for the Youth

You are no longer children, yet you have not reached the frenzied activity of adulthood. You are at a stage where you can mould history. All revolutionary change for progress of our nation has been made by youth. In order to initiate new projects, you must know history, the mistakes made and the changes brought about in the past. You must have the correct knowledge, the right judgement and the capacity to plan.

The old gang of cronies and bandicoots (rats) who have been wielding power in our country will never allow any change, nor will they attempt anything new. The establishment will continue to follow the old orthodox methods. Their interest lies in maintaining the status quo in whatever field, whether it is religion, education, science or politics. Thus stagnation sets in. If the youths slavishly follow orthodoxy and do not carve out new possibilities, they are doomed to frustration. Turning to escapism through excessive indulgence in physical and mental pastimes, they will try to exhaust themselves in dissipation of physical, mental, psychological and intellectual energy with such activities as smoking, drinking, drugs and loud noise – which you call music.

Is there a way out? The answer is you have to go through a programme of planned study of culture, values and history. It is not enough to imbibe only what the media gives because that is not knowledge, but modulated propaganda. You must learn to judge for yourselves, then form your own convictions and have the courage to live up to them. Your plans and visions must come from within, based on your own understanding of the world, your patriotism, your love for the society, and your loyalty to your country – although not necessarily to the government. Even one such leader can bring about a great change. Your youthful vigour and intelligence must not be allowed to go in the wrong direction.

The training of the brahmacārīs in Sandeepany, then in the Himalayan Sandeepany, was an essential source for the continuance of the vision to reach the society. After Swamiji taught the first group, the students received their training from various qualified teachers. This practice guided their commitment to the teaching, rather than to the teacher. In this way, they were better prepared to face their Mission work independently, rather than depend on a Guru. They needed this self-sufficient confidence to face the challenges that life would surely present them when they were assigned to the various cities and towns. Even so, they were all part of Swamiji's family and he advised and encouraged them whenever he met them during his travels.

In Swamiji's own words –

Vision for the Brahmacārīs

Serve the society. Close your eyes to everything else. Serve the society and find your fulfilment in that service. By the quantum of work that you have done and the quantum of service that you have done, you will be able to analyse how to improve that service, how to give out better work, and how to improve upon yourself. That is all!

Your words will have no effect unless you are able to live the ideas you are teaching. If you don't live them yourself, your words will have no value at all. Just noisy sounds will come out! So, learn to live your sādhanā properly. In your life, make sure your relationships and your responses to the world outside are all ethical, moral and good – then your words will have an effect.

Now go and spread the message. The next batch will be coming and we will train them. When they are here, we must be able to point to you and say, "See how these people are doing such wonderful work, like them you too must work."

Hereafterwards, the Lord is with you. He will see that you get what you deserve. If you deserve a beating, people will be inspired to beat you! Irresistibly inspired! If you are good, they will be irresistibly inspired to adore you. It all depends on you! The organization can do nothing because the organization cannot be behind you everywhere, wherever you go. It all depends on you. You have been taught how to live the divine life. Now try to live it.

Your development depends upon how much you are able to give to society – then society will be inspired to give back to you. As soon as they give to you, give back to them. Thus the game goes on. Therefore, you keep nothing. Everything goes back to the very place from whence it came – but in a more creative form in service of the society.

Swami Chinmayananda's final words on his vision were written the month before his mahāsamādhi. On August 16, 1993, the editor of *Tapovan Prasad* received an article from Swamiji with clear instructions on how the Chinmaya Mission members should carry on when the Master was not present.

In Swamiji's own words –

The Mission and the Vision

God alone does nothing. He is a non-doer. Human beings alone can strive to improve the world. A human being is not able to do anything alone. He or she needs the blessings of God – the blessings of nature.

Many things we do today cannot be done without organization. Even to bless the society and to spread the values of life requires the framework of organization. In the Vaidika days, organizations were not existent; our Vedas give no sanction for the organization of religion. The Vaidika seers knew that spirituality and religion cannot be organized, that spiritual vitality can only be unfolded within the heart of an individual in perfect liberty and freedom.

But as people multiplied and the problems of the community increased, religion was no longer responding to the needs of the community. Thus in the Paurāṇika days, the various temples of India became centres of the religion. But even at that time, there were only a few of them – Badarinath, Varanasi, Rameswaram and Dwarka. Then in 500 BC, organization became more urgently needed. At that time, Lord Buddha became the first Hindu to bring structure to India's religion. He organized his team of workers in centres called Vihars. For the next six or seven centuries, Buddhism flourished and then gradually declined. Thus, the Indian spiritual atmosphere became very chaotic. Hinduism decayed, Buddhism decayed, and spiritual values also decayed.

It was then that Ādi Śaṅkarācārya appeared on the scene and brought about a rapid reorganization of Hinduism. Temples were founded and built. As temples become prominent in the society, they become instrumental in inspiring the entire community. The temples became a centre from which spiritual ideas and thoughts were spread into the community. But with the passage of time even these temples could no longer motivate the members of the community, India experienced another period of decadence.

In the nineteenth century, Swami Vivekananda again tried to organize Hinduism; he established the Ramakrishna Mission.

After Ramakrishna's and Vivekananda's time, many great teachers followed their example and founded similar missions. Each teacher was able to inspire large number of people to work together for their self-development and to perform service effectively in the community.

We must remember the principles that the Master has taught. We must keep the vision in our hearts. A mission without a vision is a sheer waste of time. Only when we see our vision clearly, and develop an attitude based on our vision, can we do what needs to be done. Serve our fellow human beings through schools, hospitals, dispensaries or social welfare centres. If we keep our vision clear in our minds and hearts, we know that we can be effective in our communities.

The world around us was not organized by us. We have not ordered the environment in which we find ourselves. Various factors contribute toward our circumstances. We have to adjust ourselves in such a way that we can efficiently and capably meet these challenges. Our only freedom is to attune ourselves to the world around us. This tuning and adjusting are not possible unless there is complete integration within us. Thus, when we develop faith in a higher Reality, then the ideal – the goal – becomes clearer.

The picture of the ideal is the concept of God for a devotee, namely, supreme love, supreme kindness, supreme mercy, beauty of beauty, strength of strength. When this concept of the ideal is maintained in our minds, we are able to understand how far we are diverging from that ideal – in our physical behaviour, in our feelings or emotions, or in our intellectual judgement. When we compromise with the ideal and act immorally, our intellect questions the mind and says, "Fool, why did you do it?" Our mind has no answer to this pang of self-accusation. We have insulted our own wisdom. This misalignment with our vision is called the prick of conscience.

To live in devotion to an ideal and to develop self-discipline is the true backbone of all religions. Whoever does this is the true member of any mission. A mission can sustain, endure and serve the society only when the members are tenderly and strongly holding on to that vision.

The ideal of a vision – the devotion to a vision – has become lost in the society, not only in Hinduism, but also in all religions of the world. Because we have allowed this to happen, we cannot pass any ideals to younger generations. Their reverence for religion is lost; they think religion is only another organization with another vested interest.

Learn to have an ideal, to keep a vision. Discover it in yourself. No one else can give it to you. True heroism is to live true to your ideal. The world may threaten you. The community will not leave you alone. But the true hero stands defiant, firmly rooted, in his or her own convictions. That one, even a single individual, inspires the entire population. Such uncompromising heroism of living up to the ideal is the very core of our avatāras.

A Kṛṣṇa. A Rāma. What is it that we glorify in them? They had heroism in their lives. Otherwise, they were like other human beings. We worship them; we revere them because they had heroism to live up to their ideals. Living up to their ideals was not easy. Jesus was crucified. Mahātmā Gandhi was shot by an assassin. What does it matter? One day everyone has to die. We were not given a contract that we would die in a hospital bed, surrounded by wife and children. Once we have found the joy and glory of life, why not die and live for that ideal? That consciousness can arise in us when the vision is clear. One who has a vision rises to the highest.

That vision is not a contract; it is not written on paper. It must be enshrined in the heart and mind of the visionary. Where there is a vision, when even a single person has developed and cultivated the courage and heroism to live up to the vision, the mission cannot die. This kind of mission can serve the society, the community, and the world.

Swami Chinmayananda's work stands as a huge banyan tree with numerous branches, spreading and protecting his family. As Swami Purushottamananda aptly put it, "Traditionally, the disciple had to go out and collect bhikṣā (food) for the Guru, but in our case Swamiji brought food to us." The spreading banyan tree produces many roots that eventually reach the earth and take root. Then they must grow and develop independently. Many of the Swamis and brahmacārīs felt strong enough to leave the mother tree and create projects according to their own talents.

Swami Chinmayananda was the pioneer that cleared the way for all those who teach the traditional Vedāntic philosophy in English, to women, and to non-Brāhmaṇas. Wherever they are teaching, under whatever organization, whether trained at Sandeepany or elsewhere, they are able to teach only because Swami Chinmayananda single-handedly braved the tide against the prohibition of teaching Vedānta to the public.

Life is ever changing; few things remain certain. Nonetheless, one thing is supremely certain – Swami Chinmayananda loved us more than we love ourselves. He wanted more for us than we want for ourselves. He wanted us to live in the recognition of our divine nature, whereas we remain content to settle for less.

Swamiji laid the foundation with over forty years of service to humanity. The glory of Chinmaya is not the organization that he formed, the āśramas that were built, the number of lectures that he gave. The glory of Chinmaya is that he touched so many people in a personal way, so that we have the courage to be more – to push ourselves beyond our mundane limitations. **Let us not forget His Vision.**

PART – IV

The Teaching

28

Satsaṅga

Verily that is whole; this is whole. From wholeness emerges wholeness; yet wholeness remains.[1]

The words of the mystics have always been difficult to comprehend. The *Bhagavad-gītā* states that, of the few who have had the cosmic vision, those who attempt to communicate this essential Truth to others are rare indeed. It is not easy to translate the Transcendental Reality into terms of everyday understanding. It becomes, therefore, a tough and often thankless task for the one who makes an attempt.

The idea of an essential divinity in and through everyone and everything is not one to which human minds can easily relate. But the truth is there have been many persons in every era who have verified the same fact – we are divine beings.

Why don't we know it? Because it is experienced in another state of Consciousness. For example, suppose there were many people who did not dream and they were the vast majority. So the minority who did experience the dream state of Consciousness would report it to the rest of the population. According to the reliability of the reporters, the number of reports, and the similarity of the experience, the non-dreaming population would begin to trust that there is a dream state of Consciousness. They might even be open to the idea that it is a potential experience for human beings. Certainly, there would be some who would want to investigate the possibility for themselves.

[1] ॐ पूर्णमदः .... ॐ शान्तिः शान्तिः शान्तिः ॥
Prayer verse from *Īśāvāsya-upaniṣad.*

Likewise, the fact that we can know our essential divinity has been reported again and again by some of the wisest, most respected individuals in the history of all religions. Each spiritual Master, in directing his words to the needs of the specific community that he addressed, gave variations of detail, emphasis and interpretation, but the essence remained the same. To give these reports in a language that could be understandable to the modern educated agnostic was Swami Chinmayananda's mission in life.

The most meaningful and delightful moments with Swamiji were each day as everyone gathered around him – on a long veranda, in a sunny sitting room, under the shade of a tree or on the floor of a temple – to unload their questions on him. Hindus came with not only spiritual and personal difficulties, but with questions concerning their heritage and customs. During these informal gatherings, Swamiji's true genius for understanding life and applying spiritual truths to living shone most brilliantly.

In the traditions of the great teachers of India, Swamiji applied the tenets of the scriptures to the needs of contemporary society. Established in the Knowledge of knowledges, he could engage anyone, anywhere, any time, to point them to the higher vision. He was willing to use any technique available to push people beyond their petty concepts of themselves – praising or joking, mocking or insulting, laughing or feigning tears. The self-conscious, sensitive ones he praised and encouraged; the egoistic, aggressive ones he cut down to size.

He was always quick to note the idiosyncrasies of the questioners whom he knew in the group and would use his observations to respond with quips and taunts intended to evoke laughter from both the group and the questioner. His sense of humour could be mischievous, but it was always backed with a purpose. When the student's mind was relaxed from the laughter, Swamiji would strike him with an immaculate logic. He thereby brought the student to a higher level of awareness as he cleared each doubt from the web of the mind.

The following section contains a series of excerpts from these informal satsaṅgas, or discussions on the Truth. The questions were not from one person, as in an interview, but from different people in the group, who brought up their own point of view, doubt or misunderstanding. Everyone then would wait with bated breath for Swamiji to shed light on the dilemma.

Often in the quest for freedom, we reject the yoke of the do's and don'ts of traditional religions, yet we go to a Guru expecting to get specific, absolute answers – a new set of rules. The Guru is dedicated to addressing the universal Truth and the techniques of reaching that Truth. Then the student must proceed in the indicated direction; the path to freedom is an individual quest.

Swamiji had a flair for serving the ball to the seeker's court and always stressed independent thinking for his students. He gave personal guidance for individual problems, but the time arrived when the student had to take the leap to that other state of Consciousness for himself – with no guarantee other than the words of the countless sages who have gone before that he would land safely.

29

Religion

Question – Swamiji, what do you consider the purpose of religion?

Swamiji – A mature man who has lived his experiences intelligently and has maintained an alert, critical attention upon the incidents of life will come to such an inner maturity that he will feel a certain unrest. He has the necessities of life, but not a complete satisfaction. He sits back and listens to muffled questions from within. "Where did I come from?" "Where will I go (as one day I must)?" "Is life an empty and meaningless accident?" "Has life a purpose?"

Religion is for this man; it provides assurance and guidance in his endeavour to answer these inner questions.

Question – You make religion sound so positive. But so many injustices and wars have occurred in the name of religion that the mature, intelligent, critical person rejects it.

Swamiji – It is true the villainy, cruelty, ambition, madness and even wars have repeatedly reached the arena of life clothed in the cloak of glorious religion. Even today it is a regrettable fashion to go mad in the fury of war and loot, kill, plunder, rape and dishonour ourselves in the name of religion. Thus religion has come to signify a danger signal to the peace loving and the honourable. But this is not religion. What prompts these fanatics to draw out their weapons and murder the weak and the helpless is not their faith in religion, but their own base and low animalism, disguised in the pious robes of religion.

Question – What you say is true, but what about those who are working in church organizations, yet never seem spiritual; that is, they lack the qualities of love and compassion. Actually, they are rather narrow-minded.

Swamiji – Remember, I said religion is for the mature person who has conscientiously lived and examined the experiences of life. Of course, the majority never question the why of the sorrows of the body and the torments of the mind. They just hurriedly discover a new set of excitements and a fresh pattern of distractions to engage the momentary fancy of the mind. They may even turn to God in the usual formalistic religions – visit churches, give to charitable causes or even build a temple. They will even run to their pews on Sunday or go to the temple for daily prayers. But all of these are only a variety of distractions to keep the mind from looking at itself, thereby escaping from its unhappiness.

Question – You have referred to religion as a philosophy which gives the answers to life, yet even in India the majority of the people who call themselves Hindus do not know the Vedānta philosophy.

Swamiji – Yes, that is true. Hinduism has in its vast amphitheatre preserved and worshipped many ideals as contained in the Purāṇas (epics), the numerous scriptures including the Vedas and the 1,001 interpretations of these scriptures. All of this overgrowth has so effectively concealed the real beauty and grandeur of the tiny Temple of Truth that today it is hidden behind its own banners.

A true religion has two important limbs – the ritualistic injunctions and the philosophical support. Most of us generally accept the former as religion. But the rituals and formalities are mere superstitions without philosophy; philosophy reinforces the external practices of the formalities and blesses them with a purpose and an aim. Even so, philosophy without any actual practice is madness. Ritual and reason must go hand and hand.

Religion promises no magical change in the nature of the material objects or in the pattern in their various arrangements. The world will remain the same and circumstances will continue to function according to the eternal law, whether or not one has spiritual insight. Religion lends the faithful ones a psychological balance and spiritual poise to enable them to face the inevitable vicissitudes of life.

Question – Then a person who condemns other religions cannot have a true spiritual insight.

Swamiji – No. All religions have the same goal. Once the individual realizes this goal he can never ridicule others nor fanatically proclaim that his is the only way. Humility, not fanaticism, is the character of one who has realized the Truth. We are all one; there is one God.

Question – How does one acquire the faith that you mentioned?

Swamiji – Faith springs from understanding. It is a conviction that grows from understanding. Therefore, one develops it by study of the scriptures and reflection on the ideas given there. As the conviction grows, desire to experience the highest state grows.

Question – Is faith really necessary?

Swamiji – Yes, just as it is necessary for any endeavour in the world. You must have faith that the work you are now doing will bring results in the future – at least the paycheck. But faith is already in everyone; even Rāvaṇa (a demon king) had faith in his power to gain glory for himself.

So having faith in the Lord; you gain the Lord. It cannot be a vague, wandering faith, but based on a true intellectual understanding of the goal to be reached.

30

God-realization

Question – How exactly would you define enlightenment, this final goal of life that all of us are seeking?

Swamiji – Enlightenment is Liberation; Liberation of the individual personality from the embrace of the world of matter. Give up this sense of the individual 'I'; it is the only way to wake up. The truth is we are Nārāyaṇa (God), but the precious stuff has been rotting in the sense world for so long that it looks like iron. Gold oxidised with sensuality has to be rubbed and polished until it is clean. That's all.

Question – You say that we are pushed around by our desires based on past experiences from which we gained a bit of joy, so we repeat the same situation to repeat the joy. But what about the desire to get liberated, where does that come from?

Swamiji – It just happens! After tasting the joys and sorrows of the world, you drop all desires for the world, then divine Bliss is there – your essential nature.

Question – So you would consider the desire to obtain Liberation is an 'okay' desire?

Swamiji – True, it is an egocentred desire, as are all desires. However, this is a higher desire, so you may keep it. When all desires have been removed, it will die of itself because it cannot exist when all desires have disappeared. Do you see? Carefully now. All desires are gone. Then how can there be a desire to remove desires? If all desires are gone, you have reached the goal. It is the same with sleep; the desire for sleep dissolves with sleep.

The great Śrī Ramakrishna, who had such a genius for telling practical stories to point out spiritual truths, gave this example. You are in a jungle and you get a small thorn in the flesh of your arm. You look around and find a larger thorn. You pluck it off the branch. Then with the larger thorn, you dig out the smaller splinter. Now when it is removed from your flesh, will you keep the larger thorn? No, you'll toss away both of the thorns. So you use this higher desire as a tool, but, when the goal is reached, you won't keep it.

Question – What is samādhi like?

Swamiji – Śama-dhī – the 'dhī', intellect, becomes 'śama', quiet. At this time the karma drops from you. The world of experience – and, therefore, the one who experiences it – is not there.

It is not in the cosmos, not in a place in the universe. It is a different realm – no time, no place.

Question – Why doesn't the mind stay in samādhi?

Swamiji – Mind can never be in samādhi; mind is a thought flow. So your question contains a contradiction in terms. It is like asking why doesn't a living body lie down dead? After you have the insight that Brahman (God) is All, the state of samādhi is not necessary. To the God-realized one there is no going in or coming out of samādhi.

With Īśvara darśana (the vision of the Lord) comes the true Knowledge that God Is. . . that the I-concept is false. The devotee, in a flash of illumination, realizes the divine play of seeing, hearing, smelling, tasting and touching is also nothing but the manifestation of Brahman. When the ego dies away, nothing remains but an infinite homogeneous Bliss experience, which is God.

Question – So realization is an actual experience that, no matter who experiences it, will always be the same.

Swamiji – Yes, exactly the same. If you stick your finger in the light socket, what is your experience? Will it be different from his or hers? No. All experiences of the finger in the light socket will be the same. But you must do it for yourself!

The Guru has experienced God-realization and his experience will not do you one iota of good. You must contact the divinity for yourself, the divinity that is one and the same in everyone.

Remember. The finger must be put in the socket! (He makes a gesture of putting his finger into an overhead socket.) But you want to sit there with your pencil taking notes. 'Let me see what voltage did you say this socket is?' 'Will it be the same experience if I put my finger in a socket in a different country?' I tell you it is the same – Indian electricity, British electricity, African electricity. It is all the same everywhere. Having experienced American electricity, you will not have to go to India and experience it there. Upon experiencing American electricity, you have experienced electricity everywhere.

Electricity yoga! Yes, you must make direct contact, but you sit there and watch another brave fellow. He approaches the socket, then he slowly. . . and carefully. . . sticks his finger into the socket. "Oh! Ouh! Aah!" he shouts as he is knocked away by the force. Sitting there you think, 'This is the secret. This is the experience – Oh! Ouh! Aah!' Then you stupidly sit there and repeat this new mantra – Oh, Ouh, Aah – thinking that it is going to give you some benefit. No, I tell you – never! You must approach the socket, lift the finger, and make the contact. Then will you know electricity yoga. This is the only way you will benefit.

Question – How can I be sure that there is a benefit? After realization won't I have the same nagging husband, demanding mother-in-law, whining children?

Swamiji – They will all be the same, but you will see them differently. Once you realize the Truth within you, you will also see that all the plurality and diversity of creation springs only from that very Truth. Having that knowledge, nothing can ever really disturb you again.

Question – How will I know if I have reached the highest? Couldn't one make a mistake?

Swamiji – Where there is God, there the I-sense cannot be. Where the I-sense is, there God is indeed far away.

In fact you will not reach the highest because you will not be there to experience it. Only God meets God.

Question – Can't you describe your personal experience, so we will know when we have had the true experience? I remember several holy men have told of some cosmic experiences.

Swamiji – I have nothing to say of personal experience because it is ridiculous to do so. It is only yogīs who claim various experiences en route, not at the time of nirvikalpa samādhi. In pure Being there is no experience.

Question – But there must be some indication of a Realized person...

Swamiji – Here is the golden rule, you will know 'All this world is my Consciousness in different forms.' It is like entering a dream in full waking Consciousness. You have been dreaming, but you awaken from the dream. Then you re-enter the dream state knowing that you are the waker, the person who has awakened. What will be your attitude towards the comings and goings in the dream? In such a position, you are not compelled to do or not to do; you are just being entertained in the dreamworld.

By no other sign can you say that one is Realized.

Question – Once Realized; always Realized?

Swamiji – Yes.

Question – But there are some teachers who do such self-centred, foolish things, even though they seem to have insight that would only come from direct, personal experience.

Swamiji – Then it was a partial experience. Take an example – I have lain down on the sofa for a nap and am just going to sleep when the phone rings. I shake my head a couple of times, get up and answer it – "Hello".

Hearing my sluggish, sleepy voice, the caller questions me – "Were you asleep?"

"No, I had lain down, but I had not yet gone to sleep."

"Oh, then you were awake?"

"Well, no. I was not really awake."

"What do you mean, you were neither asleep nor awake."

"Well, you see I was no longer awake, but I had not really quite gone to sleep yet. I was at the doorway of sleep, but I had not completely entered into it."

Sleep is a condition of the mind when it transcends completely into a different Consciousness. The transcending must be one hundred percent. It is the same with the transcendental experience; you completely merge into your true nature of Sat-Cit-Ānanda (Truth-Consciousness-Bliss).

Question – If we are Sat-Cit-Ānanda, why did we leave it?

Swamiji – You never did!

Your looking for God is like a ceramic vase looking for clay! Nārāyaṇa says that he is with us 365 days of the year, but we do not recognize Him. It is because we are only looking outward at the sorrows in life.

It's a mental adjustment. About face! Look within!

Question – Why do some realize this Truth, while others do not, even though they both seem to be putting forth the same effort?

Swamiji – The effort is made at preparing the mental apparatus. If too much willpower is used, it is fighting against nature. Neither can there be suppression. Suppression is not perfection. So the mind and intellect are prepared before the actual attempt to transcend them is made. The mental machinery must be carefully adjusted to receive the higher message; otherwise the result will be like one of our Indian rocket experiments. The countdown is complete, the button is pushed, there is a blinding light, and a great mushroom cloud billows forth. When all the smoke clears, there is the rocket still sitting on the launch pad!

In America the rockets take off and in India they make a lot of noise, light and smoke. What is the difference? It is the amount of work and effort that was put into the machinery itself. Not that in India, rockets won't work if they are properly prepared. So it is necessary to have an integrated, pure, disciplined mind.

Question – I have been meditating for four years. I now think that I have been wasting my time because I knew nothing about the Reality you are speaking about in the classes. Does this mean I just have not purified the mind enough?

Swamiji – It need not mean that. You have detached your mind from the world of objects, but then you had no knowledge of how to direct it. You have to know what you are searching for to set your course. You are now learning how to take off!

Question – When will the rocket take off? That is the question.

Swamiji – When it happens! In the text (*Gītā* – chapter 9) the Teacher indicates what is behind the flux of the world of matter. When you see this unity, that is the first rocketing. The objects of the world dissolve into the oneness when you reach the higher state; that is the second rocketing. In full realization, you see both modes – the One in the many and the many in the One.

Question – Where does the concept of God's grace fit into the picture?

Swamiji – We all have it equally. When the car is going along the highway, it may break down, even though it has plenty of gasoline. Will you curse the gasoline? No, the problem is in the vehicle itself.

Sunshine is everywhere, giving its light to all – the rose garden, the songbird, the mosquito and the garbage dump – without any discrimination as to type, race, colour, usefulness. The sun's grace is there, but you sit in your house with the shutters closed complaining that it is dark. Open the windows, and the blessing of the sun will flood in.

Question – Do you experience this divine state all of the time?

Swamiji – Experience is of the body, mind and intellect. I am being; I am not experience. I allow experience to exist around me. I am subtle like space, untouched by anything.

It can't be said that I am in It or out of It, but I am never away from It.

31

The Spiritual Student

Question – When should one begin on the spiritual path?

Swamiji – NOW. . . We exile ourselves from spiritual practice by our own fears. The Christian feels – I am a sinner, born in sin, packed and labelled for sin. This negative mind is in the majority of us. Because we are foolishly waiting until we are good enough, we never begin. So spiritual practices are meant to make us as good as we want to be.

Question – But I mean are there certain qualities that a person needs to ensure success?

Swamiji – The seekers must have the necessary courage to inquire. We must not just accept all statements of Truth merely because some ancient and learned sage has declared them. Both our head and heart must assimilate any new ideas before they can really be our own. We hear or read an idea, then we must reflect on it until the light of understanding dawns in our own bosom. In fact, only by this contemplative process can any philosophical creed readily reach the heart to guide us in our day-to-day life and its transactions.

Question – But some of us come and listen to you and make an honest attempt to live up to the ideals, but we fail to experience this true Reality that you are pointing out. Perhaps we were not ready for the spiritual path.

Swamiji – Certainly, as in any field of study, the candidate for Self-realization also must have certain preliminary qualifications if he is to benefit from discourses on Vedānta. When we hear the grave term – 'the fourfold qualifications' necessary for a student of Vedānta – spoken of, we are apt to feel uncomfortable. Upon a closer analysis, however, we shall find that we already have developed these qualities in facing our ordinary life. They now must be refined and focused in another direction – toward spiritual endeavours.

The first of the qualifications is a capacity to discriminate the Real from the unreal, the true from the false, the essence from appearance, the object from its shadow. Who doesn't have this ability? We are not mere worms and animals. We are a cultured society of men and women who are continually applying our power of discrimination in our everyday life.

The second qualification is detachment; that is, the quality of the mind that enables one to be detached from false and painful things. Do not be frightened away with some weighty concept of dispassion. Who among us doesn't have it? When the intellect has come to a sure and definite understanding, and is consequently fully aware that a given thing is but a shadow and valueless, the mind naturally detaches from it. For example, you marry a lovely princess in a dream. When you awaken you cannot maintain your love and attachment for her. The moment you are awake, you realize your dream love was a falsehood. This detachment, gained as a result of personal knowledge, is dispassion.

These two qualifications – discrimination and detachment – are necessary for an understanding of Vedānta. When they are present, the other nobler qualities of humankind, which are the third qualification, automatically arise and link up with the fourth qualification – an eagerness to experience your own essential divinity.

Question – So we have these qualifications to some extent, but maybe they are not developed enough.

Swamiji – Yes, now you must apply these qualities to the higher realms of thought. The purpose of the Upaniṣads and the *Gītā* is to guide us from the outer levels of our personality into the innermost sanctum, the seat of the Infinite, reigning in all glory.

A student of Vedānta will start his inquiry with the external world – from where has the world come and where it will go? Once we understand the outer world, our inquiry will be into our physical body and its five sense organs. To a man born blind, there is no form. To a deaf man, the canon appears to be only smoking, not roaring. In order to enjoy tastes and smells, one needs a tongue and a nose. If we were to take away the five senses, there would be no world for us. That is, our concept of the outer world is gained through the gateway of our sense organs.

Next the inquirer will start to investigate the function of his or her mind and intellect. So step by step, he continues examining from the gross outer world to the subtler realms within. These external coverings can be said to encase the Reality within. Our physical body, with its sense organs, is the grossest encumbrance; then there is the vital air sheath, which consists of the breath and the subtle powers the body uses to maintain itself. The mental sheath is even subtler, then we have the intellect sheath, then the bliss sheath, the seat from which the joy element bubbles forth.

One attempts to reach and recognize face to face, the subtlest of the subtle, the Self. This is the moment of true meditation when the robes of these gross layers of our personality vanish and our true nature is recognized.

Question – But what if one just honestly does not have the qualifications to understand Vedānta that you mentioned. What can be done?

Swamiji – There are spiritual exercises given in the scriptures, such as in the last chapter of *Kaivalya-upaniṣad*. After the Teacher has imparted the entire Upaniṣad revealing the one behind the many, a student is sitting there with a blank face, wondering 'When is the Upaniṣad going to begin.' He hasn't understood a single concept.

In his infinite compassion, the Teacher tells this student, "I am going to give you this one very special verse. You chant it throughout the day as you are doing all your activities, whether you are walking, bathing, eating or even taking part in some sensuous pleasure. You just go on repeating this verse, for, it is an antidote for all sins. If you repeat this verse continually for thirty days, it will wipe your mind clean of all its past." The Teacher knows that when the student is able to accomplish this exercise he will then have the mental purity to understand the Upaniṣad.

Question – What about the path of devotion? Where does it fit in?

Swamiji – All spiritual disciplines are to make the mind meditation worthy. For the body, you have karma-yoga. You do your work with all actions dedicated unto the Lord. For the emotional mind there is bhakti-yoga. You give your love to the Lord; only he can return love in equal measure. For the intellect there is jñāna-yoga. You study and inquire into the scriptural ideas. There is not even one question that the intellect can ask that Advaita (non-dual) Vedānta cannot answer. Vedānta covers all possibilities, so that the intellect is finally blasted beyond logical thinking.

In the path of devotion when you have the attitude, 'I surrender all to him', the Lord comes down to you. In the path of the intellect, you attempt to reach the Lord with your understanding. 'I'll do it myself; I'll come to you' is the attitude. But this coming up or going down is all the same. If you are moving closer to the Lord, the Lord is coming closer relatively to you.

32

Meditation

Question – Swamiji, why is it important that we meditate?

Swamiji – Man is mind – meditation works on the mind itself. Realization is the long-term goal of meditation. You will wake up from the dream of the ego into the Infinite.

Question – But my mind never seems to be quiet enough to meditate.

Swamiji – Meditation is for making it quiet. When you meditate look at the depth of silence between your thoughts, just as if they were two waves of the ocean. When you are repeating your mantra, you are constantly looking to that silent depth between each repetition. Even in our daily life, we jump from one thought to another, never noticing the silence between the thoughts. Use any two thoughts; even any two vulgar thoughts will do. The substratum of silence remains the same.

Question – But we are still the observers, that is, we are observing silence.

Swamiji – You've been reading too many books. How can there be an observer when there is nothing to observe? Dive into the gap; it is your gateway.

Question – What about the vāsanās (innate tendencies)?

Swamiji – What vāsanās? Who's got the vāsanās? You have to go beyond these intellectual concepts. Intellectual study is only for the purpose of finding out that there is a Truth beyond the intellect. In satisfying the questions of the intellect you get thrown beyond it. As the pole-vaulter goes over the top, he does not keep the pole. He lets it go.

Just sitting still with the body motionless will calm the mind, at least, a relative quiet. Drop all worries, they will be there waiting for you afterwards. It is just like after you have slept, you wake up to the same old problems.

Question – But some days it is so difficult even to sit still!

Swamiji – You must watch your mind during the day. If someone has hurt you or criticized you, meditation will be difficult. Your mind will go back to that situation when you sit to meditate. With intellectual discrimination, you must let the mental bruise go at the moment it happens. Tell yourself that the insult is not true of your true Self; it is only true of the material that hangs around you. Why bother to defend it? Let it go.

Question – If I know the higher, I don't really need to meditate. But if I don't know it, how can I meditate on something I don't know?

Swamiji – All scriptures say God cannot be described, so all scriptures attempt to explain the inexplicable. Even though all use the same words to describe this higher Reality, they are not exact descriptions; they are indicators. You hold your mind in the indicated direction – that is meditation. The mind ends.

Question – When should I start meditating twice a day?

Swamiji – If my child were to ask me, "When should I eat my supper?" My answer would be "Not now, my son." The very question clearly indicates that my child is not hungry. If my son runs to the dining room and demands supper, threatening to stuff himself with cookies if the food is not served, then I will say, "Son, it is now time to eat." When I hear from you that you have already started an inspiring session of meditation in the evening, I shall send you permission to meditate twice a day.

Question – But is meditation for beginners?

Swamiji – No, meditation is not meant for beginners. They will be sitting to sleep, that is all. Of course, the resulting rest may be of some physical benefit, especially to you restless Americans, but not spiritual.

Beginners must strive to make their mind and intellect quiet, calm, serene, single pointed and sincere. This can be achieved in your daily activities, by performing them with care and attention.

Be a mirror! Reflect everything; keep nothing. No matter what passes in front of the mirror, no image remains. KEEP NOTHING!

33

Vegetarian Diet

Question – This may be a trivial question, but. . . Is vegetarian food essential for the spiritual path?

Swamiji – First of all, no question is trivial. If it is a question that is bothering you, it is an important question to you. It is, therefore, important for the teacher, since his job is to help you discover and solve your own misunderstandings. If he brushes aside any sincere question as trivial, he is not doing his work as a teacher.

This is not a license for the student to sit down and manufacture questions. You should first think about your doubt and crystallize it in your own mind. In this way, many times you find the answer within yourself. If it does not surface, you should not feel shy about asking the question.

Now, to return to your question about diet. It is not essential that you eat only vegetarian food for your spiritual evolution; however, the experience of many seekers of Truth indicates that vegetarian food helps in keeping the mind balanced for contemplation.

Question – So it can be an aid in attaining peace of mind?

Swamiji – Yes. Food has certain effects. Not only is our physical body built and maintained according to the food we eat, but our inner nature is also conditioned by it. The gross part of the food produces the energy for the physical apparatus, while the subtle part contributes to our thought energy.

When you have a nightmare, the first question the doctor will ask is, "What did you eat last night?" Rich, spicy, hard to digest foods produce mental roaming and confusion, which manifest in wild dream thoughts. Also, it is a long established practice in all the religions to fast for a period to enhance meditation power. No food, no thought. It is a technique to get a sample of the meditative state.

If on a particular day you are having a difficult time controlling the mind, eat fruit on that day. Test for yourself what the result is.

Question – It does say in the *Gītā* that to have a sāttvika (pure) mind, one should eat sāttvika food that increase strength, health and life force. So it would seem that we should make the effort.

Swamiji – Yes, the diet can be used as a means of self-control and discipline. As you progress in spiritual contemplation, you will become more sensitive to life – all life in all forms. One day as you are looking at a piece of chicken floating in a bowl of soup, you may suddenly think, 'Hey, this is the same chicken that I was feeding in the backyard yesterday. How innocently it looked up to me as its provider and friend, never realizing the ulterior motive behind my generosity.' You may begin to feel that the chicken is accusing you as a traitor – you who have seized it and buried it in your stomach.

Once this type of sensitivity arises in your own mind, you need no explanation of how or why for maintaining a vegetarian diet; you simply stop eating non-vegetarian food. So it is not a question of right or wrong; it is a question of your own sensitivity.

Question – (a Hindu gentleman) – Actually, even Rāma ate meat.

Swamiji – Yes, so this is your chance to be better than Rama! Several of our ancient ṛṣis did eat meat. They were living in the cold climates of the north, so that was the food available to them in the winter. That animal energy was necessary to combat the cold climate. Now there are trucks carrying food to the mountains and better heating is available, so meat is not necessary.

I must warn you against any fanaticism in regard to food. Religion is not a matter of the kitchen. More important than external purification is inner purification. Śrī Ramakrishna put it very succinctly, "If a man loves God, though living upon the flesh of a pig, he is blessed; but wretched is the man who lives on milk and rice, but whose mind is absorbed in lust and gold."

34

Temples

Question – Why do we have temples, or churches?

Swamiji – Where is the Government of India, please? Is it not everywhere, supporting everyone of you? It is a democracy, of the people, by the people, for the people. But to contact the Government of India, one has to go to the offices in Delhi, even though the Government of India reaches all corners of the country. In the same way, God is everywhere – all pervading – but if you want to contact Him, run to the nearest temple.

Question – So if you are not able to find God everywhere, that is the place to look?

Swamiji – Temples are places where you practise what you have studied in the scriptural textbooks. They are gymnasiums for the mind. If you tell me, "Swamiji, everyday I go to the gymnasium and come back, but my health is still not improving," I will respond, "Go for another six months."

Then if your health still has not improved, I will inquire, "What do you do there in the gym?" And I will know exactly what the problem is when you reply, "Swamiji, I go into the gymnasium and sit down there and watch everybody." Similarly, you may go to the temple, or church, and watch everyone to see what they are wearing and what they are doing. Then there is no chance for your mental ailment to improve or cure itself. You have to go there and apply your mind to the idol. Remember, it is a mental gymnasium, not a physical one. Surrender the mind in devotion unto the Lord. He will purify it and return it back to you.

Question – Give it back in better shape?

Swamiji – Yes, definitely. Lord Kṛṣṇa says, "Surrender your mind, I will clean it and give it back to you." But we are always occupied with asking God for some solution to our problems. "Hey, Kṛṣṇa! My father is not well, make him all right!" "Oh, Rāma! Please give me the promotion this time." Our mind is soaked with our own petty problems even when we are in the presence of God in the temple.

A temple is a place where his presence can be contacted directly. Think! A receiving set is necessary to hear the broadcast from Delhi. The sound waves are available in the ether everywhere. But if you want to enjoy the music, you must have a radio and tune in properly to that particular station. The temple is a place conducive for fine tuning of your mental equipment in order to receive the divine message.

35

Guru

Question – What is the role of the spiritual Teacher?

Swamiji – Your individual innate desires are your own personal debt. The total of everyone's innate desires is the national debt. Spiritual Teachers function only at this total level. They come in response to the crying of the people for an escape from suffering and for an understanding of the meaning of life. The Teacher comes to guide them.

When I point out the direction to the bazaar, you must get up and go. If you sit here and hang on to my pointing finger, you will never experience the joys of the bazaar. When the Teacher directs you, you cannot sit there hanging onto his words.

Everyone has to go in that direction for himself; no Guru can do it for him. When you put sugar in your coffee, you must stir it in or the coffee will still be bitter. I am putting the spiritual ideas into your mind, but to get the sweetness, you must stir them with the process of your own independent reflection, away from the support of a Teacher.

Question – Is it necessary for a Guru to give us a mantra?

Swamiji – If you understand Vedānta, it is not necessary. It would be like a person reading Shakespeare who suddenly asks his teacher to teach him the alphabet.

Question – But Gurus can give some experience of that Reality beyond comprehension. There are many such reports.

Swamiji – Experiences through a Teacher are dependent on the Teacher – a tourist visa. But the customs officials are always there at the gate. You are trying to sneak through with your load of vāsanās (innate tendencies). They will catch you and kick you back out. You have to make it on your own. You must become a citizen of that consciousness.

So it could be that the Teacher provides the environment so you are able to have some experience to make you wake up. In this way, you will have the courage to start the spiritual practices for yourself.

Question – But how do you choose a spiritual Teacher? We don't really know enough to judge who is a true Teacher.

Swamiji – Yes, that is correct. Students can only measure the divinity of the teacher by their own divinity. It is the same with music or dance. You have to know your subject before you can distinguish who is a Master. For this reason Ādi Śaṅkarācārya has described the qualifications of a Guru in *Vivekacūḍāmaṇi.*

Today, many who teach do not know the ultimate experience themselves. Many know more of Śaṅkara's commentaries than Śaṅkara himself. He may have forgotten something he wrote, but not these people; they are like tape recorders. Will a tape benefit from the words recorded on it? They never start spiritual practice themselves; they just talk about it. But don't worry, you can still benefit if you listen to their words and apply them to your life and sādhanā. The words of the scriptures themselves are the Guru.

Question – What about these new techniques that some Teachers have come up with?

Swamiji – Avoid them! Sanātana-dharma has no new techniques. The ancient sages discovered the laws of nature with their immaculate logic and sacred inspiration. These laws have never changed and never will. If, in your university physics class, a professor expounds his new theory of relativity, you will listen as if it is a joke, to humour him. But when you take the state exams, you will use Einstein's reasoning, not the crackpot professor's personal theory. If any Guru tells you of his great new technique – "Take off your clothes and dance" – you run!

One year this self-proclaimed teacher has one technique and the next another one. We don't need new techniques. We need to apply the knowledge that has been verified by generation after generation of sages. The problem is in ourselves; we want things to be easy and fun. That is why we run after these new methods. So spirituality is turned into a pursuit of sensual pleasures. You never improve, and the Guru gets a couple of new cars. What has been accomplished?

Question – In your early discourses, you said that your Teacher, Swami Tapovanam, was speaking through you. Was that true?

Swamiji – It was a means to keep me detached. The ego is ever ready to jump up and spoil any endeavour, particularly a spiritual one. Therefore, by constantly giving credit to my Guru, there was nothing with which to build up my ego. From another point of view, it is true – it is his wisdom speaking through me – his commentaries, his stories. My wisdom is not separate from his. Anyway, all true wisdom is one... not mine nor his.

Question – Did you have a choice about your mission of teaching Vedānta?

Swamiji – No, no choice. Not on one level. It was not really my plan or my decision. But that is not to say that we do not have free will. I could have said 'No' to the urge.

36

Ego

Question – What about the ego? Where does it fit in Vedānta?

Swamiji – Ego is not a noun, but a verb. It is nothing but a bundle of past actions and reactions. Who are you? You are this record of actions and reactions from your birth until now. So you carry this stinking bundle on your shoulders and accuse the world of stinking. The Lord is only asking you to give this bundle to Him, nothing else. Throw the bundle down and look at the world without this muddy poison. Drop this ego. Where it is dropped, divine experience arises.

The ego survives in us only so long as we entertain thoughts. Any amount of removing the negativity will not completely cleanse the mind. All dictations from within are from the mind and will be conditioned by the residual desire prompted thoughts. Even our desire to lead a spiritual life can bloat the ego if we begin patting ourselves on the back at how good and positive we have become.

When all thoughts are dropped, the ego is dropped. Only then the dancer's steps will be in unison with the background music. The rhythm of our actions will be pure and divine if deep within us is the constant detachment from the idea that 'I' am performing this action, and 'I' am to reap the rewards of this action.

Question – What about the techniques we have in the United States, such as the est (Erhard Seminars Traning) training? There is a definite experience of 'I created the whole thing – I am totally responsible.'

Swamiji – Yes, it is an enlightenment. However, there is no preparation of the mind; therefore, it is not the real thing. It is something gained, an experience of power. This is an illumination of the ego. Enlightenment is never gained; it comes.

Question – I have noticed that many of the graduates of the 'est' training do not have the love that the scriptures talk about.

Swamiji – Yes, look how disturbing they are to others – just like the rākṣasas (extroverts) in our Purāṇas. However, est has enabled many to have the courage to face life and make a success of it. Vedānta is not contrary to having a successful life. Worldly success can be a necessary step. These methods of the West are very useful as a means on the path, but one must not confuse the means with the goal. One must beware of all these new techniques. That is the value of Sanātana-dharma as taught by our ṛṣis. It has been tested and re-tested throughout the ages.

(This afternoon Swamiji was sitting in his cottage in the Sandeepany Āśrama. He leaned back and looked out of the window at the bright orange blossoms of a gulmohar tree.)

Swamiji – We have such lovely flowering trees in our āśrama garden. It is indeed nice to look out and see the lovely flowers.

Question – The sight of flowers gives us sublime happiness!

Swamiji – Yes. If we cannot find the sublime happiness within ourselves, then flowers are a means to invoke it. Yes, Vedānta explains that these bits of bliss are only a small reflection of the one great Bliss, our real nature.

Question – If that's so, why do I fog it up?

Swamiji – Because that is what that 'I' is for. Go beyond the ego.

Question – Is it possible for a Self-realized person to become re-attached to the ego?

Swamiji – Yes, there are several examples of it in our Purāṇas, but the attachment is temporary. When one wants, one can get out of it easily. However, an ordinary individual working in the world finds it difficult to drop the attachment when some circumstance hooks his mind to the lower ego. He must always be cautious of that 'devil'.

Question – You Hindus are always harping on the ego! What's wrong with it?

Swamiji – What's wrong with it? You tell me what's wrong with it! It is an obstacle. It limits you.

Put a wooden beam one and a half feet wide and thirty feet long on the ground. You will walk across it; even bike across it. But raise it to the fifth floor between two buildings and you will not take a single step on it, even if we were to offer you one hundred dollars. You would look down and you would become afraid.

What is it that fears? What is it that inhibits? THINK!

Why is it that in the parlour of your own home you can talk on a subject with your own friends for hours – rattling on until you even bore them. But put you on a platform in front of five thousand people to speak on the very same subject, what happens? You freeze up. You only have to put your thoughts through your mouth; you are only to repeat the same words you spoke in your own home. Such intelligence you were displaying for your friends! But where is all of your intelligence now? You have the knowledge, but when the moment comes to use it, it is not available.

Take another example. A doctor is to operate on his own son. He has performed this same surgery hundreds of times. But the thought – this is my son – comes into his mind along with anxiety for all the possibilities of all the things that might go wrong. Because of his emotional reaction, he is unable to perform the surgery and has to turn the knife over to an associate. He has the knowledge, but at that moment what happened? If it were you or I on the table, he would have taken the knife to us without a second thought. He would not even have imagined any future complications. Later, he could even claim – "The operation was a success, but the patient died!"

To live and act in the world without ego and ego-centred desires is the secret of success. The *Gītā* is a practical manual, an instruction book, to enable us to make the inner adjustments necessary to conquer this universal ego disease. In the Eastern cultures, it has been through an inner adjustment that happiness has been found.

In the Western cultures, happiness has been sought by making outer adjustments, continuously rearranging the world with the idea that some particular combination will bring happiness – new wife, new car, new children, new job. It's endless! The inner adjustment must be made so that the intellect is available to do any work, or to face any crisis.

Question – But I do feel like I should do something to improve the world.

Swamiji – You improve yourself! That is the real challenge! Wanting to help others – that is ego too. You think you are going to bring the experience of the Ultimate down to the physical reality? It is already here! That is like wanting to go to the moon to bring space back to earth.

37

The Nature of the Mind

Question – Swamiji, just how do we purify our mind from all these negative tendencies – anger, for instance?

Swamiji – It is as if the mind is made up of soft matter. So, as each thought passes through it, an impression is left on the mind stuff, just like a scratch. Then when similar thoughts are repeated, the scratch deepens into a canal. Every subsequent thought wave has a tendency to flow through that ready-made canal. So if the canal is made up of good thought waves, then a good character is maintained and strengthened by the subsequent thought waves flowing irresistibly in that direction.

Let us take a concrete example to examine the working of the mind. If you have a tendency to get angry and want to eliminate that tendency you should first feel sorrowful or repentant about it. Then you will have already conquered the anger to some extent. If you merely suppress it, the potential pent up anger will come forth at a later date.

But, if you are intelligent, you will divert that anger energy into some profitable activity. You should not succumb to the anger weakness by meekly saying, "It is on account of my karma."

Carve out a new canal in your mind with continuous good thought waves. Repeat to yourself – 'I love all. I am very, very tolerant.' Go on repeating the self-suggestive thoughts – 'I am kind. I never get angry. I am always tolerant.' Afterwards, in a very short time, you will observe that you have no anger at all in your mental make-up.

So first, you must recognize your mental tendencies (vāsanās). Be fully aware of your weaknesses. Man is mind. Personality is the very composition of the mind. Because of these vāsanās of the mind, we live in a state of constant reactions to the outer objects. The quality of one's experiences depends upon the mind that is brought to the circumstances. The mind is what it is, only as ordered and set by the various impressions it has gathered in its various transactions in life. Thus, when we have purified and chastened the motives and thoughts in the mind, we have purified our mind.

Question – What is the role of truthfulness that spiritual Teachers often emphasize?

Swamiji – The path to Truth is laid with truth. When you lie, there is psychological split caused between the mind and the intellect. For example, because you are feeling lazy, you call the office to say that you are sick. The intellect knows one thing, yet is hearing another. This causes a self-cancellation, so that when the intellect states something, the mind says the opposite. Eventually when you desire something, the opposite happens. Mind and intellect are to be your servants, but they must work together to produce the desired results.

Question – When I set a goal, life seems to set up obstacles to make it difficult.

Swamiji – Yes, life can test you to see if you really mean it. You have decided to study hard and achieve the high grades you need on your exam so that you will be admitted to Madras University. As soon as you have determined your goal, a cousin's wedding comes, friends drop by, free movie tickets are offered – they all come to take you off course. You have to say, 'No, this week I'm studying, next week I'll be available.' You must connect with that goal and always keep it in your mind.

Question – It seems like many times when I want something very much that it doesn't happen. Then when I say to myself, 'Never mind, I really don't need it,' what I wanted comes along.

Swamiji – Your mental energy must have been tied up; you were too tense. When you decided that it did not matter, the mind relaxed so it could do its job.

The mind is your servant. But we don't treat it like one, so it becomes the master. When I was in college in Lucknow, three of us were living together in an apartment. We decided that if we pooled our money we could easily afford to have one servant between us. We found a suitable person and hired him.

On the first morning, one of my room mates arose and asked the servant to draw him some warm water for a bath. Then, as the servant was heading for the bathroom, I, having just discovered that I was out of cigarettes, came out of my room, handed him a rupee note, and told him to run down to the corner for some cigarettes. There he was – stuck halfway between the front door and the bathroom – not knowing which way to turn, when the third fellow emerged from his room. "Quick, get me some breakfast. I'm late for my class!" he ordered the servant. Now what could the poor fellow have done under the circumstances? He could only quit – he walked out on us!

In the same way we are constantly giving too many, and often conflicting, orders to the mind. That is why you must pick your goal, give the mind its orders, then go quietly about your duties until it has time to get the assignment accomplished. So relax, this is what you did not do.

Question – It seems like whatever one is doing, but particularly when attempting to practise a spiritual life, the attitude of the mind is crucial.

Swamiji – Yes, keeping the mind in balance enables its best performance in the outside world, while at the same time it lessens accumulation of agitation that make spiritual practices difficult. Spiritual devotion is the easiest method for maintaining a balanced mind throughout the day. Do your work in a prayerful surrender to the Lord. This is the best method for a peaceful mind, whether you are a Christian, Muslim or Hindu. Tune your mind to Him, then the knowledge that you have, will flood through you. Everything you do will have a special beauty.

In this complex world, mind becomes confused, then becomes overwhelmed and agitated. It needs an anchor to hold on to. Surrender to a higher ideal, silently. No need to tell anyone what you are doing.

Question – My mind never stops running. What can I do?

Swamiji – Mind does not stop because it is the mind. Mind is a thought flow. If it were to stop – no mind.

If it runs out all over the place, tell it, 'never mind'. If it still keeps running, let it run while you watch what joy it really receives. When it gets bruised and sad, tell it with the intellect – 'Didn't I tell you there was no real joy in it! But I let you see for yourself.'

As it gains more and more joy from the spiritual life – the reflection on the wisdom of the Upaniṣads and meditation – the mind will seek pleasure less and less in the outer world. The gap between the intellectual knowledge of what you should do and the actions of your body depends on your own innate vāsanās. Until you have understood the true values of life, do not trust the mind. You have been leading a sensuous life and your mind has had the upper hand for many years; it will justify any behaviour for you. This devil mind can speak as the voice of God. The true inner voice must be cultivated carefully.

Mind is not to be changed; it is to be transcended.

38

Miracles and mind-reading

Question – Swamiji, are you able to read our minds?

Swamiji – God forbid! Who would want to waste their time raking through the garbage in your minds?

Question – But there are times when we have a question in our minds and you do answer it, either in the satsaṅga or the lectures, even before we have enough nerve to ask it.

Swamiji – Yes, that may happen. That's the way the universe works. When a lesson is to be learned, the appropriate situation arrives. A question is there, and then the answer comes.

It's not from an effort or some trick on my part; I'm an instrument. Sometimes the solution could come from a stranger on the bus. But because I'm a Swami, everyone thinks I'm using some special power. Because of a strong desire of some student, the answer spontaneously manifested through me. It just looked like reading of the mind.

Question – What about the times when you say something and it happens that way? It does appear as if you do know the future.

Swamiji – I mentioned something and because it happened to correspond to your desires you all got together and accomplished it. Think of how many times I have suggested projects that no one has carried through.

Question – But miracles can happen. What about those yogīs who can levitate, be buried alive, all sorts of far out things?

Swamiji – There was an incident between Śrī Ramakrishna and one of his disciples. It seems the disciple came to him one day proclaiming: "Master, Master, I have learned to walk on water. It took me three years of constant concentration and work, but I have mastered it." Of course, he was expecting some great complimentary words from the Master.

"Fool", replied Ramakrishna. "You can get across the river by paying only a nickel to the boatman. If you had spent that same time and concentration on investigating who you truly are, you would now know your divine birthright."

For one who knows there is no creation – why would he bother to manipulate the creation?

39

Creation

Question – Swamiji, why did God create this world?

Swamiji – What world?! What makes you think I see the same world that you do?

Question – Well, I don't know about that. But there is a creation here. Why?

Swamiji – This is an incorrect question, yet you are not the first to ask it. Even in the Upaniṣads, it has been asked again and again. "Why" is never answered in scientific inquiry. Science inquires into the how and what of things and phenomena. Why gravitation force? Why electricity? Why this earth? Why the sun? These questions are never answered by science. To question 'why' is to question the motive, and motive hunting is not the job of science.

My advice to you is to write this question on a piece of paper, go straight to God, and ask him why He created this world! I guarantee you that when you are there you will not remember this doubt! Any question about God and his motives assumes the existence of a questioner different from God. When the seeker reaches that state of God-consciousness, this world is no longer seen as different and separate, as something to be understood – the question and the questioner disappear along with the entire world of creation.

Question – That is very difficult to comprehend.

Swamiji – Think! It is a change of Consciousness. It is like in a dream when you don't know you are dreaming. You form your dream experiences from your mental impressions gathered in the waking world. As a dreamer, this dreamworld of various joys and pains is very real. Suppose the dreamer wants to know why all this variety exists in this dreamworld – why these misgivings, these sufferings, these confusions? The only answer to give him is – "Wake up and discover that the entire dream creation is in your mind alone. Realise that you are the waker!" Once awake, the waker realizes the total unreality of the dreamworld.

In the same way, this waking world of plurality is like a dream of all-consciousness. Once you realize that you are nothing but the supreme Consciousness, which is one without a second, this creation with its questions and answers dissolves itself.

Since this question 'why' is a most speculative region of thought, no final answer can be given. One hypothesis is that the creation is a consequence of God's nature as love to provide a new quality of Consciousness. The creative activity of God includes embryonic beings, you and I, having a simple Consciousness, even though we are still infinite and eternal. The maturing of these beings, so that they come to know their inherent divinity – it is already there, but they do not know they possess it – could be the basis of the whole cycle of creation.

How can they know their infinitude if they do not know the finitude? How can they know the meaning of immortality if they do not know mortality? How can they know omnipresence if they do not know limitation? This very special knowledge of their true nature has to be won by a process of descent into the prison of space and time. Then there is a gradual ascent, in which Knowledge and ultimately omniscience, is won.

Question – But how did this creation happen?

Swamiji – When someone asks me how it happened, it clearly shows me that they are not yet fed up with life and are not ready to come out of it. There you are helplessly flogging around in a cesspool and you are wondering, "Who pushed me in?"

"How did this cesspool get here anyway?" You question me. You get out of it first! Then you won't have to worry about how you got in.

Question – But the Hindu scriptures do explain creation, don't they?

Swamiji – Yes, there is the explanation of the process – there occurred a grossification of elemental material from space, to air, to fire, to water, then earth. The gross only comes from the subtle as a tree comes from a seed. But the question remains – from what raw material did these five emerge?

In our scriptures, there is not just one creation story. Each sage told his bluff story in order to clear the confusion of a particular student. He pointed only to the apparent creation – the creation in the student's mind. These explanations were to clear a particular question and for that purpose alone. That is why there are so many different theories. Ādi Śaṅkarācārya claimed that he counted eighty-two different versions in the scriptures. No theory is correct. They were a kind of lullaby to set a mood, to soothe the student's mind. No mind – no creation.

Question – So you could say that they did not understand creation themselves?

Swamiji – It's not a matter of understood or not understood. For the Realized sage there is no creation. Ask a sage who is unbound how bondage came and you will never get an answer. He will reply, "What bondage? Who is in bondage?" On the other hand, ask a person who is still bound by the world and how can he answer – he isn't out of it himself. So there you are – no answers available!

Question – You say creation is ordered by the innate desires, or vāsanās, of those in the creation. I can see how one desire leads to another, but when did the first vāsanā appear?

Swamiji – When? That is an aspect of time. Vāsanās are the footsteps of experience – in time. For example, you are walking on a beach by the sea. You place your foot on the wet sand, then you put your other foot on the sand. At this moment, there are no footprints. Only awareness is present, or a sense of 'I'. Then I raise my foot up and place it down again. This action leaves the first footprint – the first impression, vāsanā has manifested. At this very moment, there is something other than 'I'.

Carefully now. Time has not begun. Time is the interval between two thoughts. Now there is only one footprint impression, so an interval has not yet occurred. So when I lift my other foot and leave the second footprint, time begins. That is why the first unit of time is called a 'second', not first.

Or you could put it this way. The creative power had an urge to create. The first thought was 'I', just as when we awake out of sleep, our first thought is 'I'. Only then do the rest of our thoughts, emotions and objects of our world begin to roll out into existence. In the same way after this first thought of 'I', the Lord manifested all aspects of Himself. Then He identified with these many aspects. That is the reason we each have the essential divinity within us.

Question – So our particular creation is unique to us and created by us?

Swamiji – Your creation is a play of your mind. Roll it up, carry it under your arm and move in the world as a master.

Question – But the world is so real, I can't understand why you call it a dream.

Swamiji – It is not a dream, but when you wake up into the higher level of Consciousness, it is like a dream. Whether the world is real or not depends on your standpoint. Try to tell the dreamer in a dream that he is only dreaming. He will never understand. He has to wake up from that dream Consciousness.

Question – What about dreams? Are they really helpful in getting insight into one's mental creation?

Swamiji – Dreams are regurgitations of the mind. Why would you want to pick through that rubbish? Mahātmās never dream because they have no undigested experience! Dreams come from incomplete actions and thoughts during the day. They are suppressions and repressions that have gone into the mind undigested. There is no need to dream if you consciously and completely face each situation during the day. Neither should you sit imagining during the day, giving power to the mind. If you do something bad, don't go around feeling guilty because of some concept of middle class morality. Get to the source of your mental bruise and let it go. Until you have the ability to accomplish this continuous mental cleaning during the day, you can complete two rounds of the japa beads with your mantra before you go to sleep at night. This practice will bring up all the undigested thoughts of that day.

In this way, you will go directly from the waking state into deep sleep without passing through the corridor of the haunted house. The brain only rests during deep sleep, so if it spends the night roaming about from one dream to another, it never really recoups its energy to work at its full intellectual capacity. A mind working constantly day and night becomes dull, or mad.

Neither should you bring your dreams to the waking world, there's already enough confusion in your waking life. Forget them. You must keep your mind available for the work you are doing. Have you noticed dreams are always remembered by idle people? "I dreamed I had an accident; I keep remembering it," you tell me. You have more faith in the dreamworld than this waking reality. So have an accident in your dream, but don't bring it into this level of Consciousness!

Question – But life is such a circus! I can't accept that it is my creation – it really has no sense to it.

Swamiji – You only have one life. Why don't you live it like a king? You call it a circus, but it's all for your enjoyment. Why don't you enter the show with a front row ticket whenever you want? You can sit there in your cushy box seat with popcorn, cotton candy, Coca-Cola and watch the show – your creation. Then get up and walk out whenever you want! But if you are the buffoon, always going around like a clown, everywhere you go will be a circus.

Enjoy life! But step out of it to the peaceful environment of your inner Self whenever you like! You are the master!

40

Evil

Question – Where did evil come from?

Swamiji – In the beginning there was no evil. God did not create evil – it was man's contribution. Evil is equal to selfish, self-centred actions. The moment you feel that you are only a separate individual functioning in the world for your own happiness, any activity you perform will be poisoned by selfishness.

All the great religions of the world – all of them – declare that there is a greater intelligence that created the world. But none of them have any answer when you ask – "If God is perfect and beautiful and he created the world, where did evil come from?" No religion in the world has a convincing answer. They would say it is the devil's work, as though there are two forces in the Infinite – one is a good and the other is bad. In such crucial points Ādi Śaṅkarācārya's contribution in logical analysis has been most satisfactory. Even today the most scientific of men find it convincing.

His theory is that creation is only a projection of the mind. The Infinite ever remains one – the eternal Existence 'is' as it always has been, is and will be. Although the changing phenomenal universe is only a projection of the mind, it appears to the mind that this world of plurality is real. The convincing arguments by which Ādi Śaṅkara induces the seeker to reject the names, shapes and forms in the search for the subjective essence and reality are spectacular. Anyone with an ounce of intelligence who follows Ādi Śaṅkara's logical method cannot help but be convinced.

Ādi Śaṅkarācārya was extremely practical; he gives a relative reality to this world. Using the ocean as a model, he points out that its waters include the constantly changing waves that rise and fall against each other and crash on to the shore. Yet beneath the moving waves abides the pure water from which the waves rise, which supports the waves, and into which the waves disappear. The changing surface and the changeless depths are all intrinsically one essence.

In wisdom alone can this oneness be recognized. It can not be comprehended by our sense organs. We can only observe the waves on the surface of the ocean. However, when we contemplate the fundamental substratum of the ocean, we come to realize that it is only water itself that lends existence to the multiplicity of waves, their thunderous roaring, and the froth and foam produced by their clashing. They are all only expressions of the very dynamism of the silent columns of waters that constitute the depth of the ocean.

Question – You have said in class that sin is nothing but agitation in the mind. If I kill somebody and it does not leave any turbulence in my mind, does it means that I have not sinned?

Swamiji – If I kill a person I am branded a murderer; I am arrested and punished. But if a doctor kills a person during surgery, he is not arrested. Why? In the case of the doctor, the killing was attended by the motive to save a life. The action born of the desire to serve another does not leave any agitation in the doctor's mind.

If you kill someone, it will be out of some self-centred motive; the fellow was wanting your girl, or disturbing your peace, or destroying your property. The motive makes the difference.

In fact, sin is the measure of the angle of deviation between the desires of the mind and the intellect's best judgement. The intellect chooses what is right and points out what is wrong. But if the mind is not synchronized in agreement with the intellect and follows its own inclinations towards the purely pleasurable, then the actions that follow will be the complete opposite of the intellect's advice.

Question – Knowing what is good, why does man go on and do the opposite?

Swamiji – There are two separate distinct paths in life – śreyas (good) and preyas (pleasant). Man is confronted with the choice of pursuing one of these paths at every single moment of his life. The path of the pleasant, as the name suggests, pleases, fascinates and entices us. It caters to our sensual nature, and therefore, produces immediate pleasures. Ultimately, these trifling satisfactions will putrefy into ripples of disappointments and sorrows.

In striking contrast, śreyas is detested by the mind in the beginning. Even so, since it is based on sound religious precepts and injunctions, it leads to greater happiness and a genuine sense of fulfilment. We are mature people who have tasted life, and know the path that leads to a fuller happiness. We must live these convictions.

Question – So if sin is the deviation between the desire of the mind and the conviction of the intellect, then desire must be the culprit. How do we get rid of it?

Swamiji – Desire... The wavering of the mind, expressing as an uncontrollable impatience to gain something is called 'desire'. This desire is the very devil in us that compels us to compromise with our own values and tempts us to perpetrate sins. The greater the desire, the stronger the power of the pull toward the sinful and the low. Whenever the mind's instinctive cravings are not synchronized with the intellect's discriminating ability, there will be turmoil and sorrow. So desire enshrouds our wisdom.

Question – So you could say that the path of the good is the realm of the intellect, and the path of the pleasant is of the mind?

Swamiji – Yes, you would be correct. So how can a true integration between the mind and intellect be brought about? Only by surrendering this ego, with its sense of ME and MY wants, to a higher goal or ideal maintained by the intellect. This merger and harmonious integration is called yoga. Only when the mind and intellect join together in accord does peace prevail, only then does man become fit for the contemplative flight, which transcends both these mental instruments.

Question – What about those times, when in spite of one's intellectual convictions, one just cannot control oneself. We are just bound and determined to do something that we know will cause sorrow, but seemingly cannot help ourselves?

Swamiji – You take the attitude that it is just an experience to teach the mind its lesson; you stand back observing as an uninvolved witness. Afterwards, when the mind starts its whimpering over its pains and disappointments, you just tell it that you gave it what it wanted – now it can just suffer. You have no sympathy for it whatsoever! You are the observer of the drama.

Question – You say that God is within us, so every action whether it is bad or good is done by God. Why then are we punished?

Swamiji – We are punished because we are not performing the action with the full realization that the Lord is acting through us. God can only do divine actions. Divine actions can have no bad reactions, which you call punishments.

Bad actions are done when the actor is motivated by likes and dislikes, selfishness, lust and greed, which are attitudes that develop as a result of ignorance of the fact that the Lord resides within each of us. When you act as a separate egoistic entity, you are punished. When you surrender to the Lord in you, and thus allow the Lord to act, there is no punishment. Kill this little 'I' and live, see, think and act as the great 'I'. All actions preformed by such a perfected agent of action can only be divine actions.

Also, your question contains a contradiction. You say that every action – good or bad – is performed by the God in you, and in the very same breath you wonder why you are punished? If God is the doer, why not accept that God is the one who is punished? Shouldn't the one who performs the bad actions be the one who is punished? In self-surrender, when the ego is completely eliminated, there is neither an independent actor nor sufferer in you. Then only is your proposition that God is the doer true. This conclusion can be verified by your experience, when in self-surrender, you have completely eliminated the ego.

41

Karma

Question – Is God responsible for all? How can there be such a character? I can't buy that this creation is all a cosmic joke. From where I'm sitting, it's not that funny!

Swamiji – When I am driving a car, there are two forces – a blind force of gasoline and the discernment of the driver controlling and steering the vehicle. Now when the driver drives at 80 miles per hour on these terrible Indian roads, he will of course go off the road and crash into a tree. Can we say that the crash is the responsibility of the gasoline by the grace of which the car was moving?

In the same way the Life Principle gives us life, but what we do with it is up to us. If we are wanton, useless fellows, the life energy curses us. If we evolve to know the Truth, the life energy blesses us. So force is the same, we are free to do what we want with the energy – it's up to us. It is self effort based on free will.

Question – If it is true that the Reality is only the pure infinite Self, why are we here?

Swamiji – Everywhere I go I hear this question, especially from you teenagers. And I myself must have asked this question of my Teacher a hundred times. It is a natural, logical doubt. If there is a kind, all merciful Lord and the total phenomenal world is projected from that Lord, then why are we suffering in it? The general answer is that the question is wrong; therefore, the answer is not available.

The other day a friend and I were going along the road talking of the latest politics and the upcoming elections – the topics of the day – when somehow the subject moved to philosophy. "I wonder why we are here in this world," my friend mused and I could not answer him.

As we were walking along we came to a movie theatre that was playing the latest film. When I saw it, I asked him – "Have you got enough money for a ticket?" Since he replied "Yes", and I also had enough money in my pocket, I said, "Oh, boy! Let us go to the movie." We purchased our tickets and entered the theatre.

The movie had already started, so we did not have to wait in line. When we stepped inside the theatre, we found ourselves in utter darkness. The usher approached us and looked at our tickets, then with only a pencil of light he carefully guided us down the steps to a particular corner where he pointed to our two seats. We sat down. My friend was very interested in the film; therefore, he started looking at the picture and getting lost in the drama. Remember, this is the same fellow who was just asking, "Why are we here?" When he was fully engaged in the plot, I tapped him on the shoulder and said, "Hey, friend, why are we here?"

Who compelled us to go to the movie theatre? Isn't it a fact that if we, in the movie theatre, remember the world outside, we cannot enjoy the movie? We must completely forget home, husband, wife and children. If there are lights in the theatre, neither will the film have any meaning. Think of it – it must be in ignorance, in total darkness, that we sit down and watch.

Now 873 people are there in the theatre on that day. Do you think that all of them are seeing the same picture? Some are there to enjoy the plot; others for the beauty of the scenery; others are interested in the gorgeous costumes the actors are wearing; still others want to observe the techniques of photography. Distinctions are made, some identify with the hero, some with the heroine; another is getting excited because the murderer is going to murder. Each observer, according to his personal interests, interprets and appreciates the picture.

Now the more I ask my friend, "What are we doing here?" the more he tells me, "Keep quiet!" He doesn't want any disturbance at all. Again I ask him – "Why? Why are we here?"

It can only be for two reasons. Number one, we go to the movies for entertainment. So for our enjoyment, we go to the pictures. Or I may go to the movie if I feel that I may study something that I don't know – to learn something. Enjoyment and education are the only two reasons that you go into the dark place called the movie theatre. You pay your hard earned money voluntarily!

Once you are watching the movie, you may realize that the picture is boring, or it is filthy. You accept that you were fooled by the colourful advertisements. My friend, you have the right to get up and walk out. Under the Constitution you have all the freedom to get out of the show – at any time. But none of us will go! Even if we leave, we will just get a cup of coffee and a tasty cake and come back for the next show. We don't want to miss anything!

Fun and learning, these are the two things for which you and I have come here. We have come voluntarily; nobody has pushed us. You thought it would be a wonderful experience, for 'I' am infinite, eternal, immutable. What is the use of this power? I will express myself and make myself into many.

So you look at the wide screen of life and go on imagining – lovely pictures. There is only a blank movie screen. Nothing is moving; only images, coming and going, produce the illusion of movement.

The more you think about it, the more you realize probably this is the reason there is so much fascination for movies. They duplicate what we are doing everyday. We generate image after image. "This is my enemy number one." "This is my beloved." And within six months, "That beloved is now my number one enemy, and that enemy has become my beloved." These projections and subsequent agitations occur because the Truth is not known.

Question – So that is why the word 'karma' just means action – the apparent action that keeps the show going?

Swamiji – If there is no desire, there is no action. If there is no action, there is no fruit, or result of an action. Neither is there an actor to receive the result. Only when you put yourself on the level of 'I did this' and 'I did that' do you pull yourself down into the web of cause and effect.

Stand above it. Observe consciously and alertly the play of nature. Don't worry, the world will play on without you!

So our actions will have but two motives – first, by doing something, I hope to gain a reward; or by not doing something, I plan to miss a punishment, that is, to avoid some suffering or pain. Don't forget even meditation is karma, an action; meditation also drops away.

Question – What about the practice of karma-yoga for spiritual evolution?

Swamiji – When I put a pinch of salt in a tank of water, it will have no salty taste. When I am acting only for the sake of myself and my wife, then the bond of karma is stronger; if I am acting for sake of the nation, then desire gets diluted. Eventually, even the desire for working for the nation will drop away. Just as when I maintain a desire for sleep in my mind, I automatically drop all other desires and go to sleep. The desire for sleep ends in sleep.

Karma-yoga is a practice to exhaust the innate vāsanās. There is less agitation if I am thinking of my nation instead of my family.

Question – How do we know there are these vāsanās?

Swamiji – How do I know everyone has different tendencies? I just ask each one in the room to write down his three greatest desires. They will all be different. The Swami wants an āśrama. The teenager wants a motorcycle – his desire is to make some noise and attract attention. (Laughter) Yes, it's natural desire for a teenager.

The Lord says, "Don't blame me! I'm only the contractor; you gave me the blueprint." If you complain about your life, He'll just pull out the blueprint and tell you, "Sir, I did it according to your plan."

So you have to change the blueprint. That is self-mastery.

Question – Swamiji, what about accidents?

Swamiji – There are no accidents. For each effect there is a cause. Sometimes we do not immediately recognize the cause, but if we examine the situation carefully we will see there was a unique series of incidents contributing to every accident.

One bright, sunny morning Mr. Rao and Mr. Bose suddenly met each other in their respective vehicles at the southwest corner of Connaught Circle precisely at 10:06 a.m. The attending officer called it an accident. But was it? Upon examining the evidence, we note that Mr. Rao had slowed down to admire a beautiful girl on Park Street or he would have been past that spot at 10:06 a.m. Whereas Mr. Bose was happily driving along, singing cheerfully, when he realized that he was late. He pressed the accelerator, thus arriving at the intersection exactly at that time. Actually, their meeting at that precise moment was the result of a hundred such incidents, Mr. Rao's wife did not serve breakfast on time, Mr. Bose drank a second cup of coffee and so on.

Question – What about when a hundred persons are killed at one time, like in a plane crash?

Swamiji – Why do you wonder at the death of one hundred when thousands are dying every minute? It is only because they are not in one place that you never notice it. But when one hundred die together, it will make the newspaper headlines and everyone notices.

Question – Does an Enlightened person have karma?

Swamiji – I, having committed a crime in the south, move to the Bombay area, install myself in an āśrama and live here contentedly hidden away as a Swami. However, the clever police in Kerala discover that this very same Swami Chinmayananda, now decked out in the orange cloth of a sannyāsī, is the one and very same scoundrel who robbed a bank in Trivandrum last year.

A police officer is sent to the āśrama early one morning to arrest me. Upon inquiring at the gate, he is directed to my cottage where he finds Sivaram, my personal assistant, at the entrance. When the officer shows Sivaram the warrant for my arrest, he is obviously shocked, but very politely he asks the officer to wait a moment while he calls me. He comes and knocks on the door of my bedroom and calls out, "Swamiji! Swamiji! An officer is here to see you." When no answer comes from my room, he quietly puts the extra key into the lock, opens the door and slips into my room.

After a seemingly long delay, Sivaram returns to the veranda and assures the officer, "I'm sorry. I'm afraid he is not here."

"You mean he is gone?"

"Yes, he is gone". replies Sivaram.

"Where will I find him?" The officer has added some urgency to his voice.

"Well, he is here".

"You just said that he was gone!"

"Well, what I mean to say is that he is here, but he is gone," answers Sivaram in his meekest tone.

"Let me see him this minute!" demands the officer.

So Sivaram quietly leads him through the door to the bed where lies the dead, cold body of the Swami. What can the officer do? He returns to the station, marks 'File Closed' on the bundle of records and tosses them in a box.

Laws are for living creatures, not dead ones.

Question – So the law of karma is in the dream too.

Swamiji – Yes, certainly. However, the life of the body goes on. The sages have described it as an arrow shot from a bow. Birth began the course of this life. Just as you cannot catch an arrow in mid-air, for, it will continue toward its target, the body will not suddenly disappear at God-realization. Certain experiences that the body experiences are referred to as prārabdha karma; they are inevitable because the arrow has been shot and it is heading for its target – death of the body in this case.

Question – So the Realized one is not affected. It's all the same to him?

Swamiji – That's right. You go to sleep tonight and dream that you are in prison with no decent food, no decent clothing and no decent heating. You wake up. You realize you were dreaming; you know that you are the 'waker'. Right?

Question – Yes.

Swamiji – Then you go back to sleep and go back into the same dream, but this time you remember that you are the waker and this is only a dream. What will your reaction be to the cold and hunger now? You may still groan and fuss about them, or maybe not. It's all the same.

Question – What about this good karma that we hear so much about?

Swamiji – Both good actions and bad actions are for your own happiness – I want to help the poor because it makes me so happy – that attitude. An ego is involved. The gold chain binds just the same as the iron chain.

Question – What about predestination?

Swamiji – Accepting predestination is fine as a mental attitude – if you accept everything as destiny. But we call failure destiny, and success we call 'I'. Destiny is what you meet in life; your free will is how you meet it, the attitude you have and the action you take.

42

Death

Question – Swamiji, what happens after death?

Swamiji – What? Here I am sitting in flesh and blood – at least I think I am, will someone pinch me please – and you ask me about death. My boy, Vedānta is a science of life! (He turns to the rest of the group.) This fellow already knows about life – he has discovered it is useless. Now he wants to know if there is something better after death! (After the laughter dies down, he continues.)

Okay. . . Where will each of you go after you leave this satsaṅga? We will disperse according to our own individual desires, some will go home, some to the coffee house, some to the liquor store. Likewise, when you drop the physical body, the remaining mind-intellect personality will be propelled by its most powerful desires to experience enjoyments not available to physical human beings. The time spent in that particular place, which you call heaven, depends on the puṇya or merit, you have earned on earth. When you go on a vacation you stay in a five-star hotel – for how long? You enjoy until the money in your pocket is depleted. Money gone; you return. Puṇya gone; you return according to your unexpended residue of vāsanās.

Question – It is strange. We know that we are going to die, yet somehow we never really believe it.

Swamiji – Some people come to me and tell me that they will not do a certain thing, like driving or flying, because they are afraid they will die. "How stupid! How can you be afraid you are going to die? Of course you are going to die," I tell them.

Do you think that by avoiding this or that you will be able to avoid death? We are going to die, all of us – it's inevitable. One of our great sages has labelled it the most curious idiosyncrasy of mankind. Even though we see death all around us, we never think that it will happen to us. Therefore, we never bother to prepare for it. (After a thoughtful pause, he adds with a chuckle) Everybody goes. Some go quickly and some not quickly enough!

Question – Swamiji, just how is it that the subtle body (the mind-intellect personality) separates from the physical body?

Swamiji – Okay, if you insist! But I assure you that I'm on firmer ground when I am talking about life!

Actually, to understand the process of death, first one needs to understand life's processes. You and I are living as long as Consciousness illuminates our subtle and gross bodies. We are dynamic and energetic as long as the Life Principle manifests in us.

After death the body does not function, but not because the supreme Consciousness has ceased to exist. To say that Consciousness does not exist at the time of the body's death is to violate the basic tenet that Consciousness is omnipresent.

At death the illumination of the Consciousness that lends its sentience to the Life Force in the gross body ceases. This withdrawal reduces the body to biodegradable matter, which in the course of time rejoins its source – the five elements of earth, water, air, fire and space.

Question – So the gross body has been eliminated by this withdrawal of Consciousness, but the subtle body remains. Where?

Swamiji – The subtle body is composed of the mind and the intellect. The mind and the intellect manifest as thought flow. A flow or movement automatically implies a direction.

Now think! The direction of our thought flow is dictated by the vāsanās left by our previous actions. Thus it is these tendencies that determine the time and place of our next birth when the mind and intellect will transfer to the new body.

Question – My son died at the age of fifteen. Why?

Swamiji – Now think carefully. Because of a desire to see a movie, I went to the movie theatre. I buy my ticket, enter the auditorium, and sit down. Suddenly I realize that I have already seen this film. Won't I get up and leave? Or suppose that I suddenly remember that Mr. Murthi, who owes me twenty-five rupees, is going to meet me this very evening to pay me. Again, I will get up and walk out.

Now, how do you know whether these fifteen years were all the experience needed in this environment? How often does a person change cars? When he considers that it is used – to a rich man that may be every year, to a poor man every ten years. So when the use of a particular vehicle was accomplished, the child left. He didn't cry at going. No one does. We who remain feel sorrow because of our loss or inconvenience.

Question – Is it true that if you repeat the Lord's name when you are dying that you will achieve Liberation?

Swamiji – Yes, it is said in our scriptures – Your last thought will determine your next birth, or escape from rebirth. But who, after living a greedy, self-centred life, will think of the Lord at the moment of death. No one, I assure you. It is for this reason that so many Hindus name their children by one of the Lord's names – as insurance. So when you are on your deathbed, you may not think of the Lord, but at least you will call your son to your side, "Oh, Nārāyaṇa!" But this will not work either, for, it is a state of mind, not some words, that the scriptures are referring to.

So the best insurance is to pass your life in contemplating the divine qualities of the Lord and seeing his beauty in and through all of creation. Then you will be sure to think of the Lord at the moment of your death.

43

Reincarnation

Question – Swamiji, is it necessary to believe in reincarnation?

Swamiji – First, reincarnation is not a belief, it is an assumption of Hinduism. Religion must be supported by a philosophy that logically explains what I see and experience around me and its relationship to the higher Reality. It is not necessary to accept the theory, but how else would you explain the differences, the injustices, that you see in the world. If the explanation for one man being born as a leper's leprous son and another as a king's kingly son, be the free will of God, then God becomes a power mad, lusty, partial Lord who blesses and curses according to his eccentric whims and fancies. This is against the observed rhythm and order that exists in all of nature.

Question – So reincarnation is a theory to explain why one man is born a king and another a beggar.

Swamiji – Yes. Man is a rational being who inevitably seeks a cause in every effect, and expects an effect from every cause. When man sees about him types, modes, kinds and classes without number and observes that the experience of life as lived by two individual organisms is never the same, he naturally seeks a reason for the diversity. A Buddha, a Rāma, a Rāvaṇa (a demon king) – all had their own individual experiences of life, even though they were all sons of their respective royal fathers. Thus to every given set of external circumstances, each entity reacts differently and each undergoes his unique experiences.

When the disparities in life do not arise from any visible cause they must be the effect of some invisible past cause or causes.

Thus we arrive at the theory of reincarnation. If actions performed in the past bear fruit in the present as experiences, then we can conclude that we must have had embodiments in the past also.

Question – Why don't we remember any of our past lives?

Swamiji – Luckily, through the infinite mercy of God, nature has put a veil on the details of the past. Now, I ask you a question, what did you have for lunch last Saturday at noon?

Question – It must have been some vegetables and rice because that is what I always eat, but I don't remember precisely.

Swamiji – So you didn't bother to remember? So when we eat, at that time we enjoy the food. Afterwards we forget because we have better things to do in life than to remember what we ate last week. You are the product of all that you have eaten, but, fortunately, the details are not available. In the same way, we don't remember all our previous births. Thank God that we cannot remember! One wife and the present children are enough of a problem! Can you imagine having the concern of 1,000 wives and 10,000 children?

Although you do not remember all the thoughts and experiences you had in the last birth, the subtle impressions they left are still with you. They have, in fact, provided a motivation or a driving force for another manifestation, another birth as a human. So you are a product of all your past experiences; it cannot be otherwise. It is not by accident that you are what you are, and I am what I am. We are all products of our own past. We Hindus believe in the reincarnation theory to explain these differences. But you do not have to extend the cause and effect pattern back to past lives. You can just look for the pattern in your present life. That's enough.

Question – I am not happy with my job because I have discovered that my boss is corrupt. He is requiring that I mislead some clients.

Swamiji – Walk out!

Question – But I have to think of my family. Jobs are difficult to find these days.

Swamiji – If you have to work in this environment for the sake of your family, surrender all to the Lord. You follow the boss's exact instructions only. Carry out the tasks assigned to you exactly as he instructed, then mentally drop it. Don't worry about it or talk about it.

If you were really an honest person, you would not have been the one asked to do something dishonest. Corrupt, dishonest people quake in the presence of honesty. If you had been totally honest, the boss would not have had the guts to ask you to do something dishonest. Goodness has a positive beauty about it. Remember, it was your own past impressions that brought you to this situation. Now you have an opportunity to improve your attitude. All is for Him alone, good or bad.

44

God

Question – Swamiji, is there really a God?

Swamiji – Those denying God are only denying their own misconceptions of what God is. Some investigation into that which you are denying is necessary, or the denial is useless. This is a scientific age – on what evidence do you base your denial?

It's easy to say you don't believe a 'rakatah' exists. I ask you what is a 'rakatah.' And you tell me you don't even know. It is just some sound.

The word 'God' is only a sound. What does this sound symbolize? That is what each one must investigate for oneself.

Question – What would you say God is?

Swamiji – God is Truth. God is that which remains constant in past, present and future; all else is false.

Question – But is God really running the show?

Swamiji – If God is sitting and writing our individual histories – all these sorrows and tragedies – he must be a mental pervert. Right?

This idea of God is a poetic point of view; it has no philosophical support. The Creator endows the mental and physical equipment and situations in the creation according to your own instructions, so that you can expend your own desires.

The three great Hindu Ācāryas (Teachers) accept the Upaniṣads as authority. They agree that the goal of life is God-realization, not experience in this finite world. All agree on the path and the goal; they only differ in the relationship between the individual and the Divine. Śrī Madhva, the Dualist, says that you are eternally separate from the Divine. He is correct – when you are identified with the body, you are eternally separate from God. Śrī Rāmānuja, the propounder of qualified dualism, claims that you are an aspect of God. You are a drop of the ocean, but the drop can never know the ocean. He too is accurate – when you are identified with your mental self, you are a part of the whole. Ādi Śaṅkarācārya, the preceptor of Advaita Vedānta, declares that you are identical with the one. According to him, you are the eternal, essential divinity transcending both the physical and mental instruments.

Your relationship with God depends on your point of view. When you are standing on a mountain peak looking down at the temple in the valley, you are separate from the temple. When you go down from that mountain and enter into the temple gates, you become a part of the temple complex. However, when you enter the sanctum sanctorum, you and the Lord of the temple are one.

All three standpoints define your relationship to God. The relationship may change, but God remains the same. We cannot say that only Śaṅkara's non-dualism is valid. Remember that Rāmānuja and Madhva also based their philosophy from the same fount of Hindu scriptures. Their interpretations seem contradictory because their philosophies were addressed to a certain society in a particular era.

This elasticity is the strength of a perpetual, healthy culture. A culture cannot be ironbound; it must have the freedom to express itself according to the environment and circumstances in that culture at that historical time. The community must be able to look to the cultural values for solutions to its problems. Those problems will change because the world continues changing. Each one of us is composed of a physical, mental and intellectual personality, yet our physical demands can be totally different from the needs of our forefathers. Our emotional concerns may be different from those of our fathers; our intellectual aspirations can change completely in each generation. When these internal requirements shift, a condition is created in which the old modes of living in society are no longer useful. Only an efficient, flexible culture can establish a new means of satisfying the current needs in order to generate contentment in the community.

The ability of our culture to accommodate, contain and provide solutions to new problems is the brilliance of the Hindu culture and the reason for its long, long history. This enduring quality is not because of the Masters who have come from time to time, but rather the true vitality of the culture has been its capacity to produce such geniuses. They were the means through which the culture was expressed and interpreted to the society.

We at Chinmaya Mission faithfully follow Ādi Śaṅkarācārya's logic that establishes man's relationship to the fundamental Reality, which lies behind the plurality, but we do not ignore the other points of view. Dualism and qualified dualism are necessary because, not only are we to appreciate the intellectual vision of 'one without a second', we have to reach out and go there. This has to be accomplished in our own bosom and we must slowly plod on from our present level.

On some days you may be in a mood of the dualistic type where you feel that God is something to be worshipped. At other times, you may feel that you are indeed a part of God, like the qualified dualists. The moments that we can soar into the heights of non-dualism to personally apprehend the oneness of God and ourselves are rare indeed.

Question – But duality does exist. Right now I am this and That is That.

Swamiji – Of course, duality exists. You are observing it everyday. Can you deny the nose on your face? When you are at the level of the body, there definitely is duality. Pleasure and pain are in duality. So are spiritual pursuits. When a Buddhist monk sits under a tree to reach Nirvāṇa, then Nirvāṇa is something other than himself – that is duality too.

Question – But just what is the relationship of God, mankind and the world?

Swamiji – It is very difficult to find words to express the exact relationship. Words are finite, and finite words cannot express fully the Infinite. Therefore, we must attempt to convey the Truth through an illustration, which can only bring forth the principles. Then we have to mentally chew and digest the imparted ideas, so that the illustration may yield its sacred sweetness to us.

The relationship that exists between the individual, the world and Creator is explained by the example of a piece of cloth in which a decorative pattern is woven, like one of the tapestries we use for wall hangings. Now this piece of cloth is made of threads passing in and through it. The threads make up the patterns in the cloth, for example, a family sitting at tea on a long veranda with trees and sky in the background. Now, for the sake of our model, this scene would be equivalent to our total conception of the world, with its oceans, mountains, continents and individuals. The pattern constitutes our world.

Now the existence of this cloth depends on what? Has it any existence other than the thread? If we were to remove the thread would there be any cloth? No, because the cloth is only the thread. However, since we look only at the patterns of the thread, we only see the portrayal of the family at tea on the cloth. But there can be no pattern without the thread.

The thread here is the symbol for the Creator – without whom there would be no creation of tapestry or its designs. Thus the whole world is established by and patterned in the Divine Principle. If we take away this Divine Principle, the entire pattern – the world – would necessarily melt into nothingness, just as the piece of cloth would end if all the threads were to be removed.

Now let us analyse this principle further. What is the cause of the thread? If it were not for the cotton, the thread would not have existed, nor the cloth, nor the figure woven on it. In cotton, the three – the thread, the cloth and the pattern – exist. Out of cotton all the three appeared, and into cotton they return when they perish. The true essence of this cloth is nothing but cotton. Remove the cotton and try to give me a piece of cloth, please!

The all-pervading supreme Reality in Itself has not undergone any alteration. Just as cotton remains cotton; it only changes its form in the tapestry. According to its stage of modification, we give it the name 'thread', the name 'cloth', then the name 'pattern'.

Thus the relationship between the created, the creation and the Creator is that there is no relationship possible because relationship connotes that at least two things exist. If we sincerely seek the exact relationship between the supreme Reality and ourselves, we have to conclude that there is no difference at all. Just as there can be no difference between the cotton and the cloth with its pattern.

Another example used in the scriptures is the spider and its web. The spider creates the web out of itself – material of the web is the very substance of the spider. In short the web is nothing but the modified form of the spider itself. Similarly, the supreme Reality is the lock, stock and barrel of this atrocious looking mechanism of saṁsāra (the creation).

"There is only Reality. Wake up and discover who's suffering!" says the dream Guru to his dream student. Then the individual, the world and the creator all merge into that One.

45

Biography

Author – Swamiji, while I have been travelling around India with you during this past year, I have met many of your family and longtime devotees who have told me many stories about your life – even your childhood. So I started jotting down these different episodes that people recounted to me. As the material grew, I decided to start using it as the basis for a biography of your life.

He looked at me with a dull gaze, his lips drawn down, in silence.

I finally broke the long pause by interjecting another comment – "It will be inspiring to many."

"Not to me, I am sure!" he asserted with a roll of chuckles. "I know it all. Except the date that I was born, they had to tell me only that."

During the satsaṅga, he had been discussing the consultation of horoscopes for marriage arrangements with a family a few minutes before my comment, so now he added, "Horoscopes are always done. There must have been one cast at my birth."

"Yes", I replied. "Padmini (his sister) told me that there was one cast at your birth. The astrologer predicted that you would be a great person, but he did not mention that it would be in the spiritual field. Certainly no one suspected that you would become a Swami."

"Oh", he quipped. "I thought it said I was going to be a clerk. You know that's how I spend my days. Six to eight hours daily with correspondence." He paused and looked aside.

"My dear girl, a Swami has no biography or autobiography. He has no date of birth. How can one go into the origin of a river?"

Everyone present remained in silent suspense to see if he was going to reject the idea.

After another long silence, he finally replied, "Well, if you must do it, make it good! Of course you'll have to tell about all the great miracles I have performed! Yes, everyone thinks that the test of a holy man is not the life he lives, but whether he can perform some miracle. So I had to prove myself too! "

"There was the day I produced an elephant – right there in the middle of Rama Rao's living room. A huge monstrosity of an elephant appeared right before everyone's eyes. Everyone was so excited at such a wonderful thing. Oh, such a wonder! Then they started to look around to see how they were going to get it out of the room, through those small doors – well, you do know what happens if an elephant stays in one place too long! That was the moment for my disappearing act! I quickly slipped out the door!"

Everyone was doubled over with laughter as he continued, "Don't forget to tell about that time I healed a man. Poor soul came to me with dysentery. He came to me, a Swami, when he should have gone to a doctor. But never mind, I picked up a banana off the tray, whipped it through the air, so that it looked like I had picked the banana out of the air – at least it did to those in the back of the room, and to those who were half asleep.

Then the old men ate the banana and of course it made him sicker. He got so sick that he was forced to go to the doctor and get proper medicine, as he should have done in the first place. So after taking the prescribed medicine, he was better in a few days. But he will always be sure that his improvement was due to the grace of the Swami. Nothing else had healed him."

"Name it 'Miracles that Weren't Miracles'. It should be a satire on how the Mahātmās live! Make up something good!"

Author – Well, Swamiji, I do confess I had something more serious in mind for the project. I do think that the real truth, although only of the relative world, will be useful. After all, we do live in a relative world.

He pursed his lips and remained silent. At least, he did not say "No", I told myself. So I proceeded with the project.

In spite of his silence on his personal life, in 1966, Swamiji had penned a short autobiography in response to a letter from a student. Chandra Bhanu Adiyar of Mangalore had written Swamiji to inquire about the details of his personal life. It's a great example of Swamiji's sense of humour. Here is his reply –

....

Blessed Self,

Om Namaḥ Nārāyaṇāya – Salutations!

Only because I have more interesting and useful work in hand at present, I cannot give you a complete 'Autobiography'. However, here are some positive points, which should satisfy your curiosity for the time being. Later, I am sure, you will try to shift your attention from me to the ṛṣis and make your own life beautiful and sublime.

I was born in Kerala, raised in the north, hardened in Punjab, softened in Uttarkashi, criticized everywhere, applauded in some places, but accepted and worshipped by everyone. I am a riddle unto myself.

Prattling was my profession, preaching is my profession now, and I know practice should be my future job. Everywhere I earned a lot and squandered it all in the community.

I am by training a religious man, by experience a Vedāntin, by inclination a bhakta, in temperament a karma-yogī, and in practice an integral yogī. My faith is in democracy; I am convinced by socialism; I am habituated to communism – and I am committed to the impossible theory of 'Love All'.

Thick-skinned, hard boned, I have a (suit of) mail of laughter that covers and protects both my heart and hands. Therefore, stabs do not penetrate me; spears cannot cleave me; whippings do not lash me.

I eat and drink, take regular baths, sleep, wear clothes, have no jaṭā, work for 18-19 hours a day, and preach the rest of the time. When audiences are not available, I preach to myself.

I have my lovers of Truth and many beloveds in this country and abroad. I play the beloved to the lovers, and am an enthusiastic lover to my beloveds. We together step ahead and march through love towards the Lord's Palace of Bliss and Wisdom.

Your good self may meet me easily in my 35 books, or in the pūjā room of any healthy, young Indian, whether he or she is a Hindu, Christian or Muslim. The white men adore me; the yellow men recognize me; the brown men worship me; the black men love me.

My Teacher was a divinely sweet, incandescent, noble soul. I must tell you of him when you grow a bit more.

May I hope to hear from you often – even plenty of rubbish, but sprinkled with more and more of the sensible stuff? Try it. You can. Don't be shy. This is how everyone grows.

Swami Chinmayananda
Jamshedpur, 1966.

Afterword

The biography of Swami Chinmayananda is based on first hand reports since, fortunately, most of the players in the story were still living when I collected the information over the past ten years. It was only because of their willingness to assist me that this project has been possible. In Kerala, I met and talked with Swamiji's family – his sisters, Padmini and Kanakam; his stepbrother, Unni; his senior aunt, Velya Amma; and his cousins, Achutan, Balachandran, Krishnadas, Mrs. K. K. (Vilasini) Menon and Gopinath Menon in Bombay (now Mumbai). I also talked with his former companions – K. Sankaran Marar, M. Kuddapan Menon, S. Shankar Narayan and Robert D'Souza. At Ananda Kutir and Tapovanam Kutir in the Himalayas, I talked with Swami Govindagiri and other Swamis who had known Swamiji during the years he spent there. In Poona, Shusheela Mudliar was helpful with information and introductions to the people who organized Swamiji's first yajña. Of course, the many publications of the Chinmaya Mission, compiled through the years by many dedicated persons, were indispensable in completing the project. A special thanks goes to Mrs. Leela Nambiar, Br. Siddha Chaitanya, Mr. M. K. R. Menon and Usha Menon for sending me information from India that I requested. Many others, too numerous to mention, have shared ideas and experiences with me.

I also acknowledge and express my thanks to the persons who assisted me with the editing. I am particularly indebted to Judith Richards in Houston, Texas and Leslie Sawyer in New York City for their thorough reading of the entire manuscript and their making of many essential suggestions. Nagendra Rao and Usha Menon took on the task of verifying the religious and cultural information and making any necessary corrections. Peter

Fell, Griffin Mullane, and my father, Freeman Patchen, assisted in the proofreading at different stages of the manuscript. I thank Richard Coan and Raj Srivastava in Tucson, Arizona for their assistance in proofreading the second edition.

I am also grateful for the many scholarly volumes on India, the majority by British authors, published during the past thirty years. The authors have applied an objective method as they searched through old government records, personal letters and diaries for relevant information on the Raj – the British Empire in India. Anyone interested in further reading on the history and culture of India will find the selections on the following list fascinating and very informative. They have provided me with indispensable information in compiling this biography and understanding India.

(1) The Peacock Throne: The Drama of Mogul India; Waldemar Hansen; 1972 Waldemar Hansen; Holt, Rinehart and Winston, New York, NY.

(2) The Black Hole of Calcutta; Noel Barber; 1965 Noel Barber; Houghton Mifflin Co., Boston, MA.

(3) The Great Mutiny: India 1857; Christopher Hibbert; 1978 Christopher Hibbert; The Viking Press, New York, NY.

(4) The Viceroys of India, Mark Bence-Jones; 1982 Mark Bence-Jones; St. Martin's Press, New York, NY.

(5) India Britannica; Geoffrey Moorhouse; 1983 Geoffrey Moorhouse; Harper and Row, New York, NY.

(6) Halfway to Freedom; Margaret Bourke-White; 1949 Margaret Bourke-White; Simon and Schuster, New York, NY.

(7) Gandhi; Geoffrey Ashe; 1968 Geoffrey Ashe; Stein and Day Publishers, New York, NY.

(8) Nehru, A Biography; B. N. Pandey; 1976 B.N. Pandey; Stein and Day Publishers, New York, NY.

(9) The Scope of Happiness: A Personal Memoir; Vijaya Lakshmi Pandit; 1979 Vijaya Lakshmi Pandit; Crown Publishers, Inc., New York, NY.

(10) The History of Civilization; Volume One: Our Oriental Heritage; 1935, 1976 Will Durant; Simon and Schuster, New York.

(11) Winston Churchill: Youth 1874-1990 (vol. One). Randolph S Churchill - 1966 Randolph S Churchillm Houghton Mifflin co., Bostom , MA (pp. 279-327)

Glossary

Ācārya – Spiritual Teacher, preceptor.

advaita (not divided) – The one unchangeable, indivisible Truth; the one essence that cannot be described as real or non-real. Ādi Śaṅkarācārya wrote extensive commentaries on the major Vedāntic scriptures to prove this conclusion.

Agni – Vaidika God of fire.

ammā – Mother.

ānanda – Divine Bliss and happiness. A bliss that is not dependent on the objects or situations in the world or the mind, but inherent in each individual.

Ananda Kutir – The complex of cottages for Swamis, classrooms and administrative offices that comprise the āśrama of Swami Sivananda Saraswati.

Āraṇyaka – The third section of each Veda which includes the explanations of the symbolism of the rituals and mental exercises for the contemplative life of the retiree (vānaprastha āśrama) to prepare him for the fourth stage of life (sannyāsa āśrama).

Āryan – One of noble birth or character (Sanskrit). Also, the family of Indo-European languages, therefore, the nomadic invaders who brought a language of this group into India (and Europe) between 2,000 and 1,500 BC from the northern steppes.

Arunachala Mountain – Mountain in Southern India where Ramana Maharshi resided throughout his adulthood. In the Purāṇas, Arunachala is said to be the centre of the universe.

āsana – A particular posture or mode of sitting; a seat, stool or pad for sitting.

āśrama – Monastery, hermitage, place of retreat.

āśrama – The four orders or stages of a Hindu's life – brahmacarya (student), gṛhastha (householder), vānaprastha (forest-dweller), sannyāsa (renunciate).

Atharva-veda – In general, this Veda contain rituals for dealing with practical matters of life in the world. Its philosophical section contains the *Muṇḍaka, Māṇḍūkya* and *Praśnopaniṣad.*

Ātmā(n) – The essential divinity, or light of Consciousness, in each individual; often translated into English as 'Self'. See Brahman.

Avatāra – An incarnation of the Divine made flesh in response to the collective karma of the population of a given time, not because of individual, personal karma. Examples include Rāma, Kṛṣṇa, the Buddha.

Ayurveda – A system of the ancient knowledge (Veda) of health and medicine that is so comprehensive it includes descriptions and drawings of the tools used in major surgeries. Its validity is now recognized by modern medical science.

Badarinath – One of the four great Himalayan pilgrimage centres; the Maṭha established by Ādi Śaṅkarācārya in the north.

bhajana – Devotional hymn or chant.

Bhagavad-gītā (Song of the Lord) – A major scriptural poem contained in the *Mahābhārata* epic. In the eighteen chapters of the *Bhagavad-gītā,* Lord Kṛṣṇa gives the divine Truth to his student Arjuna in the setting of the battlefield of the dynastic war between the Pāṇḍavas and Kauravas. The *Gītā* is, therefore, intended as a practical guide to persons attempting to live a spiritual life in the world, rather than for renunciates.

bhakti/bhakta – Devotion/devotee. Bhakti-yoga is the path to enlightenment through devotion to God, the Truth, or a holy Teacher.

Bhārata – India; the home of the ancient clan of Bhāratīyas, or 'Sons of Light', which was held together by a strong cultural and religious bond based on the Sanskrit Vedas. The area is believed to have extended from present-day Pakistan and Afghanistan on the west to Burma on the east, from the Himalayas to the Indian Ocean on the north and south.

bhikṣā – Food obtained by begging or asking for alms. Also, the meal served when a sādhu is invited into the home.

Brahmā (masculine gender) – The deity of the Hindu Trinity who is the Creator of the universe. Do not confuse with Brahman, see below.

Brahman (neuter gender) – The impersonal God, devoid of all qualities; the omnipresent, all-pervading, transcendent Reality. This supreme Reality is called Brahman when regarded as transcendent, and Ātman when regarded as the Life Principle in the individual person.

Brahmasūtras – One of the three authoritative books of Hinduism in which Śrī Vyāsa encapsulated the principles of Vedānta in 551 terse statements. These short verses were originally intended for ease of memorization, thereby ensuring their availability for mental reflection on the great truths of the Upaniṣads at any time or place.

Brahma vicāra – Continually thinking on the nature of Brahman, the eternal Truth.

Brahmavidyā – Knowledge of the eternal Truth, Brahman.

brahmacārī (m), brahmacāriṇī (f) – One who moves in Brahman; that is, one who continually fixes the mind on the eternal Truth. The more common meaning is student, or one who practises spiritual discipline and celibacy.

brahmacarya āśrama – The first of the four stages of life in the Hindu system. This period of life, usually from five to twenty-five years of age, is allotted to general education and the study of the Vedas for the understanding of, and preparation for life.

Brāhmaṇa caste (Brāhmaṇa) – The highest of the four Hindu castes. The priestly caste consists of many sub-castes depending on the area the priest comes from and the duties he performs, such as temple priest, family priest, astrologer, teacher, cook and so on.

Buddha (one of true wisdom) – Buddha is a title bestowed on an Enlightened Master. The Buddha in the present cycle is Siddhārtha Gautama (563 BC) who was born in a small kingdom in present-day Nepal. After renunciation of his kingdom and a long period of asceticism, he became Enlightened and began teaching. His sermons form the school of philosophy called Buddhism.

Caste – There are four castes, each with its own duties, rules, regulations and hierarchy. Within each caste there are hundreds of sub castes, variations and hierarchies. Varṇa (caste) is usually translated as 'community' by Indians, for, it means much more than a single category. It means where one is from, how one dresses, what one eats, the language one speaks. Traditionally, there was flexibility in the caste system, according to one's talent. For example, Mahatma Gandhi's father, from the grocer Vaiśya caste, served as a counsellor to a king, the traditional role served by a Brāhmaṇa. On the other hand, J. Nehru was a Kashmir Brāhmaṇa (considered a lower status in the Brāhmaṇa caste hierachy); however, he and his father were attorneys, a Kṣatriya caste function. Having had to withstand the foreign invasions of religious fanatics, both Muslim and Christian, for some 1,000 years, the Indian system has continued to crystallize and become rigid in order to protect the culture and religion.

The highest caste is the Brāhmaṇa, or priest, teacher, scholar, doctor, advisor group. By virtue of their position in the society, they have more duties and are accorded heavier punishments than the other castes. For example, in the *Mahābhārata,* a group of men had committed a crime. The Brāhmaṇa was given the death sentence, while the ones of lower castes were given sentences in prison, varying according to their caste.

The Kṣatriya caste is referred to as the warrior caste. This caste includes everyone from the king to the foot soldier, their wives and children. In modern times, they have been court judges and administrators. Only Kṣatriyas went to war, leaving the rest of the population free to carry on with their respective duties.

The third caste is the Vaiśya, or merchant and farmer category. In general, this has been the wealthiest caste.

The fourth caste is the Śūdra or service caste. Anyone who performs services in the community, such as office executives, clerks, secretaries and persons in banking, communication and medical services.

cāṇḍāla – Untouchable; one outside of the caste system. The outcastes were generally of the aboriginal native tribes.

Candrakalādhara (moon + small part + ornament) – During the churning of the Milky Ocean by the gods and the demons, 'Candrakalā' emerged on the day of the new moon. The gods prayed to Lord Śiva to wear this crescent moon on his head as an ornament with the hope that it would help cool his destructive anger.

Cochin – Port city on the Malabar coast of the Arabian Sea; also the pre-independence kingdom that included the cities of Cochin, Ernakulam and Trichur.

Congress (Indian National Congress) – Organised in 1885 with the assistance of Allan Hume, a retired British civil servant, for the purpose of giving Indians more voice in public affairs. Congress was the principal political organ in India's struggle for independence and remains the major political force in modern India.

dal – Dried beans that have had the outer husk removed. Any bean or pea may be made into a dal. Also, any soup or curry that is made from a dal.

darśana – To see or view, usually used in the context of 'beholding' a holy person or an idol.

deva (m), devī (f) (dev = to shine) – God/Goddess. All Vaidika gods are functional names of the one supreme creative power manifesting in myriad forms; therefore, these deities, or shining ones, preside over and have the power to bless various activities in the world. In the context of Vedānta, the gods are symbolic of human inner psychological powers representing one's ability to bless or curse oneself.

dharma (dhṛ = to support, sustain) – The inner essence or very foundations of a thing or being. Dharma may be translated as law, duty, harmony or essential Truth, according to the context.

dharmaśālā – Overnight abodes or hostels that were constructed by pious people or kings to provide free food and shelter to travelling pilgrims.

dhoti – The traditional men's wear in many parts of India, which is a large rectangular cloth, wrapped around the body like a skirt and tied at the waist called a luṅgī in Kerala.

Dravidian – The principal indigenous culture and language on the Indian subcontinent. It remains the source of the South Indian culture and language, Tamil of today.

Enlightenment – The direct experience that the individual Self (Ātman) is one with the supreme Self (Brahman); also referred to as Realization, Self-realization and Liberation. The Sanskrit terms for enlightenment are mokṣa, mukti and nirvāṇa.

Gandhi, Mahatma (Mohandas K.) (1869-1948) – The leader of the Indian nationalist movement who voiced the ideal of non-violence. He dedicated his life to searching for Truth and devising programmes for the improvement of the lives of the impoverished masses of India.

Gaṇeśa – The elephant God of great wisdom and strength who is worshipped first in any ritual or new enterprise. He is invoked to remove obstacles in the practical matters of success in worship or in worldly endeavours, or to remove obstructions in spiritual practices done to attain Enlightenment.

Ganga – A river flowing from the high Himalayas, said to originate in the heavens. It has sustained a flourishing Civilization along its banks for several millenniums. (Mispronounced 'Ganges' by the British.)

Gangotri – One of the four great Himalayas pilgrimage centres. It is near the source of the Ganga.

Gauḍapāda, Śrī (700 AD) – The Guru of Govindapāda Ācārya, who was the Guru of Ādi Śaṅkarācārya. He authored the *Māṇḍūkya-upaniṣad's Kārikā*, or commentary.

Gāyatrī – The most sacred verse in the Vedas (*Ṛg* 3.62.10) that invokes the Solar deity, Savitṛ, for wisdom in daily living. It has been used in daily worship and in initiation ceremonies throughout the ages in Bhārata.

ghāṭa – Slopes, steps – the steps that line the sacred rivers and temple pools to enable the worshippers to easily enter the water for a purification bath; therefore, also the most sacred places along these pools and rivers. The term 'ghāṭa' is also used for mountain ranges, such as the Western Ghats that borders and defines the state of Kerala.

ghī – Butter that has been clarified using fire.

Gītā – See *Bhagavad-gītā*.

gṛhastha āśrama – The householder, or second stage of life of the Hindu. The householder lives according to a behavioural code given in the dharma śāstra. In addition, he daily performs certain required rituals.

Guru (one who dispels darkness) – A spiritual Teacher who initiates seekers into the secrets of the sacred scriptures by the clearing of ignorance and misconceptions of life, thereby revealing the eternal Truth. Colloquially, a teacher of any specialised knowledge.

Hanumāna – The deity of wind and mental prowess. As the hero monkey who aided Lord Rāma in the battle against evil, he exhibited great qualities as a supporter of dharma and devotee of the Lord. He is, therefore, idolized throughout India, particularly in the north, in the region of Rāma's ancient kingdom.

Hara – An epithet of Lord Śiva.

Hari – An epithet of Lord Viṣṇu.

Harijana – Children of God; a term coined by Mahatma Gandhi for the untouchables.

Havana – A fire ritual accompanied by the chanting of the sacred Vaidika mantras for a communal or common purpose. In the Vaidika age, havanas were performed to give offerings of ghī, milk or grain to please the deities. With the later philosophical development of Hinduism, their purpose evolved into a method of practising renunciation.

Indus Valley Civilization (ca. 4000-1,500 BC) – An advanced Civilization in ancient India concurrent with the Babylonian and Egyptian civilizations. Numerous sites of ruins lie along the Indus river in present-day Pakistan.

japa – Repetition, usually mentally, of a mantra to exclude all other thoughts and to build the power of concentration of the mind.

jñāna – Knowledge; wisdom of the absolute Reality.

Kailash, Mount – Peak of 22,280 feet in southwest Tibet in the Kailash range of the Himalayas. The pilgrimage path that girdles it is thirty miles long and reaches a height of 18,000 feet at one point. It is also called Kamgrimpoche (Tibetan).

karma (kṛ = to do) – Action, work, deed; the sum of the effects of past actions producing results in the life of the world. According to the context, karma can be translated as destiny (the results of past actions) or duty (actions intended to produce good results in the future). In the Vedas, karma means only the action of performing the prescribed rituals.

karmaphala – Fruit, results of actions in the world.

Kedarnath – One of the four great Himalayas pilgrimage centres.

Kerala – The Indian state established after Independence in 1951, composed of the small kingdoms on the Malabar coast of the Arabian Sea in which Malayalam was spoken, including Travancore, Calicut and Cochin.

Kṛṣṇa, Lord – The ninth and most beloved avatāra. His life was immortalized with Śrī Vyāsa's *Bhāgavatam* and *Bhagavad-gītā.*

Krishnamurti, Jiddu (1895-1986) – Born in Andhra Pradesh, he was groomed as a messianic figure by the theosophist Annie Besant. In 1928 he repudiated his role as the World Teacher and, to some extent, the role of all spiritual Teachers. He spent his life principally in Europe and America writing and lecturing – being a spiritual Teacher.

Kṛṣṇāṣṭamī Day – Lord Kṛṣṇa's birthday. He was born after midnight on the eighth day of the dark moon in the month of Śrāvaṇa (July-August) in a prison in Mathura.

kula-guru – Spiritual Teacher of the household or clan.

Lakṣmī, Śrī – Goddess of wealth and good fortune; symbol of auspiciousness and grace. Also called Śrī, which means auspicious.

Lalitā – An epithet of Pārvatī, wife of Lord Śiva.

līlā – Divine play, particularly of the gods.

lungi – Malayalam word for a wraparound cloth worn as a skirt by both men and women in Kerala (dhoti in Hindi). The mundu is the top cloth worn over the shoulder.

Madrāsī – Resident of Madras (now Chennai). During the British Empire the Madras Presidency included the sourthern states of Tamil Nadu, Kerala, Mysore and Andhra Pradesh.

Mahābhārata – An epic poem of ancient India detailing the history of the evolution of mankind through the lineage of the

Bhārata family. Written by Veda-vyāsa, the poem of 100,000 verses is the longest epic poem in the world. It also contains the philosophical treatise, the *Bhagavad-gītā.*

Mahārājā – Great king; can be used as both a secular and spiritual title.

mahāsamādhi – The great or final samādhi, that is, the death of a sage. Therefore, the burial place of a sage is also referred to as a 'samādhi'.

Mahātmā – Great soul.

mālā – Rosary used for meditation. It usually consists of 108 beads with a central (meru) bead, or turning bead, to enable one to count the number of repetitions of the mantra while chanting.

Malayalam – The native language of Kerala that originated with the Dravidian Tamil although it has numerous additions from indigenous influences and from Sanskrit. It is considered to be the most sanskritised of the native Indian languages.

mantra – A sacred syllable, word or phrase that represents the eternal Truth. Mantras may be used in daily life for protecting the mind from falling into agitation and for spiritual evolution by reflecting on their significance.

Master – In India and Hinduism, the term refers to one who has mastered himself and has thereby mastered life.

Māṇḍūkya-upaniṣad – A philosophical treatise in the *Atharva-veda.* It is considered to be the most terse, yet most sublime and complete, of the Upaniṣads.

maṭha – Monastery, seminary; one of the four centres established by Ādi Śaṅkarācārya for the preservation of the four Vedas and other sacred scriptures – Badarinath (north), Sringeri (south), Puri (east) and Dwarka (west). These four maṭhas have established subsidiary maṭhas in their respective districts, such as at Kanchi and Kavir.

mauna – Silence, the practice of maintaining silence to prevent the dissipation of energy and as an exercise of discipline.

Mughal – A dynasty established in India in the 16th century by Bābara, a Mongolian/Turk; also a civilian of this dynasty.

monsoon – Seasonal rain-bearing winds that inundate most India with rains from June 10 to September 10 each year, except the southeast coast, which has rains from late November through January.

Narayana, Jaya Prakash (1902-1979) – The founder of the Congress Socialists in the early 1930's and leader of the Socialist Party. He was one of the few Indian nationalists educated in America and this experience influenced his emphasis on industrialisation in India. In 1956 he withdrew from formal politics to serve his countrymen in what he felt was a more practical manner by establishing the Sarvodaya (Upliftment of All) Foundation. His devotion to the cause of India's independence and resulting respect from the people was equal to that of Nehru.

Nārāyaṇa – An epithet of Lord Viṣṇu.

Narayana Guru (1856-1928) – Born in the low Ezhava caste in Kerala, he was a respected reformer who spent his life building temples, teaching Vedānta and preaching against social injustice.

Nehru, Jawaharlal (1889-1964) – First Prime Minister of independent India. He and his father, Motilal Nehru, were prominent leaders of the nationalist movement and Indian Congress Party from the 1930s.

niṣkāma karma – Action performed without the taint of personal desire for results or reward.

OM (AUM) – A mystic syllable that represents the higher Reality, Brahman. It begins all the sacred scriptures and all prayers. Its significance is expounded in the *Māṇḍūkya-upaniṣad.*

OM Namaḥ Śivāya (surrender + (to) Lord Śiva) – The mantra emitting the highest vibration of the seven seed sounds (such as eim, srim, krim, hrim) defined by Ādi Śaṅkarācārya in the *'Karpūrādī Stotram'*.

Pañcadaśī (fifteen) – Vedāntic text of fifteen chapters written by Swami Vidyāraṇya. It is an advanced introductory text (prakaraṇa grantha) intended to unfold all the subjects of Vedānta necessary for enlightenment, or to serve as a foundation for further study of Vedānta.

paramparā – A line of teachers established by the handing down of the eternal Truth from teacher to student.

prakaraṇa grantha – Introductory Vedāntic texts that unfold the entire subject matter of Vedānta with or without reference to any of the terse Upaniṣads. The purpose of these texts were to explain all the concepts necessary for enlightenment in simple terms, so the subject could be understood without having to resort to the study of the thick scriptures and the lengthy logical analysis typical of the scholarly approach. Some of the most known are *Ātmabodha, Vivekacūḍāmaṇi, Pañcadaśī, Vedānta Sāra, Vedānta Paribhāṣā.*

praṇām – A prostration; often used as a salutation to show respect to a holy man.

prasādam – Food, usually sweets, offered to the gods during a ritual. Afterwards, it is distributed among the participants as a consecrated offering along with ash, sandalwood paste or other items used in the worship.

Prasthāna Traya – The three foundation scriptures of Vedānta – *Bhagavad-gītā, Brahmasūtras* and the Upaniṣads.

prema – Divine, selfless love, as opposed to romantic, self-centred love.

pūjā – Worship, ritual; pūjya – worshipful.

puṇya – Good karma or merit, accumulated from good actions.

Purāṇas – Epics, or ancient legendary histories compiled by Veda-vyāsa. There are eighteen Purāṇas, each of which contains the following five topics – 1) cosmology with various symbolic illustrations of philosophical principles, 2) secondary creation after periodic annihilation, 3) genealogy of gods and saints, 4) descriptions of the great epochs, 5) history of the royal dynasties.

Raja – King; the king of a large or prosperous kingdom was a Mahārājā.

Rāma, Śrī – The eighth incarnation of Lord Viṣṇu; the hero king of the epic *Rāmāyaṇa*, who was the model of piety, morality as well as ethical behaviour in the performance of worldly duties.

Ramakrishna, Śrī (1836-1886) – A Bengali sage who accepted and demonstrated the essential unity of all religions. He was the Guru of Swami Vivekananda, Swami Brahmananda and other founders of the Ramakrishna Mission.

Ramana Maharshi (1879-1950) – A spiritual Master who left home at sixteen years of age after an experience of enlightenment to spend the remainder of his life at Arunachala Mountain, meditating and teaching those who came to him. Ramana Maharshi is considered to be the last of the line of authentic sages of the ancient tradition. Somerset Maugham, a British Playwright, visited the sage in 1938, and later used him as the model for the holy man in *The Razor's Edge.*

Rāmāyaṇa – The history of Śrī Rāma; the epic poem of 24,000 verses, written by Śrī Vālmīki. The *Rāmāyaṇa* dramatizes the trials of the individual, represented by Sītā, in spiritual evolution.

ṛṣi – A divinely inspired poet or sage; usually refers to the original preceptors of the Hindu scriptures.

Rishikesh – A traditional spiritual centre of the Hindu sages and sādhus. It lies at the foot of the Himalayas on the river Ganga.

Ṛg-veda – The oldest Veda, therefore, it contains much historical information. It is the only Veda that appears to have been partially formulated outside of India. The verses are metrical and intended to be recited aloud for the invocation of the deities during the sacrificial fire ceremonies. The *Aitareya* and *Kauṣītaki Upaniṣads* comprise its philosophical section.

roti – Flat, round, unleavened wheat bread that is baked on an iron griddle, often called chapati.

rudrākṣa – A seed from a tree found in the Himalayas that is used for the beads of mālās. In addition to its medicinal properties including regulating blood pressure, it is believed to emit a peaceful vibration conducive for meditation. The Gaurī-Śaṅkara rudrākṣa is a rare double seed that is used as the turning bead on a mālā. In addition to its rarity, the double rudrākṣa is valued as a symbol of creation, the wedding of matter and Spirit.

rupee – The Indian unit of currency; in recent years the value has fluctuated between 25 and 50 rupees per U.S. dollar.

sādhanā – Spiritual practice; any discipline performed for the purpose of turning one's mind from the world and applying it to the spiritual truths.

sādhu – A practitioner of spiritual and virtuous values; in common usage, a sannyāsī or wandering mendicant.

Sāma-veda – The third and most poetic of the Vedas, whose mantras are to be sung during the sacrificial fire ceremonies. It contains the *Chāndogya* and *Kenopaniṣad.*

samādhi (sama = steady + dhi = intellect) – A calm and pure mind in all circumstances, whether sitting in meditation or acting in the world. Also, a trancelike experience of divine ecstasy.

sambar – A thick soup made of tūr dal, vegetables, chillies and spices.

sannyāsa āśrama – The fourth āśrama in the four stages of the Hindu's life. At this time, the life in the world is renounced for the purpose of attaining enlightenment. Vows are administered by a sannyāsī renunciate.

sannyāsī – One who has renounced the world by taking the sannyāsa vows.

Sanātana-dharma (eternal Truth) – The eternal principle of life that is the essence of all religious teachings; that knowledge, which remains unchanged in all periods of time and states of Consciousness. The religion based on the Vedas, which is best known by its foreign label of Hinduism.

Sanskrit – That which is well or completely done. The oldest language of mankind; the language of the original Hindu scriptures, developed for the communication of spiritual ideas and concepts, not for dealing with worldly or mundane concerns.

Sarasvatī – Goddess of speech and learning who is the consort of Brahmā, the Creator.

Sat – The essence of being, the essential, the true.

Sat-Cit-Ānanda – Term used to express the ultimate experience of oneness – Sat = Truth; Existence; Cit = Intelligence, Consciousness; Ānanda = divine Bliss.

satsaṅga – Association or nearness with the virtuous; therefore, discussions with, or time spent in the presence of spiritual Masters.

sattva (n.), sāttvika (adj.) – One of the three modes (guṇas) of manifestation: sattva = calm, peaceful; rajas = active, agitated; tamas = dull, inactive.

Sāvitrī – The divine Solar deity, or the vitalising power behind the visible sun, immortalized in the Gāyatrī Mantra.

Self – The nearest English equivalent of the Sanskrit word 'Ātman', the essential divinity of an individual.

sevā – Noble, altruistic service.

sevaka – One who does sevā, or service.

Śaṅkara – An epithet of Lord Śiva; see Śaṅkarācārya, Ādi.

Śaṅkarācārya – Title given to the head of each of the four maṭhas set up by Ādi (first) Śaṅkarācārya and their subsidiaries.

Śaṅkarācārya, Ādi (730-820 AD) – The great Master of Advaita Vedānta who synthesized the Vedāntic teaching with clear commentaries, wrote many scriptural books, as well as composed beautiful devotional hymns; commonly referred to by the name Śaṅkara. He renovated and established temples and founded maṭhas in the four directions in India for the preservation of the Vedas.

śāstras – All the scriptures of the Hindu religion.

Śiva – The third God of the Hindu Trinity who is entrusted with the task of destruction, thereby enabling regeneration.

Śivarātri – Śiva's night – the fourteenth day of the dark half of the month Māgha (February) on which a rigorous fast is observed in honour of Lord Śiva.

Sringeri – The maṭha in the south with which Swami Chinmayananda was connected through the lineage of Swamis with the name ending of 'ananda Saraswati'. Śrī Abhinava Vidyatirtha Mahaswamigal was the past Śaṅkarācārya at Sringeri.

Śruti (śru = to hear) – The holy scriptures that were heard by the ancient ṛṣis through direct revelation; the Vedas.

Śrī (m), Śrīmatī (f) – A title of respect used in direct address or in writing; equivalent to Mr. and Mrs. in English.

Swami (m), Swamini (f) – The title used by a sannyāsī who has taken the vows of renunciation; literally one who is with oneself.

Swamiji – Term used when directly addressing a Swami, the suffix 'ji' added to a name indicates respect in direct address.

Tamil – The language of the Dravidians of South India, from which Malayalam is derived.

Tamil Nadu – The state of South India in which Tamil is spoken; its capital is Madras (presently Chennai, its pre-British name).

tapas – To shine, blaze or converge inner heat. Austerities on the physical level include yoga postures; on the mental level, consistent concentration; on the intellectual level, applying the concentration and thought to a divine ideal.

Tapovanam Kutir – The hut at Uttarkashi overlooking the river Ganga that was the residence of Swami Tapovanam in his later years.

Tilak, Bal Gangadhar (1856-1920) – One of India's first prominent nationalist leaders. His efforts towards India's total independence earned him the title of Lokamanya, 'Respected of the people'. His efforts were rewarded by a term of six years (1897-1902) in British prisons in India. He developed the ideas of passive resistance, boycotting of British goods, organization of mass opinion, and other political tactics that were later adopted by Mahatma Gandhi. Because of his words, 'Swaraj (self-rule) is my birthright,' he has been called the Patrick Henry of India.

Trivandrum – Capital city of Kerala in the former princely state of Travancore.

Tungabhadra river – A sacred river that flows through Mysore and part of Andhra Pradesh to merge with the larger Krishna river in Andhra Pradesh.

Turīya – The substratum in which the waking, dream and deep sleep are perceived in the phenomenal or waking point of view; for convenience, it is referred to as the fourth, or Turīya, state of Consciousness. It can be compared to water, which appears in the three states of ice, liquid and steam.

Upanayanam – The sacred thread ceremony for the bestowal of the Gāyatrī Mantra. The ceremony for the purpose of 'bringing near or leading to' the Truth is performed by a priest and presided over by the father of the boy being initiated. India's law-giver, Manu, states the appropriate age for the receiving of the thread as five years for a Brāhmaṇa, six for Kṣatriya, and eight for a Vaiśya (Code of Manu 2.37-38).

Upaniṣad (seated below) – The culmination, or philosophical section, of each of the four Vedas that reveals the essential oneness between God and man. These treatises are believed to have been compiled from 800 to 500 BC. They were meant to be taught by an Enlightened Teacher to students of a humble and receptive attitude, that is, both mentally and physically 'seated below'.

upāsanā (seated near) – Being near to the Lord through continual mental visualisation of his form.

Uttarkashi – The Himalayan mountain village that has been the residence of many sages, including Swami Tapovanam.

vānaprastha āśrama – The third stage of a Hindu's life. As a forest dweller, he lives in semi-retirement at the edge of the family estate where he is separate from the family, but available in an advisory capacity as his sons take over his former duties. He passes the day in contemplation and study of the Āraṇyaka section of the Vedas.

Varanasi – Considered the holiest city in India by the Hindus. Its historical name was Kāśī. (Re-named Banaras by British).

vāsanā – Innate tendency. These subconscious tendencies colour all levels of our personality – our perceptions, emotions, thoughts and actions. It is postulated that they are brought with us into this life from previous births.

Vedānta (end of knowledge) – System of non-dualistic philosophy based on the Upaniṣads, which are found in the last section of the Vedas. Vedānta proves the non difference between the individual Self (Ātman) and the supreme Self (Brahman).

Vedas – The four principal books of sacred knowledge – *Ṛg*, *Yajur*, *Sāma* and *Atharva*. Each Veda is divided into four sections to guide the four āśramas (stages) of life. The first, or Saṁhitā section contains the many mantras, which are hymns, prayers and formulae to be used in the various rituals during the gṛahastha āśrama. The second, or Brāhmaṇa section is commentary on the meaning of the mantras with directions for their use in various rituals to produce results in worldly endeavours. The third section consists of treatises for contemplation and study including the symbolic meanings of the elements of the rituals. These mental exercises are meant to be used by those of the vānaprastha āśrama. This section is, therefore, named the Āraṇyaka or forest treatises. The fourth section contains the philosophical treatises, the Upaniṣads, intended for the final realization by those in the sannyāsa āśrama.

The Vedas can also be divided into the three subdivisions of karma, upāsanā, and jñāna. The karma section is concerned with correct action in the world and contains both the Saṁhitā and Brāhmaṇa sections. The upāsanā division for worship and spiritual contemplation consists of the Āraṇyakas. The jñāna, or knowledge, division consists of the Upaniṣads.

vidyālaya – School.

Viṣṇu, Lord – The God of the Hindu Trinity who is responsible for the maintenance and preservation of the creation. It is He who incarnates from time to time as an avatāra to guide and uplift the evolution of creation. Often referred to as Nārāyaṇa.

Viṣṇu Sahasranāma – Hymn containing the one thousand names, or manifestations, of the Lord Viṣṇu.

Vivekacūḍāmaṇi – An introductory text of Vedānta (prakaraṇa grantha), written by Ādi Śaṅkarācārya, that explains all concepts, topics and terms contained in the Upaniṣads.

Vivekananda, Swami (1863-1902) – Leader and founder, with Swami Brahmananda of Śrī Ramakrishna's disciples and of the Ramakrishna Mission. He received a standing ovation at the First World Parliament of Religions in Chicago in 1892, which assured his success as a Teacher of Vedānta in America.

Vyāsa, Śrī Veda – The poet-seer who compiled the oral tradition of the sacred teachings into written form, thus preserving the Vedas and Purāṇas. He also wrote the *Brahmasūtras* and the *Mahābhārata.* The date of his life and whether there was more than one Vyāsa is disputed. Hindu tradition holds that there is a Vyāsa, one who compiles the Vedas, born in every cycle of creation. Kṛṣṇa Dvaipāyana was the Vyāsa of the present cycle.

yajña – Fire sacrifice or ritual. Yajñas may be performed for the evolution of the world and/or the purification of the mind. In the Vaidika period, members of an entire community gathered for the purpose of a great sacrificial ritual to invoke the blessings of the gods for worthy endeavours, such as peace in the world and the welfare of the community and its prosperity through an abundance of cattle and crops. The scriptures also prescribe five daily yajñas (rituals) for householders during the gṛahastha āśrama.

Swami Chinmayananda modernised the context of yajña to mean 'any social, communal, national or personal activity that the individual undertakes in a spirit of self-sacrifice and dedicated service.' In his lectures, jñāna-yajñas, ignorance was sacrificed in the fire of Knowledge through the study and contemplation of the scriptures.

yajña-śālā – The site in which the sacrifice or yajña was performed; therefore, the hall where the knowledge of the Upaniṣads was given out.

Yajur-veda – The prose mantras of this Veda are intended to be uttered while pouring the oblations into the sacrificial fire. Its philosophical section is divided into two parts – the Kṛṣṇa or black section contains the *Taittirīya, Kaṭha, Śvetāśvatara, Mahānārāyaṇa* and *Maitrāyaṇī Upaniṣads.* The Śukla or white section contains the *Īśa, Bṛhadāraṇyaka, Jābāla* and *Paiṅgala Upaniṣads.*

yoga (yuj = to join) – All techniques and attempts by a spiritual aspirant to directly experience Enlightenment, that is, identity with one's essential Self (Ātman). In the Western world, yoga has been interpreted to mean physical exercises to achieve quietude of the body and mind.

yogī (m), yoginī (f) – One who has attained the final goal of identity with the essential divinity, or in most cases one who is attempting to do so.